SANTA ROSA

A TWENTIETH CENTURY TOWN

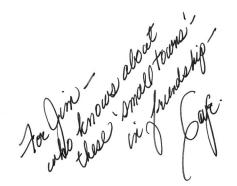

For Jim —
who knows about
these 'small towns' —
in friendship —
Gaye.

GAYE LeBARON & JOANN MITCHELL

historia, ltd.

Acknowledgments

Designer
Brad Cott

Photo Editor
John LeBaron

Editors
Cathy Vertuca
Mary Fricker
Diane Holt

Typography
Digi-Type, Inc., Santa Rosa
Joann Cassady
Mandy Masciarelli

Printing
Lithocraft, Inc., Santa Rosa
Jack Fairclough
Eric French
Jolynn Bodlak
Warren Long

First Printing
(Limited Edition of 5,000 copies)
Copyright 1993 by Historia, Ltd.
All Rights Reserved

ISBN 0-9615010-2-2
Printed in the United States
of America

Library of Congress Catalog
Card Number 93-79227

The authors gratefully acknowledge the interest and assistance of the following:

Henry Trione; Norma and Evert Person; the *Press Democrat* with special thanks to Dr. Alison Head, library director and Mike Parman, publisher; the Sonoma County Library, especially Winifred Swanson and Audrey Herman; Bo Simons for access to the Wine Library photo collection; the Santa Rosa Chamber of Commerce; City of Santa Rosa, especially Kitty Frisbie of the City Manager's Office and John "Stan" Lindsay, director of administrative services; Sonoma County Clerk Eevie Lewis; County Recorder Bernice Peterson; the Sonoma County Museum and director J. Eric Nelson; Luther Burbank House & Gardens, particularly archivist Lynn Collins; the Sonoma County Historical Society; Sonoma County Law Library, Marilyn Josi, librarian; the Santa Rosa High School Foundation; Will Batey, library director, Santa Rosa Junior College; Dave Dorrance for access to NWP Historical Society; John Hacku, curator, Ripley Museum; Sharon Stockham and the Exchange Bank; Frank Norman, MD for sharing his medical history; the Santa Rosa Fire Department, particularly Brian Elliott and Jim Davis; John Burton for access to his research on Grace Brothers Brewery; and Saturday Afternoon Club members Barbara Race, Beth Agnew, and Dorcas Allison.

We thank Phoebe and Sherman Boivin, Martha Comstock Keegan and Dennis Keegan, Jette Cochrane Rodman, Marie Lauritzen, Rose Otani, Dolly Pearce, Helen Rudee, Dorothy Shea, the late Eleanor Silvershield, Marian Caratti, Maurice Wood, Glenn Klein, Bill Money, Doris Kennedy, Fred King, Irene Faoro, Bob Bache, Song Borbeau, Carole Dunn, Shirley Rodota, David Frey, Mike Grace, and the late Virginia Grace for sharing information and their photo collections.

For detailed information we are indebted to: Joe Vercelli, Vern Wood, R.W. Bussman, John Crevelli, the late Walt Tischer, the late "Nin" Guidotti, the late Harold Bruner, Donald Head, Robert Glover, Bob Becker, Mabel Crawford, Don Silverek, Norma and Jim Voss, and Harry Lapham.

In addition we are grateful to the following individuals who lent their professional, academic, and clerical aid: our friend and former partner Dee Blackman, editor Catherine Barnett, attorney Dwight Allen, Prue Draper, Jenny Harris, Suzanne LeBaron, Vonnie Matthews, Jan Cheek, Greta Larsen, Carolina Spence, Art Volkerts, Ruth Rockefeller, Tom Chown, and John Schubert.

And finally, for his patience and his humor, we thank Jim Mitchell.

Table of Contents

historia, ltd.

—Press Democrat Collection

The ruinous earthquake and fire of April 18, 1906 reduced downtown Santa Rosa to rubble. Recriminations about structural flaws and the quality of the bricks and mortar from which the business district was built would continue for a decade. But the damage was done. No city on the North American continent had ever been hit harder by earthquake than Santa Rosa was on that fateful spring morning. It would be fifty years or more before residents, borrowing a leaf from San Francisco's book, would take survivors' pride in the extent of the disaster.

The immediate prospects, however, were gloomy. But it is not so easy to kill a town, as Santa Rosa was to prove in the days and months that followed. Although soldiers sent from a neighboring town to stand guard over the ruins of Santa Rosa's business district amused themselves by staging a mock burial ceremony for the little city, its history was not ended.

Members of Petaluma's Company C of the California National Guard were sent to augment Santa Rosa's Company E, most of whom had their own post-earthquake chores to attend. Company C soldiers were billeted in the Reorganized Latter-Day Saints Church on Fifth Street, between A and B streets—the church whose spire, rising over the ruins, is so prominent in many earthquake photographs.[1] When the Petaluma soldiers' duties were ended, they marched in solemn procession, carrying a coffin across the lawn of the ruined courthouse. The boys from Petaluma, a town that had long regarded Santa Rosa as its natural rival in politics as well as commerce, clearly intended the coffin as a cruel symbol of the death of the town.

The citizens were not amused. Petaluma had gone virtually unscathed in the earthquake and the very presence of the "South County militia" was galling. Even without the Petaluma connection, such high jinks would not have endeared the soldiers to a community which was in no mood for jokes.

Santa Rosans were living under martial law in a virtual heap of bricks and boards. But they were proud, and they considered the military presence an affront to their integrity. "If you wish to go on business through the lines you can have a soldier escort you to the place and back," a Santa Rosa woman named Jessie wrote in a letter to relatives at the end of April.[2] "The only shot fired was at a dog mistaken for a prowler," another survivor would recount with well-remembered defiance years later.[3]

As if to defy its tormentors, the town refused to stay buried. It was, in fact, a vital and bustling community in the days that followed the disaster. The mood was a mixture of joy and despair. People believed dead were found alive. The makeshift newspaper, printed on a borrowed press, spread the good news: "Mrs. Dr. Stuart," caught in San Francisco, was reported "home safe." Mrs. N.L. Jones was not dead, but "doing nicely at the residence of Dr. Lain." Mrs. L.C. Cnopius, believed fatally injured, was improving.[4]

Petaluma's militia, top left, called to guard the ruins of Santa Rosa's downtown after the 1906 earthquake, musters in front of the Latter-Day Saint's Church on Fifth Street.
The domeless Sonoma County Courthouse, at right, is the backdrop for a tableau of workers clearing rubble from Santa Rosa.

The view of the fallen courthouse from Third and B streets photographed by Clarence Flesher.

The reconstruction of Santa Rosa has a jigsaw puzzle quality, pieced together from letters and advertisements and personal narratives. Histories of Sonoma County written by those who lived through the event each tell the story with a different tone. Ernest Finley's 1937 history, compiled to commemorate the opening of the Golden Gate Bridge, tells of San Francisco's damage in 1906 but fails to mention Santa Rosa, with the exception of an occasional oblique reference in biographies of individuals who were involved. Honoria Tuomey devotes a short chapter in her 1926 history to the earthquake—or, more correctly, to earthquakes in general, since Tuomey glosses over the Santa Rosa disaster in favor of a learned treatise on natural phenomena written by a college professor in 1890.

In his 1911 history, Tom Gregory ranges from mock-heroic to wry humor. The earthquake occurred, writes Gregory, on "a California spring-dawn when nature is in the last restful moments of night slumber and dreams are rounding to their finish." And he tells of ex-Councilman Michael McDonough, the landlord of the Grand Hotel, who was "shaken out of his apartments in the hotel…his piano went with him, the two survivors landing on the sidewalk…very much jangled and out of tune…. After the dust was blown away, Mike was revealed, patriotically and modestly draped with the national ensign, sitting on the wreck of the instrument—like the Roman Marius on the ruins of Carthage."

For all his flights of fancy, it is Gregory who gives us the clearest picture of the reconstruction, for his book was published just five years after and the memories were fresh and clear. It was a squad of sailors with their officers, one of whom was a physician, dispatched from Mare Island Navy Yard, who did much of the terrible work of clearing the wreckage and recovering the dead. Once the debris was raked off the rails of the streetcar tracks that ran down Fourth Street, flatcars from both the Petaluma & Santa Rosa and Northwestern Pacific lines were rolled downtown and loaded with rubble.

"Everybody worked," said Gregory. "All hands, virtually, were out of a job and broke. It was more practical and more philosophical to shovel brickbats and ashes onto a platform car than to stand around sadly contemplating the ruin of office and shop. The storekeeper with no store to keep kept his soft hands blistered dragging metal beams, plates and gaspipes out of piles of wreckage….Youthful attorneys with no cases before the court until the insurance companies began to 'welch' on the fire losses, took a summer school course in railroad construction and the method of filling in grade-cuts with train loads of debris from burnt cities. Manual labor was the only recognized profession…But in that day of gloom there was heard no complaint. There was no responsive audience for a complaint."

As soon as the ruins had cooled, merchants went digging to pull out merchandise, damaged and undamaged, to stock temporary stores. "Pitifully primitive," is the way Gregory describes these establishments. Wood frame buildings on back streets that had been vacant for years were opened and swept. Lumber from the yards out of the fire path made hastily-constructed shacks. Grocers sold every bit of salvaged food without, according to Gregory, raising prices or taking advantage of the situation. "There has been recorded," he wrote proudly, "no act of selfishness, no act of lawlessness, and not an act discrediting Santa Rosa during those trying days. Her people stood together."

People were rapidly returning to business as usual. Schools reopened April 30, the wood frame buildings of the Fourth Street School and the stone high school on Humboldt Street having been inspected and found safe. (Later the Burbank School on Ellis Street was found to be damaged.) City officials set up headquarters on a table on the Hinton Avenue sidewalk in front of the destroyed City Hall. County officials pitched a tent on the lawn of the collapsed courthouse and kept office hours. Congressman Duncan McKinlay rushed home from Washington, D.C., leading a wave of politician-visitors.

By May 1, people were coming to town to pay their taxes, and the Southern Pacific trains connecting Santa Rosa with Sacramento, Oakland, and points east were running on schedule. A special train to Santa Rosa brought Secretary of Commerce Victor H. Metcalf, President Theodore Roosevelt's personal Red Cross representative, a number of generals and California Governor George Pardee.

Despite the official head-shaking and clucking at the extent of the damage, Santa Rosans closed ranks. Newspapers and the business community, fearing the mock burial would become financial reality, conspired to tell the world that everything was just fine and dandy.

To some small extent, this was true. Surrounding farms, on which the economy depended, were not seriously damaged. Except for scattered livestock and more than one cow "gone dry" from fright, rural life was uninterrupted. Residences in the town, generally wood frame buildings, had twisted and fallen off their foundations, but most were still livable and worthy of repair.

"Several hundred houses, residences, are damaged," our letter writer Jessie reported, "and a great many (at least 100) will have to be taken down entirely—some are on the ground—others about to fall. Very few houses in town but have the plaster all broken and fallen off." Still, with the exception of the residents of the downtown hotels, there were surprisingly few homeless, and those quickly found shelter in the neighborhood boardinghouses or private homes.

A call went out for the loan of "invalids' rolling chairs" for the injured. The carpenters' union called a special meeting to mobilize for reconstruction. Doctors and lawyers salvaged their files and opened offices in their homes. "The business street now is the north side of Fifth and people have offices in tents and a few have built temporary stores and restaurants," Jessie wrote to her sisters in Sacramento.

Max Rosenberg's Red Front store was back in business in ten days in a hastily constructed shack on Mendocino Avenue. The Red Front's post-earthquake stock consisted of "the contents of eighteen trunks of drummers' samples" which had been found buried in the ruins of the St. Rose Hotel. The trunks themselves served as counters in the temporary store for more than a year.[6]

Things were moving quickly. On April 25, the *Press Democrat* leased a lot previously occupied by a Chinese washhouse on Mendocino Avenue near Fifth Street, gathered a cylinder press and a supply of type, ordered a new Mergenthaler Linotype machine, and moved into its new quarters on May 1. By May the saloons, which had been ordered closed immediately by Mayor John Overton, were permitted to reopen when a delegation of tavern owners appeared before the City Council to complain the enforced closure was diverting their business to other towns. There was still a semblance of martial law, however, and the bars were closed by 6 p.m.

Some residents simply packed up and left town, although that news was seldom reported. When the St. Rose

A monument in Santa Rosa's Rural Cemetery honors those who died in the quake.

—Timothy Baker, Press Democrat Collection

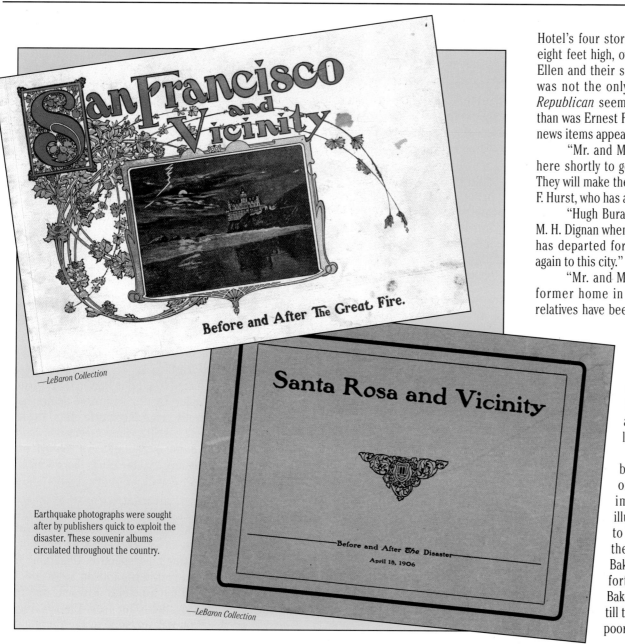

—LeBaron Collection

—LeBaron Collection

Earthquake photographs were sought after by publishers quick to exploit the disaster. These souvenir albums circulated throughout the country.

Hotel's four stories crumbled into a pile of rubble about eight feet high, owner Alexis Chartrand took his wife Mary Ellen and their seven children and moved to Fresno.[7] He was not the only defector. Editor A.B. Lemmon of the *Republican* seemed less reluctant to write of departures than was Ernest Finley in his *Press Democrat*. The following news items appeared in the *Republican* in May:

"Mr. and Mrs. A.J. Hurst and their family will leave here shortly to go to Los Angeles to reside permanently. They will make their home with their son and brother, Ottie F. Hurst, who has a good position there."

"Hugh Buram, who was clerking in the drug store of M. H. Dignan when the recent disaster overtook Santa Rosa, has departed for his home near Fresno. He may return again to this city."

"Mr. and Mrs. M.E. Baker have departed for their former home in Troy, N.Y. Since the earthquake their relatives have been insistent that they return and they are not certain whether they will remain in the east or not."

"Mr. and Mrs. J. Bamford and family went to Ukiah this morning and will remain there a short time. Mr. Bamford will engage in business here again as soon as he can secure a location."[8]

The Jess Bamford family did come back to Santa Rosa to reopen his bakery on Third Street. But, like so many, their immediate response was despair, as illustrated in a letter from Victoria Bamford to her sister in Potter Valley: "Downtown there is not a store left and our poor old Bakery is a thing of the past.... Jess was very fortunate, he left his can of money in the Bakery and yesterday he and Art McCord dug till they got it out.... Some of the rich men are poor today. And Santa Rosa is gone."[9]

Meanwhile, Santa Rosans were enormously proud of their unselfishness. Nurses and doctors worked long hours without pay. Laborers and out-of-work clerks worked together to rebuild. Almost everyone was broke and out of work, so they helped each other. One of the sources of great pride in the community was that, of all the hundreds of thousands of dollars collected for California earthquake relief, Santa Rosans declared they needed only $40,000 to get back on their feet.

One reason for this positive approach was economic. No one wanted to spread the word that people were leaving town in substantial numbers or that there was any reason at all for investors to be wary of Santa Rosa's future. City Council minutes and newspaper stories, veiled in clouds of boosterism, do not tell the real story of the months that followed April. The city fathers, however, knew the truth.

The first official day of business after the quake was June 4, following a series of city-proclaimed legal holidays which made it possible for people to get their financial affairs in order. By summer, the council was receiving reports the Santa Rosa assessment on the tax rolls had decreased by $341,865 from the 1905 figures, while the county as a whole had gained $12,905.[10] Financial setbacks were not the only aspects of the earthquake that were purposefully underestimated. Historians, digging through official records eighty years later, would be able to prove the death toll in Santa Rosa was nearly double the announced figure of sixty.[11]

Advertisements provide clues to the fearfulness that produced a new caution. Hahman's Drug Store installed the town's first plate glass window in new Santa Rosa. The City Council passed new building codes. Fire escapes were added to apartment houses; a "modern" housing system; replaced the residence hotels where so many had died. Basalt blocks from the nearby Annadel quarries became the building material of choice, replacing bricks. All this was duly noted in the official records. But no one ever said why. Few spoke the word "earthquake."

No one was fooled by all this bravado. Santa Rosa's grim situation was widely known. So was the determination with which the citizens faced the future. The November bulletin of the Pacific Coast Travelers' Association contains an emotional description of Santa Rosa's courage in the face of disaster, beginning: "Santa Rosa is the pluckiest city in California."

At the end of the fiscal year Mayor John P. Overton issued a report from the Relief Committee that put the tragedy in some economic perspective. Donations from companies, cities, and individuals totaled $60,608.18. Two donations of $10,000 each headed the list, one from Standard Oil Company, the other from the *Los Angeles Times*. Every donation was included in the report—$25

The first floor of the new Overton Hotel on Fourth Street. Santa Rosa became a forest of steel reinforcements as the downtown was rebuilt.

—*Chamber of Commerce Collection*

from the Mendocino County town of Covelo, $17.50 from the citizens of Eureka, Nevada, $300 from Weaverville and $70.72 from Chadron, Nebraska, to name just a few.[12]

The money was spent in predictable ways: $2,020.69 for cash relief for the injured, funds for a free lunch counter on Main Street to feed the rescue workers, money for inspection of sewers and chimneys, money for extra police work. The generosity of Captain Bertrand Rockwell, a grain merchant from Kansas City who had come to visit his daughter and her banker husband James Edwards, was noted. Captain Rockwell, said the report, "gave money to assist in rescue work, paying cash every evening."

The Relief Committee concluded its accounting with an acknowledgment of the thousands of individual charities not included, estimating some 2,500 people received donations of food and clothing from friends and strangers alike. There were further kindnesses from neighbors, illustrated by such gestures as Sebastopol's loan of its new fire truck, loaded on a flatbed rail car and sent to Santa Rosa, which were not reflected in the Relief Committee's report.[13]

A year-end summary of 1906 in the *Press Democrat* calls it, somewhat obliquely, "one of the history-making years of the age in Santa Rosa." Editor Finley, characteristically, points ahead with optimism. There were $1 million worth of building permits issued in the city between May and December, he said, and "magnificent building blocks, more attractive and substantial than ever, adorn the city's thoroughfare, some completed and occupied, others nearly so. Right on through the new year, rehabilitation will continue and all will be well by this time next year."

Finley's optimism was well-placed. By midsummer, businesses were permanently relocated or engaged in construction. Pedersen's was doing considerable business in linoleum, carpets, and "earthquake-proof" furniture for the new stores. Banker Frank Brush had plans drawn for a new building on Mendocino Avenue to house, among other

enterprises, Keegan Brothers clothing store. Funds were being raised by St. Rose's "mother church" in Tomales for repairs to the damaged building built in 1901 by stonemason Peter Maroni. The stone church had actually suffered comparatively little damage due to Maroni's skill as a mason and to pastor John Cassin's insistence on steel reinforcement. Maroni was hired to repair the tower and to do the necessary stone work on the Western Hotel at the California Northwestern railroad tracks.

The Odd Fellows began work immediately on a new building. The Dougherty-Shea Building was rebuilt. The Native Sons proceeded with building plans made before the earthquake. The destruction of the Athenaeum building cost the town not only the theater of which it was so proud but the post office as well. The theater was never rebuilt, but a new site was selected for the post office, at the corner of Fifth and A streets. The first post-earthquake

REPORT OF RELIEF COMMITTEE SANTA ROSA, CAL., 1906

Mayor Overton's report, at right, showed receipts and expenditures from April 20 to July 31. U.S. cities were generous in their support of Santa Rosa.

The skeleton of the new courthouse in Santa Rosa's plaza was a visible sign of the town's recovery.

"entertainments" were moving pictures shown at the Rosalie Theater in the old church building on Fifth Street on June 14. There were big crowds at each of the two showings. The Victory Skating Pavilion in Grace Brothers Park reopened in July.

Citizens were still jumpy from the hundreds of aftershocks which followed the quake. "We have had slight shocks here for two weeks but are getting used to them.... We are all well and getting our nerves settled," wrote Jessie in early May, "but at night I dream of earthquakes and wake up thinking there is one." Santa Rosans were ready for the pronouncement of a distinguished and exotic visitor. Dr. F. Omari, a professor at the Imperial University in Tokyo and, according to the *Press Democrat*, "the inventor of that most remarkable instrument, the seismograph," came on an inspection tour of earthquake damage to Northern California. He stayed in Santa Rosa as a guest of Kanaye

Nagasawa, the Japanese vintner at Fountaingrove Ranch, and before he left he told residents they need not fear earthquake again. His statement to the press: "An earthquake of such proportions as you had here on April 18 means the removal of an immense underground weak point so that a district strongly shaken by an earthquake is really settling down to a safe and stable position and is regarded seismically as a safe place. As a matter of fact, there has been no instance in which great earthquakes have happened successively at one and the same place."[14]

Once the quaking stopped, the main concern was that the new town be better than the old one had been. Finley urged his readers to be forward-looking in their rebuilding plans. "Sonoma County will have to build a new courthouse, and the county will have to be bonded for the purpose.

It was business as usual as soon as the dust settled. Above, Lee Brothers drayage company's post-quake office. Below, Santa Rosa's "shacktown" City Hall

While we're about it, we might as well build it right. A modern, up-to-date structure is the only thing that will fill the bill."[15] Finley's editorials were more than upbeat. "It is very probable," he wrote in early July, "that if it had not been for the earthquake and fire, Santa Rosa would have had to wait a long time for a new post office."

The pattern of redevelopment would prove to be fortuitous in coming years, as the automobile replaced rail travel and the term "highway" became a household word. The earthquake provided the opportunity for Santa Rosa to adjust its traffic patterns to accommodate the future means of transportation. The business district which had swung westward to meet the railroad in 1870 gradually turned back to a north-south orientation, taking up its place as an important way station for the increasing traffic from San Francisco north. Both newspapers called for the establishment of new street lines and wider thoroughfares suitable to cars and trucks.

The period from 1906 to 1908 was a busy one. The rhythm of hammer striking nail set the tempo, and the enthusiastic optimism of the newspapers set the mood. By the spring of 1908, the new courthouse was in place in the square, and the new post office was under construction. The Exchange Bank, which had reopened after the quake with a cabin erected in front of the vault that was virtually all that was left of the bank structure, was rebuilt. So was the Santa Rosa Bank.

The cornerstone for the courthouse—the same cornerstone laid in 1884 for the ruined building, now chiseled with a new inscription—was put down at the corner of the skeletal structure-in-progress with great ceremony on April 9, 1908. "A spectacular scene," is what the *Press Democrat* writer called the events of the day. "The immense crowd blocked Hinton Avenue and the places of vantage ground in front and at the sides of the building. It had the aspect of a summer day and the bright gowns of the women and children and the light attire of the men lent a radiant dash of color. Back of the Grand

—Chamber of Commerce Collection

A flower seller offers some cheer to weary Santa Rosans from his makeshift florist shop next to the library on Fourth Street.

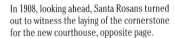

In 1908, looking ahead, Santa Rosans turned out to witness the laying of the cornerstone for the new courthouse, opposite page.

Lodge platform the Sir Knights [Knights Templar of the Masonic Lodge, which presided over the formalities] were grouped and their showy uniforms lent finish to the picture."

The copper box enclosed in the cornerstone in 1884 was opened for the Board of Supervisors the day before the new stone was put in place. It contained the usual complement of daily and weekly newspapers and rosters of elected officials, as well as an assortment of business cards, coins, and an Indian arrowhead. The contents were replaced with current additions and a historical sketch of the great earthquake written by Herbert Slater.

Supervisor Herbert Austin presided at the ceremony. Judge Emmet Seawell "spoke eloquently...review[ing] the significance of historical events in which Sonoma County had figured." The "grand orator" was Judge Albert Burnett, who spoke at length of the great rebuilding enterprise and the spirit of the citizens.

It would be two years before the courthouse, designed by architect J.W. Dolliver and built by the San Francisco contracting firm of Rickon-Ehrhart, would open for business. The process did not go smoothly. There was argument over the amount of money spent and charges the new building was of shoddy construction and not earthquake proof. The district attorney, Clarence Lea, was called to mediate the issue and declared it safe. Dedication day was May 6, 1910.

Housing patterns changed. Many of the small hotels where so many died in the earthquake did not rebuild. Permanent hotel residents found flats or apartments in converted homes. The two large hostelries, the Occidental Hotel and the Overton Hotel, dominated the downtown area. The economy was still shaky, although such a word would not have been uttered. In his year-end report on December 31, 1906, editor Finley accentuated the positive, tallying the miles of additional water and sewer mains and the new wider streets.

The rebuilding and enlarging of the flour mill, the shoe factory, the woolen mills, and the wineries; Grace Brothers Brewery plus their new enterprise, Santa Rosa's first creamery; National Ice Company's ice plant on Sebastopol Road; the expanded cannery; a new skating rink and a bathhouse and swimming pool on A Street near Fifth; and the $280,000 bonds passed for the construction of a new courthouse—all seemed to be indicators Santa Rosa had taken the worst fate had to offer and bounced right back. After an unexpected and unpleasant interruption, it was time to get on to the 20th century. ❧

—Finley Collection

The corner stone of the new

Sonoma County Court House

is to be laid on

Thursday, April 9, 1908, at 1:30 p. m.

by the

Grand Lodge of Masons of California
assisted by the Santa Rosa Lodge

You are hereby invited to join with us in the performance of this ceremony

The parade will be formed at the corner of Fifth and Humboldt Streets at 1:30 p. m.

Moving Forward

Hoof beats, the creak of wagon wheels, and the whistles of the trains were the sounds which passed for traffic noise at the turn of Sonoma County's century. Although Santa Rosa's first automobile, a "Schelling," created in a Fourth Street bicycle shop, was on the street in 1899, it would be a decade and more before the chug and cough of the early gasoline engine would smooth to a hum and become a familiar background noise in the town.

The train whistle dominated all but the remotest corners of the county. There were up trains and down trains, from San Francisco and Oakland; there were in trains and out trains, from Sebastopol, Forestville, and Two Rock. There were trains which hauled paving blocks out of Rincon and Sonoma valleys, and boxcars filled with apples, prunes, and barrels of wine to meet the Central Pacific for eastern markets.

There were trains carrying people—salesmen from San Francisco, Denver, and Chicago; students from the western part of the county commuting to Santa Rosa High School or Sweet's Business College; baseball teams from Petaluma coming to play the local "nine." There were young men passengers who worked as messengers for banks, carrying satchels of cash and bonds, or for the freight companies, chaperoning important cargo from sender to receiver; businessmen bound for San Francisco or Oakland; families visiting married sisters in San Jose; young couples going on their honeymoon.

People met the trains. Families came to meet soldiers coming home from far-off places, sons and even a few daughters, home from college. Stages, later autobuses, to carry passengers to parts of Sonoma County where the trains did not go, met every passenger train arrival and endeavored to connect with every departure.

Santa Rosa's street railways converted to electricity in 1905 when the Petaluma & Santa Rosa Railroad bought the lines as part of its transit system. The streetcars went along Fourth Street from the plaza to Humboldt and Benton streets, and south along Santa Rosa Avenue to the fairgrounds and South Park, and west to the Olive Street neighborhood.

In retrospect, the number of passenger trains seems staggering. In 1906, the north-south main line known at that time as the California Northwestern (It had been the San Francisco & North Pacific and would become Northwestern Pacific in 1907.) carried 100,814 passengers to and from Santa Rosa, a city of less than 9,000 residents. The new P&SR enjoyed increased traffic as shoppers and farmers and students switched to the more convenient electric line. But it was also first to be affected by the motor car. In 1912, for example, the line carried 760,725 passengers on its interurban streetcars. In 1916 the number dropped to 619,729.[1]

Still, in 1927, the year the P&SR opened its new mission-style stucco depot at Fourth and Wilson streets, there were twenty interurban streetcars from the electric line's "great white fleet" in and out every day. At the stone depot at the western end of Fourth Street, ten Northwestern Pacific trains from San Francisco, some ending in Santa Rosa, some going on to Eureka or making connections to the Russian River area, passed through daily—with added excursion trains to the river resorts on weekends. From the North Street Southern Pacific depot there was one passenger train arriving and departing daily, two on Sunday, serving serious travelers who were bound for the Central Pacific and points east.

There were few secrets in the days of train travel. The depots were meeting places, a train trip a social event. Everyone knew who went to the city on business and probably, with plenty of time for close questioning, what that business was. Certainly, the railroad employees knew.

Waldo Erickson graduated from Santa Rosa High School in 1927 and took his first job with Northwestern

Going to town along the Sonoma road in 1910, a Rincon Valley rancher approaches Brush Creek.

—Beth Winter Collection

Pacific as a baggageman. There were only two things he didn't like about the job, Erickson would later recall. "I didn't like shipping corpses—we shipped a lot of corpses; remains is what they were called and they had to buy a ticket and pay excess baggage." He didn't like actors much, either. "There were two theaters in Santa Rosa then, the G&S and the Cline, which had vaudeville shows.[2] Every vaudeville performer came with half a motortruck load of luggage."[3]

Lydia Curtis was the first woman hired in NWP's Santa Rosa office. Later, after forty-one years on the job as clerk and agent, she would remember the long hours a rate clerk spent searching Interstate Commerce regulations and freight tariffs, which were constantly changing. Passenger rates and routings were equally complex; a round-trip ticket to Chicago, painstakingly handwritten, might drag on the floor when unfolded.[4]

NWP was created in 1907 as a partnership venture between Southern Pacific and Santa Fe—a compromise agreement reached after the two western giants had battled each other to a standstill for control of the route north to Eureka. It was a challenge from a third railroad, Western Pacific that brought the adversaries together. The old "Donahue Line," first into Santa Rosa and still the north-south route as the California Northwestern, was part of the package. Southern Pacific had purchased the CNW Railroad Company in 1903.[5]

Northwestern Pacific's "down train" at the Santa Rosa depot at the end of Fourth Street. The depot was the heart of the town. In 1927 there were ten trains daily to Santa Rosa from the Bay Area.

—*Fred A. Stindt Collection*

The jointly owned NWP built the tracks north to Humboldt County, along the tortuous Eel River route, in 1913, taking turns in controlling the operation of the line, until 1929 when Southern Pacific bought the Santa Fe half and NWP became a wholly owned subsidiary of Southern Pacific. NWP, Southern Pacific's most profitable arm, employed some 500 people in the railroad yard in Tiburon and had a reputation as the most efficient freight handler in the United States before World War II.

The "juice line," as the Petaluma & Santa Rosa Electric Railway was known, prospered through the early years of the century. In addition to its freight line service from orchards and poultry farms, its interurban trolleys plied the countryside from Two Rock to Forestville, bringing passengers—ranchers on business, housewives for shopping, students for school classes—directly into the shopping districts of Santa Rosa, Petaluma, and Sebastopol. Farmers found the electric line convenient. Stops were less than a mile apart, and cans of milk bound for the Petaluma creamery or crates of eggs for San Francisco delivery routes could be loaded from a trackside platform within wheelbarrow distance of the chickenhouse or barn. Pick-ups in early evening made it possible for fresh farm products to meet the NWP trains and the ferries to be in San Francisco kitchens by breakfast time.

But the P&SR, quick to expand, was financially fragile. The San Francisco Northern Railroad Company became a partner in the P&SR in 1914 with plans to extend the electric line north to Healdsburg and south to Cotati. Those lines were never built and the next few years were rocky ones for the company, which was now jointly owned by bondholders and stockholders. In 1918 the First Federal Trust Company, as trustee for second mortgage holders of the P&SR, filed for foreclosure, a friendly action brought for the purpose of refinancing. This reorganization carried the electric railroad to 1932, when it was purchased by Northwestern Pacific. Passenger service was discontinued and the tracks up Fourth Street removed.

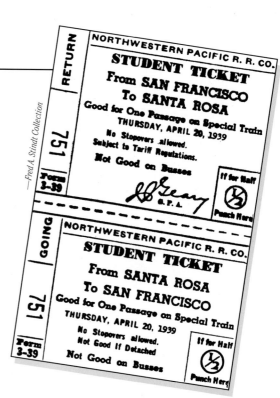

—Fred A. Stindt Collection

Southern Pacific's depot on North Street burned in 1932. It was never rebuilt and the railroad line to Sonoma closed soon after. The line had been built in 1888 to connect Santa Rosa with the Central Pacific. It was known in the 19th century as the "McDonald Line," for fruit broker Mark McDonald, its principal advocate.

— LeBaron Collection

—Finley Collection

The railroads were dangerous. Crossings claimed the lives of the unwary or the unlucky with fearful regularity. If the noise of the early automobile engines did not obscure the warning whistles, the reckless abandon of the new mode of transportation overcame caution.

The P&SR crossing of Sebastopol Road, the SP crossing of Fourth Street, the NWP crossing of College Avenue—all claimed their share of lives. In 1915, when the first of the newly invented "wig-wag" signals were installed at the College crossing and the Ninth Street crossing, they were heralded as protection against the "death traps" the railroad crossings had become.

But even with the new signals, there were frightful accidents. In 1921, two motorcylists were killed by an SP freight on Fourth Street. And, while there were only minor injuries, a train-car collision at the same crossing caught the attention of the community. Riding with brewery owner Frank Grace in his Cadillac when it was hit by a train were his four young sons, Tom, Bill, Jim, and John, plus their friends Allen Campbell and Warren Richardson.

Train wrecks were far less frequent, but even more fearsome. On a Monday evening in August of 1910, the good fortune of Sonoma County's first "through" railroad, known as "the lucky road," ran out. The up train, carrying Santa Rosans and Petalumans home from the city, collided with a southbound work train at Ignacio, killing twelve people and

The distinctive "headgear" of an electric engine, above, marked the Petaluma & Santa Rosa Railroad, known familiarly to railroad men as the "juice line." On the opposite page, an NWP passenger train, southbound to Santa Rosa, slices between orchard and vineyard near Geyserville in 1955.

18

injuring twenty. It was the worst railroad disaster in the area north of San Francisco Bay.[6]

The accident occurred when the conductor on the California Northwestern work train miscounted his northbound trains, mistaking the Sonoma train for No. 6, the passenger train bound for Santa Rosa . He signaled his engineer the track was clear and the work train pulled off the siding at Ignacio onto the main line. As it came around a curve, No. 6 was dead ahead, stopped on the main line tracks, all brakes set. The work train was traveling at thirty-five miles per hour. Eyewitnesses said the two engines "reared into the air" on impact.

Remarkably, both engineers survived the crash, although they were seriously injured. It was the occupants of the smoking car who died, trapped in the mass of twisted metal when the baggage car directly in front of them was pushed into their car by the force of the collision. Eleven of the twelve dead where killed outright in the "smoker."

The hero of the day was a Catholic priest from a parish in Benicia who was on his way to visit his family in Healdsburg. The Rev. Lawrence Jago, according to newspaper accounts, armed himself with an axe and cut his way into the smoker, pulling dead and injured from the wreckage, offering prayers and last rites along with first aid.

In Petaluma, a band had been playing in the square on lower Main Street as a crowd gathered to hear a speech by Congressman Duncan McKinlay. The first indication something had gone wrong was the caravan of automobiles speeding through a town where an auto was still the exception rather than the rule. When people in the crowd recognized the occupants as doctors from Santa Rosa, there was a near-panic. It was John Olmsted, editor of the Petaluma Argus, who brought the news, rushing from the newspaper office to stop the band and announce the disaster. "The meeting was called off," the Argus later reported, "Mr. McKinlay not caring to talk politics at such a time."[7]

It was the nature of the Sonoma County communities that nearly everyone seemed to know someone who was coming on the up train. Frantic citizens jammed the telephone lines and crowded into the newspaper offices, seeking information. Editor Olmsted called it "the most terrible night since the days of the great earthquake." Petaluma physicians rallied to follow the Santa Rosa medical contingent. Dr. Samuel Bogle, county physician and administrator of the County Hospital, left with Congressman McKinlay in the first car. Other physicians and nurses followed—as automobiles could be secured. When not another working automobile could be found in Petaluma, anxious citizens took buggies and headed south for the accident scene.

Attorney Frank Meyer was the first passenger to reach Petaluma. His account of the smoking car, telescoped "like a paper bag," and of passengers pinned in their seats, unable to escape, proved no exaggeration. Santa Rosa's first eyewitness was Monte LeBaron, who was not in the smoker but in a coach car. Escaping with minor injuries, LeBaron ran the mile and a half to the town of Ignacio to report the disaster and to telegraph his family he was safe.

The dead included Pincus Levin, a partner in Santa Rosa's tannery business; Herman Bayer, owner of the Model Saloon in Santa Rosa's Exchange Bank building; two young Petalumans who were riding as messengers, Wilkie Emerson and Will Poehlmann; T.W. Richardson, a Petaluma store manager; journalist George Riley; John Wilkinson, a San Quentin guard; Neil Neilsen, a Black Point resident; and five salesmen—two from Rockland, Illinois, two from San Francisco, and one from Berkeley.

The sale of automobiles was slow going in the early years of the century. The two Schelling autos built by bicycle mechanic George Schelling and his blacksmith-machinist brother Alex in 1899 introduced the concept of the gas-powered vehicle to the community. Their one and only customer, Dr. James Jesse, drove his Schelling courageously, if not well, through the streets on his

A "Great White Car" of the P&SR's interurban fleet, below, picked up rural residents in front of their western Sonoma County ranches and deposited them in downtown Santa Rosa.

At right, an early model of the P&SR trolley passes along Fourth Street in front of the Exchange Bank in 1915.

—Finley Collection

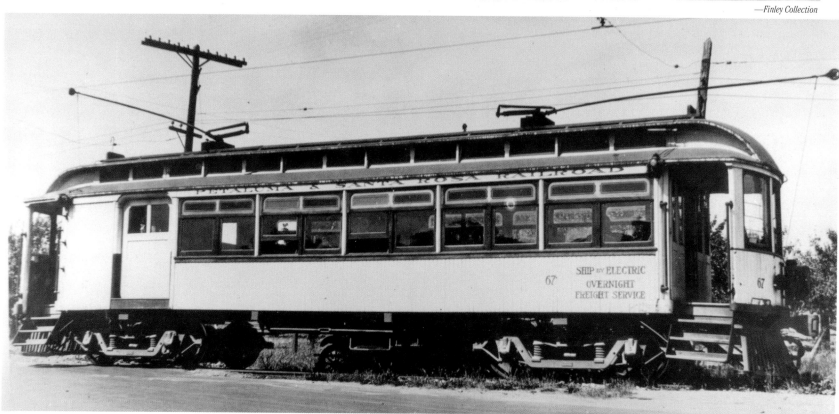

—LeBaron Collection

missions of mercy. Actually, Dr. Jesse was adequate as a driver, it was as a stopper that he failed. The forward progress of the Schelling could be halted only by disengaging the gears, a system the physician had difficulty mastering. He once drew a crowd as he made several trips up and down Fifth Street while trying in vain to get the vehicle out of gear. He finally stopped by swerving to avoid a vegetable cart and tipping the Schelling on its side, its wheels still going around.

George Schelling foreswore his own rudimentary design for a superior model in 1901. The Oldsmobile, a lightweight one-cylinder car which sold for $650, was in volume production and Schelling became Santa Rosa's first auto dealer, selling the Olds product from his bicycle shop on Fourth Street. His enterprise was soon joined by the town's other bicycle shop, the Santa Rosa Cyclery. Its manager, Fred Wiseman, destined to build the county's first airplane, took on the REO dealership, selling Ransom E. Olds' "improved" automobile, the one which bore his initials.

Santa Rosa had its share of speed demons. Young men like Wiseman and his friend Ben Noonan went as fast as they could go on bicycles, switched to automobiles as soon as they were available, and then took to the air when that became a semi-viable option. Noonan had earned local distinction by mounting his bicycle to race a train to Sebastopol and win in 1899. In 1909 he achieved further glory when he drove a Stoddard-Dayton to victory against professional race drivers from all over the state in the first-ever California Grand Prize Race.[8]

The race was a catalyst for the increasing interest in the automobile in Sonoma County. Santa Rosa was selected as the starting and finishing point for the fifty-two-mile endurance run. The course was over dirt roads (there was little else at this early date in transportation history) north to Healdsburg, around that town's plaza to Geyserville, east to Dry Creek Road, and then south through the Dry Creek Valley to the Santa Rosa road and the finish line.

There were fourteen cars entered. Drivers came from as far away as San Diego, hired by automobile manufacturers' representatives to drive for the glory and publicity a win would bring to their cars. There were two Stoddard-Daytons. One of them was Ben Noonan's car but, until twenty minutes before the race began, he had no plans to drive it in the competition. He had lent it to Houts Auto Company, the Santa Rosa Stoddard-Dayton dealer, with the agreement the company's professional, a driver named Peters, would be at the wheel.

Noonan was seated at a table at the Hotel Lebanon, dressed in his best Sunday suit, eating his breakfast, when someone from the Houts Agency rushed in to say the plans had gone awry and he must come and drive his car or both

At right, the participants in California's Grand Prize Race of 1909 get off in a cloud of dust from the starting line in Santa Rosa. Below, George Schelling and his family pose in a 1909 model Studebaker near their home on Washington Street. Schelling, who built Santa Rosa's first automobile, was also the town's first Studebaker dealer.

—Claire Dowling Collection

—*LeBaron Collection*

Stoddards would be pulled out of the race. The second Stoddard was driven by Noonan's good friend and fellow speedster, Fred Wiseman.

Noonan ran to the garage, which was in the first block of Mendocino Avenue, put overalls and a jumper over his church clothes, climbed into his machine, and advanced to the starting line. Hundreds were there to cheer the drivers on their way. Hundreds more, perhaps thousands as the newspaper reported, lined the roadsides and crowded around Healdsburg's plaza. The day before the fourteen drivers had driven their big machines slowly through the streets of Santa Rosa, leading the annual Rose Carnival parade. On race day all roads had been closed to regular traffic and the town was crowded with the occupants of 150 touring cars from the Bay Area, most of them driven by members of the San Francisco Motor Club, which co-sponsored the race along with the Sonoma County Automobile Association.

Santa Rosa's Hudson dealer, below, displays his new models along Main Street. Early automobile dealers engaged in stunts such as driving to the top of Bennett Peak to promote this revolutionary new means of transportation.

—LeBaron Collection

The "autobus," shown as it leaves the Santa Rosa depot, circa 1930, and Santa Rosa's beloved "little yellow bus"—a nickel a ride—which began service in 1929.

—*LeBaron Collection*

—*Robert A. Burrowes Collection*

Santa Rosan Angelo Rossi at right, was a pioneer in motorcycle racing in Northern California. One of his many champion riders was Earnest Heine, shown astride Rossi's racing-model Indian.

The race was won in one hour, five minutes, and eighteen seconds. It was survival of the fittest machine. Only six finished. The Pope-Hartford sheared off a timing gear at the start and never left the line. The Thomas, driven by Evan DeJong, dropped out just before the ten-mile mark after losing a rim and a tire. A.J. Welch's Packard picked up a nail coming back through Healdsburg. The Speedwell, driven by an Englishman named Gordon, also suffered from "punctures." The Comet had two flat tires at the same time. Both Stearns, favorites at the start of the race, dropped out with mechanical problems.

The survivors were not without their trials. The Tourist, driven by a man named Ely, lost thirteen minutes when a tube broke in the ignition and dropped into the flywheel. Ely stuck with it and finished, albeit sixth and last.

—*Sonoma County Museum*

— Press Democrat Collection

Fay Sheets, driving the Acme, lost a tire off the front wheel and drove the last sixteen miles without it to finish fourth. The second-place car, a Stevens-Duryea driven by a man named Ontank, finished with a frame cracked almost in two pieces. Wiseman, who stopped to fix a broken rod on Dry Creek Road, took advantage of the Acme's lost tire and finished third. Frank Murphy's Buick finished fifth.

None was more splendid, however, than Noonan's run. New to automobile racing, he used his knowledge of the roads, gained in thousands of miles of bicycling, to advantage and kept what the newspaper described as "a thrilling speed." He was two minutes and twelve seconds ahead of the Stevens-Duryea. Draped in garlands of flowers, he was cheered by the crowds as he passed. His car was photographed from every angle by a man hired by the Houts Auto Company.[9]

There would be many more motor races in Sonoma County, on both roads and tracks. Santa Rosa automobile enthusiasts boasted about having "the fastest flat track for auto racing in the world" in 1912 and made plans for a "Barney Oldfield Day" in early November when the great race driver would compete on that track. Rain canceled the race, but he came again in July of 1913 and covered the mile track in forty-nine and two-fifths seconds in an exhibition run.

In the late 1930s, twenty-two of the fifty cars entered in a "Tin Lizzie Derby" on the horse track at the fairgrounds piled up in one of the most spectacular crashes of the age. There was only one injury—a broken arm.

Motorcycle races brought the best of the Indian, Thor, Excelsior, and Merkel riders to town.[11] Angelo Rossi, born in Kenwood in 1900, aspired to be among those riders. He began racing motorcycles when he was still in his teens, working for a cycle repair shop in Oakland. In 1922, when his boss refused him a few days off to compete in a race in Fresno, Rossi quit his job, went to the race, and came home to Santa Rosa to open his own motorcycle shop.

Even after Rossi retired from professional racing, his shop continued to sponsor racing bikes and developed important race riders, including his son Don, Ernest Heine, Al Scoffone, and Dick "Bugsy" Mann, who was twice grand national champion. Ang Rossi Motorcycles, a business which passed to his sons and grandsons, was among the pioneer leaders in motorcycle sales. Rossi helped organize the North Bay Motorcycle Club in 1939. The organization's clubhouse would later be renamed for him.

In 1921 and '22, Sonoma County made an attempt to enter the big-time auto racing circuit with the construction of the Cotati Speedway. The banked board track brought Indianapolis 500 winners like Tommy Milton and Ralph DePalma and the great Oldfield to compete for purses of up to $25,000.

In its two seasons, the Cotati Speedway drew trainloads of spectators from all over the Bay Area and caused traffic to back up for many miles at the ferry docks as the racing enthusiasts made their way home.

It was a 100-mile "Tin Lizzie Derby" at the Santa Rosa horse track in the late 1930s which put another Sonoma County entry into the racing record books. The first of what was to become an annual event, the Model T race drew fifty cars, with dozens of Sonoma County drivers in addition to auto sportsmen from all over Northern California. In the 80th lap, two cars locked wheels and skidded on the dirt track. The cloud of dust they raised obscured the vision of the drivers behind them and they piled up, one after another. Spectators, who couldn't see for the dust, heard the screech of brakes and the sounds of metal hitting metal.

When the dust had lifted, there were twenty-two cars in the smash-up. Drivers and mechanics would call it miraculous that the only injury was a broken arm, suffered by driver Gino Buffi of Healdsburg. There was no fire, despite the fact that the track was flooded with gasoline.

When the wreckage was cleared away, the race went on. The winner was nineteen-year-old Andy Triacca of Santa

The Cotati Speedway, a banked board track, brought Indianapolis drivers and Bay Area crowds to Sonoma County for two busy seasons in the 1920s.

—*Charles Kruse Collection*

Rosa. He avoided the pile-up by crashing into a fence and came away with only a spike in his tire. He was able to continue on his spare—one of only twenty-five drivers to finish. He drove the final lap at a daredevil fifty-seven miles per hour and took home the prize, which was $350.[12]

Later, in the 1950s, drag racers would compete at a strip on the auxiliary airfield in Cotati built by the Navy in World War II. Sports cars, too, would race on the Cotati Raceway course. Hardtop racing was a popular post World War II sport on tracks throughout Northern California, including the Santa Rosa Speedway northwest of the city.

Two decades into the new century, the automobile would become commonplace, no longer the exception to the transportation rule. Once begun, the automotive juggernaut would be as impossible to stop as Dr. Jesse's Schelling. Within forty years there would be a road system throughout the county and the state, the inner bay and the Golden Gate would be bridged, and the all-powerful railroads would be fighting for their very existence.

In May of 1912 the Santa Rosa City Council passed its first traffic ordinances. Autos and motorcycles must be muffled. They must also have lights to turn on after dark. Cars were to stay to the right when meeting another car, pass on the left, and, according to the newspaper, honor "a number of other desirable changes from the old order of things which daily caused much confusion." Special Officer Nielsen was empowered to arrest speeders and to be compensated for this service at the rate of $2.50 for each fine levied.

The early car dealers were a colorful lot. In 1911, William Davis of Davis-McNee Auto Company announced he would drive to the top of Bennett Peak in a Mitchell 20. The

The garage owned by Charlie Kruse and Sam Bertoli at 113 Third Street, above, was a busy place in 1922. The Grand Garage, at Third and Main, below, was a landmark for Santa Rosa "autoists" for many years.

hill was steep enough, he pointed out, to require four horses to pull a wagon to the top. His 30 horsepower auto, with five passengers aboard, actually made it to within seventy-five feet of the peak. The stunt was considered a great success.

Car owners, referred to as "autoists" in a Grand Garage advertisement in 1912, bragged as much as the dealers. Hop broker Chris Donovan (who went so far as to name his 1913 Cadillac touring car, calling it "Navonod," which was his name spelled backward) came home from a trip through the Sacramento and San Joaquin valleys to issue a full report to the newspaper, including the news the entire trip had been accomplished with "nary a puncture."

The automobile had come to stay. By 1915, there were enough cars on the streets of Santa Rosa to produce complaints about traffic. "Auto speed burners" were wearing out College Avenue. There were two full-fledged automobile dealers and six garages in addition to the bicycle shop auto agents. In 1916 a taxi service was offering trips to anywhere in the city for 10 cents. By 1918, businessmen were talking about the need for an "auto park" for travelers. Tourism was becoming an industry.

However, the horse and buggy days were not quite over. There were still four livery stables still operating in Santa Rosa: the old and established Fashion Stable on Main Street, which had room for 100 horses and boarded many for the "carriage trade," McGregor & Sons, McAlpine's, and Myler's. Three harness makers—Bauman's, Belden & Hehir, and O.G. Smith—and a couple of busy horseshoers remained in business. In 1916, Traffic Officer Ragain stopped a Rincon Valley woman for driving her buggy without lights and was set upon with a buggy whip.[13]

In the 1920s, America took the automobile to its heart. In January of 1921 President Warren G. Harding offered the strongest endorsement to date by choosing to use a motorcar for his inauguration parade in place of the traditional presidential carriage. In Santa Rosa, the streets

Above, the Santa Rosa Auto Camp, across Mendocino Avenue from Santa Rosa High School, circa 1930.

L.G. Bonar's Independent Oil Company on Roberts Avenue, below, sold gasoline to pioneer motorists in 1915.

fairly roared with the sound of gasoline engines. The city hired a motorcycle police officer in 1920 to pursue the motorists which were impossible for a policeman on foot or bicycle to catch.

The automobile had not only revolutionized transportation, it had added a whole new dimension to the business community. The auto park had become a reality. Located on the site of the former Veterans Park at the end of McDonald Avenue, it was considered one of the best in the state, with a kitchen equipped with nine gas plates on pre-pay meters, a reading room, and a large pavilion. According to a newspaper article in July of 1921, showers were planned. Filling stations with attendants in white uniforms sprouted like mushrooms along the state highway. In 1924, there were twenty stations in Santa Rosa.[14]

In one week in May of 1923, there were thirty-one autos sold in Santa Rosa, the newspaper reported; the very next week, twenty-two more—one Cadillac, three Chevrolets, eight Fords, one Gardiner, two Dodges, one Olds, two Nashes, one Studebaker, and three Hupmobiles. In 1923, inventor Abner Doble, who would later make his home in Santa Rosa, broke ground for a new plant in Emeryville where he produced his revolutionary Doble Steam Car. Doble built just forty cars, the last one in 1932. He was an exacting man and the cars were engineered to perfection and sold with a warranty much like that of the Rolls Royce. But the cars cost $10,000 and the Crash of '29, which ended production of many less-expensive automobiles, ended the Doble Steam Car.[15]

In 1923 bids were let to operate four passenger buses over the principal streets of Santa Rosa as a city franchise. In 1929 a service calling itself a "motorized street car" began to ply the streets—a ten-minute ride for 5 cents.

———

Roads had always been a political issue, from the days when stagecoach drivers took county supervisors on wild rides along precipitous ocean cliffs to point up the need for better maintenance. From 1902's cattle drives down College Avenue from the SP depot on North to Noonan's Meat Company west of the NWP tracks, to the day in 1949 when the new section of Highway 101 through Santa Rosa was opened, the politics of traffic became increasingly more important in Sonoma County, as in all of California.

The rutted wagon roads followed the old Indian trails from the hills and valleys to the bay and the ocean, although the early settlers were generally headed in the opposite direction. As the county became more heavily populated, connecting roads reflected the original government surveys which divided the county into townships and sections rather than land grants.

As more sophisticated horsedrawn conveyances followed civilization to the Pacific Ocean, roads were smoothed by grading and graveling for the new century. And the advent of the automobile created a demand for many more improvements than could be made by a man with a horse and wagon and shovel.

City streets were graded and bridges built to accommodate the weight of the new machines. An automobile bridge across Santa Rosa Creek on A Street was built in 1924. In 1925 the city paved more than eighteen miles of city streets. Everyone was an expert. In 1927 residents of Howard Street threatened a lawsuit if the city insisted on paving their street with "Willite" rather than concrete. Three streets were given "boulevard" status that year, meaning cars must stop before crossing or entering these thoroughfares.

In the relatively flat lands of Sonoma County, redesigning the old rights-of-way for the automobile presented a challenge. There was no drastic change in routes. Petaluma Hill Road, one of the most heavily traveled routes of the 1800s, continued as the main north-south highway. The old road from Santa Rosa to Sebastopol, which was first graded in 1874, remained the way west. The first roads in the county had been on the

On the opposite page, a crash on Sonoma Highway, 1930s.

—Private collection

coast, the Russian sled roads of the early 1800s becoming the stage routes which connected the inland towns with the shipping points at little bays and "doghole" lumber ports from Bodega Bay to Fort Bragg.

The politics of road building, however, were as important as the routes. Citizens demanded road improvements from their government leaders, who were faced, at the same time, with the independent spirit of pioneer ranchers who routinely built fences across rights-of-way and tore up bridges when they needed lumber to repair a barn.

The first California state highway bonds were authorized in 1910, but the state could sell only a quarter of the first issue and each county was left on its own. Responsibility for roads in Sonoma County was divided

Horse-and-buggy days lasted well into the 1920s in Santa Rosa. The Fifth Street Stables was only one of several livery stables still doing business ten years after the automobile became popular.

—Finley Collection

according to supervisorial district. Each district had a roadmaster, a political appointee. There were continuing charges, in all districts, that supporters of incumbent supervisors received preferential treatment. Some charged one could determine the political stand of the owner of a ranch by the quality of the road passing his driveway.

In 1912 the Santa Rosa Chamber of Commerce began lobbying the legislature for road improvement measures in the county. By October of 1914, cognizant of the growing importance of the automobile and Sonoma County's reputation as a link in what Bay Area residents called the "bad road ring" of rural counties surrounding the urban area, businessmen formed the Sonoma County Good Roads Club, with eleven committee members pledged to improvements. The same month, as if to prove the allegations, the company operating the first autobus from Santa Rosa to Petaluma announced the service was being eliminated because of poor road conditions.

The beginning of the war in Europe in 1914, and the general uneasiness over what lay ahead for the United States, curbed financing and put road plans on hold. It was the onset of World War I, however, that brought about the first comprehensive road map for Sonoma County. Nervous county officials asked the county surveyor, M.P. Youker, to map all the automobile routes in the county for security purposes. When the war was over, Youker's map took on a pattern of colored lines, reflecting the move to establish an organized and maintained county highway system. Meanwhile, local officials continued to put pressure on the governor and legislature for construction of the north-south state highway.

One project, planned before the outbreak of hostilities in Europe, was accomplished. The first section of the north-south route to be paved in Sonoma County, the fourteen miles from Healdsburg to Santa Rosa, was completed in 1914.[16] The Petaluma-Santa Rosa section took longer. In 1916, state surveyors began work to establish an entirely new right-of-way, eschewing the old wagon roads. But the nation's entry into World War I delayed any decision or start of construction for two years. And the citizens were restless about the delay. An editorial in the *Press Democrat* in 1916 complained bitterly that Sonoma County had been assured, when its share of the bonds were purchased, work would be finished in time for the Panama-Pacific Exposition of 1915. "Very few tourists got to this part of the country," said the editorial. "They couldn't."[17]

The Bay Area was closing in on Sonoma County. In 1917, the Black Point cutoff was opened with accompanying fanfare, including a dinner and rodeo in Sonoma. The Petaluma to Santa Rosa section of Highway 101, following a valley route parallel to the old Petaluma Hill Road and Stony Point routes, through the town of Cotati, was finally opened in the fall of 1918. With some thirty-five miles of state highway in place, it was time to turn attention to the connecting county roads.

—*Chamber of Commerce Collection*

—LeBaron Collection

Winners of the Indian marathons of 1927 and 1928. At left, inset, Mad Bull, winner of the first race, with the "Princess of Happy Camp" and Flying Cloud (number 2), winner of the second race.

*T*he '20s were the decade for promotions and slogans. Bert Kerrigan was making Petaluma the "World's Egg Basket" and another promotional genius, Charley Pyle, hired by the REA, was putting the Redwood Empire on the map of the United States. One of his great successes was an "Indian Marathon," first run in 1927, in which Karoks from the upper Klamath River in Del Norte County competed against Zunis from New Mexico, reputed to be the world's best distance runners.

The wire services covered the event with enthusiasm. Pyle would later report to the REA that an average of 300 words per day appeared in newspapers all over the world in the week the runners were on the road. There were eleven contestants who left San Francisco's City Hall. Seven of the eleven finished the race, averaging sixty miles per day. Crowds lined the highway all the way, even in some of the remotest sections of northern Mendocino and southern Humboldt counties. Seven days, twelve hours, and thirty-four minutes later, a Karok named Mad Bull crossed the finish line in Grants Pass, Oregon. Despite his fleetness of foot, Mad Bull used his winnings to buy into the automobile age, spending $1,000 on a new car with his name painted on the door.

The race was so successful Pyle staged another a year later. This time there was at least one Sonoma County entrant, a Wappo chief named Hummingbird, who called on his people for support. The Wappos staged all-night dances to "induce good will for their runner." Santa Rosa's colors, however, were carried by Chochee, a Zuni. This time Flying Cloud, another Karok who had finished second in the first race, won, cutting twelve hours off Mad Bull's time. Mad Bull dropped out in Cloverdale, suffering abdominal cramps and "severe chafing."[18]

The county's Better Roads Bonds totaling $1,640,000, the first funds for such an endeavor, passed overwhelmingly in May of 1919. Before work began, the question of who controlled the roads had to be settled. A county engineer was appointed, entrusted with establishing a county road system. This decision occasioned a storm of controversy. The question of road control would be a major political issue into the 1920s.

Meanwhile, road crews continued to work doggedly on road improvements as politics and uncertain financing allowed. In the 1920s, the state highway was paved with concrete from Petaluma to Healdsburg.[19] The county had built concrete roads to Sonoma, to Freestone, through Sebastopol, and waterbound macadam roads from Freestone to Valley Ford, from Sonoma to the Napa County line, Alexander Valley Road to Franz Valley, and on Westside Road along the Russian River. Eastside Road was dirt, as were all the roads in the north part of the county and the route to Calistoga, after the Petrified Forest. The road from Bodega Corners to Bodega Bay was gravel.

None of these projects lacked for controversy. One example was the protest which arose in 1920 when the county proposed the new Sonoma highway abandon the road through Rincon Valley in favor of a route on the other side of Santa Rosa Creek, parallel to the railroad. The proposed new route would follow Sonoma Avenue, pass McDonald's reservoir (Lake Ralphine), the tiny community of Melitta, through the center of the old McDonald stone quarry and above Wymore's redwood grove. It was an unpopular choice. Apart from the surveyors who proposed it, it seemed to have no proponents. The people of Rincon Valley wanted to keep their road. The residents of Sonoma Avenue didn't want the traffic. The protest was effective. The route which became Highway 12 followed the old drive up the center of the valley.

The coastal stage route was still unpaved, following the route over Meyers Grade, although the county had hired two men who would become the "deans" of county roads, Marshall Wallace, later county engineer, and Chester King, road commissioner. They lived at Jenner and worked through the '20s building a new road to Fort Ross. A 1929 travelers' advisory rated the Shoreline Highway (Stinson Beach to Fort Bragg) as "vastly improved since last year. Joint inter-county road district now under way."[20] The cliff-hanger portions in Sonoma County, built with pick-and-shovel labor and a Fresno scraper, became State Highway 1.

By 1929, State Route 1 (later 101), designated the Redwood Highway, was paved from the Sausalito ferry terminus to Cloverdale with new twenty-foot-wide pavement from Penngrove to Santa Rosa. Work was continuous on much of that north-south route. Travel information promised fast dirt roads in sections where reconstruction was underway.

Roads were still the big political issue of the North Coast in the 1920s. Attempts at road building beyond Sonoma County had been sporadic and widely scattered. As the population grew (and became more vocal) in northern cities like Eureka and Crescent City, there was a growing demand for a major highway lengthwise through the state. The Mail Ridge Road along the rim of the Eel River canyon was a dry-weather route, suitable only for pack mules in rain and snow.

The counties kept whittling away at a path through the wilderness and, by 1920, there was a road of sorts from San Francisco to Eureka. It might take four full days to make the trip and it was distinctly a "take-a-shovel" route marked with broken axles and springs, boiling radiators and multiple flat tires. The route north of Eureka was even worse.

The citizens grew restive about the comparatively small amount of state and federal money being allocated to North Coast roads. In 1920 county supervisors and businessmen met in Santa Rosa to begin a mutual effort

There was only one way across the bay before 1937 and that was by boat. The San Francisco ferry left from Sausalito. Below, the ferryboat *Santa Rosa* slides down the ways at the Alameda shipyard in 1938.

—Gambini Collection

—Chamber of Commerce Collection

toward better transportation. They called themselves the North Bay Counties Highway Committee, a name which was changed within the year to the Redwood Highway Association. Once the highway was built, the organization broadened its program to include the promotion of tourism on the new highway and became the Redwood Empire Association.

The new highway was dedicated by 1924 and celebrated wildly throughout the decade. Photographers had a field day as the REA planned one promotional event after another.

The first autobus over the highway stopped in Santa Rosa for a photo with Luther Burbank. The 472 miles from Marin County to Josephine County, Oregon, including the famous "Avenue of the Giants" where the road wound through giant redwood trees in Humboldt County, were touted as the new vacation paradise in newspapers, magazines, and newsreels. By 1929 the REA travel information service could put on a positive face and report that 460 miles were "either paved, oiled or graveled. The beauty of the scenery and the equable climate makes up for any delays or temporary discomfort caused by this short twelve miles under construction."[21]

In 1933 the City Council of Santa Rosa turned the street maintenance of Santa Rosa, Hinton, Exchange, and Mendocino avenues over to the state as part of California's highway system. The result was a "new" Mendocino Avenue fifty feet wide from Fourth Street to College Avenue with nine-foot sidewalks on both sides.

President Franklin Roosevelt's make-work programs of the Depression-era 1930s resulted in welcome attention to Sonoma County's roads. An office of the National Re-Employment Service opened in Santa Rosa in 1933 and, by fall, several hundred people were working on road repair and bridge construction projects under the auspices of the Public Works Administration.

Until 1937 there were two ways to get to San Francisco from the area north of the bay. And both of them were by boat. Train passengers left the rails at Tiburon or Sausalito. The first autobus routes from Santa Rosa met the ferries. Motorists had the choice of Southern Pacific auto ferries to the Ferry Building or the first fleet of Golden Gate ferries to the foot of Hyde Street. Passengers heading for Oakland and the East Bay caught a ferry at San Quentin Point which took them to Richmond.

Named for the cities they served, the ferries provided dependable service, even in high seas. According to 1927 timetables, there were ferries every forty minutes from San Quentin to Richmond and every half-hour from Sausalito to San Francisco. By 1932, proponents of the Bay Bridge project were quieting opposition with statistics showing the bay was overcrowded with ferry traffic.

While daily commuters were rare, the crowds on the ferries returning to San Francisco and the East Bay were always formidable on Sunday nights as tourists returned to the urban area after weekends at the Russian River, a hike on Mount Tamalpais, or just a pleasant drive through the orchards and vineyards of Sonoma County. It was not unusual on a summer Sunday to find a line of autos snaking along the highway, which then skirted Richardson Bay, from Sausalito into downtown Mill Valley. A special event, like a rodeo in Sonoma or a race with big-name drivers at the board track in Cotati, could cause a traffic jam all the way to Petaluma if the ferries were running a little late. On the Fourth of July weekend in 1920, the *Press Democrat* reported a Santa Rosa man waited four hours and forty minutes to get his car on a ferry coming from San Francisco to Marin County. Thousands of autos, he said, were headed for the Russian River resorts and thousands of train passengers as well. The 8:15 p.m. up train arrived in Santa Rosa at 10:15 p.m, its six coaches filled with holiday revelers bound for the Russian River.

Lines for the Richmond ferry, swelled by college students from Marin and Sonoma counties heading back to

In 1927 Northwestern Pacific ordered three new diesel-electric powered auto ferries to compete with the fast service offered by Golden Gate's streamlined fleet. The new boats were the *Santa Rosa*, the *Mendocino*, and the *Redwood Empire*. The *Santa Rosa* was completed first, and its launching on March 17 was a festive occasion for the citizens of the namesake city.

Several hundred Santa Rosans traveled to the dry dock in Alameda via a special train to Sausalito, where they boarded the steamer *Tamalpais*, equipped with a fifteen-piece band for the occasion, for the trip across the bay.

Both Mayor John Overton and Chamber of Commerce President Frank Doyle spoke at the launching ceremony. But the honor of christening the 251-foot steel-hulled ferry went to a child. Twelve-year-old Jean Ayers, chosen as "Miss Santa Rosa" for the occasion, broke a bottle of proper Prohibition-era grape juice across its prow as the boat slid down the ways and the *Santa Rosa* was afloat, the moment recorded by a contingent of newsreel cameramen and press photographers.[22]

The *Santa Rosa* and her sister ships, launched in subsequent months, worked the bay for only eleven years. In 1938, a year after the opening of the Golden Gate Bridge, NWP discontinued ferry service and, the following year, sold the boats to the Puget Sound Navigation Company of Seattle, where the *Santa Rosa* became the *Enetai*.

Berkeley, meant waits of an hour or more on the long pier at San Quentin until the mid-1950s. College students were the savviest of ferry riders. Whether they were coming from the North Bay, Vallejo, or Martinez, they soon learned to walk the line of cars until some sympathetic soul let them ride on in the back seat, paying the 50 cents due for an additional passenger, instead of the $2 fare for walk-ons. The money saved could be spent on berry pie and coffee in the top deck restaurant.

It seems something of a miracle that the Bay Area's two great bridges could be financed and built at the height of the Depression. The San Francisco-Oakland Bay Bridge, the world's longest steel bridge up to that time, was completed in 1936, spanning the eight and a quarter miles separating San Francisco from the East Bay.[23] The Golden Gate, the wildest of all of the North Coast's transportation dreams, became reality with its opening in May of 1937. It was the culmination of a plan that began in Santa Rosa in 1923 when the Exchange Bank's Frank Doyle, president of the Santa Rosa Chamber of Commerce, called the first meeting of a group which would be known as the "Bridging the Golden Gate Association." Delegates from San Francisco and the North Coast counties sat down for the first time to discuss seriously the possibilities offered by a world-famous bridge builder named Joseph Strauss and a dozen visionaries who had written and spoken of bridging the Gate since the latter part of the 19th century.

In May of 1923, the enabling legislation for the formation of a special bridge district, carried by Assemblyman Frank Coombs of Napa, passed in the legislature. The bill provided the opportunity for twenty-one Northern California counties to join the district that would finance the bridge. When the politicking and protesting and voting were over, six of the twenty-one agreed to be part of

"Miss Santa Rosa," twelve-year-old Jean Ayers, christens the ferry named for her town in March of 1927. Several hundred Santa Rosa citizens made the trip to Alameda for the launching.

—LeBaron Collection

—Chamber of Commerce Collection

An early artist's concept of the bridge over the Golden Gate. The first meeting of the "Bridging the Golden Gate Association" was called by Santa Rosa banker Frank Doyle in 1923.

—Chamber of Commerce Collection

not only the pressure to save trees, but the birth of a trucking industry once the bridge was built.

Lake County, like others of the eligible counties which did not touch on either the bay or the Redwood Highway, declined to participate. Besides, its citizens would reap the benefits of the bridge without taxation. Then, with the timber interests sighting in on the economic issues, Mendocino County leaders reconsidered. In September of 1925, they voted to withdraw from the bridge district and petitioned Secretary of State Frank Jordan to refuse to certify the district, arguing the Mendocino signatures on the petition were now invalid.

The issue went to the State Supreme Court. The district's contention was that signatures, once presented, could not be withdrawn, and the court agreed. In December of 1926, the court ordered the Secretary of State to certify petitions of six counties which formed the Golden Gate Bridge & Highway District.

It was an oddly shaped geographic entity consisting of the contiguous counties of San Francisco, Marin, Sonoma, and Napa, with a strip along the Redwood Highway through central Mendocino County excluding most of that area's timberlands. Leaping over Humboldt, it included all of Del Norte County, thus extending to the Oregon border.

"It is a district of extremes," writes John van der Zee in his book on the history of the bridge, *The Gate*, "including some of California's most densely and least populated counties, affluent and poor, rustic and sophisticated, an organization created for a single and temporary purpose, which has somehow managed to survive for more than sixty years."[24]

This unique district and Strauss's controversial "dream bridge" were subject to intense scrutiny in the next three years. The first of six hearings on costs and financing was held in Santa Rosa in November of 1927. There were safety concerns to be answered and government agencies, including the Coast Guard which worried about interference with maritime traffic, to be satisfied. The

the district. Mendocino County was the first to join. The supervisors there voted to participate on January 7, 1925. Marin County was second, its vote coming on January 23. Sonoma and Napa counties were close behind.

In Humboldt County, the timber and lumber interests were strenuously opposed. They saw the bridge as an avenue to boost tourism, which would in turn increase the interest in keeping the giant redwoods as a tourist attraction rather than a timber source. It was no surprise, therefore, when Humboldt's supervisors voted against joining the district. Nor was it a surprise that the powerful Northwestern Pacific and Southern Pacific railroads opposed the construction of the bridge. Not only did SP operate the lucrative ferries that were the only way across, but the railroads were greatly dependent on the timber industry for freight business. In addition, the railroads owned substantial amounts of timberland adjacent to the railroad rights-of-way. There was still another reason for the railroads to work against the bridge: They could foresee approved design would become one of the wonders of the modern world—a spectacular steel suspension bridge 4,200 feet long, with 746-foot towers, the largest bridge towers ever built up to that time.[25]

The engineers and architects, realizing they were involved in a structure that would create interest far beyond the area it served, paid careful attention to the aesthetics of the bridge design. The color of the bridge was intended from the outset to be a warm and distinctive contrast to the blue-gray waters and chill fogs of San Francisco Bay. There were many mixtures of vermilion and burnt sienna tried. Paint companies were invited to submit selections. In the final decision, it was the color of the protective undercoating of red lead which seemed to suit the bridge in its setting. The color of the outer coat would match it.

The politics of bridge-building were all about growth, of course. Writing in the October 8, 1934 issue of the *Republican*, merchant Fred Rosenberg, who owned the biggest department store and the tallest building as well as much of the downtown property in Santa Rosa, summed up: "Santa Rosa and Sonoma County are on the verge of the greatest development and growth in [their] history…with the Golden Gate Bridge soon to be opened the city faces the prospect of more tremendous growth than ever before. I visualize the Santa Rosa of the future as 'another San Jose'—a thriving business metropolis in the center of a prosperous agricultural region."

With the well-financed opposition fighting at every turn, the Golden Gate Bridge became a mission. When the railroads and the timber interests threatened a boycott of the *Press Democrat*, Ernest Finley, who had stood beside Doyle since the beginning of the project, wrote himself into the history of California journalism in a resounding response: "Damn the circulation! The bridge must be built!"[26]

Once the cables were rolling, the saga of the bridge was a tale of danger and adventure worthy of Jack London. Special precautions were taken; doctors prescribed diets for the men who worked "up top," to counteract dizziness, and workers were given special goggles to help them with the "snow blindness" caused by the fog and the reflection of light on the water. Still there were mishaps. Equipment foundered and deep-sea divers performed miracles of retrieval in the rough waters of the narrow channel. A freighter, off-course, struck a nearly completed trestle. Platforms collapsed. Safety ropes parted. Before the bridge was complete, eleven workmen died—but fourteen others were saved from certain death by the heroics of their fellow workers. These men formed an exclusive organization known as the "Halfway-to-Hell Club."

The bridge opened in the spring of 1937 with a week-long Golden Gate Bridge Fiesta. Auto caravans rolled in from eleven western states, Canada, and Mexico to take part in the celebration. Their delegations joined in a parade which included 100 bands, five from Sonoma County's high schools, and 100 floats, including one from each town in Sonoma County. On Pedestrian Day, May 27, some 200,000 people walked back and forth across the bridge in a twelve-hour period. That evening a cast of 3,000, headed by baritone John Charles Thomas, presented a musical pageant, "The Span of Gold," at Crissy Field.

The following day the ceremonial chain on the San Francisco-Marin county lines was cut by San Francisco Mayor Angelo Rossi, Golden Gate Bridge and Highway District President William T. Filmer, and Santa Rosa's Frank Doyle, designated "The Father of the Golden Gate." When the last link fell, 500 planes from the aircraft carriers anchored off the Gate roared over the bridge in salute. And, in Washington, D.C., President Franklin Roosevelt pulled a switch in The White House which turned on a green light at the toll plaza, a signal for the drivers in the line of waiting cars that stretched for miles at both ends of the bridge. Three hours after the green light flashed, the Pacific fleet steamed under the bridge in a parade of ships ten miles long, officers and men on deck, saluting the achievement.[27]

Frank Doyle got much credit for his part in the bridge planning. He was honored by having the San Francisco approach to the toll plaza named Doyle Drive and by being accorded the privilege of taking the first ride across the bridge in an automobile. The ride had occurred two months before the opening, when Doyle had come to inspect the progress. Knowing the elderly man's dedication to the project, a bridge worker slipped behind the wheel of Doyle's car and drove him across the still-unopened bridge. The first woman to drive across the Golden Gate, who waited until opening day, was Mrs. J.A. McMinn of Healdsburg. She was following the lead of another Healdsburg woman, Mrs. E. Lange, who, a year before, had dressed in men's clothing to walk across the catwalk of the Bay Bridge when it was newly constructed.[28]

The transportation impact on the North Coast counties was immediate. But the long range growth would wait on other world-shaking events—such as World War II.

――――――

Airplanes were little more than science fiction at the start of the 20th century. News of the Wright brothers' feat at Kitty Hawk in 1902 did little to change the lives of most residents of Santa Rosa—with a few notable exceptions.

Fred Wiseman, manager of a cycling shop and dealer in early automobiles, had raced bicycles and motorcars. Like his friends Ben Noonan and Henry Peters, Wiseman was interested in anything that would go faster. In 1909 the thirty-three-year-old Wiseman paid a visit to the Wright brothers' bicycle shop in Dayton, Ohio, saw their first plane, and came home to Santa Rosa to build his own, using pictures because he had no blueprints. His friend Noonan, a partner in his family's wholesale meat company, financed the project. Hall-Scott Motors Co. built the engine. After he built it, Wiseman still had to learn to fly it.

By 1910, innovators were following the lead of the Wright brothers, building aircraft that would stay aloft for record two-hour and three-minute flights, aircraft that

could exceed the speed of aerial balloons. One of these was Wiseman, who, with the help of Peters and Noonan, had fashioned a flying machine (the newspaper had yet to use the term "aeroplane," preferring instead "airship" or simply "machine") which he had flown on the Laughlin Ranch at Fulton where it was being built. In 1910, Wiseman first attempted a public flight at the Fourth of July celebration at Kenilworth Park in Petaluma. The flying machine attained an altitude of fifteen feet for 200 yards before it crashed into a fence.

Early in 1911, Wiseman announced he was ready. He would fly his "machine" from Petaluma to Santa Rosa—non-stop. The entire county paused to consider this feat, and to wait and watch. The newspapers made much of the event. Wiseman would carry three letters from civic leaders, a package of groceries from Hickey & Vonsen in Petaluma to Kopf & Donovan in Santa Rosa as a goodwill gesture between the merchants, and several copies of the *Press Democrat*, which he would "deliver" along the route. This would later prove to be the world's first airmail flight, beating by one day a British pilot who flew mail across a river in India.

The 12:30 p.m. takeoff from Kenilworth Park on February 17 drew a crowd of spectators and a reporter, who saw "the huge contrivance rising easily and shooting out over the fence and across the park like a bird, and heading in the direction of the county seat."[29]

The actual flight took two days. Wiseman had negotiated only four and a half miles when his engine failed and, narrowly missing a windmill, he landed in a muddy field near Denman's creamery. The second day he made better progress, dropping *Press Democrats* to subscribers as planned, although his average altitude was 100 feet.

Although Wiseman completed the flight the second day, he never made the fairgrounds. About three-quarters of a mile short of the city limits, he turned the plane's nose upward to clear some trees and the engine stopped. Just minutes short of his goal, Wiseman once more landed in a

—*Gabriel Moulin Studios, San Francisco*

GOLDEN GATE BRIDGE FIESTA

San Francisco

OFFICIAL
PEDESTRIAN DAY
MAY 27, 1937

1856 *Souvenir* 25c

Golden Gate Bridge & Highway District

1856

ADMIT ONE PEDESTRIAN
GOLDEN GATE BRIDGE

muddy field south of the Enz dairy. A parade of automobiles roared out from town to welcome him.

The flight, later certified by the Smithsonian Institution as the first time mail was carried by air, was cause for great celebration in Santa Rosa. Clambering out of his rudimentary aircraft onto the dirt of the field, Wiseman handed over his historic messages. From Petaluma Mayor George P. McNear to Santa Rosa Mayor James Edwards: "Petaluma sends greetings and best wishes to Santa Rosa by Aviator Fred Wiseman." The second letter was from McNear to John P. Overton, Santa Rosa banker and Chamber of Commerce official. It read: "Petaluma invites Santa Rosa to her Industrial and Pure Food Exposition." The third letter, from Petaluma postmaster John E. Olmsted to Santa Rosa postmaster Hiram L. Tripp, would prove crucial to historians in establishing the Wiseman flight's first-place ranking in the history of air mail. "Dear Sir and Friend," the letter read. "Petaluma sends, via the air route, congratulations and felicitations upon the successful mastery of the air by a Sonoma County boy in an aeroplane conceived by Sonoma County brains and erected by Sonoma County workmen. Speed the day when the U.S. Mail between our sister cities, of which this letter is the pioneer, may all leave by the air route with speed and safety."

Wiseman, who traveled up and down the Pacific Coast that year demonstrating his aircraft and flying in several early air races, did not pursue a career in aviation. Within the decade he retired from his pilot's seat, telling friends he "didn't see any future in flying."[30]

Santa Rosa's first "flying field" was a dirt airstrip a mile south of town on the Petaluma road. While it had a surprising amount of air traffic, there was no attempt at establishing an official airfield in town until 1928, when the Chamber of Commerce took an option to buy 127 acres of the Fountaingrove Ranch from Kanaye Nagasawa for an

airport. The following year it was leased to Richfield Oil Company, who improved the runways and erected a blue and yellow beacon tower.

Until that time, aviation had been more for fun and wonderment than for serious commerce. Townspeople followed the exploits of Wiseman as he competed in early air races. They gazed skyward in 1912 when aviator Weldon Cooke made a successful flight directly over the town, reaching an altitude of 2,500 feet. In 1914, pilot H.N. Blakely reached 6,500 feet flying over Santa Rosa on his way from San Francisco to Cloverdale for the Citrus Fair. Blakely, the newspaper reported, flew at speeds up to "almost a mile a minute." On the way back to San Francisco after the fair, the plane's engine died and it dived into San Francisco Bay.

Santa Rosa's Frank Doyle, above on the right, was accorded the honor of cutting the chain that officially opened the bridge. There were many "official" openings, including a signal flashed from President Roosevelt to allow traffic to flow. On the page opposite left, a crowd estimated at 200,000 people walked the bridge on the day set aside for pedestrians.

*T*here was some disappointment the day before pilot Fred Wiseman's historic arrival in Santa Rosa. Word of the overnight delay was slow to arrive and Santa Rosa's school children were dismissed to go to the fairgrounds to watch for the plane that didn't come.

After the first day's mishap, the *Press Democrat* established an early warning system to alert residents to Wiseman's approach. On the front page of the February 18, 1911 edition, along with the news story of the "Wiseman, Birdman" flight, was this message:

"If you hear the whistles blow and the bells ring this morning, or if you hear a series of bomb explosions, you will know that Wiseman has successfully passed Cotati, six miles south of this city, and at that point has signaled the *Press Democrat's* lookout that he expects to be able to continue the flight on to Santa Rosa. The engineers in charge of the works at the local factories will cooperate with the *Press Democrat* today and endeavor to prevent a repetition of yesterday's disappointment and inconvenience to the public. No signals will be forthcoming until Wiseman and his machine have reached and passed Cotati, the last station to be passed on the trip coming this way, and the first station below this city going south. This is the *Press Democrat's* original plan, but it was not the plan followed yesterday."

Pioneer airplane builder and pilot Fred Wiseman and his wife Alice at a Cloverdale air show in 1911. At upper left, Wiseman at the controls.

Blakely leaped into the water and swam away to be rescued. The plane did not sink.

Despite dangers (a sergeant was killed in 1919 when an Army plane and a Navy seaplane collided during an aerial demonstration in Santa Rosa), people flocked to see the daredevils who flew in and out of California towns through the decade of the teens—men such as Leon Ferguson, the aerial acrobat who was the star of the 1920 Sonoma County Fair, performing such feats as his famous wing walk, inventing new thrills daily for fairgoers. One day he hung by his toes from the wing skid in the air in front of the grandstand, the next he stood on his head atop the airplane. On the final day of the fair, attempting to stand atop the plane while the pilot looped-the-loop, Ferguson was killed. The plane hit an "air bump," he lost his balance and fell to his death. His father was watching from the grandstand.[32]

Barnstormers like Sam Purcell, who had instructed pilots for the Army in World War I, came to offer citizens a taste of aerial delights. Purcell stopped off at the flying field in 1919 so his Pacific Aviation Company biplane could take all the curious and courageous for flights over Santa Rosa, Healdsburg, and Petaluma. The promised elevation was 2,000 feet. The cost was $10. Nor were these aeronautical adventures without risk. In 1920 a passenger plane taking the public on a pleasure trip crashed, seriously injuring the wife of city assessor Lester Brittain and newspaper man C.W. Etheredge.[33]

One of the barnstormers was a local boy. Shirley Brush, the son of Santa Rosa banker Frank Brush, was a professional pilot, making his living at work for the California Raisin Association of Fresno, dropping samples of Sun-Maid raisins over special events in California. In 1919, after a raisin-bombing mission over the crowds gathered in San Francisco for the arrival of the Pacific Fleet, Brush came home with a flourish. He flew over Santa Rosa in his Curtiss airplane, performing loops and dives over the city before coming in for a landing at the flying field. "Almost as soon as he was out of the plane on the ground,"

the newspaper reported, "automobiles began to arrive from town, filled with curious persons and friends.... Starting at 9 o'clock Thursday morning, Mr. Brush will carry passengers in his plane...and there are dozens of residents who have already announced their intention of making an air voyage with Mr. Brush."[34]

The development of aviation through the 1920s was exciting, front-page news. The first mail plane flew from San Francisco to New York in 1920. Robert Fowler, who had flown his Bluebird on the first transcontinental flight, flew from Santa Rosa to San Francisco that same year in just forty-three minutes. World records for air speed and distance were being broken almost as fast as they could be set. In 1924 three Army planes flew the Pacific. In 1925 four Sonoma County aviators, all members of the Sonoma County Aero Club, raced from Sebastopol to Richmond, a contest won by Arthur Starbuck. But 1927 would be the banner year. Sonoma County residents knew this when George Sherwood, a former Santa Rosan, flew from Los Angeles to Santa Rosa, landing in Sebastopol, actually, in just four hours. And the world knew when, in May, Charles Lindbergh took his *Spirit of St. Louis* from New York to Paris, becoming the first aviator to fly the Atlantic alone.

Later that year, there was a valiant effort to encourage the hero known as "The Lone Eagle" and "Lucky Lindy" to fly over Santa Rosa on a planned trip from San Francisco to Portland. In a telegram, the *Press Democrat* suggested his known reverence for the resting places of the "famous dead" would be served if he flew over the home and grave of Luther Burbank. But it didn't work. Lindbergh flew north on the eastern side of San Francisco Bay, in the general direction of Sacramento.

The "new, improved" airport on the Fountaingrove property at the northern edge of town was celebrated with a two-day grand opening air festival in 1929. There were air races and an air show and exhibitions by flying record-holders. The president of Richfield Oil flew in from Los Angeles in the company's $125,000 Fokker monoplane.

At left, the Cotati Flying Field in 1925, and, below, Mike Guglielmetti and his friend Charles Offutt, Petaluma, after a mishap in Lake County in 1920.

The "Flying Guglielmetti Brothers" became hometown heroes as the age of aviation advanced. Merino "Mike" Guglielmetti taught himself to fly in an ex-Army "Jenny" in 1920. He then taught his younger brother, John, establishing a Santa Rosa "team" known as "Big Goog" and "Little Goog" to pilots all over the state.

Mike had his share of narrow escapes. He crash landed in a plowed field near Kelseyville in the early '20s, upending the small plane. He and his friend Charles Offut, a Petaluma Hudson dealer, were uninjured. But Offut was with him on another adventure when, on a flight to Winters, Mike spotted his brother Julius standing in the yard of his ranch house near Dixon. He was putting the plane through a series of stunts as a salute to his brother when a fire extinguisher came loose from its fastenings while the plane was upside down and struck Mike on the head. Offut, riding in the passenger seat, did not realize the pilot was unconscious. He thought the nose dive was another stunt — until the plane was fifty feet from the ground. Offut escaped the crash without injury. He and

brother Julius pulled Mike from the wreckage, with serious head injuries.

Mike and Johnnie both took jobs with airlines when the stunting days were over. Soon John Guglielmetti was setting air speed records, and Mike was carrying passengers for Maddux Air Lines. He upended a Ford tri-motor in the mud on the "soft" runway of the Santa Rosa Municipal Airport in the early '30s, but none of the five passengers was injured.

After Maddux, Mike flew for United Air Lines. In 1941, both he and Johnnie left the air lines to ferry bombers to England for Lockheed Aircraft, which was manufacturing the planes for the Royal Air Force. In February, on a run from Southern California to England, Mike's bomber hit a radio tower near the landing field in El Paso, Texas. He was killed. On the ground, watching, having landed just ahead of his brother, was Johnnie Gugliemetti.

At his death, pilots lauded Mike for his efforts on behalf of aviation and credited him with an important role in the development of air transportation in the West.[31]

FLY
OVER SANTA ROSA
— IN A —
FORD TRI-MOTORED AIR LINER
12 PASSENGER

FRIDAY, JAN. 18
STARTING AT 11 A. M.

Through the efforts of the Santa Rosa Chamber of Commerce and Theodore Roosevelt Post, American Legion, arrangements have been made with the Maddux Air Line to make scenic flights over Santa Rosa and surrounding country.

— FROM —
SANTA ROSA
MUNICIPAL AIR PORT
on Healdsburg Highway

For information enquire at Santa Rosa Chamber of Commerce, Frank Berger's Cigar Store, or at Air Port

Fare $5.00
MARENO GUGLIELMETTI, Pilot

Santa Rosa's flying field in the 1920s. Many aviation pioneers came from Sonoma County.

Mae Gardiner, the young Santa Rosa woman chosen as "Queen of the Air," wore a rhinestone-encrusted flying helmet in place of a crown. A Western Air Lines passenger plane with twelve aboard flew in from Oakland, a promise of future commercial air service. The airport facility was heralded as "the first step of the north of the bay counties in the march of aviation progress."[35]

The first scheduled air service from Santa Rosa to Oakland and San Francisco was Empire Airways, begun in 1929. Al Bondi was the owner. Ted Peoples was the pilot. Peoples made the flights south in forty minutes. His mistake was made going the other direction. In 1931 he was arrested by Prohibition agents for flying liquor to Covelo. A subsequent jury trial in Covelo Justice Court found Peoples not guilty. The trial was the biggest event of that year in Round Valley. Stores closed and 500 people attended, according to newspaper accounts.[36]

The partnership between the city and Richfield Oil lasted six years. Santa Rosa aviators Ingles Puffer and Fred Lencioni, owners of Santa Rosa Air Service, leased the airport from the oil company in 1934, on a month-to-month provisional basis. Depression-plagued city officials debated whether to continue leasing the field, where there were six airplanes hangared, or take over the management as a strictly municipal enterprise.

In August, 1935 the City Council, with federal public works money available for improvements, decided the city should run the airport. The ninety acres remaining in

—*Jimmie FitzGerald Collection*

airport use were purchased, along with the hangar, pumps, and underground fuel tanks, for $12,500 through the Chamber of Commerce's option. The chamber offered the property to the city when it became apparent federal funds would be available for a work-relief program at the airport only if it were in municipal ownership. In January of 1936, WPA funds totaling $63,000 for runway extensions and improvements were approved through Congressman Clarence Lea's efforts.

Lea, who represented the North Coast in Congress, was a strong supporter of air travel and a pioneer in aviation legislation. As early as 1924, Lea was part of a group recommending the closing of Chrissy Field on San Francisco's Marina in favor of building a large military airport in Sonoma County. While Chrissy Field survived, Lea remained the biggest booster of air facilities in the North Bay through the Depression era and into the war years.

The first commercial airline, Pierce Brothers Air Service of Eureka, put Santa Rosa on its regular run from Humboldt County to San Francisco in 1936, and the Santa Rosa Municipal Airport was re-dedicated to its new life in November of that year. Fred Lencioni, with his new partner, Jack Barham, continued to operate the Santa Rosa Air Service from the flying field, with an ever-increasing number of newly licensed and student pilots. In 1937 the city named its airfield for Fred Steiner, city manager, who died a few days after the airfield dedication. Mayor George Cadan unveiled a drinking fountain and bronze plaque memorializing Steiner in ceremonies in January. The dedication meant a change in the airfield's designation, on aviation maps and the records of the Bureau of Air Commerce, to Steiner Field.

Air travel had changed markedly since the early barnstormers stopped off at the dirt strip south of town, but enterprising pilots were still in business. In 1938, hundreds of Santa Rosans lined up at the airport to buy joy rides from Fairfax Flying Service, a Kansas City company offering a choice of aircraft—a "huge" tri-motored all-

Crowds turned out at the Santa Rosa Municipal Airport in the 1930s to take a ride over Santa Rosa in a tri-motored "air liner."

metal airliner, a racy little Ryan monoplane, and a four-passenger Cessna.

In 1940 there were two "Grade A" airports in the county and four landing fields. The Santa Rosa airport (Apparently no one called it Steiner Field, despite the official designation.) was home to seven privately owned planes. Flying services had thirty private students and ten students in the Santa Rosa Junior College aviation program. Flying services also averaged about twenty pleasure flights per month at $1.50 per person.[37]

Congressman Lea's efforts to get federal funding for a large regional airfield continued. One of Lea's legislative triumphs was the creation of the Civil Aeronautics Administration, the forerunner of the Federal Aviation Agency. It was under the auspices of this agency, which governed non-military aviation in the nation, that he worked, through the late 1930s, for the establishment of a government airport in Sonoma County. Site selection had caused a delay in his plans when, in December of 1941, the air force of Japan attacked the United States fleet in Pearl Harbor. Three days after the attack, condemnation began on an airport site seven miles northwest of Santa Rosa. The government designated it as the Frank Laughlin site, although a large part of the Slusser Ranch and many other properties —sixteen owners of the original plan for 464 acres—were involved.

The $280,000 condemnation suit filed in Sonoma County Superior Court on December 10 was for just 320 acres, because the county opted to get the first runways established and seek land for expansion later. Most of the site was in hop yards and prune orchards. It was a second choice, the Navy having blocked a CAA purchase of the Piezzi Ranch west of Santa Rosa because it was too close to a planned Naval airfield in the Leddy tract. Local hopes for the $280,000 appropriation had dwindled with that decision.[38]

The declaration of war changed everything. CAA officials conferring by telephone with county supervisors immediately reactivated the funding on the condition a site be selected and condemnation begun within twenty-four hours. The county, however, would have to wait for its airport. The site was transferred to the Army and became Santa Rosa Army Air Field, first an auxiliary base for Marin County's Hamilton Field and then a fully commissioned training base for fighter pilots. Army engineers were surveying runways sites by December 16.

———

No facet of life in these United States changed as much as transportation did in the first half of the 20th century. While railroads remained vital to the area during World War II, the automobile, aided by the unprecedented lobbying efforts of the trucking and oil interests, sealed the fate of the railroads.

The demise of the railways was not as dramatic as their beginnings, although in some instances mournful passengers gathered for "last day" ceremonies. December 31, 1931 was the day streetcar service from Olive Street to McDonald Avenue in Santa Rosa was discontinued forever.[39] The P&SR's regular passenger service stopped in 1932. The last passenger train on the P&SR tracks was in April of 1941, a hodgepodge collection of electric cars and wooden rail cars pulled by an NWP steam locomotive. It was a sentimental journey for excursionists, who traveled the whole route, with a side trip to Two Rock.

The electric service just made it through World War II. The rolling stock was worn out and, branch by branch, section by section, the electrical system was abandoned and the overhead trolley wires were torn down. January 24 of 1947 was the last electric freight outside the Petaluma area—a carload of horses for the Liberty stop. The Liberty-Two Rock run was abandoned and torn up in September of 1952. The grain, dairy, and poultry hauling was being done by truck.

Southern Pacific discontinued passenger service on its Sonoma Valley line in 1928 and, in 1932, abandoned its North Street depot after it was damaged by fire. In 1934, SP discontinued freight service to Schellville and, the following year, removed the rails from Los Guilucos Station to North Street. The right-of-way through the walnut and prune orchards east of Santa Rosa became, after 1950, the route of Montgomery Drive. Freight for the Central Pacific now went to Schellville by way of Petaluma and Novato on NWP.

Santa Rosa became a one-railroad town. But Northwestern Pacific was very important to the county when World War II curtailed the availability of both rubber and gasoline. Along with the rest of the nation, Sonoma County once again relied on railroad traffic for freight and passenger service. Northwestern Pacific maintained a passenger service to Santa Rosa throughout the 1950s. As with all trains, the one-two punch of the automobile and the Depression had hit hard.[40] Steam locomotives had given way to diesels in the 1930s, taking some of the romance from the rails.

The automobile changed much more than the way we came and went. It changed our landscape and our habits.

The spa-like resorts, often at the sites of hot springs, where families came with trunks to spend the summer months, were replaced by the motoring vacation. Auto camps, courts, and motels replaced hotels. Livery stables gave way to service stations on nearly every corner of the business district. Horses, so much a part of everyday life at the start of the century, disappeared from the streets and were kept and tended for fun instead of necessity. Horse-lovers formed riding and driving clubs. Train buffs formed organizations dedicated to the memory of the days when rails ruled. Both were nostalgic, a kind of mild protest from people who weren't in such a hurry to see the old ways disappear.

Train and truck, in their turn, were very important to Sonoma County's agriculture-based economy. Air service was always sporadic at best, and the county's growers relied, first on rails, and then on well-maintained highways to carry their products to the urban markets. ❧

The automobile changed America's traveling habits. The auto camp of the '20s and '30s evolved into the "motel," a composite word made from "motor" and "hotel." The Cedar Shake Motel opened on the Redwood Highway at Santa Rosa's northern edge in the 1940s.

—Earl Gwynne Collection

In the spring of 1917, after three years of anxious reading of headlines and dispatches from places with unfamiliar and unpronounceable names, Santa Rosans went off to war.

Company E, Santa Rosa's unit of the state militia, was the first group to be called. They marched down Fourth Street sixty strong with the Santa Rosa Band, hurriedly assembled, playing a military air. The 352 students of Lincoln School, marshaled by their principal, Miss Minnie Coulter, lined the street, waving American flags. At the depot they boarded the Willits Southbound Express, the 10:07 down train, and joined their regiment at the Presidio of San Francisco.[1]

Their commander was Capt. Hilliard Comstock, a tall, handsome Santa Rosa attorney. His lieutenant was another lawyer, Thorn Gale, who missed the send-off being, as the newspaper reported, "confined to his home with the mumps." He joined his comrades later at the Presidio. The first sergeant was Everett Campbell. There were three other sergeants, Donald Geary, Burton Cochrane, and Frank Churchill. The roster of troops read like a fair sampling of the Santa Rosa telephone directory—Rued, Crist, Sullivan, and Trembley, two Volpis and a Pozzi. They were joined at the Presidio the following week (the very day, in fact, the United States entered World War I—April 6, 1917) by Petaluma's Company K, fifty-two men under the command of Second Lt. Joe Haran, marching through solid masses of people to the train. Four young Petaluma men, caught up in the excitement, joined the line of march and enlisted at the Presidio.

By fall of 1917 there were three contingents gone to war, escorted to the depot by the Home Guard and the Civil War veteran members of the Grand Army of the Republic. The later groups went to Camp Lewis, Washington, for training. The newspapers reported their departure in the innocent "making the world safe for democracy" spirit that was heard throughout the land.

The war in Europe had been slowly creeping into Sonoma County's daily life since it began, officially, in the summer of 1914. Relief funds were raised for the starving Belgians. The Sonoma County Medical Society sent financial aid to Belgian doctors. Growers and fruit brokers combined to send a train carload of dried fruit to war victims. Gavin McNab, an official of the California Development Board, spoke at a dinner at the courthouse suggesting agricultural counties of the state offer asylum to the farmers of Belgium.[2]

Daily dispatches about the torpedoing of ships shared the front pages of the *Press Democrat* and *Republican* with the politics of America's position. As was true throughout the nation, there was considerable ambivalence. The report (April 16, 1915) of President Woodrow Wilson's neutrality speech shared the front pages with a warning to the citizens of Santa Rosa to "take shelter if German planes appear."

Members of Santa Rosa's Company E, called to war, pose for an army photographer at Fort Mason, San Francisco in 1917.

—*Jette Cochrane Rodman Collection*

Horse buyers, acting on behalf of the U.S. Cavalry, paid frequent visits to Santa Rosa, seeking to purchase mounts from the several horse farms in the area. One of the most important horse breeders, John H. Rosseter of Wikiup Ranch, was well-acquainted with war damages, having lost his "magnificent stallion, Sunflower," two mares in foal, and an expensive brood mare when the Germans sunk the American ship *Manhattan*.

The war brought the growing antipathy to things German to a head. German names were wiped from the records. In Petaluma, Bremen Street became Liberty Street. In Santa Rosa the Germania Bar became the Eagle Bar, the Germania Hotel the Union Hotel, and the Bismarck Cafe the Red Cross Cafe.

There was constant vigilance against German spies. In many instances this meant any resident with a German accent, or even a German name, could come under suspicion. A pronouncement in the newspaper in May of 1918 warned, "Every German or Austrian in the U.S. unless known by years of association to be absolutely loyal, should be treated as a potential spy."

A loyalty oath was required for workers in California Packing Corporation's cannery, which employed 700 workers, most of them Italian, in the

By the time the United States entered World War I, Santa Rosans had practiced their farewells. This crowd gathered at the railroad depot in 1916 to see the men of Company E off to Arizona. The militia had been summoned to duty to protect United States citizens and property from the incursions of Mexican rebel Francisco "Pancho" Villa and his raiders.

—Comstock Family Collection

*T*he men of Company E were well-accustomed to packing their kit bags. They had returned from Nogales, Arizona, just six months earlier, where they had joined American troops in guard duty along the Mexican border. Some of them had made the trip in 1912, responding to the call for men to fight the Mexican revolutionary band of Pancho Villa. By 1916, military pursuit of Pancho Villa by "Black Jack" Pershing and his troops had resulted in anti-American mob sentiment in several Mexican cities. When Americans were taken prisoner in an uprising in Chihuahua, the federal government had called out the guard and Santa Rosa men had responded. Sent off by what the newspapers called "The greatest demonstration in Santa Rosa history," the "soldier boys" headed first for Camp Hiram Johnson in Sacramento, at the end of June 1916, and then to their tents along the border near Nogales.

When the Mexican campaign ended in the fall, Company E came back to Sacramento, paying a home visit for Santa Rosa's Admission Day parade in September. They were all home "permanently" in time for a celebration banquet October 7. This time they stayed until late March, 1917, about a week before the U.S. entry into World War I, when they left for Camp Lewis, Washington. Sergeant William Davidson, who had served on the Mexican border with Pershing, was given a hero's sendoff in the *Press Democrat*. "He will go north," wrote the editor, "in his old uniform." However, Company E did not see action in World War I. They were sent to the French fighting front on November 15, 1918, four days after the Armistice, where they remained until the following March.

Santa Rosa reserve officers who served in World War I. Left to right, Burton Cochrane, Harold Davenport, Lt. Peterson and Junius Gale.

At far left, Santa Rosa soldiers stand guard along the railroad tracks near Nogales on the Arizona border in 1916.

summer of 1918. Government officials were fearful of interference with food supplies to the military. Still, more than 115,000 cans of fruit were packed at Santa Rosa's "big cannery" that season without incident. And the Italian community turned out in October for a Liberty Bond rally at La Rose Hotel to raise $10,000 for their new country.

The well-publicized vigilance produced tension, fear, and anger among immigrants. The first violation of the regulations outlined for enemy aliens was registered in Santa Rosa when an Austrian woman from Oakland was found with a large dagger which, according to the newspaper report, she promised to use on the first American who insulted her.[3]

Radio, still in its infancy, was viewed as a potential problem. Commercial radio was virtually unknown although Dr. Charles Herrold, a San Jose man, had put the first station "on the air" in 1912. (Known first as "San Jose Calling," it became KQW and eventually KCBS, San Francisco.) Undoubtedly, it was picked up in Santa Rosa by dedicated amateurs who had set up elaborate receiving and broadcasting sets to play with the new medium.

Immediately after America's entrance into the war, the government, fearing broadcasting facilities would be

Hilliard Comstock, kneeling at far left, wrote to his family on the back of this picture postcard: "Here's a very poor picture of myself and Frank C. [Frank Churchill, standing at far right] in our tent pitching squad. We pitched this tent in one minute and fifty-six seconds." On the opposite page right, is another photo mailed home by Hilliard Comstock showing men in his company at practice on the machine gun range.

—*Comstock Family Collection*

used to transmit information to the enemy, ordered all amateur wireless plants dismantled. Six weeks later, when news of the "3,000-mile" transmitter discovered and seized on the top of Hood Mountain was announced, even grumbling crystal set owners admitted there may be a need.

One whose German name and apparent sympathies brought notice was a Vineburg man who was arrested after witnesses reported he was "noting topography from Glen Ellen to Vineburg." His bold statements in support of German military power, an Iron Cross in his valise, and a letter found in his possession saying, "There are only a few of our kind left but we can do a great deal," did not help his cause. Nor did the map showing railroad tracks and bridges through the Sonoma Valley, with special attention to the late Jack London's ranch and the country estate of Adolph Spreckels.[4]

Not all the incidents were as dramatic. In March of 1918 two Santa Rosa women, Mattie Reardon and Mrs. W. Sorenson, were charged with "disturbing the peace and disloyalty" after they made a noisy exit from a "war address" by City Attorney Gil P. Hall, one of them saying, "I don't want to hear no more of that war talk."[5]

L. J. Johnson, who was heard to suggest "American soldiers are only picnic soldiers, good for parades," was advised by the court to invest $200 in War Thrift Stamps as penance. A neighbors' quarrel in Bennett Valley became a federal case when a registered alien, B. Mundkowski, was reported for waving a gun. He was charged with possession of firearms after his neighbor testified Mundkowski was "also pro-German."[6]

With America's entrance into the war, the latest enlistment became the news of the day. Harold Bruner left his job in his father's art store to become a sergeant in the Aviation Corps. Mervin Burke went to France as an officer, serving in Paris on a general's staff though he was, according to the *Press Democrat*, "not yet twenty." In the tiny community of Preston, north of Cloverdale, the boast was that all the young men of Preston—nine of them—were serving in the armed forces.

Not all the heroes carried guns. Bert Hope, the son of a Healdsburg minister, left the University of California with the first group of volunteers to drive an ambulance in France. He would earn the War Cross for his bravery. Dr. Jackson Temple sold his interest in Santa Rosa Hospital and went to war. Dr. Ovid Tuttle was commissioned a first lieutenant and went off to serve as a dental surgeon. And not all were men. Sonoma County women nursing at the Stanford Naval Base Hospital Unit

A trio of Santa Rosa officers on World War I duty. Left to right, Hilliard Comstock, Burton Cochrane and Frank Churchill.

were sent to "a foreign country"—Santa Rosans Margaret Rued, Hazel Bruner, Eliza Tanner, Ruth Overton, and Berthleen Caldwell, Jessie Coon, Geyserville, and Rae DuVander of Windsor.[7]

They would end up in France, most of them. Some, like Frank Denham of Company E, lost their lives. Others, like William Heinrich, who gave up his job as a bellhop at the Overton Hotel to fight, was badly gassed, so badly complete recovery was termed doubtful. The Hills brothers of the Gold Ridge district, five of them, were all together in a French trench when a shell hit. One was killed, his four brothers were injured. Even those who returned unscathed were changed enough to alter the history of their community.

The cliché of the American farm boy in "Gay Paree" could have been invented for Sonoma County soldiers. World War I came upon Santa Rosa as it did any of thousands of farm towns all over the nation. Santa Rosa had less than 10,000 people, most of whom cheered for their departing sons with high hopes and flags and patriotic songs. Those who returned came back seasoned travelers, bringing home tales of foreign lands with a rakish *Vive la différence!* changing Santa Rosa, if not instantly then gradually, from an insular community that neither knew nor cared for global concerns to a more cosmopolitan town ready to take its place in the bigger world.

Letters from Sonoma County soldiers, with the now-familiar "Somewhere in France" at the top, were published in the *Press Democrat*, providing the first inkling of changes to come. "I know it is narrow-minded," wrote Pvt. Joseph Dearborn of the 144th machine gun battalion, "but their customs are certainly queer—and I think it worth being shot at to see it all. You can't imagine the education there will be in it if we stay here long."[8]

Marine James Williams discovered "French fries" and other foreign delicacies: "Sunday I went out to dinner with a little French girl. I had beef steak, French fried potatoes, bread, wine, and coffee so I fared pretty well. She was a nice looking girl but I had some time talking to her. She didn't understand anything. She has got a little store. I may bring her and the store back with me. Ha ha."

Lt. Fred Duhring of Sonoma, in charge of an ambulance section, was astonished at the scope of the German language. "The roads we drive over now are all plastered with German signs to point the way. In some places they use an immense sign with words on it of never less than twenty-five letters each. It would take a well-educated Hun fifteen minutes at least to read one of them." Pvt. Merlin Meeker discovered the French *café*. "They have open fronts and small gardens in front with tables. They do not drink quickly, but sip and talk. The town has places dating back to B.C., almost."

Cavalry Lt. Frank Sedgley did some shopping, the better to impress his Cloverdale neighbors on his return. "I ordered a winter suit cut along French lines. It is being made by the oldest tailor in Saumur whose father and father's father were tailors here for L'Ecole de Cavalrie. French tailors make our uniforms more baggy than those in America. They have brass hooks at the waist under the arms to hold up our Sam Browne belts, have leather lining on the inside of the breeches' legs for horseback riding. I have a pair of riding boots, that the King of England is jealous of. Only I keep spearing myself with my own spurs and catch them on steps going downstairs. Veery, veery undignified, n'est pas?"[9]

When Tin Pan Alley asked, "How you gonna keep 'em down on the farm?" it was a question that seemed pertinent to Sonoma County life.

On the home front the Red Cross, disbanded after equipping the men of Company E in the Spanish-American War, reorganized. With the call-up of Company E, a meeting was organized by civic leader John Plover at the home of Santa Rosa's social "first lady," Isabelle McDonald, to establish a unit of the Red Cross. In less than a month, the chapter had 475 members, in two months 1,100, and within six weeks, nearly 1,300 people had enrolled. Mr. and Mrs. Selah Chamberlain (the former Edith McDonald) donated $1,000 to the treasury. Kanaye Nagasawa, the owner of the Fountaingrove Ranch, sent $50 from Japan, where he was visiting relatives.

Red Cross workers organized the entire community. The enlistment of Red Cross nurses, for hospital service and availability in case of emergencies, began. The chapter would have eighty-eight nurses on its "ready" list by 1918. Santa Rosa High School domestic science classes made hospital and refugee garments, hot water bag covers, and "comfort" bags for the wounded. The manual training classes at the high school made 150 canes for military hospitals. School children were set to knitting for soldiers and nearly 1,000 knitted articles were produced, a source of some community pride. Mrs. Fred (Byrd Wyler) Kellogg headed a committee collecting used clothing for Europeans and shipped eight large cases in early 1917. When the ship carrying the gifts from this "Overseas Club" was torpedoed, members collected more.

Everyone had collections of scrap metal, rags, foil, and rubber. School children were assigned to collect fruit

—American Legion Collection

*I*rving Klein, who came to Santa Rosa after the war to go into business, was one of the few survivors of the celebrated "Lost Battalion." Klein, born in Hungary, immigrated to the United States in 1907 at the age of fifteen. He enlisted in the Army in 1917 and, in September of 1918, was a corporal in the 77th Division which went into the Argonne Forest to relieve the Rainbow Division.

When the French army unit to the left collapsed, Klein's battalion and another American battalion were flanked by the Germans. Klein was a hero from the start of the battle, assuming leadership in an assault, under heavy fire, on three enemy machine gun positions. Four days later German bullets found Klein, damaging a leg and destroying his left elbow.

For seven days, Klein's battalion was pinned in the Argonne woods under enemy fire until the 207th Infantry broke through and rescued the survivors. Of the 679 men, only 194 were alive. Klein was one of just eighteen survivors in his company. Of the 250 men who had gone in with him, 232 had died.

For his bravery and his leadership under fire, Klein was awarded the Distinguished Service Cross as well as the French Heroic War Cross and the Italian War Cross. At Letterman Hospital in San Francisco, where he was sent to recover, he met two Sonoma County residents, Dr. Cuthbert Fleissner, the physician Klein always credited with saving his arm, and Army nurse Charlotte Nalley of Healdsburg. They talked to him of their homes and he visited them, and in 1921 he came to Santa Rosa, opening an auto parts store on Main Street. When he lost his business in the Depression years, he opened a cigar store on Fourth Street and, after Prohibition, added liquor to his stock. Klein's Liquors later moved to Santa Rosa Avenue just south of Third Street.

Klein became a leader in the local and state veterans' organizations throughout the first half of the century, serving as commander of Theodore Roosevelt Post, American Legion, in Santa Rosa in 1925. For a record fourteen years, under three governors, he was a member of the California Veterans Board.

—Press Democrat Collection

Santa Rosa soldier Hugh McMenamin in training camp. Like many others called to WWI, McMenamin never left the United States.

—Paul Caratti Collection

Below, the men of Santa Rosa's Company E are introduced to gas masks in the spring of 1915.

—Comstock Family Collection

60

pits and nut shells, commodities readily available in orchard-dotted Sonoma County, because a carbon created by burning these pits was being used to neutralize the effects of poison gas used at the front.

One of the first meetings of the chapter was formally addressed by Dr. Jackson Temple, who advised housewives present to monitor their garbage carefully as their first contribution to the war effort. "Keep broken glass and tin cans out of the garbage," he told the women, "as they are fatal to pigs and it is essential to the war effort that we are able to feed our garbage to the hogs."[10]

When Father John Cassin, pastor of St. Rose, donated a pair of high-powered binoculars to the military, he received a thank-you letter from Assistant Secretary of the Navy Franklin Roosevelt. A Santa Rosa real estate man, John Lamb, received commendations for the number of sweaters he knitted for soldiers.

On November 7, 1918, Santa Rosans joined Americans everywhere in a celebration of a false armistice, based on premature news reports that Germany had signed an armistice agreement. Four days later, November 11, the celebration was in earnest. The *Press Democrat* reported: "Santa Rosa was awakened from its usual Sunday night repose shortly after 3 o'clock by the blowing of whistles, blowing of horns and the screech of auto horns as the news became public of the signing of the armistice."

By 4 a.m. the streets were filled with people who had dressed and driven downtown to learn if the war really had ended. An impromptu, pre-dawn parade up Fourth Street was followed by a larger parade in midmorning, when residents of the surrounding countryside had arrived. The Santa Rosa Band and the Boys Drum and Bugle Corps assembled for the occasion. The fire chief brought out the "auto chemical" engine and rang its warning bell. Mayor J.C. Mailer addressed the crowd and everyone joined in the singing of "America" and "Columbia." In the afternoon a delegation of Italian-

Americans appeared on the streets carrying the Italian and American flags, parading about town amid cheers.

The only celebrations were impromptu by necessity. There could be no formal gathering, for the news came at a bad time. The same newspapers that carried the news of the armistice contained a bold-faced, black-bordered warning of the danger to the community from a new enemy, the Spanish influenza.

By early October of 1918, when the end of the war was in sight, the virulent disease that began in the trenches of

An ambulance made of flowers, with the red cross in red roses, was an entry in Santa Rosa's 1917 Rose Parade.

—*Press Democrat Collection*

—*Chamber of Commerce Collection*

United War Work Campaign

This is to certify that

Clark Mailer _____ of Fremont School

having completed his payment of One and 12/100 Dollars from his own earnings, toward the United War Work Campaign Fund, is therefore, enrolled, as one of the "VICTORY BOYS" and is thus helping to provide comfort, and cheer, for an American Fighter through, the work, of, the seven, organizations represented in the campaign

YOUNG MEN'S CHRISTIAN ASSOCIATION
YOUNG WOMEN'S CHRISTIAN ASSOCIATION
NATIONAL CATHOLIC WAR COUNCIL
K. or C.— JEWISH WELFARE BOARD
WAR CAMP COMMUNITY SERVICE
AMERICAN LIBRARY ASSOCIATION
SALVATION ARMY

Ralph G. Coyle
STATE SECRETARY

Geo. F. Ballard
LOCAL EXECUTIVE

J.R. Mott
CAMPAIGN DIRECTOR GENERAL

A.H. Whitford
DIRECTOR DEPARTMENT CAMPAIGN DIVISIONS

"A MILLION BOYS BEHIND A MILLION FIGHTERS"

Schoolboy Clark Mailer received a certificate for the dollar he contributed to the United War Work Campaign.

Europe and spread quickly through both allied and enemy camps had reached Sonoma County. At home, the first news of the epidemic came in wire service dispatches and, more urgently, in the news of illness and deaths of Sonoma County soldiers in Army camps in the eastern United States.

In Santa Rosa citizens heeded the warnings to avoid crowds but by mid-October the siege had begun. Movie studios announced there would be no new film releases until further notice, anticipating the closure of theaters. Teachers were instructed to watch students for symptoms and send them home immediately. Brothers and sisters of influenza victims were banned from the classroom. Meanwhile, the disease was spreading. New York City reported half a million cases by mid-October and reports of epidemics in South Africa, South America, and Australia were in the news.

Closer to home, Mare Island Naval Base in Vallejo, issued its first official warning on October 9, 1918, suggesting precautions were advisable. The symptoms— chills, fever, depression, weakness, dizziness, severe headache, backache, pains in the muscles and joints, coughing, and nasal congestion—would come to be familiar

ones to following generations, but the fierceness of this first "flu," as it came to be called, cannot be understood in modern terms. There was no sulfa, no penicillin, no antibiotic. Medicine was nearly powerless to stop the deadly side effects. "Spray your throat and nostrils with a solution of ten percent argyrol, use boric acid powder as a snuff and keep away from crowds." That was the government dictum.[11]

The first to become ill in Sonoma County were people who were living, like the soldiers of World War I, in close quarters. A dozen or more men working on Highway 101 and living in a road construction camp on Cotati Boulevard near Wilfred were reported to be "down," a term which would become all too familiar in coming weeks. At the Salvation Army's Golden Gate Industrial Farm and Orphanage at Lytton the children "took" the flu at the rate of seventy-five per day until 175 of the 250 youngsters were ill. They included ten-year-old Helen Groul, whose death, on October 16, was the first in Sonoma County attributed to influenza.[12]

Before another week had passed there were 150 people ill in Santa Rosa. In the pages of the newspapers, the obituaries began "sudden illness" and "pneumonia," fooling no one. A young sailor home on furlough buried at Shiloh Cemetery; Everett Grove of Windsor dead at twenty-six; Lakeville pioneer Edward Dowd dead after a two-day illness; Earl Jamison, the Northwestern Pacific agent, dead. Finally, reporters stopped evading the truth and started citing influenza as the cause of death.

Schools were closed; the Cline and the Rose theaters went dark; club and lodge meetings were canceled; children were forbidden to play in groups on the street; and Sonoma County was joining the rest of the world in burying its dead.

It was a disease that spared the weak and took the strong. Despite the early tragedy at Lytton orphanage, children, for the most part, survived. So did older people. Young adults, strapping young farmers in their twenties and thirties, soldiers in top physical condition, young mothers—these died in great numbers. Pregnant women seemed particularly vulnerable. Multiple deaths in families were frequent, as were multiple family funerals. Brothers and sisters died in the same day, representatives of three generations died within a week of each other—first, a young mother; two days later, her mother, and a week later, little Alice Gray. At Sonoma State Hospital, fifty patients died within a week.[13]

Those who remembered the Spanish flu would call it "the scariest thing I've ever known." Family life broke down. Whole families were stricken, sometimes four or five sick in one room to spare others in the household. Small children ran unattended in the streets because their parents were too sick to care for them. The Red Cross worked overtime, appealing continually for volunteers to care for the sick. A young man who had nursed his mother for four days and nights fell desperately ill when she died. A mother who worked to support her five children was in need of food when she became too ill to work.

Santa Rosans responded. Hotels and restaurants provided hot meals. Butcher Paul Noonan donated twenty-five pounds of soup meat every day. Wildwood Dairy brought three gallons of fresh milk to the Red Cross office every afternoon. Farmers stopped by with live chickens to make broth, or a bushel basket of potatoes. "Can you cook a custard or make a glass of egg nog?" Red Cross officials asked in the newspaper columns. Nearly every housewife who was well enough, came through.

The streets took on an eerie look. By the first week of November, gauze masks were compulsory, by city ordinance. Not only were store clerks and bank tellers required to wear them, but pedestrians who appeared on the streets of

4th EXTRA

1:00 P. M. **THE PRESS DEMOCRAT**

VOL. XLV   SANTA ROSA, CALIFORNIA, MONDAY, NOVEMBER 11, 1918   NO. 173

ARMISTICE TEXT

LOCAL EXEMPTION BOARD GETS ORDERS

WASHINGTON, Nov. 11, 3 a. m.---By the Associated Press.---The world war will end this morning at 6 o'clock, Washington time, 11 o'clock Paris time. The armistice was signed by the German representatives at midnight. This announcement was made at 2:50 o'clock this morning The State Department's announcement simply said: "THE ARMISTICE HAS BEEN SIGNED"

—*Press Democrat Collection*

Santa Rosa or Petaluma without them were subject to a fine and/or a jail sentence. Northwestern Pacific required masks for its passengers.

Drug stores advertised atomizers and Dobell's solution for spraying the throat and San Tox Wine of Cod Liver Oil and Iron to "fortify the system" against disease. Dibble's department store assured customers in ads that shopping there was safe—"Not one of our salesladies has been ill."[14]

Frances Grimm was ten years old and a boarding student at Ursuline College. "At its early stages," she wrote in her account of the epidemic, "the Sisters told us to write our families not to visit us. Day scholars stayed home. There was no school for them.

"In early 1919 I took sick. After a bad night, Sisters called Dr. Jesse. He came at 5 a.m., ordered the school closed and told the Sisters to send the boarders home. The Sisters phoned my mother—we owned a hotel and saloon in Duncans Mills. She came down on the first train, which got in here about 8 a.m. There was no place to take me. Mom went to Charles Dunbar [civic leader and former assemblyman] but he had no place. Finally Sister Mary Frances suggested a building used for laundry. It had been partially destroyed in the earthquake. No nurses were available. When my mother tried to get a nurse she took a cab to Sebastopol to see Ruth Burns. She was busy. Then [she went to see] Rose Donnelly and when she went up on the porch, there were three bodies waiting to be picked up. It was a tragedy!

"She finally found one. Her name was Rose Patterson and she worked twelve hours. By that time Sister Antonio and Sister Agnes had come down with it. My Mom helped during the day and returned to the Occidental Hotel at night. Before she left for the night, Sister Mary Francis insisted she have a couple of straight shots. Mom said it saved her from the flu."[15]

Burgess Titus, who compiled his recollections of his years in Santa Rosa in a memoir he called "I Remember When," remembers when, in 1918, he worked at the American Bakery on lower Fourth Street and "Mr. Whitaker and I and all the people who came and went wore cloth gauze masks over our noses and mouths. Each person felt the flimsy cloth would ward off the terrible influenza bug that was traveling rampant around the whole world.

"We would watch a wagon or a truck go slowly down Fourth Street and, although we could not see the bodies under the black cloth cover, we knew there were seven or eight people under it we had known, or known something about. It was said they were being taken to the brewery ice house to be put in cold storage until they could be properly cared for. It would always seem like the big strong people would be the first to fall to the scourge; and many of them had come home from the War in Europe, only to be cut down by the flu bug."[16]

Social life came to a standstill. "Another churchless Sunday," the *Press Democrat* headline read.[17] Marriage licenses dwindled and what ceremonies were performed were scarcely celebrations. Only the bride's mother and brother were present at one reported nuptials. Santa Rosa's health officer, Dr. R.M. Bonar, issued directives daily. "Don't attend funerals—say it with flowers." "Don't travel and if you must use your own conveyance." "Don't visit sick friends." He also appealed to families of the sick not to wait until night to call a physician. "They're all overworked and need all the regular rest they can get." The telephone company, too, made an urgent appeal to customers to stay off the telephones except when absolutely necessary. Many operators were sick and the ones available needed to be ready for calls to physicians.

District Attorney George Hoyle and the Board of Supervisors debated the wisdom of simply "closing the county," that is, declaring a general quarantine barring Sonoma County to travelers. People from the Bay Area, fearful of the disease, attempted to "escape to the country" and occupied resort cottages at the Russian River and in Sonoma Valley. The summer cabins were cold and damp in November, resulting in pneumonia and the spread of the disease in the rural areas. The outstanding exception was the community of Bloomfield where the hometown physician, Dr. Bruce Cockrill, announced with great pride there had been "not a single case" of Spanish influenza.[18]

There was a respite at the end of November. The city lifted the mask ordinance. Schools reopened. But by Christmas week, the disease had a resurgence. There were bans on public dancing, the mask law was reinstated, and by the first week in January, all public meetings were once again prohibited. Stores were closing early. The downtown was deserted.

Still, Santa Rosa fared better than most smaller towns, possibly because more physicians were available. Another factor was the Red Cross, which did heroic work. When an emergency hospital opened at the Saturday Afternoon Clubhouse in January of 1919, Adelaide Parsons, in charge of staffing for the Red Cross, put out a call for nurses and the call was answered. Jessie Weeden was the supervising nurse. She had nothing but praise for the volunteers— housewives, business college students who did nursing duty, teachers who used the high school kitchen to prepare hot meals for the patients. The doctors, said Weeden in a newspaper interview, sent people to the hospital when "they

Burgess Titus, standing at left with his brothers Nathan and George in 1918, would later share his vivid memories of the terrible days of the Spanish influenza in Santa Rosa.

—*Leland Titus Collection*

—*Press Democrat Collection*

GAUZE MASKS

WELL MADE FROM STERILIZED ASEPTIC GAUZE

15c each

We have just received a supply of gauze, and if you prefer to make your own masks we can supply you with the best quality at

25c per yard, or a 5-yd. package for 90 cents

•••••••••••

LUTTRELL DRUG CO.
DEPENDABLE DRUGGISTS
Free Delivery.

PHONE 3   527 Fourth St.

CLINE THEATRE
AND
ROSE THEATRE

Closed for one week by Board of Health as a precaution against influenza epidemic. Will reopen when safety of the public is assured.

WATCH FOR COMING ATTRACTIONS.

Fryer's Abietene
WILL SAFEGUARD AGAINST
SPANISH INFLUENZA

Don't wait till you feel it coming on. Spray throat and nose frequently with ABIETENE. See window and get your bottle at Rutherford's. Fifth and Mendocino.

TO STOP SPANISH INFLUENZA
—— The germs multiply with great rapidity, so spray five times an hour with

FRYER'S ABIETENE
Rub Abietene Ointment on throat and nose and put ointment up each nostril. See window and get your bottle at

RUTHERFORD'S : : 5th and Mendocino

Teenager Vernon Silvershield, left, in 1918 with his bicycle and his gauze mask, required by law, during the flu epidemic.

Welcome Home

November 11, 1919

Santa Rosa's day of honor to her Service Men

Welcome Home Edition
THE PRESS DEMOCRAT

SECOND SECTION

PAGES 9 to 16

VOL. LXVI SANTA ROSA, CALIFORNIA, TUESDAY, NOVEMBER 11, 1919 NO. 115

Published Tuesday, Nov. 11, 1919
Sonoma County's Welcome Home Day
In Honor of Her Service Men

A History of the Part Played by Sonoma County's Men and Women in the World's Greatest War. A Record Which Should be Preserved.

felt they must die." The untiring work of the hospital's hastily assembled staff, she said, saved most of them.[19]

Finally, in mid-January 1919, the epidemic abated. The *Press Democrat*, on January 17, reported only six new cases of influenza during the past twenty-four hours. The tone of the news story was upbeat. This lowered number was considered a very hopeful sign. The emergency hospital closed on January 26. By February the schools had reopened (there had been two five-week closures) and on February 4, for the first time since October, Santa Rosans attended church services—to pray for those who had not survived and to give thanks they themselves had lived through this terrible time.

More people died of the Spanish influenza worldwide than were killed, on both sides, in World War I, the most costly war, in terms of human life, in the history of the world. By the time it subsided in 1919, twenty million people were dead. Death records show a total of 175 persons died of influenza in Sonoma County in 1918 and 1919.[20] While these figures alone indicate a death toll higher than the monumental earthquake of 1906, they are not truly indicative of the damage done by the disease. Death from pneumonia resulting from the flu would have to be sorted out and added. Many thousands more would die in the following years of tuberculosis and other related respiratory diseases resulting from the pandemic virus.

In November of 1919, one year after the Armistice, the *Press Democrat* published a special "Welcome Home" edition. Again, it was hard to separate the war from the epidemic. After the "roll of honor" list of the thirty-seven Sonoma County citizens who died in action, as a result of wounds or in aircraft accidents in the war, there were the twenty-two names of men and women who died of influenza in the military service.

Still, the anniversary publication struck a positive pose—celebrating the triumph of democracy and the patriotism and generosity of Sonoma County residents, who invested $12,500,000 in Liberty Bonds for the war effort, over-subscribing four of the five county quotas. The small-print list of all the men and women who served filled a page, as did the good work of the Red Cross in Sonoma County.

While the special edition was meant to herald, not change but the return to business as usual, there is little question World War I opened towns like Santa Rosa and rural counties like Sonoma to a greater world; and—what was so important to agriculture and to business—a larger and more diverse marketplace. 🙢

Good Years, Bad Years

The 20th century was filled with promise for Sonoma County agriculture. In the first three decades that promise was fulfilled beyond the wildest dreams of the pioneer farmers. By 1920 a dozen major crops, widely diversified, combined to make Sonoma the eighth ranking county in the entire nation in agricultural production.[1] First in wine grapes; first in eggs and poultry; second in prunes, canning cherries, and hops; an acknowledged leader in apples, dairies, and livestock—the litany of products rolled proudly off the tongues of those whose task it was to extoll the county's virtues. The "boosters" of the 19th century, the writers of letters home, who had foreseen bountiful harvests from the fertile virgin land where grew wild grass tall enough to hide a man on horseback, who had lobbied for a railroad to send their crops to market, were proven right on all counts.

Dairy cows were the county's enduring producers of agricultural dollars. Since pre-railroad days when farmers shipped their surplus calves and butter out of Bodega Bay to the San Francisco market, dairying had been at or near the top of income production lists. Small creameries in the coastal communities of Valley Ford, Bodega, and Bodega Bay gave way in 1913 to a cooperative creamery headquartered in Petaluma that could control market and pricing and keep the dairymen prosperous through difficult times. Dairy products from the Petaluma Cooperative Creamery created an ever-widening market for the Swiss, Italian, Portuguese, and Danish dairymen who populated the rural areas of southern and western Sonoma County. In October of 1931 Sonoma County was tenth in California in dairy production. By mid-century, the Petaluma Cooperative Creamery had 1,100 "owners" and was the second largest in the state.[2]

In a time when butterfat was the measure of milk, Jerseys consistently won the awards. There were several important Jersey dairies in the Santa Rosa area, including that of Florence and Al Gilardoni of Fulton and Lullaby Farm, the dairy east of Santa Rosa run by the Murray

brothers. Lex and Bob Murray were the dairying success story of the 1930s. The sons of Laura Murray began building their Jersey herd while they were still Future Farmers at Santa Rosa High School. Lex started a milk route as an FFA project in 1934 with cows he borrowed from a Tomales dairyman and from his agriculture teacher, George Bath, who was a rancher in addition to his faculty work. Lex then purchased two registered cows for $150. His brother Bob joined the dairy operation when he entered high school. By the mid-'50s, Bob Murray was milking 120 cows on 220-plus acres on Summerfield Road and his mother's fifty-acre farm in town, on Franklin Avenue.

Others among the prize-winning dairies were Guy Mann's ranch in Freestone, Ernest Finley's ranch on the Laguna near Sebastopol and W.H. Kimes's ranch in Windsor. Santa Rosa High School's agricultural program produced a series of winning livestock-judging teams. In 1923, a team

Dairying was a leading producer of agricultural dollars in Sonoma County from the earliest settlement days. In Santa Rosa, in the years before World War I, close-to-town ranchers ran morning milk routes, competing for the business of city dwellers. Below, Louis Pedrotti stands proudly at the entrance to his farm in the Todd District in 1915. At right, the Bellevue Dairy's milk delivery service of Emerson Brown.

—*Finley Collection*

—*Turrill & Miller Photo, Finley Collection*

—Leonard Talbot Collection

Santa Rosa High School's 1923 livestock judging team won the state championship and placed third in international competition. Left to right, Don Weatherington, Frank Vought, William Braun, and Wesley Jamison. SRHS student Leonard Talbot, at right, demonstrates his abilities as a crop judge. His mother, Talbot recalled, always referred to his Future Farmer activities as the "Corn Club."

—Finley Collection

from Santa Rosa composed of Wesley Jamison, William Braun, Harry Vought, and Don Weatherington represented California and won third place in cattle judging in an international livestock show. In 1928, Santa Rosa's team, led by instructors Bath, Phillip Becklund, and Walter Patchett, won the state championship; and in 1934, with Wesley Jamison as their coach, a SRHS team with Richard Gray, Lex Murray, and Noble Ledson won the national title in a dairy-cattle judging competition in Kansas City.

Santa Rosa's southern neighbor, Petaluma, was the "Egg Basket of the World," a title drawn from the hundreds of chicken farms that clustered around the town and the many prosperous hatcheries that followed the 1879 invention of a prototype multi-egg incubator and brooder house by a pair of Petaluma men.

The incubator had been the work of a Canadian immigrant with a penchant for "tinkering" named Lyman Byce and his fellow inventor, a Petaluma dentist named Isaac Dias. The brooder house that would house as many chicks as the incubator could hatch was built by Christopher Nisson, a Danish farmer whose ranch was near Two Rock and whose Pioneer Hatchery would become one of the largest in the world. These inventions, and the availability of grain for feed, created a boom in fryers and eggs in Petaluma that would last for eighty years.[3]

Statistically, Petaluma's chicken and egg production in the first half of the century was staggering. In the 1920's, Petaluma shipped more than 22 million dozen eggs, not only to San Francisco and the Bay Area but on to New York, where the label "Petaluma Extras" commanded a big price, and to Hawaii, South America, and Europe.[4]

There were nineteen commercial hatcheries in Petaluma, with capacities ranging from 100,000 to 1.8 million eggs; nine feed mills, six egg-packing plants, three poultry-processing plants, and an incubator factory.[5] There was also a Main Street shop called the Chicken Pharmacy. This

—Private Collection

business, devoted to medicines to cure the myriad diseases and conditions that plague poultry, was opened in 1923 by druggist J.E. Keyes and remained a viable business, through a succession of owners, until it closed in 1954. Robert Ripley, a "Santa Rosa boy" who had achieved success as the creator of a cartoon panel of oddities called "Believe it or Not!", gave the Chicken Pharmacy fame and, in fact, turned it into something of a tourist attraction.

In 1930, there were 4,314,279 chickens counted in the agricultural census of Sonoma County. Chickens, predominately white leghorns, being raised on small farms spreading out from Petaluma to the Sonoma Valley and north to Fulton, accounted for 40,967,437 eggs shipped from the county that year. In 1935, poultry products, valued at $11,200,000, were the richest of the county's farm crops.[6]

The "World's Egg Basket" title, painted on a sign welcoming Highway 101 travelers, was the work of Bert Kerrigan, a master promoter who was hired as Petaluma Chamber of Commerce manager after World War I. Kerrigan's specialty was slogans. He had created the "Milk from Contented Cows" for Carnation.[7] It was Kerrigan's advice, which Petalumans adopted with a vengeance, to forgo all other industry and commerce and concentrate on chickens.

For three decades, Kerrigan's idea worked like a charm. But the move to corporate agriculture and risk-capital farming after World War II would spell disaster for the small chicken rancher. In 1949, at the peak of its production, Sonoma County shipped 48 million dozen eggs, one third of all the eggs sold in California that year. By the mid-1950s, competition from Southern California, where producers kept 100,000 hens laying "round-the-clock" in environmentally controlled cages, had served notice to the rural farmers that their long, low, redwood chicken houses, so much a part of the southern Sonoma County landscape, were obsolete.[10]

Santa Rosa's fame and fortune were drawn from orchard, vineyard, and hopyard. Of the three major

Chickens accounted for the fact that the largest agricultural community of Jewish immigrants west of the Delaware River gathered in Sonoma County after 1904. Immigrant Jews from Eastern Europe, particularly those who had not prospered in the large East Coast cities where they first settled, came to Sonoma County in surprising numbers in the first half of the century. Social scientists who have studied this group conclude it was an ideological commitment to a rural lifestyle which started this Jewish back-to-the-land movement.[8]

Sam Melnick, an immigrant from Lithuania, came to Petaluma in 1904 and bought seven acres and 500 pullets. He and the other early Jewish farmers had visions of a community where Jews could live in dignity and health. They wrote letters, loaned money, offered advice, and helped others get started. Between 1917 and 1921, forty Jewish families came to southern Sonoma County, which became, in the words of one historian, "a major center of Yiddish culture within the United States."[9]

After World War II, there was another "wave" of new farmers. Some were refugees from Hitler's Europe, others were garment workers pushed out of New York and New Jersey by the mechanization of their industry. By 1949, there were more than 200 Jewish families on small chicken ranches around Petaluma, Penngrove, and Cotati. Some were Zionists who had come to learn how to raise chickens, planning to transfer their knowledge to a kibbutz in Israel. But most were people who celebrated the idea of owning farm land, which had been prohibited to them in their homelands.

It is impossible to separate the Jewish chicken farmers of Sonoma County from their politics. Many had been politicized in their native countries, by the pogroms and by conditions in revolutionary Russia. Whether they were Orthodox, Progressive, Socialist, Communist, or Zionist, part of the appeal of chicken farming was that it was politically acceptable.

—*Sonoma County Library*

that the sandy loam of the Russian River bottom land, the Laguna de Santa Rosa and its tributaries, Green Valley Creek and Mark West Creek, was suited to hop production. In addition the coastal fogs that cooled the evenings seemed to produce larger hops with more lupolin which would bring a better price than Central Valley's crop. By 1930 more than three million pounds of hops were being grown, "toasted," baled, and shipped from Sonoma County each year.[11]

Until the 1950s, hop vines lined the roads from Santa Rosa to Healdsburg, Fulton, Mark West, and Windsor, west to Forestville, and through Alexander Valley, and the distinctive stone hop kilns became as familiar on the landscape as the valley oaks.

The names of the hop ranchers—Steele and Proctor, Talmadge and Wood, Fenton and Bussman and Maddux and Peterson, Slusser and Laughlin, and Finley and Grace—were the same as the names on the streets and roads around Santa Rosa. Thomas Hutchinson grew hops on his Annadel farm on the highway to Sonoma; Harrison Finley's hop kiln was a landmark on Mark West Springs Road. Vern Wood was only a boy when his father moved from Sebastopol and bought a little ranch on Hall Road to raise hops. The brokers—Chris Donovan, Ben Hall, Walter Richardson, George Proctor, Milton Wasserman (who was manager of the local office of William Uhlmann Company, one of the world's largest hop brokers), Robert Madison (who bought for Max Wolf Co. and served as Sonoma County's assemblyman during World War I and was later a city councilman)—were among the political and social leaders of the town.

Hops were a risky crop. The comparatively small acreage required to supply enough hops for the world market made prices fluctuate wildly. A crop failure in one part of the world could drive prices over $1 a pound one year, while news of new plantings or a high yield could send them below 10 cents a pound another. In beer, said market-wise hop growers, "the cap cost more than the hops." Still,

agricultural endeavors that created the economy of the town, hop growing was the king.

Hops grow on a tall vine, a member of the cannabis family, a cousin to the marijuana plant. The hop vines twine and climb along strings or wire trellises attached to poles. The fruit of the hop vine, scaled and shaped like a small pine cone, is harvested, dried in kilns, and used in the production of beer. A yellow resin-like substance called lupolin found at the base of the scales, or "bracts," is what gives beer its distinctive bitter flavor.

Hops grow well in rich, moist soil such as that found along rivers and creeks. The county's first hop growers, Amasa Bushnell and Otis Allen, had harvested a crop in Green Valley in 1858. Those who followed their lead found

The Chicken Pharmacy on Petaluma's Main Street, upper left, dispensed medications for poultry ailments from 1923 to 1954.

fortunes were made—by grower and broker alike—in Sonoma County's "hop years," roughly 1880 to 1950.

Hop pickers were very important to the process since hops are extremely perishable and must be picked quickly once they ripen. The grower has a thirty-day window in which to pick, dry, and bale his harvest. In Mendocino County, where hop land followed the Russian River from Ukiah to the town to which the crop gave its name, Hopland, Pomo Indians picked the hops. In the early part of the century, the Indians came every year to Santa Rosa to pick, camping west of town and working at the call of a "boss" named Tom who contracted with the growers for his band

of pickers.[12] Chinese workers, men only, who came from San Francisco for the harvest season, were supplied by laborer contractor Tom Wing, the undisputed head of Santa Rosa's Chinatown. They stayed in the Chinese boarding houses along Second and Third streets. Japanese workers, who came from Hawaii, became as expert at working the hops as they had been in the pineapple and cane fields and were much in demand for planting and training the vines as well as for the harvest.

In addition, families from San Francisco and the East Bay came to pick, regarding the work as an excursion or country outing. These urban pickers generally camped on

Workers at the Jones hop kiln on Westside Road in 1909. Top to bottom, Ernie Small, Clarence Bruer, Fred Birkhoffer, Floyd Bollinger, Warren Jones, and Carl Peterson.

The inset photo is a close look at the bracts of the hop vine, the top crop of the early century in the Russian River Valley.

—LeBaron Collection

—Sonoma County Library, Healdsburg

73

the ranch where they were employed in an enclave that took on the aspects of a summer resort in the evenings, when they sang and danced around a campfire. Housewives and high school students picked hops for extra money, working alongside the migrant workers to get the job done.

Robert Bussman, whose family was among the last of Sonoma County's hop growers, talked about the pickers who came to the ranch on Woolsey Road, near Mark West Creek. "We used to have between 350 and 500 people on the ranch during the hop harvest. They came from all over the state—Pomo Indians from the mountains, 'Okies' and 'Arkies,' gypsies, longshoremen from the docks of San Francisco...." Like many ranchers, Bussman provided a camp. His was in the pear orchard and consisted of tents ranging in size from the one-man six-by-eight-foot variety to twelve-by-fourteen-foot family-size platforms with walls made from the cloth used in the kilns. "We set up showers and had four Maytag washers, redwood tables and benches and stoves for cooking we made out of square gas tanks obtained from junk yards and auto wrecking places. Electric lines were strung up for lighting. A grocer from Santa Rosa would set up a store during the harvest where you could get fresh meat and staples.

"So you see," said Bussman, "it was a big campground, with a kind of a carnival feel. As I recall, there were some good banjo and guitar players." During the Depression, his grandfather, Pete Bussman, distributed cards with directions to the ranch on one side and an invitation to "Tell your Friends." On the other he made his pitch: "Hop Pickers Wanted, 90 acres, Vacation with Pay." Said Bussman: "He would describe the camp facilities, with free rent and wood, hot and cold water, lights and so forth. This attracted a lot of pickers who would come back year after year. We had two and three generations of families picking hops for us over a span of twenty or thirty years."[13]

The importance of getting the ripe hops into the kiln put the grower at the mercy of the pickers. With quick and competent pickers who filled their sacks with only hops and not dirt clods to increase the weight, a grower could earn a good living on a twenty-five-acre hop ranch. Many families got rich on fifty acres. And some ranches, like the 185-acre Wohler Ranch, were considered immense. Smaller hop yards, eight, ten, twelve acres, customarily grew "low-pole" hops, on wooden poles no more than seven feet high, which not only cut picking costs but negated the need for a large capital outlay for the fifteen, eighteen, or twenty-foot steel poles and wire trellises.

Big or small, the grower depended on the decisions of the hop buyers. The "price of hops" was an important factor in Santa Rosa life. It was a topic of regular news stories and of dinnertable and streetcorner conversation. For example, a newspaper story on an August Sunday in 1917, a year when hop prices had bottomed out at about 8 cents per pound, was headlined "Growers Are Awaiting Confidently 20¢ Hops" and began: "With hops selling at $17\frac{1}{2}$ cents per pound Saturday there was unusual excitement among both dealers and growers on the streets during the afternoon hours."

Most growers were financed by the brokers, who often owned an entire crop by harvest time, sometimes contracted as much as three years in advance. Hop contracts and their agreed-upon prices were filed annually with the county assessor's office. "It didn't matter what you wanted for your hops," said Vern Wood, remembering a year when "Dad held hops waiting for a $1.25 a pound and took 9 cents."

Despite the tensions, the hop harvest was an exciting time. There were picking contests and speed contests and many a flirtation between the young women pickers and the "high pole," usually a local lad with some athletic ability whose job it was to scale the poles and drag the vines down to picking height.

Prohibition's impact on the hop market was injurious but not fatal. It began with a surprising leap in hop prices, predicated on the British demand for hops at the end of World War I. The roller coaster started with the wartime

—Virginia Grace Collection

At right, hop pickers on the Grace Ranch in Alexander Valley celebrate the end of the harvest. Below, hop kiln workers load sacks of dried hops.

—Finley Collection

liquor laws that first reduced the alcohol content of beer to 2.75 percent and then shut the breweries (December 1, 1918) to conserve grain, laws that were battled valiantly by California legislators including Congressman Clarence Lea. Lea spoke out against legislation which would outlaw the manufacture of beer and wine but not the sale, and which still allowed foreign imports. Such a law, he warned in testimony before the Senate Agriculture Committee, would ruin the grape and hop growers. He opposed the prohibition of wine and doubted the wisdom of striking down the beer business. "The money put into the hop business should be considered," he told the Senate committee, calling attention to the fact that American barley was being sent to France and England for the manufacture of beer there. "There is a certain inconsistency to that," said Lea, understating for emphasis the feelings of his agricultural constituency, who knew all about vulnerability. While grape growers pondered alternate uses for their wine grapes, hop men had a saying: "There are two things you can do with a hop. Throw it away. Or make beer."14

The growers, fearing the worst and knowing at this time that a national prohibition was a likely future prospect, joined with Sacramento Valley hop growers in forming a statewide organization, which held a mass meeting at the courthouse in Santa Rosa in the summer of 1918. Chaired by banker Frank Brush, with broker Milton Wasserman as secretary, the growers elected Dan Carmichael, mayor of Sacramento, to go to Washington and plead the case of the hop men. The lobbying was intense. The Sonoma County Farm Bureau wrote President Woodrow Wilson about the plight of the hop and grape growers, asking that at least they be given some time to dispose of the crop due to be picked within the month. But Carmichael's mission was not successful. U.S. breweries were making plans to build plants in China. The Department of Agriculture was suggesting that at least one-third of America's hop land be planted with vegetables. Growers and brokers alike agreed that the outlook was glum.

Then surprising events occurred. In November of 1918 "Colonel" C.C. Donovan, generally referred to in the *Press Democrat* as the "Hop King," offered three growers three-year contracts—for 1919, 1920, and 1921—at 35 cents a pound. The "Colonel" was on a buying spree, preparing to export his hops. England was buying California hops to put her breweries back in business after the devastating war. Other brokers jumped on the export wagon. Bob Madison bought the last of Lake and Mendocino counties' supply and started offering three-year contracts. Pete Bussman signed with him, as did the Ballard Ranch in Healdsburg and Santa Rosa grower Chester Von Grafen. There was considerable excitement among the growers. "Some growers who had not intended to grow hops anymore," said the *Press Democrat*, "now that long-term contracts are being made, will set out yards again."15

By spring, new records were being set weekly with hop prices. All the brokers were bidding for the coming fall crop and buying high. George Proctor paid 32½ cents. John Miller,

Hop picking was hot and dusty work. At far left, women pickers strip hop vines on a ranch near Healdsburg.

At right, A Sacramento newspaper artist's caricature of Santa Rosa's politician/hop broker, Assemblyman Bob Madison. The "something up his sleeve" refers to his prowess as an amateur magician.

ROB'T MADISON OF SANT ROSA, VETERAN OF THE INFLUENZA, HAS NOTHING IN SIGHT, MAYBE HE HAS SOMETHING UP HIS SLEEVE.

—King Family Scrapbook

STATE READY TO ORGANIZE HOPGROWERS

State Market Commissioner to Take Over Management of Campaign to Sign Up the Growers

—King Family Scrapbook

whose crop was jointly owned by the Exchange Bank and the Bank of Italy, conferred with his "partners" and rejected an offer of 57 cents in July. "Hop growers," observed the *Press Democrat*, "are assured a fine thing for at least three years in spite of national prohibition." The Trembley brothers sold to Milton Wasserman for 50 cents a pound; Frank P. Grace made a deal with Bob Madison. By September, when hops were bringing 70 cents—the highest since the glory days of the 1880s—the *Press Democrat* was reporting each record with jubilation: "The honest farmer is coming into his own this year with many of the crops grown in Sonoma County." But, the editor admitted, it seemed more serendipitous than usual, terming the state of the hop market "peculiar" as he reported on four-year-old hops, baled and stored and "considered practically worthless," being bid at 35 cents per pound.

"New" hops hit 84 cents in October, paid to William Peter Slusser and Ben Steele by broker William Richardson, and the last of the locally grown 1919 crop went for $85\frac{1}{2}$ cents. Hop men, said the newspaper, were "now at the pinnacle of prosperity." That turned out to be prophetic. Buyers wouldn't pay that price again until World War II. The hop fields of Kent were back in production by 1920 and, in addition, English breweries were quite testy about the condition of American hops, protesting that the California product was filled with leaves and dirt. In 1921, pickers were issued a stern warning about a propensity to weigh-in heavier by larding the hop basket with clods and twigs, in other words, "picking dirty." "We are living in a prohibition country, and if you pause long enough to reflect that if European dealers stop buying California hops, as they have threatened to do, hop growers must go out of business. If you go to work in this field you are making a contract with us to do first class work and if you pick dirty the contract is broken and we must part company at once."[16] But the "peculiar" hop market was over and what lay ahead was true Prohibition—and Depression.

Joe Maddux, whose family grew hops at Mark West, remembered: "Prohibition knocked hell out of the hop market. Prices went to 5 or 6 cents a pound. But the hop ranchers hung in there and when the war started the price soared to a $1 a pound and better. They were baling and selling the sweepings off the floor."[17]

The boom started by World War II lasted through the post-war years. In contrast to World War I, when the legislature shut the breweries to save grain, the government couldn't do enough to encourage the hop growers. "When the Germans marched on Czechoslovakia," said Vern Wood, "the world hop supply was cut by a lot. They offered us all the steel we needed, gas coupons, anything to keep growing hops so the servicemen could have their beer." Prices went to $1.25.[18] These were the years when "hop money" was a familiar term in Santa Rosa, when stories were told of growers who spent most of the winter at fancy San Francisco hotels and traveled abroad in grand style. Some of the growers built big homes on their ranches. Others, like the Steeles, lived in town and "commuted" to the hop yard. Bob Bussman's family lived on Monroe Street, but "My father was out at the ranch [on Woolsey Road] by 6 a.m." he recalled. "He liked to go to the hardware store first and Dixon Hardware opened at 5:30."[19]

Then, in the 1950s, the business went as sour as a bad batch of Grace Brothers' "Brew '52." Within the decade, hops disappeared from Sonoma County. Raford Peterson brought in the last hops from the landmark Wohler Ranch in 1956. The Bussman Ranch harvested its ninety acres until 1961. Soon there were no more. Several factors contributed to the loss of the hop industry. One alone could not have done such damage. First was the price, which declined after World War II. Many hop men blamed this downtrend on the changes in American drinking habits. Beer became too popular, some would say. A writer for "Hopper," an industry magazine, decried the changes.

"At this point I must bring up a dismal threat to the glory of American beer. Right now, the threat is a cloud on the horizon, no bigger than a braumeister's belly, but if the trend continues, beer will lose more and more of its distinctive quality and become strictly a thirst-quencher in the same category as Hires Root Beer and Seven-Up. Today about 70 percent of the beer—and much of this is sold by delicatessens, grocers and supermarkets—and the bulk of packaged beer is bought by women.

"Worse yet, women have begun to drink beer. Also, increasing numbers of boys and girls in the bobbysox circles, who have undeveloped palates and the taste standards of a jellyfish, have begun drinking.

"The result is that brewers have found out that in order to cater to this trade, they must take the backbone out of beer. A well-hopped beer is considered bitter by the sissy and female market. A good hearty brew, with plenty of barley malt extract in it, is considered heavy—and fattening."[20]

A Sebastopol hop grower, long retired, shared the writer's opinion on the damage done to the quality of beer by women. "Rosie the Riveter," he said, "went to war and learned to drink beer with the boys. That was the beginning of the end of the Sonoma County hop business."[21] The "Rosie the Riveter" factor hit the coastal hops before the valley hops. Not only did the coastal fogs produce bigger hops with more lupolin, but they differed from the valley hops in that they were "seeded," a term that means there were male hop vines planted here, "about every tenth hill" said Vern Wood, to pollinate the vines. The "male" hops were unproductive and valley growers did not like to bother with them, preferring to use the seedless variety that did not require pollinization. Brewers could tell you the difference was in the taste. The seeded hops had more of that lupolin that gave the beer its bitter flavor, a higher "hopping ratio," they called it. It was that difference, plus size, which had made the pre-WWII hops from Sonoma, Mendocino, and Lake counties more valuable. Now, with a trend toward lighter-tasting beer, it was quite the opposite. The seedless hops were in greater demand.

The second reason was a soil condition called downy mildew. Most hop land, being moist and dense, was always susceptible to this mildew, which often rendered the land useless for several seasons. After World War II, the nation's chemical companies, left with an excess of ammonia from the manufacture of ammunition, promoted the use of nitrate as fertilizer. Sonoma County hop growers, despite the fact that they had been dry farming successfully, bought the pitch. They began to irrigate and use the ammonia fertilizer in the water. The dampness produced a downy mildew that destroyed the crops and, what was worse, stayed in the soil.

—*Dauenhauer Family Collection*

What Eli Whitney did for cotton planters, Florian Dauenhauer did for hop growers. Dauenhauer, far left, a Santa Rosa hop man with a penchant for "tinkering" invented a hop picking machine in 1939 that revolutionized the labor-intensive hop industry.

Hop buyers, seeing the Sonoma County situation as potentially disastrous, began to look to eastern Washington, in the valleys around Yakima, where the soil froze in the winter, nine inches down, killing any residue of mildew left from the previous season.

Finally, there was the invention, by a clever Santa Rosa hop grower, of a machine that would pick hops. Florian Dauenhauer's hop picker, a structure which separates the hops from the vines fed into it, was tested on the ranch he and his brother Joe leased near Sacramento in 1939. The machine worked so well that other growers trucked their hops to it. Dauenhauer returned to Santa Rosa, moved his machine shop into his father's old garage, and built eight new machines. He also started the patent process on his invention. In 1944 his patents were granted and he was on his way to revolutionizing the hop industry—and hastening the decline of the Sonoma County hop business.

Where a fifty-acre hop ranch had been considered a large holding, given the picking problems, the machine made large tracts of hops possible—1,000 acres and more could be picked before the crop went bad. Sonoma County, where small farms had been established as the pattern in the 1850s, had no such tracts. The open spaces of the upper Sacramento Valley, eastern Washington, and northern Idaho were planted with hop vines. Sonoma County's "hop years" were over.

The distinctive towers of a hop kiln rise among young orchards near Healdsburg in the early 1950s. The Russian River is in the background in this southeasterly view. Growers often replaced hop vines with prune trees when hops disappeared from Sonoma County.

—*Redwood Empire Association*

Wine grapes and hops were Sonoma County neighbors, closely bonded in adversity in the "boom and bust" years between world wars. Much as hop growers greeted the new century with optimism, so vineyardists and winemakers in Sonoma County were as mellow as a barrel of old Zinfandel when the 20th century dawned over some 20,000 acres of Sonoma County vineyards.

Ocean fogs and volcanic soil had combined to make this the cradle of California viticulture in the 19th century. Technically the Russians can be credited with bringing the first wine grapes, experimenting with European varietals at their farms near the coast. General Mariano Vallejo, the military governor of California under Mexican rule, made his contribution to winemaking, although with the mission grape, which had little future in the world market.

The contributions of Count Agoston Haraszthy, the Hungarian political refugee who wrote the book, literally, on California viticulture, have been well documented.[22] The fact that his own vineyards were in Sonoma County provided an incentive for would-be vintners to try their hands here. Pioneer vintners like Charles Krug, who later moved to the Napa Valley, began their work in Sonoma County. Another European immigrant Andrea Sbarbaro founded Italian Swiss Colony, destined to become the world's largest winery. And "citizen of the world" Thomas Lake Harris, the founder of the Fountaingrove Utopian Community, used his connections with the members of his Brotherhood of the New Life to create a market for his Santa Rosa wines in New York, London, and Edinburgh.

There were two levels of Sonoma County viticulture in the first part of the 20th century. First, the prestige wine from Fountaingrove, Italian Swiss Colony, Santa Rosa's DeTurk Winery, Korbel Champagne Cellars in Guerneville, and the Sonoma Valley winery Haraszthy founded, Buena Vista; second, the barrel wine produced by the many, many small wineries and shipped by rail to eastern cities. Both were vital links in the county's agricultural economy.

The Northern California wine industry had survived a potentially disastrous infestation of phylloxera, the root louse that had dealt such a severe blow to France's wine production in the 1880s and traveled to the United States in the 1890s. At the turn of the century in Sonoma County, where thousands of acres of vines had been uprooted, grape growers were replanting enthusiastically with grafted, resistent rootstock, enjoying their county's enviable position as California's leading producer of both wine grapes and wine.

The years between 1900 and the start of Prohibition were considered by early winemakers to be Sonoma County's Golden Age. They were producing about two-thirds more grapes than neighboring Napa County and increasing the acreage each year. Grape acreage climbed from 21,000 to 42,000 by 1920 and the number of wineries, most of them

Grape pickers work a vineyard for Italian Swiss Colony at Asti, circa 1915.

—*Finley Collection*

BRANGER

Fine *Wines*

California

SHERRY

ALCOHOL 20% BY VOLUME

DISTRIBUTED BY BRANGER VINEYARD

BOTTLED BY EL GAVILAN WINERY

SANTA ROSA, CALIFORNIA

—Mitchell Collection

Bottasso & Son Winery on Sonoma Mountain Road, about a mile off Bennett Valley Road, was one of many small family wineries surrounding Santa Rosa in the years before Prohibition.

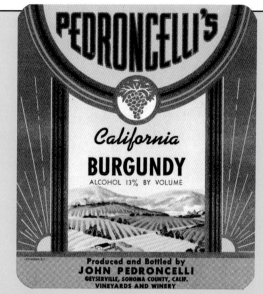

PEDRONCELLI'S

California

BURGUNDY

ALCOHOL 13% BY VOLUME

Produced and Bottled by
JOHN PEDRONCELLI
GEYSERVILLE, SONOMA COUNTY, CALIF.
VINEYARDS AND WINERY

— Pedroncelli Winery

Bercut-Vandervoort & Co., Inc.　　Sole Agents for the U. S. A.

★★★★★★★★★★★★★★★★★★★★★　VERITAS　★★★★★★★★★★★★★★★★★★★★★

ALCOHOL 12% BY VOLUME　　　　　　　CONTENTS 4/5 QUART

FOUNTAIN GROVE

CALIFORNIA

CHAMPAGNE

NATURALLY FERMENTED
IN THE BOTTLE　　　　　　　　B R U T

PRODUCED AND BOTTLED BY

Fountaingrove Vineyard, Santa Rosa, Sonoma County, California

—Sonoma County Wine Library　　　　　　　　　　　—LeBaron Collection

81

small, family vineyards and backyard presses supplying barrel wine to urban markets, was estimated at 256 in Sonoma County alone.[23]

Sonoma County's four "marketing giants" of the time, comparatively speaking—DeTurk, Fountain Grove, Korbel, and Italian Swiss Colony—were still making the bottled wines that had won prizes in European competitions since the 1880s. And they were surrounded by literally hundreds of small wineries, most of them on ranches owned by immigrants who planted a few acres of grapes for their own use, learned there was a market for it, and kept a wine press in the shed. The wine they produced was mostly a blend called, politely, "Italian mix" and, more often, "Dago

Rolling out the barrels at the Baldocchi Winery on Piner Road, circa 1918.

—Baldocchi Collection

red," shipped out of the county in barrels stacked on railroad cars.

If Prohibition came as a surprise to these winemakers, it shouldn't have. The ban on the production of alcohol in World War I was a warning. But California still enjoyed its "frontier mentality" which, together with the attitudes of immigrants who considered wine a necessary part of a meal and of life, made the notion of outlawing its production and sale seem far-fetched.

What was a surprise, and would remain a surprise to agricultural historians of the future, was the increase in grape production after the manufacture, sale, and consumption of alcoholic beverages were indeed outlawed by the 18th Amendment to the Constitution.

Grape growers did not have the escape valve for their product that the hop buyers found in Europe. Or so they thought. French, German, and Italian vintners were not clamoring for California grapes. Hurried statewide conferences were held and the State Board of Viticulture began compiling statistical information on alternate uses such as raisins, fresh grape juice, grape syrup, vinegar, and industrial alcohol. None of these offered a welcome solution in Sonoma County, where vineyards were planted for wine and wine only.

Yet, a future statistician, creating a graph of grape production in Sonoma County, would draw a line that climbed steadily upward from 1900 to a peak from which it quickly declined to a 50-year-low in the 1950s. The time of the peak is the surprise: grape acreage in Sonoma County reached its all-time high in 1925, six years into Prohibition.[24]

The truth is that winemaking continued in the United States on three fronts. Grape juice for home consumption was never outlawed and, after a time and pressure from East Coast immigrant groups, a law providing that families could make wine for home use was passed. Wine for medicinal purposes and ecclesiastical wines, both sacramental and rabbinical, were never outlawed, although permits were required, which only a few chosen

Piner District rancher Dewey Baldocchi poses on the steps of the U.S. Capitol. Baldocchi and attorney Nick DeMeo made a successful trip to Washington in 1942 to plead that North Coast grapes be excluded from government price ceilings.

winemakers obtained. And finally, winemaking continued illegally all over the nation. Just as the hidden stills needed sacks of sugar to supply the bootleggers who distributed their liquor, so the illegal winemakers needed carloads of grapes to keep the presses filled.

In 1922, grape growers were getting record prices for the fruit of their vines, $105 per ton, 15 percent more than the previous year and three times more than 1918, the previous record year. By the end of September of '22, forty refrigerator cars were rolling out of Santa Rosa daily, sending 300 tons of grapes per day to the East Coast market.[25] Delighted grape growers abandoned all thought of premium vintages and were ripping out the more pretentious Chardonnay and other thin-skinned, delicate vines to replant with the sturdy Zinfandel, Alicante Bouchet, and Carignane grapes, tough-skinned varieties that produced a sourer wine but were guaranteed to survive the rail trip.

Winemakers did not share the grape growers' good fortune. Hundreds of thousands of gallons of the "wine of the region," which had just begun to flirt with premium varietal grapes when Prohibition came, were poured out, making the creeks run red and, some say, giving the Russian River a pinkish tone as it flowed west from Healdsburg. Stories passed through generations of winemakers' families tell of neighbors coming with buckets and dishpans to catch the wine as it ran from the vats into the closest streams. Some, satisfied with a lighter vintage, dipped from the streams themselves. In 1920, according to a *Press Democrat* news story, there were three million gallons of wine in vats in Sonoma County wineries with no market in sight.[26]

When the decline occurred—and it did, sharply, in 1926—it was caused by overproduction. When grape prices rose in 1920, '21, and '22, the growers were overcome with optimism. Prohibition wasn't going to destroy their livelihood, they thought. It was going to make them rich. In their eagerness to supply the demand of Eastern markets,

they overplanted. The harvest of 1926 far exceeded the demand. Northern California produced more wine than all the rest of the United States combined in 1926. Prices dropped, by more than half to $45 a ton, and grapes rotted on the vines. The worst, feared earlier, had finally happened.[27]

Even though the possibility of repeal of the 18th Amendment (which did occur in 1932) offered new hope, many had already replaced their vines with prune trees. And the nation was in the throes of the Great Depression, which had dealt the staggering market its death blow. What laws could not do, economics had done. People could not afford to drink. The forty-year decline in the Sonoma County wine industry had begun. By 1933, there were just seventy operating wineries in Sonoma County.[28]

The grape growers who stuck it out faced new problems, including the federal government's plan to deal with surplus grapes. The U.S. Department of Agriculture's ProRate Act of 1935 was designed to save the growers of raisin and table grapes in the Central Valley. On the North Coast, where growers of wine grapes were struggling to hang on, there was no longer a surplus. They could sell all the grapes they were growing for wine. Although the prices were not wonderful, the growers were optimistic. In 1938 they made a concerted effort to make the government understand the differences in California's grape-growing regions. A trio of Santa Rosans, grapegrower Dewey Baldocchi and attorneys Charles and Nick DeMeo, made a journey to Washington, D.C., that proved historic for the industry. They not only succeeded in convincing the USDA that wine grape regions should be excluded from the ProRate laws but, by thus requiring a statement of origin for grapes, created the first appellations in the nation.[29]

Later, in 1942, when the government was calling for price ceilings on California grapes, Baldocchi and Nick DeMeo set off for Washington once more. This time their mission was to convince the government that the price ceiling would be disastrous for North Coast vineyardists,

*T*hrough the 1940s and '50s, the hardier winemakers persisted and prospered: Foppiano and Pedroncelli in Healdsburg, Sebastiani in Sonoma, Korbel in Guerneville, Martini & Prati in Santa Rosa, and certainly Italian Swiss Colony, which had been deemed the world's largest winery in 1937, with a capacity to produce 8,500,000 gallons. Louis Foppiano, one of the acknowledged leaders, recalled the beginnings of the Sonoma County Wine Growers Association, which was formed in those "middle years."

"I remember that 1946 was the year we started getting together because it was the year before Della [Bastoni] and I got married. I don't recall exactly who the first people were. There were nine or ten of us, including Isabelle Simi Haigh, August Sebastiani, Elmo Martini, one of the Frei brothers, Rita Cambiaso, Abele Ferrari, Bill Bagnani of Geyser Peak, one of the Korbels, and a Pagani or two.

"Most of what we did was just problem-solving. We all had about the same concerns—moving inventory and selling wine. In those days there were a lot of laws left over from the Prohibition era, and we spent a lot of our meeting time discussing what to do about them, and calling on our legislators for assistance. Once in a while we'd have a speaker come up from the Wine Institute or one of the glass companies. Some of the wineries were just starting to put their product into bottles, so we always needed help in that direction. Most of our members were farmers interested in learning about the new grape varieties being introduced by the University of California, so one of their experts or one of the local nurserymen would talk to us about what they thought would be the important grapes and how they should be planted and tended.

"For a while the association was very active. Our dues were low, just $25 a year, and our structure was a little informal. I was the first president and I began to feel a little like FDR as I was re-elected for term after term. We got better organized as we went on and became a little more formal. For a couple of years it was touch and go, but we held on through the '50s, and even printed a map to show people which wineries had tasting rooms and where they were."[30]

— *Geyser Peak Winery*

—*Geyser Peak Winery*

whose yield per acre was only a fraction of what was produced in the irrigated Central Valley table grape regions. The success of their lobbying expedition can be measured in results. The proposed ceiling had been $30 per ton. The ultimate market price that year for North Coast grapes, once the agreement was reached with the Office of Price Administration not to establish price controls, was $70 per ton. Grape growers credited the efforts of Baldocchi and DeMeo with saving the North Coast wine industry, which would revive beyond any of their highest expectations in the last third of the 20th century.[31]

It took a long time to recover from the combined one-two punch of Prohibition and Depression. Prohibition had changed America's drinking habits. Hopper cars of grapes, left standing on railroad sidings waiting for eastern buyers, had to be filled with hardy fruit. But the tougher grapes left customers with the lingering taste of sour wine. Some people, certainly, drank less or gave it up altogether. Many discovered they had a taste for hard liquor. The cocktail hour of the '40s and '50s did not include wine.

Prunes, generally, replaced hops. Some had already combined. Pete Bussman and his sons, William and Ellsworth after him, had sixty-five acres of prunes beside their hop yard. Bussmans had a three-tunnel dehydrator on their Fulton ranch and dried prunes commercially until Sunsweet came in. Farm laborers often worked both crops. At the Bussman Ranch the crews completing hop baling would start immediately running the dipper on the dehydrator. The same families often picked both crops. Many preferred to work the prunes, since the fruit is shaken from the tree and picked off the ground. The fact

—Martini & Prati Winery

—Chamber of Commerce Collection

that they could work in the shade compensated for the kink in the back.

Prune ranchers owed a debt to Luther Burbank. The "funny" fruit became an important crop in Sonoma County after Warren Dutton leased some land in Santa Rosa in the spring of 1881 and asked nurseryman Burbank, just six years removed from his native Massachusetts, to deliver 20,000 French prune seedlings by fall. The transaction, which other nurserymen had deemed impossible, proved to be not only the beginning of a new agricultural endeavor but of the Burbank legend as well.[32]

The first World War provided a giant boost to the prune business as the government purchased tons of the dried fruit, which traveled well, to ship to American forces overseas. After the war, export of the fruit to European markets kept prices up. In 1920, prunes brought 25 cents per pound, a new high. Germany, recovering from the ravages of the Great War, was a large buyer of Sonoma County prunes in 1924.[33]

Although Mark McDonald had been active brokering Sonoma County prunes, and his packing sheds near the Southern Pacific depot on North Street (purchased by Grace Brothers in 1927 as the brewers diversified in Prohibition) were among the largest in the state, it was Healdsburg, not Santa Rosa, that became "The Buckle of the Prune Belt." By the 1950s the Sunsweet company dried and packed more than 17,000 tons per year at its Healdsburg facility. But Santa Rosa supplied its share with bountiful prune orchards east of town, alternating with walnut orchards along Santa Rosa Creek, extending into Rincon Valley.

The first real commercial orchard in Sonoma County had been planted in Santa Rosa in 1875 by Charles Juilliard. He had a few of just about every type of fruit growing on the thirteen acres on the south side of Santa Rosa Creek near his home.[34] His venture was experimental in nature, an attempt to show the wisdom of

diversification from the grain crops that were wearing out the rich county soil.

What Juilliard's experimental orchard showed was that apples grew well in the mid-Sonoma County climate. But the credit for pioneering the early apple that would make Sonoma County a leader in apple production goes to the Russians who brought Gravenstein seedlings from Europe to plant on the hillside above Fort Ross in the early part of the 19th century. Seventy years later, rancher Nathaniel Griffith planted Gravensteins on his land on Laguna Road and consulted with his friend Burbank about the best ways to increase the yield on this highly flavored apple. And just as Griffith, who earned himself the appellation "Grandfather of the Gravenstein," was setting out to prove that Gravensteins could make money for orchardists, a Sebastopol "tinkerer" named Joe Hunt devised a dehydrator that worked very well on apples. Gravensteins, it was determined, dried well, retaining much of their famous flavor. Griffith's interest became an industry as neighboring growers planted Grav orchards in

—Finley Collection

At top left, a harvest of Sonoma County prunes, drying in the sun. Below, flats of prunes are delivered by wagon to the sulphuring shed.

At far right, the interior of the cannery in Santa Rosa, circa 1907.

CALIFORNIA PACKING CORPO
PLANT NO 5

*T*he cannery was the hub of Santa Rosa's westside in the fruit packing season. A descendant of the Hunt Brothers original plant, it had become California Packing Corporation's Plant No. 5 when Sebastopol's Hunt family moved its fledgling food empire to the Sacramento Valley in 1900. In 1909 a portion of the original cannery burned in the fire that destroyed the Santa Rosa Woolen Mills. By 1917, Cal Pack (the now-famous Del Monte label) was working in a three-block complex between the railroad tracks and Santa Rosa Creek with a new building facing Third Street.

The cannery had a distinctly Italian flavor. John Oliva was plant superintendent from 1904 to 1920. His successor was his nephew, Charles Carniglia. Their work force was drawn from the neighborhood, an area known as "Italian Town" to uptown Santa Rosans since the earliest immigrant families built hotels and grocery stores along Wilson Street and neat frame houses with bountiful vegetable gardens and wine presses in the basement on the streets west of the tracks.

Sometimes the workers went directly from boat to cannery. Many of them didn't speak English and relied on cannery management for help far beyond the working day. Carniglia, and Oliva before him, helped workers get their citizenship papers, helped them find housing, translated official papers for them. It was, in many ways, an extended family. The cannery workers met and married and brought their babies to the plant's child-care facility across Third Street, known fondly as the "Kindergarten Cannery." They weren't all Italian, but most were immigrants. There were Portuguese, some Irish, and at least one black woman, Lucy Moore.

The cannery season started in April and ended in October, processing apples, plums, peaches, tomatoes, pears, cherries, and berries. The berries were the most fragile, and the short berry season meant the longest days, with workers on duty to midnight washing and

sorting berries for canning. Cal Pack ventured into truck gardening also, raising spinach and peas on leased property in Valley Ford for canning in Santa Rosa. In addition, they canned peas from Ignacio and tomatoes from the Sacramento Valley. Much of the produce came by train—pears from Lake and Mendocino counties, apples, berries, and cherries from Sebastopol, and peaches and plums from Geyserville and Cloverdale.

Westside youngsters often "hijacked" the berry and cherry trains coming in from Sebastopol, jumping aboard when they slowed for a country road crossing to ride to the cannery sidings, feasting on handfuls of the sweet,

ripe fruit along the way. Some of the produce, by the 1920s, was coming by truck. Long lines of flatbed trucks full of cherries and other fruit often lined the street on summer evenings, waiting their turn to unload.

The cannery closed in 1928. Ranchers had replaced berry vines with orchards, and there were apple-packing sheds open nearer to the source. Freight rates, both in and out of Santa Rosa, became prohibitive and Cal Pack transferred much of its Santa Rosa business to a new, larger plant in San Leandro, closer to the Bay Area population center.

The Third Street building became the Poultry Producers' plant. Lena Bonfigli, who owned the Battaglia

Hotel across Sixth Street, bought the superintendent's house and converted it to apartments. The hundreds of Italian immigrants who got their start at the cannery were left with memories—both good and bad. The hours were long. The pay was mostly piecemeal, and low. Sometimes workers would work sixteen hours and earn $1.70 per day. In lean times, families charged groceries all winter at Italian grocery stores like Forni's on Wilson or Bacigalupi's on Fourth and paid when the cannery opened in the spring. They also made friends there, learned English there, and, from their start in the cannery, settled into Santa Rosa life.[35]

—LaVerne Avila Collection

the rich Gold Ridge district soil, while Joe Hunt and his sons parlayed the dehydrator into a cannery on Santa Rosa's railroad tracks and a food processing empire known as Hunt Brothers.[36]

With the skill to grow Gravensteins and the technology to preserve them, apple growers profited much as prune ranchers did as World War I opened the county to the world market. The prospect of profit attracted new investors in the rolling hillside land of the west county. All around the town of Sebastopol, the apple orchards blossomed and bore fruit, and apple processing became a multi-million-dollar business in the years before World War II. Some of the success of this endeavor can be measured in terms of transport volume. In 1928, a year when the crop was estimated at double the previous year's yield, Southern Pacific tallied 1,800 carloads of Gravensteins from Napa and Sonoma counties shipped to eastern and southern markets.[37] After Griffith came a generation of "apple men" who built this orchard empire.

R.E. Oehlmann, who began with a forty-acre orchard, two cows, and a team of horses in 1919, expanded his holdings until he owned several large ranches in Green Valley and founded Manzana Products, the largest of three independent apple canneries in the county. Oehlmann was the first chairman of the Early Apple Advisory Board.

Oscar Hallberg, whose apple interests included a dryer and a cannery and a juice processing plant, built the first cold storage plant in the county, with a capacity of 100,000 boxes. His brother Alfred had a smaller dryer and grew cherries and berries as well as apples. James O'Connell and his partner, Al Garcia, were among the largest dried apple processors; the Barlow family is generally credited with starting the first commercial applesauce business in the United States.

Will Hotle, a partner of Lew Hart in the Gold Ridge Orchard, was also an officer in the Sebastopol Fruit Company, a shipping co-op. Gold Ridge was considered by many to be the finest fruit ranch in the county. Hotle grew many varieties of apples, which he had planted in the early part of the century, in addition to cherries and berries. After his death, the orchards passed to his daughter, Miriam Hotle Burdo.[38]

Carl Silveira and Jack O'Connell formed a partnership in the early '40s, processing apples in downtown Sebastopol until they bought the old Barlow Cannery on Occidental Road. The Frei Brothers, Louis and Walter, came from a winemaking family but also owned one of the largest orchards in the county. It was near Vine Hill Ranch, owned by A. H. Morgan, whose Gravensteins were nearly always the earliest to market, sometimes as early as July 5, a source of admiration and comment from his fellow growers.

Russell Taylor was a buyer for S&W Foods, Macomber's, and other food companies. In 1944 Taylor, who

LaVerne Nelson, not yet two years old, stands watch over a harvest of berries at her Grandfather Wells's strawberry fields at Summerfield Road and Sonoma Avenue, circa 1917.

owned a large trucking company in addition to his fruit brokerage, introduced Sonoma County apples and pears to buyers for Gerber Baby Food, a rapidly growing market, with happy financial results for orchardists.[40]

Well into the 20th century, farmers were still experimenting with field crops that would grow well—and sell well. In 1924, the Rural Relationship Committee of the Santa Rosa Chamber of Commerce was working with the Farm Bureau in the investigation of several prospective agricultural pursuits, including the establishment of a silkworm farm near Santa Rosa, which never came to pass, and turkey raising, which would become an important industry in the second half of the century.

The fertile soil, temperate climate, and proximity to the urban centers of the Bay Area made truck gardening, as it was called even in the days before there were trucks, a viable option for Sonoma County farmers from the time the potato was exchanged for gold dust in the hungry new boomtown of San Francisco. There were several interesting, if short-lived, ventures into both lettuce and artichokes, crops that would eventually become agricultural mainstays in the valleys near Monterey Bay.

A post-World War II attempt to grow artichokes in the fields between Bodega Bay and Salmon Creek was not successful, nor was an earlier foray, in 1929, into Jerusalem artichokes as a cash crop. The latter had corporate backing.

Ike Parsons hauls his nephews behind his tractor on the ranch where he raised prize draft horses and fruit. The orchards were in the valley below the family's hillside home on Santa Rosa's northern edge. In the 1920s, when this photograph was taken, Montecito Road was a private driveway that ended in the Parsons yard.

—*Boivin Family Collection*

—LeBaron Collection

The herds of blooded livestock that were driven across the plains by early Sonoma County settlers in the 1850s were the basis of thriving livestock enterprises that expanded to include sheep raised for both lambs and wool. Livestock ranchers prospered well into the 20th century. In the peak year 1949, cattle and sheep accounted for more than $6 million of the county's agricultural production. Above, a late 1920s' crowd views prize dairy cattle at the annual Valley Ford Cattle Show, customarily attended by the governor of California.

Pabst Dietary Company opened a cannery in Santa Rosa in 1929 to make soup from the "sun-chokes," which were being advertised for their health benefits. The cannery opened with eighty employees in November of 1929, just a month after the stock-market crash, and was greeted with fanfare in the community. The Chamber of Commerce hosted a luncheon for 200 at the Occidental Hotel to celebrate the first harvest and welcome the Pabst company.

But 1929 was a drought year, and the harvest produced 'chokes that were substandard. Most were rejected by the company. The cannery closed, and the only legacy of the farmers' brief venture into this crop was a court fight over the terms of the marketing agreement with Pabst.[41]

In 1931, mustard greens were hailed by the newspaper as the important new crop. In January of that year, twelve tons of the greens, with the brand name "Ship Shape," rolled out of Santa Rosa in a refrigerator car, bound for Eastern markets. Research indicates that the "Ship Shape" project lasted one season, perhaps one shipment, only.[42]

The following year, it was lettuce. In June the first carload of lettuce raised on the Williams Brothers and Webb vegetable gardens near Cotati was shipped from Santa Rosa to the East Coast, heralded as an agricultural "first" for Sonoma County.[43] The Cotati plains would be planted in coming seasons, with a variety of crops, all grown for seed at the Waldo Rohnert Seed Farm. Waldo Emerson Rohnert was the founder of an international seed business with headquarters in Hollister, where there were enormous silos filled with vegetable seeds awaiting shipment all over the world. The 3,000 acres of flat land on the old Page Ranch between Cotati and Santa Rosa was a satellite farm, run for Rohnert's son Fred by manager Tex Carley. In the 1930s, half a million dollars worth of lettuce, beet, radish, onion, and carrot seed was produced there.[44]

Some of the experimental agriculture ventured far afield. In 1936 A.F. Wagar of Santa Rosa attracted statewide attention with his California Giant Frog Farm where he grew two varieties of edible frogs—Giants and Leopards. Some of the Giants grew to be twenty-eight inches long, a bonus for frog-leg fanciers. The "Daddy," Wagars measured with pride at thirty inches.[45]

In the final analysis, however, the products that kept Sonoma County in the top ranks in agricultural production were the ones that started early and endured. Dairying was foremost among these, although not without its controversies. Hoof-and-mouth disease proved costly to Sonoma County dairymen in 1924. California embarked on a five million dollar campaign to eradicate the disease. In Sonoma County, a permit was required to move animals. In 1935 state and federal officials added California to the long list of states where testing for tuberculosis was required of dairy cows. Despite the standardizing of pasteurization procedures, TB remained a health problem. In the first year of testing in Sonoma County, 8,360 of the 34,000 cows tested were determined to be infected and consigned to the slaughterhouse. The government indemnified dairymen at the rate of $20 maximum per cow over the price offered by meat packers. In Sonoma County, where dairy cows were worth up to $60 per head, there were financial losses. Critics, mistrusting the scientists' assurance that TB was transmitted through milk, called the testing program a "meat packers plot."[46]

One of these critics was Joe Talbot, a champion for the rights of farmers, whose column "This Week" appeared in the *Press Democrat* for more than twenty-five years, until the week of his death, at the age of eighty, in 1935. Talbot was a Granger and a Bennett Valley farmer whose father, Coleman Talbot, had crossed the plains in a covered wagon to settle on the Bennett Valley land in the 1850s. Known as "The Sage of Bennett Valley," he offered solid news about crop conditions and the market outlook, told his readers when to plow and when to plant, and supplemented his "almanac" with tales of the "old days" and his pithy observations on national politics and the economy.

World War II brought new markets for Sonoma County fruit. Santa Rosa resident Edson Merritt was a key figure in the increasing importance of fruit-growing in Sonoma County in the early part of the century. His first job in Santa Rosa, before 1900, was as a bookkeeper for Hunt Brothers. Later, while employed as a banker (for both Santa Rosa Bank and Santa Rosa National Bank), Merritt organized his own fruit brokerage, specializing in prunes and other dried fruits, and in 1922 became manager of the Sebastopol Apple Growers' Union, which marketed the bulk of Sonoma County's apple crop.

Merritt, who was recognized as an authority on fruit marketing, made annual trips to eastern cities in the interest of the Sonoma County fruit trade. He is credited with establishing nationwide markets for the Gravenstein apple.[47]

Many of the important apple growers engaged in diversified farming. Just as many of the ranchers in the Healdsburg area grew pears and prunes side by side, so the west Santa Rosa and Sebastopol ranchers often grew hops on the low edges of the hilly apple land. Marvin Wasserman was a good example of diversification. Known primarily as a successful hop buyer, he also owned one of the largest prune orchards in the area. It was not uncommon for a rancher to have the "Big Three"—hops, apples, and

Fruit broker Edson Merritt's warehouse at Seventh Street and the Northwestern Pacific tracks, circa 1910. Merritt and Mark McDonald Jr., whose warehouse was on North Street near the Southern Pacific depot, dominated the fruit brokerage business in the early years of the century. Merritt is credited with establishing a national market for Gravenstein apples.

—*Turrill & Miller Photo, Finley Collection*

prunes—on a single ranch. And maybe cherries, which were in demand for canning and for the creation of maraschino cherries, the sweet nugget in those popular post-Prohibition old-fashioneds or the non-alcoholic Shirley Temples.

In the first half of the century, there were more than 120 cherry growers in Sonoma County, ranging from farms with two or three trees in the yard to the 100-acre El Centro orchard in Occidental.[48] While farmers grew many varieties, including Bing, Tartarian, Lambert, and a name that had echoes of the Civil War politics, Black Republican, the predominate variety was the Royal Ann, which was in demand for maraschinos. Cherry buyers were Lyons-Magnus and S&W, processing in Sebastopol, and California Packing Corporation at its Santa Rosa cannery. The cherries were shipped from the plants in barrels, packed in brine. In 1930, Congressman Clarence F. Lea pushed hard for a tariff

on Italian maraschinos, which proved a great boon to local producers. Cherry orchards extended from the Gold Ridge district all the way to eastern Santa Rosa. One large orchard on the bank of Santa Rosa Creek, owned by the Hahman family, was removed in 1950 to make way for Santa Rosa Memorial Hospital.

If Santa Rosa's new hospital was built in a cherry orchard, new Santa Rosa was built where walnuts once grew. The walnut orchard east of Santa Rosa, known at the turn of the century as Walnutmere, the country home of Henry Vrooman and his wife Emily, was reputed at one time to be the largest walnut orchard in the nation. Emily Vrooman is generally credited with planting the orchard in the late 1890s and with pioneering some early varieties of walnuts in the United States. Walnutmere sold in 1919 to Samuel Hartley of Fresno, who continued to grow walnuts for commercial use. The French Mayette and Franquette nuts lent their names to streets as homes replaced the trees. It was a harbinger of things to come.

Sonoma County clung to its leadership position among the nation's agricultural counties through the Great Depression. Its eighth rank among the richest farmlands in the country in 1920 slipped some but not a lot, to tenth in 1936.[49] But the size of the farm was shrinking. The average Sonoma County farm in 1900 was 213 acres. In 1930 it was 118 acres.[50] And the rise of "agribusiness," the corporate farm, after World War II would impact these small farmers—the family chicken ranch, the fifty-acre hop yard. Most of all, it would affect the grower who had a few acres in pears, a few in prunes, a few in apples, and just enough hops to capitalize in a good price year.

In 1946, with poultry still the leading money crop in the county, the total farm value was $75,865,000. It would not reach those numbers again in the next decade. By 1955 the value was $70,278,000, which was a $429,000 increase over 1954, a jump attributed in part to increased accuracy in the

The valleys and hillsides surrounding Santa Rosa, Sebastopol, and Healdsburg blossomed through each springtime with apples, prunes, and cherries as the principle orchard crops.

surveys. Dairy products were challenging poultry's leadership and hops had all but vanished.[51] In his annual report for 1955, the county's agricultural commissioner Percy F. Wright said: "Many growers are still searching for a pay crop to replace removed hop acreage." Sweet corn, strawberries, and green beans were the leading contenders.

In the Russian River Valley and on the hillsides around Sebastopol, apple and prune growers held fast through the post-war transition. A look at the crop report on apples, both fresh and dried, for odd-numbered years shows upward movement in total income:

1949—$2,236,000
1951—$2,708,000
1953—$5,565,000
1955—$4,031,000

Prunes were more uncertain:

1949—$3,855,000
1951—$3,837,000
1953—$2,577,000
1955—$7,654,000

Cherries, too, seemed to be holding their own. The crop report for 1949 shows a total of $325,000 in cherry income, from both fresh and processed. In 1955, it was still $330,000. But walnuts, counted among the leading crops in the glory years of the '20s, were the first orchards to convert to subdivisions and faded quickly in the crop lists. In 1949, walnut income, already diminished, was $157,000; in 1955 it was $15,500.[52]

It would be twenty years or more until the new "wine age" dawned in Sonoma County, when vineyards would march in file over the land that had been hop yards and prune orchards. Close to Santa Rosa's borders, houses, not hop vines, were growing—faster than all the prune trees Luther Burbank could have produced. 🐦

—Press Democrat Collection

The harvest of agricultural dollars was the basis of commerce in early 20th century Santa Rosa. It was a farm town. The hardware and feed stores opened before dawn to accommodate customers who needed a sack of grain or a tool to make fence repairs. And it was a market town, where "buyer" was a term of respect, where rail cars filled with fresh fruit rolled in from the western county in the summer and fall and carloads of dried and processed fruit headed east to meet the transcontinental railroad.[1]

The earthquake of 1906 dealt a severe blow to Santa Rosa commerce. Four months after the earthquake, a group of Santa Rosa businessmen, most of them still trading in tents and shanty-stores, met in Judge Albert Burnett's courtroom in the temporary courthouse to form a Chamber of Commerce. The stated purpose was "for the common cause of enlarging the city's commercial importance and attractiveness." The unspoken goal was to convince both clients and investors there was life in the old town yet.

And there was life. Many of the city's landlords and merchants had come out of the disaster determined to make it better than before. Maurice Prince owned several buildings on Fourth Street that were destroyed in the earthquake. He not only rebuilt but added a second story to each of the two new buildings. The new Doherty-Shea Building at Fifth and Mendocino also came out of the disaster with a second story.

The railroads joined the expansive mood, building a long spur track along the edge of the Ridgway property, connecting the Southern Pacific from its terminus on North Street to the Northwestern Pacific near its crossing on College Avenue. The connection ended the necessity of hauling East Coast and Southern California freight to Ignacio and Schellville to connect with the Central and Southern Pacific.

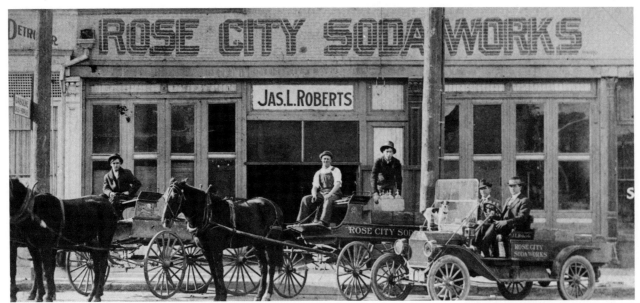

—Eleanor Haney Collection

The town was refitting for the automobile but business in post-earthquake Santa Rosa was still a horse-and-wagon enterprise for a decade. Young Tom Campion loads bottles of Queen Charlotte seltzer or Rose City sarsaparilla in front of the soda works in the first block of Main Street, circa 1910.

While the early months of the chamber's organization were spent putting a happy face on a grim situation, by the start of 1908, there was genuine reason to smile. In the first year and a half the city appeared to have made remarkable strides toward recovery, building, as it had before, on its solid agricultural base. The cannery was running on its original site, as were the fruit packing and drying companies.[2] The Santa Rosa Woolen Mill was once again producing blankets for the eastern market, having increased its capacity by 25 percent in the rebuilt structure.

In 1910 newspaper stories boasted that the locally produced blankets were being sold at the prestigious Wanamaker's Department Stores in New York and Philadelphia. Two flour mills were in full operation, as were the two tanneries and the shoe factory. The return to prosperity of Levin's Tannery and the Santa Rosa Shoe Factory suffered a setback in 1910 when fire destroyed both buildings. Once again, the local business community, anxious to keep the jobs these firms provided, rallied to aid the rebuilding. The city was careful to control the location

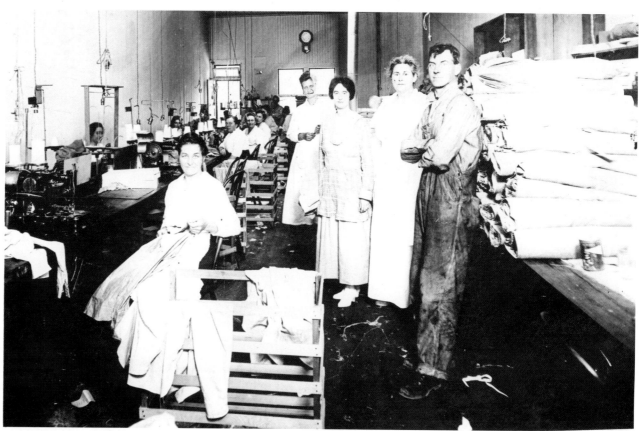

The Cameron Shirt Factory on Fifth Street was a branch of a Napa company. Mollie Albertson is seated in the center foreground of this photograph made in 1913. May Walker stands second from right. During World War I, the shirt factory made khaki pajamas for soldiers.

—*LeBaron Collection*

97

OVERTON HOTEL

*T*he first members of the Chamber of Commerce truly counted. They counted tourists and business revenues and new industries and new residents. They were committed to spreading the word that Santa Rosa was, in the words of the early brochures, "a charming home city." But their priority was the creation of jobs. In 1908, the chamber offered "free industrial sites to manufacturers who would locate in our city."[3]

While there was no rush of new industry to take up the free land, there was a steady increase in the number of businesses and both newspapers were effusive in praise of commercial enterprise. In 1911 the Santa Rosa *Republican* published a special "Sonoma County Development Edition" with ten pages of descriptive prose about Santa Rosa businesses and businessmen. Both the Occidental and the Overton hotels were in new buildings, both under the ownership of the Santa Rosa Hotel Company owned by the Bane brothers, Frank, John and Charles. La Rose Hotel, owned by Batiste Bettini, made a point of reporting the cost of construction ($35,000) with a reassurance that the building was made of stone and reinforced concrete. The Germania Hotel in the 100 block of Fourth Street had a new proprietor, Karl Schmid. The Roma Hotel offered comfortable rooms and "the best 25 cent meal in the city." The same offer was made by The Western Hotel, in "a new and splendid building," being operated by John Fumasoli and Antonio Lepori.

Restaurants, except for hotel dining rooms, were scarce. It was not an age of dining out, unless one was traveling. But saloons were plentiful, all of them serving Santa Rosa-brewed Grace Brothers steam and

By 1911 the two "uptown" hotels, the new Overton, shown at upper left, and the Occidental, which stood on opposite corners of Fourth and B streets, had both been purchased by the three Bane brothers. The Overton would later become the Santa Rosa Hotel.

At left, the directors of the new Chamber of Commerce pose in front of the office. Note the sign on the window: "Strangers Welcome."

lager on tap, along with such bottled beers as Yosemite, Buffalo, Enterprise, and an occasional Budweiser. Old Crow was advertised as the choice whiskey of the day. The drinking establishments included the New Corner at Third and Main, owned by S.H. McKee; the Oberon, owned by Frank Brown and Louis Gnesa; F.G. Wright's Cozy Corner at Second and Main; the Panama-Pacific owned by Zaveri Arrigoni, recently arrived from Fort Bragg; Cavagna and Fenacci's OK Saloon; the Crystal Bar in the first block of Fourth Street owned by Trotter and Ferrari; Jesse Brunk and Les Brittain's well-established Palace Bar, described as "homelike;" Swank's Saloon, another longtime establishment across from the depot at the foot of Fourth Street; and the Louvre, owned by William Hearn.

There were two cigar stores, La Brazoria, owned by John Mercier, and Muther & Son. Frank Muther, the city's fire chief, had long manufactured his own cigars, in two price ranges, the 10-cent Golden Crown and the FM, described as "a bit cigar." There were also two bottling works, William Hudson's Santa Rosa Bottling Works, the county's pioneer in carbonation, located at West Third Street and Roberts Avenue, and, new since the earthquake, Rose City Soda Works, owned by James Roberts, which made Rose City Ginger Ale, Cream Soda, and Queen Charlotte Seltzer, in addition to "mineral waters, oyster cocktails and carbonated drinks of all kinds." There were two candy stores, each with ice cream parlors. One was owned by J.V. Ewing, who had run a general store in Forestville and would go on to be postmaster in Windsor, and the other by A.D. Skinkle, who had purchased Chester Sherman's well-known candy store in 1910.

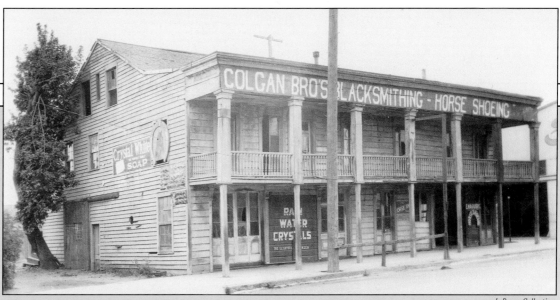

—*LeBaron Collection*

The Main Street building at upper right, had been the stagecoach stop and hotel known as Santa Rosa House in the 19th century. By 1910 it had been converted to a blacksmith shop and was considered a landmark.

Customers and one small dog line up for service from bartender "Shorty" Ferletti at Girolo's U.S. Saloon.

—*Traverso Family Collection*

99

of the new tannery, being sensitive to complaints about the smell of the old one.

By 1908, Bertoli Brothers' macaroni factory was fully operative again. So was Grace Brothers Brewery, two new ice plants—which were so important to fruit processing and shipping—and several wineries. The planing mills, lumber yards, and foundries necessary to supply what had become a post-disaster building boom were prospering. George Reilly's manufacturing plant alongside the NWP line made cement pipe for draining the new street system. Reilly's firm also supplied the stonework for the new post office building and the new courthouse.

Edward H. Brown was the chamber's first secretary. In 1912, in the first annual report available in the chamber's archives, Brown outlined the steps being taken to increase the population. There was considerable emphasis on exhibits—exhibits showing the prosperity and charm of Santa Rosa were displayed at the Los Angeles Land Show and the State Fair that year—and on direct mailings. According to the report, "100,000 pieces of literature" were sent all over the United States to interest prospective homeseekers.

Opposite page, J.K. Fergurson, top photo, and Ira Pyle, standing at right in the lower photo, were sent on a goodwill tour of the country by the Chamber of Commerce in 1913. The mission: to let prospective residents know that Santa Rosa was alive and well.

—*Trombetta Family Collection*

The Santa Rosa Macaroni Factory, 1921. Second from right is junior partner Floyd Trombetta.

Brown measured his success in the 1912 report: "The greatest testimonial that we are bearing fruit from our efforts is that today there are more real estate men in business in Santa Rosa than there has been in the history of the city by over two hundred percent and I think I am safe in saying that they are all doing good business."

The success of those efforts to lure residents, however, may be measured by another, more exacting, gauge. Between the census of 1900, albeit allowing for a decrease after the earthquake, and the census of 1940, Santa Rosa's population increased from 6,673 to 12,605, less than 90 percent in forty years. Compared to the leap from 500 to 5,000 between 1850 and 1890, the difference is clear. It was the slowest growth period in Santa Rosa history.4

Still, the real estate men were busy. And the push was being made against the odds. The earthquake had received worldwide attention. An argument could be made that the recovery required nearly forty years or that there might not have been recovery without an organized effort. And certainly the town's relative prosperity could not have returned without leadership.

In 1913, the chamber sent two businessmen, Ira Pyle and J.K. Fergurson, off on a goodwill tour of the country. Their mission was to extoll the virtues of Santa Rosa and induce people to move here. Frank Doyle and Frank Brush wrote letters for them to carry along, statements of the bankers' faith in the town's future. The bankers were the civic leaders of this period and one of them, Doyle, would continue to claim that title until his death forty years later.

Frank Doyle was still, technically, the cashier of the Exchange Bank in 1913. But he already had assumed the duties of the president, a title which would pass to him at the death of his father, bank founder Manville Doyle, in 1916. And Doyle already wore the mantle of community trust. He was at the forefront of the Chamber of Commerce organization, for no one knew better than a

—*Press Democrat Collection*

banker how much depended on an orderly and optimistic renaissance in Santa Rosa.

The year after the earthquake, at a point when Santa Rosa businessmen were least able to weather a financial crisis, the local banks were able to survive the statewide Panic of 1907 in which many banks failed. The Sonoma County Clearing House organization, of which Doyle and his father were leaders, provided the cooperative security necessary. The Exchange Bank was, in fact, one of the few to welcome the tighter banking laws and demand for larger reserves set forth in the resultant Banking Act of 1909. The 15 percent reserve was less than the Doyles' institution had been maintaining all along. The Exchange Bank was recognized as a leader in the state's financial community.

—*Finley Collection*

*F*rank Doyle appears in the annals of Santa Rosa as its principal visionary. He was the one who painstakingly negotiated leases with Fourth Street businessmen for the widening of the business street by fifteen feet in the reconstruction. That done, he turned his attention to the condition of Sonoma County's roads and became a persistent force for new road construction. Again, looking beyond, he became a charter member of the Redwood Highway Association, a group formed to plan and to lobby the state for construction of a highway from San Francisco Bay to Grants Pass, Oregon. Finally, that interest in transportation as a necessity for commerce caused him to call the first meeting to discuss a proposal to bridge the Golden Gate.

Doyle was a champion of agriculture, understanding it as the mainstay of Santa Rosa's economy. He served on the boards of smaller banks and of utility companies and headed cultural, social, and fraternal organizations. It would be difficult to overstate Frank Doyle's impact on his community.[5]

Brush was Doyle's opposite number at the competing Santa Rosa National Bank. He also was the son of the president and held the title of cashier. More of a wheeler-dealer than the conservative Doyle, Brush owned a substantial amount of property including ranches in Rincon Valley, Windsor, and Sebastopol, rangelands for his stock in Mendocino County, and orchards in the Sutter Basin.

His home on "upper" Fourth Street near University Street was large and considered quite fancy for the times.[6] The bank building, at the corner of Fourth and Hinton on the east side of the square, was relatively majestic for Santa Rosa financial institutions of that period. Brush became something of a hometown hero in 1905 when, as the founding director representing Santa Rosa on the the the board of the Petaluma & Santa Rosa Electric Railroad, he flung himself across the tracks of the competing California Northwestern to stop the CNW's steam engines from scalding P&SR crews who were installing a grade crossing to bring the electric line into town. Brush's part in the incident, which became famous in railroading as the "Battle of Sebastopol Avenue," raised him to a somewhat exalted position in the community.

Unlike Doyle, Brush would not retain his position of leadership and respect. In 1918, under a cloud of scandal, he resigned his bank position and two days later was arrested by United States marshals and charged with embezzling, along with two other employees, $728,000 in bank funds. The bank closed, constituting "the largest in the history of national bank failures on the Pacific Coast," according to the *Press Democrat*. A portion of the funds, some $110,000, was money Brush's bank was holding for local residents who had subscribed to World War I Liberty Bonds in a drive of which Brush was chairman. It would be years before all the bondholders would know the fate of their investment. In 1922, Congressman Clarence Lea's legislation passed both houses of Congress to provide relief for the subscribers of Santa Rosa National Bank.[7]

Indicted on thirty counts, totaling $204,000, Brush pleaded guilty and was sentenced to ten years in the federal penitentiary at McNeil Island, where he served four years before being paroled. On the day before his guilty plea on May 1, 1919, Brush's explanation of the financial disaster appeared on the front page of the *Press Democrat*. He cited his own financial losses—$100,000 on the P&SR Railroad and $200,000 on a building project destroyed by the earthquake—as reasons for his crime. He could have handled these, he said, had it not been for the lean years before the world war. "So twice fate intervened. If it had not been for the earthquake I would still be Frank A. Brush, the prosperous man of affairs. If it had not been for the war, I would not now be broken under a burden of shame."

Other community leaders who emerged after the earthquake and guided Santa Rosa through thirty years or more of recovery were Joseph Grace and Ernest Finley.

One of the Grace Brothers of local beer fame, Joe Grace was more patrician than his brother Frank. While Frank ran the brewery, Joe was balancing the books, buying land, and becoming a gentleman farmer with hop yards and fruit, rice, and cotton ranches throughout the county and the state. In 1908 he became president of the powerful Pacific Coast Hop Growers' Union. He had just begun to assume a leadership role that would make him a member of Santa Rosa's most powerful trio—with Doyle and Finley—by the 1930s.

Ernest Finley was thirty-six years old in 1906. He had purchased the *Sonoma Democrat* and merged it with his tiny weekly *Santa Rosa Press* in 1898. Until he bought the *Republican* in 1927, he had worthy competition from Allan B. Lemmon and the two previous owners of that newspaper who consistently offered readers another political view. After the two newspapers came under one ownership,

Promotion was the key word of early 20th century California. Santa Rosa boosters took their show on the road with this traveling "fair."

—*Grace Family Collection*

One of Santa Rosa's success stories of the first half of the century was Grace Brothers. The Grace Brothers beer label was established in 1897 when brothers Frank and Joe Grace, who owned a grocery store at Fourth and A streets, bought the old Metzger Brewery on Wilson Street between Second and Third streets. The wooden brewery building burned shortly after the sale and the brothers replaced it with the first of several brick structures on the creekside site.

Grace Brothers steam and lager beers, both barrelled and bottled, became well known throughout the state. And Grace Brothers Park, the beer garden at the end of the streetcar line, with its maple spring dance floor for rollicking German polkas, was a favorite gathering place for young people. The site of the 19th century Kroncke's Park,

which had drawn Bay Area clients by the traincar load, the beer garden was also a picnic spot for organizations from all over the county. As the brewers prospered, Joe Grace built a large and elegant house at Fourth and Pierce streets, next to the gardens.[8]

The beer business flourished as transportation improved and carloads of Santa Rosa-made beer rolled out across the northern part of the state. In 1918, when Prohibition began, GB, along with Buffalo and Acme, was one of the top selling labels. The brothers converted their enterprise to carbonated beverages, an ice cream plant, and an ice house during Prohibition. Their land holdings—for Joe was a shrewd investor—carried them through.

Frank Grace died in 1930 and his five sons took his place in the company. In the mid-'30s, the

"hometown" brewery reached its production peak in an agreement with a wholesale grocery company that distributed its beer to markets all over California. The Santa Rosa plant ran twenty-four hours a day and a second brewery and bottling plant was opened in Los Angeles.

The Grace Brothers Tap Room, a free meeting room where male members of Santa Rosa clubs and lodges could sample the local product, became something of an institution. So was the brewery's whistle, a hollow hoot that signaled high noon in Santa Rosa. But post-war competition was not kind to the Grace Brothers. The brewery closed in 1953 for a five-year hiatus. When it reopened, Thomas Grace, the surviving son and nephew, would head the company.[9]

Finley was the dominant molder of public opinion in the community and was, as postmaster and "kingmaker," generally considered to be among the political leaders in what was a conservative Democratic community.

The letter Frank Doyle sent with Chamber delegates Pyle and Fergurson in 1913 expressed the provincial optimism of the post-earthquake years, couched in language typical of a pre-world war American westerner: "I have traveled over a dozen States and, must say I have never found a County that has the climate we have and can produce the variety of products we can.

"We are also close to the markets of the World, bordering on San Francisco Bay. We are so located that we get cheap Electric Power, cheap fuel and when the Panama Canal is opened I look for improvements here that will astonish the natives."

Brush's letter was shorter. "In our County we have a superb climate and plenty of good land with plenty of good schools and churches and all the things that go to make a favorable community to reside in. Should they [Pyle and Fergurson] at any time on their trip need money, their checks will be taken care of promptly." There was some irony in Brush's assurances, considering his future fate.[10]

Much of the promotional success the Chamber of Commerce enjoyed in its first two decades revolved around Santa Rosa's most famous resident, Luther Burbank. He was quoted on chamber brochures: "I would rather own a piece of land the size of a good healthy house in Sonoma County than an entire farm anywhere else in the world." Burbank was exploited, some would say shamelessly, in the chamber's efforts to call attention to the town. In 1915, the chamber joined with cities up and down the coast in gearing up for the Panama-Pacific International Exposition. They planned an electric sign in San Francisco for the whole year, saying "Visit Santa Rosa, the Home of Luther Burbank." Although there is no

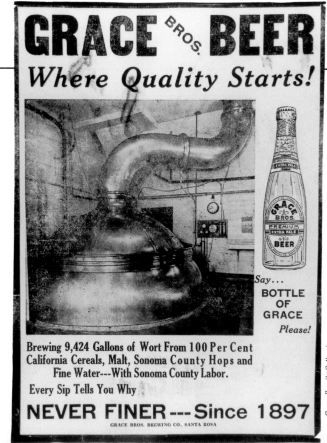

GRACE BROS. BEER
Where Quality Starts!

Say... **BOTTLE OF GRACE** *Please!*

Brewing 9,424 Gallons of Wort From 100 Per Cent California Cereals, Malt, Sonoma County Hops and Fine Water---With Sonoma County Labor.

Every Sip Tells You Why

NEVER FINER --- Since 1897

GRACE BROS. BREWING CO., SANTA ROSA

—Grace Family Collection

A beer sampling at Grace Brothers Brewery. Left to right, Jack, Tom, and Bill Grace, and a cousin, Bud Shea, who was a salesman for the company.

—Grace Family Collection

*L*uther Burbank's powers to lure visitors to Santa Rosa were indeed demonstrated beyond the wildest Chamber of Commerce dreams when America's captains of industry and invention came west to San Francisco for the Panama-Pacific International Exposition in the fall of 1915.

Excited at the prospect of meeting Thomas Edison, whom he described as the man who "shed more light on the Earth, expedited business and made home life more comfortable than any other man who has ever trod the planet," Burbank went to San Francisco to meet Edison and to invite him and his friends to visit Santa Rosa.

He sent a telegram to Herbert Slater announcing that "Mr. and Mrs. Edison and sister and Mr. and Mrs. Henry Ford will visit Santa Rosa if possible on Friday. No bands. No racket. They wish to come quietly." Slater may have been chosen to receive the notification because he was Santa Rosa's representative in the state senate. But he was also the *Press Democrat* writer who was permanently assigned to "the Burbank story," and this was to be an important one.[11]

Chamber Secretary Nagle flew into action. He arranged to have two private Pullman cars barged to Sausalito where they were connected to the northbound train. The finest automobiles in town, borrowed from their owners, stood ready at the depot to carry the visitors to Burbank's home on Santa Rosa Avenue. Along with the Edisons and the Fords came Harvey Firestone, the first man to manufacture a practical air-filled tire and an important figure in the young automotive industry. Also on the train was Ford's son, Edsel, and a contingent of sisters and cousins and secretaries.

Despite the request for "no racket," an excited town turned out to meet them.

Crowds stood along the streets and cheered as the cars passed. With Edison's permission, schoolchildren had been invited to assemble outside Burbank's house to meet the inventor responsible for the electric light, motion pictures, and the phonograph. They came from Santa Rosa's three schools—Fremont, Lincoln, and one named for Burbank—and from Sebastopol where Burbank's experimental farm was located.

The great men walked into the crowd of school-children as the big press cameras flashed and the motion picture cameras ground away. The movie photographers sent the men back repeatedly to walk the pathway. "Darn those movies," said Edison, who invented them. The crowd roared with delight. Ford shook hands all around, joking that he was "beginning to feel like a politician." He was the target of every automobile enthusiast in Sonoma County that day, accepting a design for a tractor from a Healdsburg man and a sketch of a "lifesaving suit" from the Rev. Thomas Himle, pastor of the neighboring Bethlehem Lutheran Church.[12]

Editor Finley interviewed Ford and brought an official request from the farmers of Sonoma County. They wanted him to manufacture a tractor, a "caterpiller" they called it. Ford acknowledged the importance of a gasoline-powered tractor to "encourage the planting of thousands more acres." He promised one soon, although not a caterpiller but one of his own design. The Ford tractor, he told Finley, would be on the market the following year and for "no more than $225." He was only a little premature. The Fordson tractor went on sale in 1918 and Ford shipped Burbank the first one off the assembly line as a gift.[13]

—Luther Burbank Home & Gardens

evidence that the sign was ever erected, it was an idea greeted with enthusiasm.

The world did beat a path to Santa Rosa that year. And Burbank was the key. The chamber's new secretary, Walter Nagle, summed it up in his 1915 report. Nagle was a hometown hero, having taken on the chamber job when an injury ended his baseball career. Known to the sports writers as "Lucky" Nagle, he had been a successful pitcher with the Los Angeles Angels, for Pittsburgh, and for the Boston Red Sox, retiring with a respectable lifetime win-loss record of .625. He had thrown himself into the chamber job with a vengeance. "It had been," he wrote of 1915, "a year fraught with success beyond dreams and brought scientists, statesmen and philanthropists, preeminent in every walk of life, to pay homage to our beloved fellow townsman, the matchless Burbank."[14]

A study of the chamber's scrapbooks would indicate that the obliging Burbank was summoned to stand front and center in nearly every photo the chamber made for publicity purposes until his death in 1926. Images of the white-haired gardener—with Miss Sonoma County, dwarfed by the team of giants clustered around him as he clutched a football, standing in front of the first motor stage to Eureka—attest to his patience and willingness to be of service to the business community.

<hr>

There was an unremitting emphasis on being "up to date." New electric signs created some excitement in 1912. In 1915, a Santa Rosa electrician, Clark Van Fleet, lighted most of a block of Mendocino with "one of those wonderful nitrogen electric lights." Great Western Power Company and the fledgling Pacific Gas & Electric Company competed for business between 1910 and 1920. In 1912 Great Western Power promoted "Electric Week," in which there were demonstrations for such modern miracles as electric ranges, vacuum cleaners, electric sweepers, electric egg beaters, electric tea samovars, and ozonators to purify the

—Luther Burbank Home & Gardens

air. When PG&E preferred stock was first offered in 1914, it found many eager takers. And when that company ran a free line to the County Hospital in 1915, it was welcomed as "cheaper than the fuel which had been used to develop electricity there." The utilities had come to stay.

The first commercial wireless station was installed at Himmie Jacobs' Electrical Store on B Street in 1911. "Soon," wrote the reporter who joined the crowd that came to hear it, "it will cover a 100-mile range." The local

A clear indication of Luther Burbank's importance was the 1915 visit of Thomas Edison, Henry Ford, and Harvey Firestone to his Santa Rosa home. On the opposite page, left, Burbank greets Edison at the NWP depot. Above, Edison, Burbank, and Ford sit together on the steps of Burbank's house.

<hr>

Visit
the Home of

California's

best known
Citizen

Luther Burbank

Santa Rosa
1926

amateurs got first crack at it, however. Young people like Harold Bruner, Vincent Griffith, Edgar Sugarman, Stuart Rogers, Clifford Nichols, Leslie Tolman, Frank Lawrence Jr. and Harry Fechtelkotter were the first to try.[15] Once the wireless was operative, the first half of each hour was reserved for exclusive government use; the last could be used for commercial purposes. In 1915, John Hood obtained a government wireless to bring the correct time twice daily to his jewelry store on Fourth Street. The wireless sent time signals from the observatory at Mare Island. It could, the newspaper reported, "pick up messages for 1,000 miles on a clear night."[16]

When the government released wartime controls on radio equipment, a Santa Rosa high school student named Armand Saare built a 124-foot tower at his family's home on Sonoma Avenue and broadcast code messages to other "sparks" like himself around the West. In 1921, editor Ernest Finley, a man who loved cultural entertainments,

Burbank was the center of most of the Chamber of Commerce's promotional projects. Above, he poses with dignitaries who were passengers on the first bus trip up the Redwood Highway in the 1920s.

learned that broadcasts of the Scotti Grand Opera, performing in San Francisco, were being sent from a radio set on the roof of the Fairmont Hotel.

To bring this wonder to the people of Santa Rosa, Finley hired young Saare, who rigged a 400-foot antenna from the bell tower of the fire station at Fifth near B Street to the roof of his newspaper office. Mike Pardee, a high school friend of Saare's and a cub reporter on the *Press Democrat*, was assigned to assist in the project. On the appointed evening, some 700 of "the best known people of Santa Rosa and surrounding communities" stood in the street in front of the *Press Democrat* building to hear the first radio-transmitted opera ever sung in California. The music, preceded by the results of the Pacific Coast League baseball games, was broadcast from the Fairmont Hotel station. Finley was greatly pleased. The concert "gave Santa Rosans an idea of the practical side of the radio phone," his newspaper reported. For Saare, it was the beginning of a long career. Soon he and his friend Wayne Rulofson had built a radio receiving set they called the "Sarson." Manufactured in his workshop at the family home, the Sarson sold for $125. Since Saare shared Finley's flair for promotion, the radio came with a free subscription to the Santa Rosa *Republican*. Saare Radio would supply sound for public events and provide the community with the newest wonders of the communications age for fifty more years.[17]

Finley, too, retained his interest in radio. In 1937 he put Santa Rosa's first official radio station, KSRO, on the air. The San Francisco Bay Area was a busy radio market, with KQW, (the nation's first commercial radio station, established in 1912 in San Jose), KPO, KGO, KFRC, and KSFO all coming in loud and clear on Santa Rosans' sets. A station in a city of 12,000 was considered a risky enterprise. Radio historians regard KSRO as something of a pioneer in small city broadcasting.[18] Again, it was a Finley venture. The newspaper publisher, caught up in the excitement of the Golden Gate Bridge opening, chose to ignore the final stages of the Depression.

You too

will like

Santa Rosa California

"I would rather own a piece of land the size of a good healthy house lot in Sonoma County, than an entire farm anywhere else on earth, if I had to live elsewhere"

—LUTHER BURBANK.

—Chamber of Commerce Collection

When Finley stepped to the microphone on a Sunday morning to initiate the station he called "The Voice of the Redwood Empire," it concluded two years of negotiation with the Federal Communications Commission, in which a parade of businessmen from Lake and Mendocino as well as Sonoma County had testified to their need for this radio service.

The first broadcast included the KSRO Band, led by Vincent Trombley, and the winners of a three-county talent contest. The studio was on the top floor of the *Press Democrat*'s Mendocino Avenue office building in a big room which had once been the Santa Rosa Coffee Club and later a ballroom for children's dance classes. The transmitter and tower were west of the city, in the Leddy tract, on a street named Finley Avenue.

Hilmar Cann, who worked as an engineer for KSRO for twenty years, found that a small station required much of its technicians. Cann and Ansel (Bud) Magrini, a Santa Rosa sports figure, recreated out-of-town junior college baseball games by means of telegrams sent at the end of each inning or after a spectacular play.

The telegrams were delivered from the Western Union office downtown by bike messengers who covered the three-mile distance to the tower as fast as they could, which was not always fast enough. Magrini would do the play-by-play and Cann the sound effects. When they saw the delivery boy coming, a quarter of a mile down Finley Avenue, Magrini would start his commentary about "check swings," "time outs," and "the pitcher going to the resin bag," with Cann providing the crowd noise, until the telegram arrived.

Sunday nights were devoted to classical music. "The Ernest L. Finley Hour," five hours of classic music, would endure for two decades after the founder's death in 1942.

There were several station managers in KSRO's first years, including Charles Scott, who ran the station in the post-war era. Frank McLaurin, who became manager in 1953, served in that position until the Finley family sold the station thirty-six years later.[19]

Santa Rosa's first motion picture theater, the Nickelodeon, had opened in 1902. By the 1920s, there were also Charles Carrington's Columbia and Rose, Guy Grosse's Theaterette, the Elite on Fourth Street, the Strand at the corner of Fifth and Davis streets, and the Cline at Fifth and B streets. The Cline, which would become the Roxy in later years, had replaced the Athenaeum as the center of live entertainment for the community. Vaudeville was alive and well, as were touring companies such as impresario Oliver Morosco's which, in the summer of 1922, brought Frank McGlynn in *Abraham Lincoln*, a musical program by the famous Irish tenor Chauncey Olcott, and, as a benefit for the new swimming pool, Broadway's longest running play, *Abie's Irish Rose*.

More exciting was the prospect of movie studios. Sonoma County, being rural, scenic, and close to the Bay Area, became a favorite setting for motion picture makers not long after this new art became an American enterprise. In 1914 Grauman Feature Players Corporation sent a delegation to explore a Santa Rosa studio site, and the following year Exposition Feature Players Film Corporation looked at the town as a headquarters. The industry chose other towns, notably Hollywood and for a time worked from studios in the East Bay, but did provide Santa Rosans with a

---

KSRO Program Today

Following is today's program which marks the opening of Radio Station KSRO, "The Voice of the Redwood Empire."

10:30 a. m.—Station sign on.
10:30 a. m.—The Churches' Voice, John Seagle, baritone, Samuel Kissel, violinist. Trinity Choir and Richard Leibert, organist.

George Hall's Hotel Taft orchestra.
2:00 p. m.—The Redwood Strings. George Trombley, director.
2:30 p. m.—On the Mall—Band con-

—KSRO Collection

touch of glamour—however brief. A film called *The Moneymaker* written by Sir Gilbert Parker, who was a well-known writer of the time, was made near the Russian River in 1921. A house and barn were built for the movie at Benson's Tavern. And famed director Cecil B. deMille brought his film company to Guerneville in 1925 to make an Indian epic called *Braveheart*. But after stars Rod LaRocque, Jean Acker, and Tyrone Power Sr. pitched their teepees in a riverside meadow, the industry abandoned nature for the technological wonders of the Hollywood sound set and it would be seventeen years before another motion picture director "discovered" Santa Rosa.

The G&S Theater, an enterprise of businessmen John Greeott and Eligio Strobino, opened in 1923 on B Street, the grandest of the new theaters. It was leased to Thomas Reaves, an experienced theater man from the Bay Area whose opening program set Santa Rosa on its ear. The opening night show was *Blossomtime*, live on stage with the original New York cast. Tuesday and Wednesday were vaudeville nights. The G&S was on the Pantages circuit—considered big-time entertainment in the '20s. Santa Rosa and San Jose, the newspaper boasted, were the only small cities on their schedule.

Dan Tocchini built the Strand Theater on Fifth and Davis streets in 1924; the G&S and Cline were sold to West Coast Theaters and the names were changed to the California and the Roxy. Fred Rosenberg would add the Tower Theater in 1939, an Art-Moderne structure considered the fanciest in town. The Tower was on Fourth Street, between the new Rosenberg's Department Store and the library park.

John Greeott was one of the town's busiest developers in the 1920s. A classic immigrant story, he had come to Santa Rosa from Italy at the age of twenty with "ten cents in his pocket," worked in the vineyards, bought some land, planted his own vines, and opened the Alpine Winery at the top of the Calistoga grade. He and a designer-contractor named Albert Hildebrandt teamed up to build

Sonoma County was "discovered" as a locale for motion pictures early in the century. Cecil B. DeMille filmed his Indian epic, *Braveheart*, in Guerneville in 1925. At right is star Jean Acker. Below is the Indian village DeMille's movie company built on the banks of the Russian River.

—Harry Lewis Scrapbook

—Harry Lewis Scrapbook

111

The Hoyt brothers, Henry and Frank, were among the important builders at work in Santa Rosa after the earthquake. The post office at Fifth and A streets, a busy place where businessmen met daily, was one of their construction projects. It was completed in 1910.

—Finley Collection (inset)

—Sonoma County Museum

several downtown structures in that period of expansion, including the Hinton Avenue building that would later house the Topaz Room (it was a National Cash Register Company office first), the Sonoma County Abstract Bureau, and the first two-story parking garage in town, which occasioned considerable comment at the time. On B Street, between the theaters, it was designed to shelter the automobiles of the theater patrons. It had a repair garage on the first floor and an automobile elevator that took cars up one level to be parked. (Later the building was used as a bowling alley.) In addition to the theater building, Greeott and his investment partner Strobino bought the Santa Rosa National Bank building after Brush's financial disaster.[20]

Hildebrandt, who built the Petaluma & Santa Rosa Railroad Depot at the foot of Fourth Street in 1927, also built Lafferty & Smith's Mortuary, which was next door to the garage. Other Hildebrandt construction included the Elks Club on Fourth Street, west of B; the Occidental Hotel; and the Poulsen Building, which had originally been built for the Elks and had a grand ballroom at the top of the stairs.

Brothers Frank and Henry Hoyt were also important contractors in the first half of the century, counting among their major projects the post-earthquake United States Post Office at Fifth and A streets and the Carnegie Library. The post office building, a Roman Renaissance Revival design, was one of the twelve earliest buildings built by the federal government in California. The supervising architect, James Knox Taylor, believed that government buildings should be compatible with their settings and designed each to harmonize with local history and climate, rather than imposing a "grand federal plan." The Santa Rosa structure was of granite, with Spanish roof tiles and floors of terrazzo and marble. Completed in 1910, it housed federal offices as well as the postal service and would be a community gathering place for nearly sixty years. Much business and social intercourse was conducted on the broad steps of the building at at Fifth and A streets.[21]

CAMPI RESTAURANT
THIRD STREET

Call and See "Little Pete"   Phone Black 4172

—1907 SRHS Porcupine

Most restaurants were hotel dining rooms in the early part of the century. Campi's Restaurant on Third Street was an exception. There were a few lodging rooms upstairs but the restaurant was the main attraction for Santa Rosa residents. The proprietor in 1915, at left, was Ralph Caraccio.

—Finley Collection

113

Meanwhile, competition between the town's two newspapers was sometimes friendly. Finley bought a revolutionary new press in 1914, a 20th Century Duplex capable of 7,000 copies of twelve pages per hour, printed, folded, pasted, and trimmed. In editorials, he accused the *Republican* of falsifying its circulation figures, but the competing paper was apparently prosperous and influential. The *Republican*'s editor Allan B. Lemmon—a Kansas native of a political persuasion to match his masthead—had purchased it in 1887 from Richard Cannon.[22] In 1914 the two newspapers jointly constructed a large screen on Fifth Street between Mendocino and B streets where a stereopticon flashed the results of the election to the crowd that filled the street.

More restaurants showed up in the business listings as the town became more cosmopolitan. By 1915 Barnett's Restaurant, Bianchi Brothers restaurant, the Vienna Cafe, Paul Marcucci's restaurant, and the Santa Rosa Cafe were all doing business on Fourth Street. Ralph Carracio's Campi was on Third Street. The Santa Rosa Coffee Club, at 628 Fourth Street, was unique among them. Managed by Leonard Prell, it was a membership club and the most popular gathering place for businessmen. Its success can be explained by the report presented at the annual club meeting of 1916. Members were provided with daily lunches for $12\frac{1}{2}$ cents, as well as access to the game and card tables. In 1914, according to a newspaper report, the members were spending considerable of their business time with an "automatic baseball game" installed at the club.

Women were provided a luncheon and gathering spot in 1922 when May Stephenson and Ann Martin opened the Anna May Tea Room over Baldwin's Drug Store in the 500 block of Fourth Street. This was "something Santa Rosa has felt the need of for some time," the newspaper reported, adding that the "color scheme is rose and grey."[23]

Groceries could be purchased at two kinds of stores in the early part of the century: large general merchandise establishments like George King's and Kopf & Donovan, both on Fourth Street, Cnopius Mercantile Company on Mendocino Avenue at Fifth Street, and Roof Bros. at Fourth and Wilson, which also sold coal, hay, and grain; or small, mainly neighborhood, stores such as Harden's on Robert's Avenue, Charles' on Santa Rosa Avenue, Allen and Anderson's on Orchard Street, Heim's at Fourth and North, Crocker's on Davis Street, Hall & Schurman on Main, Coltrin's on Mendocino, and Shaffer & Sons on Barham Avenue.

The largest Italian grocery was Nate Bacigalupi's store at Fourth and Davis, established in the 1880s. Bertoli

Hinton Avenue, on the east side of the courthouse, in the 1920s. City Hall is at left. The Piggly Wiggly in the Chamber of Commerce building was one of the first grocery chain stores to come to Santa Rosa. The chamber building was later reconstructed as a restaurant called the Topaz Room.

—Chamber of Commerce Collection

Brothers was at Cherry and Mendocino, Bertolani's in the 400 block of Fourth, Laguero & Bonardi at Sixth and Wilson.

By the prosperous 1920s there were bigger grocery stores. The Piggly Wiggly on Hinton Avenue on the plaza was perhaps the first of the chain stores. (When pioneer grocer Ney Donovan retired in 1927, he transferred his accounts to Piggly Wiggly.) Cleaveland Brothers was on Third; Fehrman & Peters, Cooper's Central Market, and Martin Ananiantz's New California Market were all on Fourth Street. On the west side, in the '20s, there were Forni's on Wilson, and Ridolfi's and Trombetta's in addition to Bacigalupi's, which was now owned by Nate's son Al.

Even in the money-scarce 1930s, the grocers prospered. At least two of the Italian families who started in the business—as so many did, as clerks at the Bacigalupi store—moved uptown in that decade to establish markets that would become community landmarks.

Their first venture was a partnership. Traverso & Arrigoni Market was established in 1932 when Pietro Carlo (Charlie) Traverso and his sons Louis and Enrico and their friends James and Frank Arrigoni bought Bacigalupi's Market.

Frank Arrigoni, the youngest of four brothers, was almost a Santa Rosa native. Born in Fort Bragg, where his Lombardy-born father Zaverio owned two lumberworkers' hotels, he was very young when they moved to Santa Rosa in 1910. Zaverio opened a cafe in Santa Rosa. At Lincoln School on Davis Street, Frank Arrigoni met classmate Louis Traverso.

Louie had come to town in 1922 with his father. An immigrant from Genoa, Charlie Traverso became manager of the Santa Rosa Market at Fourth and Davis, which was then owned by Enrico Muzio, a North Beach businessman who is generally credited with bringing the first "store-bought" ravioli to Santa Rosa. The young men all worked at the store after school, and when Louie graduated from Sweet's Business College, he became the bookkeeper at the market, now owned by the multi-enterprised Bacigalupi

Traverso Market, below, had settled into a remodeled house at Second and A streets in 1941. From left, Enrico Traverso, Beppi Narduzzi, Gavin Garaventa, Mike Rossi Jr., and Charlie Traverso. At right, mother Francesca Traverso, known as "Lilla."

—Traverso Family Collection

At Nelligan's Feed Store on B Street near First Street there were scales in the street beside the loading dock, to weigh truckloads of feed.

family. Charlie's younger son Rico and his mother arrived from Italy in 1927.

The Traverso-Arrigoni partnership, formed at the start of the Depression, lasted five years. In 1937, still in the "hard times," the Arrigonis, with brother Peter added to the business, moved into a market at Fourth and D streets. It had been a Skaggs "Cash and Carry" store, the precursor of the Safeway chain. The idea of an Italian market at that end of Fourth Street was innovative, although Reno and Paul Mancini ran the Court Market on Santa Rosa Avenue at Third Street. "The neighbors looked us over," Frank would remember later, "and gave us six months."[24]

A year later, the Traversos moved—also into a former Safeway store at Fourth and A, but stayed there just two years before moving to Second and A streets, where they bought an old house owned by lawyer Thorn Gale, lifted it up, and slid a market underneath. When Charlie died in 1954, the brothers continued. Mother Francesca Traverso, who lived upstairs, presided over the vinegar barrels in the back room.

"I have always thought," Louie Traverso would say, looking back over the years of partnership and friendship, "that the Italian government should give our two families

some recognition. We taught people about Italian food. Did they know what ricotta was? Or mozzarella? Or what to do with olive oil? Not until we showed them!"[25]

Despite the Skaggs and Safeways, Santa Rosa was still not a chain-store town. The home-owned Court Market on Third and Santa Rosa Avenue prospered, as did the Diamond and Pershing markets on Fourth Street. Leroy Bolce, who worked for the Zuur family in the wholesale grocery business in the 1940s, kept a list—and memories—of his clients, including Swanett's at South A and Clark streets, the 505 at Mendocino and Fifth, Espindola's on Fourth across from St. Helena Avenue, Santorini's Black & White Market on Santa Rosa Avenue, Wheeler Market, Lewis Market.

The first home-owned store to fit the new "supermarket" category was Park Auto on Mendocino Avenue across from Bailey Field. The name came from the auto court on the site, a traditional 1920 layout with cabins in back and a gas pump in front. The owner sold a few groceries in the office, a kind of early convenience store. When the Sarubbi Brothers, Dante and Bill, bought it in the '40s, they built a modern market on the site, with a butcher shop, a liquor department, and off-street parking.

The prosperity of the 1920s was based on the success of Sonoma County as an agricultural area. Many of the businesses were directly dependent on the surrounding agriculture. Nelligan & Son sold feed and grain and bought eggs at their Second and B streets establishment, which had a scale for weighing feed sacks or grain by the truckload implanted in the pavement outside the store. There was a new business building at Fifth and Riley streets for the sale of tractors and farm implements. Charles Bacon opened a Farmers' Exchange where ranchers could trade unneeded equipment.

The business transactions of 1927—the organization of the Sonoma Fruit Products Company to manufacture wine jelly and buy and sell dried fruit; the purchase of McDonald's prune packing plant near the SP depot on North Street by Grace Brothers; and the establishment of a processing plant and cannery for Jerusalem artichokes by Pabst Dietary Products—are illustrations of the relationship between town and farm.

Old business patterns were already changing by the time the quarter-century mark approached. A. Trembley had come to Santa Rosa as a wagonmaker and manufacturer of farm implements, both important services to 19th century Sonoma County residents. In the 1920s his son Alfred Trembley faced the decreasing demand for wagons and went into the insurance business. The family would later resume a modern equivalent of the old firm—an auto parts supply company. Mallory Brothers was another company that progressed with the advent of the automobile from horsedrawn vehicles to motors. The brothers J. Kiergan and Jacob T. Mallory went from blacksmithing and "wagon work" to auto repairs at their Second Street location and finally established an auto parts business that lasted, in family ownership, for a half-century. Auto parts was a new enterprise. Emil Kraft began his Diamond tire dealership and auto accessories store which would become Kraft Auto Parts at Second and Main in the 1920s, eventually taking his wife Faye's nephew, Weston Barnard, into partnership.

Charlie Bauman saw his family's harness and saddle business, begun just before the earthquake, diminishing with the increase of automobile traffic. Charlie, who was just seventeen when he took over his late father's business in 1915, was already planning ahead. He liked to tell his friends that some day cars would have plates of glass instead of celluloid windows. As the sale of his horse collars decreased, Charlie decided to go after the horseless

In the photo at right, the interior of Bauman's harness shop on Third Street in 1920. From left to right, George Veach, Charlie Bauman, Zolvy Blackman, and Katherine Bauman. Above, Bauman's expanded leather goods store on Mendocino Avenue sold custom-made automobile tops and luggage.

—Joan Perry Ryan Collection

117

—*Chamber of Commerce Collection*

carriage trade. He sold and installed leather car tops with glass windows. Customers would pay $1,000 or less for a touring car and bring it to Bauman's where, for $700, it would be fitted with a special top. In the 1920s Bauman's had it both ways, selling harness on one side of the shop on Third Street and auto tops on the other. Some of his customers patronized both sides of the business.

When automobile manufacturers offered such amenities as leather tops and windows, and even convertible tops, Bauman's changed again. Charlie added a line of leather luggage. Later, in the store on Mendocino Avenue, he would sell ladies' handbags as well. But Charlie was a horseman and he never gave up that side of his business. He began making custom saddles for people like himself, who would keep horses as a hobby. His Santa Rosa shop gained a worldwide reputation for fine saddles and orders came from as far off as Argentina. Bauman and Harry Emery, who also established a successful saddlery in Santa Rosa, kept the region's horsemen supplied.

Bauman was an organizer and charter member of the Sonoma County Trail Blazers, the Sheriff's Posse, and the Sonoma County Riding and Driving Club. His daughter, Lorraine, became manager and buyer for the family business in 1947 and became owner when Charlie died, after a heart attack on a Trail Blazers' ride in 1951.[26]

———

The 1920s was a time of great changes in business. The automobile was responsible for some of these changes, prosperity for others. Stores remodeled and rebuilt. Hotels expanded and offered luxury services. The number of restaurants increased, as dining out became a

———

At left, a trio of blockmakers and a messenger with their lunch in a basalt quarry in Annadel, circa 1910.

Above, left: Customers roll into Louis Gambini's gas and oil station at Third and B Streets as they did for more than 30 years.

— *Sonoma County Museum*

Motorists could get everything from an oil change to a root beer at the Redwood Rose Auto Center on Mendocino Avenue (the Redwood Highway) between Fifth and Ross streets in the 1930s. Montgomery Ward's department store was later built on the same site.

social event. Gasoline stations were installed on every corner. Some were owned by oil companies. Others, like Louis Gambini's, which would be a landmark at Third and B streets, were independents.

The decade of the '20s was also a decade of ballyhoo. Promoters and press agents invented themselves, and fast-talking young men saw opportunities in the new profession. One of these was C.C. (Charley) Pyle, a brother of the post-earthquake business leader Ira Pyle. Nicknamed "Cash & Carry" by his friends and clients, Pyle first came to national prominence by promoting the successful Indian marathon to call attention to the Redwood Highway in 1927. The previous year he had signed on as an agent for Harold "Red" Grange, the football sensation, who later owned a ranch near Cloverdale in partnership with Ira Pyle.

C.C.'s most lucrative account, however, was another Santa Rosan, cartoonist Robert Ripley. In '34 Pyle directed the "Believe it or Not Odditorium" at the "Century of Progress" World's Fair in Chicago. In '36, he managed Ripley's pavilion of oddities at the Texas Centennial Exposition in Dallas.

Although he was always good for an interview when he rolled into town in his "palace on wheels" to visit his mother, not all of Pyle's ventures were national successes. His attempts to launch a professional tennis league, with a series of tournaments around the country, was a financial failure. And the sixty-three-day, 3,400-mile Los Angeles-to-New York marathon he planned never took place.[27]

The land around Santa Rosa was its fortune. In addition to the agriculture which was the foundation of the town's economy, there was a substantial income from the quicksilver mines of the Russian River and Pine Flat areas and, closer to the town, the basalt industry. Basalt deposits in the hills that separate the Santa Rosa and Sonoma valleys were quarried extensively in the early part of the century, providing employment for several thousand workers, many of them immigrants.

Flynn and Tracy, the San Francisco paving block company, had its own quarry on the ridge west of Rincon Valley. Along with the McDonald, Wymore, Grey, Landgren, and Manuel quarries between Santa Rosa and Kenwood, and the Schocken and Pinelli quarries near Sonoma, and earlier quarrying enterprises near Petaluma and the first Penn's Grove railway station, Sonoma County had supplied paving

—*Press Democrat Collection*

blocks for San Francisco streets since the 1870s. The blocks—four-by-six-by-eight inches, weighing twenty pounds each—were cut from slabs of the stone that had been blasted out of the hillside deposits. They were carried in ore cars run by gravity down steep rails to the railroad station at Melitta or hauled by wagon to Annadel and Kenwood. At peak periods—according to former blockmakers—two freight-carloads, a total of 10,000 blocks, were shipped daily from each station. The by-products, basalt chips known as spolls, also were carried down the hill by the carload and sold to Southern Pacific, which used them for ballast along the railroad tracks.[28]

The blockmakers were mostly foreign-born, and most of them were trained in stonework, since blasting and chiseling were exacting tasks. Some of the early workers came from Scotland and Wales, some from Ireland, and some from Sweden. But, by the turn of the century, almost all the blockmakers were from Northern Italy. Most came from the Massa-Carrara district of Tuscany, where the world-famous marble was quarried and cut. Blockmakers were paid by the piece, usually in thousand-block lots. Wages started at $22 per thousand until the formation of a blockmakers' union upped the scale to $45 per thousand.

At the Flynn and Tracy quarry, one of the largest on the ridge, there were bunkhouses and a washroom—no toilets or running water—but the buildings served as bachelor quarters to many of the drillers, lumpers, blockmakers and finishers. This was the only quarry to provide living quarters.[29] Other workers lived in boarding houses at Kenwood, Melitta, and Santa Rosa, and rode to and from work in wagons supplied by their employers.

The advent of the automobile spelled the end of the paving block industry. Basalt streets were too hard on the delicate suspension systems of the new machines. An imported paving system invented by the Scotsman James MacAdam was more efficient and more comfortable. By the 1920s, the paving block business had dwindled. The quarries continued to be sources of the large building blocks used in

the construction of the unique Old World-style buildings that became Sonoma County landmarks.

By the mid-1920s the Chamber of Commerce had become a strong and active force for growth and economic progress. It had 449 members, of which 135 worked actively on committees including transportation, city government, social services, agriculture, and publicity. There was an active "Prospective Settlers" program in place, which worked through the California Development Association to provide contact and correspondence with residents of other states to interest them in settling in Sonoma County. In 1924, 1,150 people were wooed by the chamber in this fashion.[30]

Such enterprises as the California Carbon Paper Manufacturing Company, makers of Grand Prize Carbon Paper, established a plant here in 1921 but moved to San Francisco within two years, changing the name to Pacific Carbon & Ribbon. Plans for a pickle and jam factory on Cleveland and College were greeted with enthusiasm in 1922.

Those who came to look at Santa Rosa in 1924 would have found a solid and bustling California farm town. The county directory for that year describes it that way but adds:

"Manufactures in Santa Rosa are gaining greater importance each year. There are now three large tanneries, a shoe factory, a big cannery, several cigar factories, a vinegar factory, three large fruit packing houses, two shirt factories, two ice works and cold-storage warehouses, a brewery, three large wineries and several smaller ones, two large macaroni factories, good foundries and machine shops, many fruit-drying establishments, two factories for carbonated drinks, and many lesser industries.

"Transportation facilities are excellent, thirty-two trains arriving and departing daily on the steam roads, with electric cars and motor buses arriving and departing every hour of the day.... Streets are mostly either paved or

At left, a view of the Rosenberg Building and Fourth Street from the courthouse lawn. In the inset, the street scene is several years later, looking east up Fourth Street with A Street crossing.

macadamized, eleven miles of new paved streets having been built within the last year...Santa Rosa is one of the most prosperous towns in the State, and is growing fast."[31]

In 1928, the Pyke Company bought the clothing factory at Boyd Street and Sebastopol Road and announced plans to produce men's pants there. The Cameron Shirt Company's plant on Bosley Street was busy, with employees earning as much as $6 per day.[32]

Merchant Max Rosenberg, whose Red Front Store had gone down in the earthquake and reopened as Rosenberg's Department Store at the corner of Fourth and B streets, was considered to be one of the town's leading merchants. His son, Fred, was something of an entrepreneur. In 1921 father and son combined capital and enterprise to construct the building that would be Santa Rosa's only "skyscraper" for nearly fifty years.

In a move that was taken as a vote of confidence in Santa Rosa's future, the Rosenbergs hired a San Francisco architect, Sylvain Schnaittacher, who had trained in the studio of A. Page Brown, designer of the Ferry Building. They commissioned him to design a five-story steel-frame office building which would be, for years to come, the tallest building between San Francisco and Portland, Oregon.

The site they acquired was the northeast corner of Fourth and Mendocino, opposite the courthouse in the old town plaza. The building displaced a service station, Standard Oil's #77, which had been built there in 1916, the Piedmont residence hotel, an abstract office, a real estate office, and some second-floor quarters that housed a dressmaker and the offices of a hop buyer.

Schnaittacher designed a Romanesque structure which opened in 1922. The first tenants included Rutherford's Drug Store on the corner, F.W. Woolworth Company on the Fourth Street side—considered something of a prize—and Healey's Shoe Company on the Mendocino Avenue side, moved over from its location in the 500 block of Fourth. The 105 offices, which seemed, to many, a staggering number, filled quickly. People with no business there came just to ride the town's first elevator.

The new building towering over the courthouse and the plaza gave Santa Rosans a confidence in the future. But

The Santa Rosa Hotel and the White House, Fourth and B streets.

—Press Democrat Collection

Above, merchant Max Rosenberg, top photo, and his son Fred opened Santa Rosa's "skyscraper," the 105-office Rosenberg Building in 1922.

The corner of Fourth and Mendocino, shown at right, was the site of Standard Station #77 before the Rosenberg Building was constructed.

if they needed to look to their past, they had only to walk a block west and two blocks south of the courthouse to the wood frame house on the north bank of Santa Rosa Creek, its walls embroidered with wisteria vines.

The house, on First Street at the foot of B, had been built in the early 1850s, perhaps before the first courthouse, by a carpenter named Charlie White, who decorated it with the fancy cut-out trim so popular in the 19th century. It had been the home of the Hoag family since father Obediah bought it in 1875. There were eleven Hoag children and several of them never left home. Helen, the eldest, inherited the house when her father died, but it continued to be home to several family members.

Cushing Hoag was an insurance broker who gained a reputation as a town character by conducting his substantial business at the Exchange Bank corner, using his hat as an office. The house was his official business address. Edwin was also in the insurance business but had his own home on Aston Avenue. Lorena and Edith became elocutionists and teachers. Edith married and lived in Texas. Lorena came home and Aletha, the youngest, who was born in the house, never left home. If the house was a little run down and some of the Hoags were considered to be eccentric, it was an important part of the community. The fire horses had lived in the Hoag barn after the earthquake destroyed the firehouse. In the changing times, it was a touch of the town's beginnings. It was a landmark.[33]

A pedestrian in the business district in 1924 would have passed businesses that would continue to be part of the town's commercial enterprise through much of the 20th century. The White House, which had issued merchandise from owner William Carithers' Fifth Street home after the

123

earthquake, rebuilt at the northeast corner of Fourth and B. The White House was incorporated in '24, as W.E. Carithers & Sons, with Donald Carithers as president, William Jr. as vice president, and brother-in-law Vernon Garrett as secretary-treasurer, opening stores in Napa and Vallejo in the '30s and Petaluma in 1946. The third mercantile store was Dibble's "Women's Outfitters" furnishing everything from corsets and petticoats to evening bags. The two men's stores were Henderson's, founded by George Henderson and continued by his sons, Robert and Cyril, and Keegan Brothers, owned by the McNamara Brothers. Harvey

Sullivan, who had worked as a cash boy at Keegan Brothers in 1917, at the age of eleven, went to work as a salesman in 1929, and his brother Austin came to work there in 1935. The Sullivan brothers bought out the McNamaras in the late '30s. Shoe customers chose from R.C. Moodey & Son or two stores called Healey's—Eugene Healey's Healey Shoe Company on Mendocino Avenue in the Rosenberg Building, later owned by his son Edward, or Healey & Son, owned by Eugene's brother and nephew, William Sr. and William Jr., in the Occidental Hotel building.

One of the pre-earthquake businesses which had adapted nicely to the new town was Pedersen Furniture Co. Established in 1892 by Danish cabinetmaker Jens Christian Pedersen, the company sold furniture from the front porch and barn of a family residence on Second Street for five years following April 1906. In December of 1911 the furniture company, which now included J.C.'s sons, Obert and Fred, as partners, opened in a large rambling building on the north side of Fourth Street near D Street. The firm stayed in that location until 1953—long enough to accommodate the Pedersen "sons of sons," Fred Jr. and William, as partners—and then relocated in a new building at Fifth and Humboldt.[34]

There were two other "furniture families" in Santa Rosa in the first half of the century whose businesses extended to three generations. Nielsen Furniture at Fourth and A streets was founded after the earthquake by Christian Nielsen, who had been a clerk at Pedersen's, and his brother Anders. The Stone Company, which had stores in Petaluma, Sebastopol, and Healdsburg before opening in Santa Rosa in 1926, was owned by Grover Stone, whose sons, J. Ralph and Stewart, joined him in the business. Ralph Stone was something of a hero in Sonoma County, having distinguished himself on the gridiron at the University of California. He was a member of the Western team that won the exhibition football game at the 1932 Olympics in Los Angeles. He also enjoyed a brief film career with parts in three Hollywood football movies, including *The All-American*.[35]

Hardisty's and the Elks Club at the southwest corner of Fourth and B streets.

—LeBaron Collection

The Corrick family business began in 1916 when A.R. Corrick, known as Rae, and his wife Mabel Huckins Corrick bought into Charles Wright's book, stationery, and appliance store on Fourth Street east of Mendocino Avenue. Wright had moved there when the ill-fated Atheneum building was leveled by the earthquake. In 1918 the Corricks ended the partnership with Wright and added gifts and china to their stock. Husband and wife, with one longtime employee, Charles Oakes, operated the business through the early years. Displaced when the Rosenberg Building was built, the business moved in 1923 to a location just east of B Street. It would move along Fourth Street three more times in the next sixty years, maintaining its family ownership as Corrick son-in-law Kenneth Brown, husband of Rae and Mabel's daughter Marjorie, became a partner in 1943 and assumed full ownership in 1946 when the elder Corricks retired.[36]

The Hardisty family was new in business in 1924. The town's pre-earthquake tea and coffee merchants, Flagler's on Fifth Street, had been purchased by Joseph Hardin in 1908 and became, in partnership with H.S. Gutermute, Enterprise Coffee and Crockery in the 400 block of Fourth Street. In the early 1920s Frank Ammer purchased the business and, in 1926, sold to Lee Hardisty, who had opened a competing business farther east on Fourth Street in 1923.

Hardisty brought his nephew, Clem Hardisty, a young school teacher in Lakeport, into the business. Clem's brother, Elwin, still a student, would join the firm later. In the 1930s Hardisty's moved to the corner of Fourth and B, where it would remain for forty years, emitting evocative aromas of spice, tea, and fresh ground coffee. When Lee Hardisty died in 1942, Clem and Elwin bought the company. Clem ran the portion of the store that stocked electrical appliances, homewares, and shavers; and Elwin was responsible for china, glassware, gifts, toys, and tea and coffee.[37]

Clement Bruner had been an art dealer and purveyor of art supplies since 1899 and had rebuilt his shop—the center of artistic activity for the coastal section of Northern California—after it was destroyed by the 1906 earthquake and subsequent fire. His son Harold had joined the family business by the mid-'20s. His younger son, Merlin L. (Bud) Bruner, was one of those young people fascinated with the new technology known as radio. In 1928, Bud opened his own radio sales and repair business in the back of his father's store.

Clement Bruner achieved a degree of distinction in the art world as an agent for the well-known painter of Pomo Indians, Grace Hudson of Ukiah. He retired in 1947,

Mead Clark Lumber Company at Third and Wilson streets, circa 1920.

—*Press Democrat Collection*

leaving his son Harold to carry on the fine arts tradition. Bud Bruner's radio business, riding the growth of a new industry, moved to its own Fourth Street store in 1935, and to another, larger store on Third Street after World War II.[38]

Mailer's, Dixon, Ketterlin Brothers, and Coon & Bent were hardware dealers in the 1920s. In addition to tools, nails, plumbing supplies, and sporting goods, Coon & Bent sold stoves and ranges. Ketterlin's offered a full line of farm implements and tractors. Dixon advertised that it was "The Winchester Store." J.C. Mailer advertised simply "Everything" including water systems and Aeromotor windmills. The Levin family enlarged its hardware business in 1931 when they moved to the commodious store in the 300 block of Fourth Street that had been Titus & McKinney's Furniture Company. Of the five, Mailer's would live the longest. James C. Mailer had joined Edward Neblett, a colorful old pioneer who was Santa Rosa's first mayor, in the town's first hardware business at First and Main. They moved to the Fourth Street location in the 1870s. In 1875, Neblett died and Mailer assumed the business. He rebuilt it after the earthquake damaged the original building and passed it along to his sons, James and John, and ultimately to John's son, Clark Mailer. Jessie Frey became a partner in 1935 and the business became, officially, Mailer-Frey.[39]

Benefitting from all the building and expansion in this period were lumber dealers like Mead Clark, who opened a yard on Third Street near the railroad in 1912, and Frank Berka, at Eighth and Wilson streets, who had been selling lumber to Santa Rosans since the Civil War. Berka's was sold to E.U. White in 1925 and again in 1931 to Henry Laws. In 1940 two employees of these competing firms, who were good friends, became part owners. Elie Destruel, a trusted employee whom Clark regarded as an adopted son, bought into the Third Street business; and his neighbor Steve Yaeger, who had worked at the old Berka yard for more than ten years, became a partner to Henry Laws.

Destruel became sole owner of Mead Clark in 1952, the same year that Laws sold his interest to Yaeger and his new partner, David Kirk. The two west-end firms would be amiable competitors for Santa Rosa's lumber trade into the second half of the century.[40]

Rosenberg's Department Store, on the southeast corner of Fourth and B streets, wasn't just a clothing store. By the 1920s Max and Fred Rosenberg's enterprise was the town's largest store, selling groceries, fresh vegetables

The 1936 fire that destroyed Rosenberg's Department Store at Fourth and B streets also burned part of the Santa Rosa Hotel, a millinery shop, and several offices.

—Santa Rosa Fire Department

The new department store, an Art Moderne design by San Francisco architects Hertzka and Knowles, opened the following year.

—Earl Guynne Collection

(Max had initiated the first "free market" for Sonoma County farmers), liquor, and drugs, along with clothing.

On the morning of May 8, 1936, Floyd Davis, who drove the city street sweeper, saw the smoke pouring from the alley at the rear of Drake's Electric Shop as he rumbled along B Street in the hour before dawn. He hurried to call the fire department. In the Santa Rosa Hotel in the same block, banker Charles Parks, up at five for an early horseback ride, saw the same smoke and alerted the desk clerk. Together they hastened to wake the sixty guests, who turned out into Fourth Street clad in nightclothes and what they could grab on the way out the door.

The blaze, which may have been Santa Rosa's most

damaging fire, destroyed part of the hotel, a parking garage, a millinery store, offices—and Rosenberg's. The Rosenbergs wasted no time. Flaunting the Depression, Fred and his father Max, who had been officially retired since 1925 but was still active in business, announced within weeks that they would rebuild immediately, promising a "spectacular store" of which the community would be proud. They selected a site two blocks east at Fourth and D streets where Barber's Service Station had been. They commissioned the San Francisco architectural firm of Hertzka and Knowles to design an Art Moderne structure which proved to be the most exciting addition to the town since the "other" Rosenberg building fourteen years earlier.

In 1944, Max Rosenberg died in San Francisco. After his retirement he had taken up residence at the Chancellor Hotel, owned by his family. In 1951, Fred sold the department store to the McNeany family of Fond du Lac, Wisconsin. The Rosenberg name was retained.[41]

There were generally about eight drugstores doing business in central Santa Rosa in the the first half of the century. Gene Toschi's and Gene Farmer's pharmacies were on opposite corners at Fourth and D. Ralph Tomasco's was at Fourth and A. Through the years the names of the stores changed with the proprietors —Belden & Upp, Warboys and Dignan, Pye, Reedy, Juell, Davis, Baldwin and Stewart— but the count and the personalized service remained the same through the 1950s.

Bert Callwell, who spent seventy years in Sonoma County drugstores—from delivery boy to pharmacist—was the unofficial historian of the profession.[42] He started in 1914 at the age of fourteen, working as a delivery boy, soda jerk, and bottlewasher at Farmer's; moved to Rutherford's at Fifth and Mendocino the following year; and, at eighteen, went to San Francisco to take classes at the College of Physicians and Surgeons. His classmate was another Santa Rosan, Angelo Franchetti, the son of immigrants who ran a hotel near the railroad tracks. Franchetti had worked at Tomasco's first store.

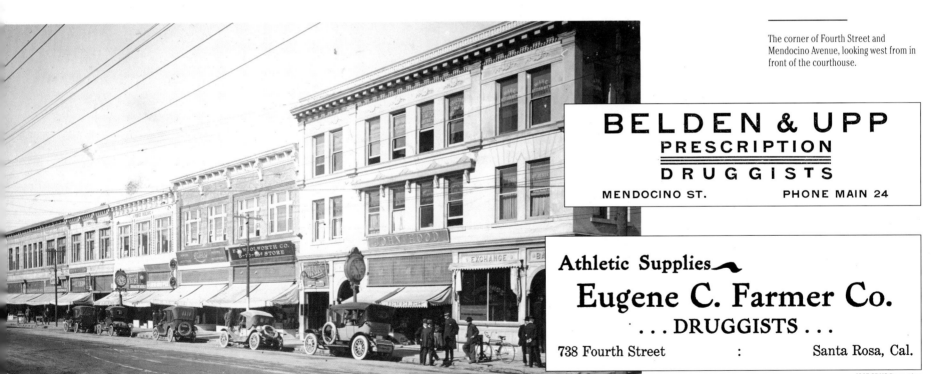

The corner of Fourth Street and Mendocino Avenue, looking west from in front of the courthouse.

BELDEN & UPP
PRESCRIPTION
DRUGGISTS
MENDOCINO ST.   PHONE MAIN 24

Athletic Supplies
Eugene C. Farmer Co.
...DRUGGISTS...
738 Fourth Street   :   Santa Rosa, Cal.

—1907 SRHS Porcupine

—Finley Collection

Callwell and Franchetti came back to town in the early '20s, qualified as assistant pharmacists, and finished their training in the downtown drugstores. Toschi was still doing business at the same place. Albert Gambini and Ray Butler owned Empire Drug. William Rutherford, who was a civic figure and had served as mayor, moved his drug store to Fourth Street, west of the Exchange Bank, before he became a municipal court judge, selling his business to the Hall Brothers, Theron and Lowell.

By the 1930s, Franchetti owned Tomasco's and Callwell had moved north, purchasing a store in Geyserville. Oliver Tuttle moved his Fourth Street business to his home on Lincoln Street in the 1940s and specialized in home delivery. And Franchetti expanded, joining with Arch Hill of Sebastopol and Graham Mann and Arch Reid to form the Medico Drug Company.

At least three of these drugstores had soda fountains, which were a traditional part of the profession. (Druggists, it should be remembered, are the ones who developed the formulas for most of America's favorite soft drinks.) At Rutherford's and Tomasco there were marble counters and stools and a soda jerk, usually a high school boy. In 1947, when Medico bought John Bacci's drug at Fifth and Mendocino and remodeled it, the new floor plan included an L-shaped counter where many in the business community took refuge during the new post-war phenomenon known as the "coffee break."[43]

While population growth was slow, Santa Rosa's business community, starting with absolutely nothing in 1906, was marching forward with the Chamber of Commerce at the fore. Santa Rosa became a state leader—listed second in retail sales per capita among California's cities in both Bank of America's 1930 census and the *Pacific Rural Press* survey in 1932.

The year 1929 began on a note of business optimism, capping a decade of unprecedented prosperity. Montgomery Ward had chosen Santa Rosa as a store location and was building a department store on Mendocino Avenue north of Fifth Street. It would be the second chain department store for Santa Rosa. J.C. Penney had been doing business at its Fourth Street location for some ten years. Metropolitan, the second "five-and-dime" chain in town, had taken a lease on a Fourth Street location.

The banks were financially sound. The Exchange Bank was generally considered the most important, due in no small part to Frank Doyle's civic leadership. Santa Rosa Bank, the pioneer bank in town, established by E.T. Farmer in 1870, had become a branch of the Bank of Italy in 1917 with the sale of the Exchange Avenue institution to San

The cannon on the corner of the courthouse lawn levels on traffic circling from Exchange Avenue to Fourth Street. In the background are the American Trust Bank and Bank of America, later the Empire Building.

—*Earl Gwynne Collection*

129

130

Francisco's immigrant financier, A.P. Giannini. Joe Grace was the vice president and manager of Bank of Italy, and a young Santa Rosa man named Joe Lombardi was "on the platform" as assistant cashier. Lombardi was the pride of the Italian community on the westside, being the first immigrant to "cross the tracks" and become valedictorian of Santa Rosa High School. He was also the first from his neighborhood to enter the University of California.

American Trust Company was the newcomer. It was the former Savings Bank of Santa Rosa, known as the "Overton bank" for the founding family, established in 1873. James R. Edwards was manager in the '20s, before he moved to the Exchange Bank in 1929. First National Bank of Santa Rosa was chartered in 1922 by Bay Area financiers Leon Herrick and Joseph Morrow. The Santa Rosa office was run by Fred Cassani, assistant cashier, and the Sonoma County directors included Kenwood rancher Charles Louis Kunde and Herbert Mueh of Cnopius Mercantile.[44]

There had been few financial concerns for Santa Rosa depositors since Frank Brush's admitted misappropriations ten years earlier. Joe Lombardi remembered one incipient run on the Bank of Italy in 1921, which was prevented by a warning. "We heard rumors," he said, "that people were going to come for their deposits. We started early in the morning, calling around to other branches, in Napa, in Petaluma. I went to the Exchange Bank, to Jim Edwards at the Savings Bank. By opening time, I had a desk covered with cash." Most of the fearful despositors, soothed by the sight of real money, did not withdraw and panic was averted.[45]

Leonard Talbot, the salesman son of farmer-columnist Joe Talbot, the *Press Democrat*'s "Sage of Bennett Valley," was among the first stockbrokers in Sonoma County. Talbot went to work for Cyrus Pierce Company of San Francisco upon his graduation from the University of California in 1922. He worked out of the San Francisco office, as did all Northern California brokers in that era, but declared Sonoma County and the North Coast to be his territory. He wasn't without competition. "There was Merrill Miller from E.H. Rawlins and a man named Jacobsen," Talbot remembered in later years. But Talbot was productive and brokerage firms competed for his skills. He worked for home offices in both Chicago and New York before he joined with another UC graduate, Duke Hannaford, in the mid-'30s to form their own brokerage house. Hannaford & Talbot had a San Francisco office and a Santa Rosa office. "We got up to fifty salesmen," Talbot would recall proudly. "We were dealing in improvement bonds, a limited market. But they appealed to the farmers. And they proved to be the strongest, proved to be the best."[46]

There were flurries of excitement in the county in the 1920s as the development of natural resources promised—but never really delivered—"booms." In 1925, a San Francisco company made a proposal to develop the Geysers "into one of the greatest power projects in the world," with Santa Rosa as the distribution center; and H.N. Witt reported that he "brought in" no less than 100 barrels of oil a day from his well near Petaluma. Both Shell and Gulf oil companies searched diligently through the next two years and Shell did lease Petaluma land for wells.[47]

These promises of wealth were exciting, but despite the impact of a national prohibition on grapes and hops, Santa Rosa remained an agricultural center—a farm town. The big businesses were still the cannery, the hardware merchants, and the farm suppliers. The stores and shops depended on the farmers and their wives. Agriculture was keeping its part in this business bargain. Sonoma County was still ranked in the top ten in the nation in total crop production. America was in a state of euphoric prosperity. California, Sonoma County and Santa Rosa were all riding the wave. ❧

The first proposal to harness the geothermal power of the Geysers was made in 1925, one of several promises of resource development in the county that created business excitement in that decade.

In the glow of idealism that followed the victorious conclusion of World War I, the prohibition movement which had been abroad in the land since the turn of the century gained momentum. Its political basis lay in the reform movements led by charismatic national figures such as William Jennings Bryan and woman suffrage leaders such as Susan B. Anthony and Frances Willard.

The anti-saloon movement and agitation for prohibitory laws which had gained considerable success with "local options" between 1900 and 1906 (particularly east of the Rocky Mountains) drew new strength from wartime zeal, fueled by a campaign to associate the drinking of alcoholic beverages, especially beer, with Americans of German descent.

The implied connection between "disloyalty" and drinking gave impetus to politicians to approve a wartime measure which was technically a food control bill, saving grain for the war effort, with a section prohibiting the manufacture of distilled liquor, beer, and (inexplicably, since it was not a grain) wine. These prohibitions lasted until the ratification of the Constitutional Amendment which would come to be known, ruefully, as "The Great Experiment," and the Volstead Act which enforced its laws.

Northern California was not a leader in the prohibition cause. The question, which historian Page Smith identifies nationally as "an East-West issue," divided California on distinct North-South lines.[1] It was more an agricultural matter in the rural north than a matter of conscience. This was particularly true in Sonoma County, where there were 256 wineries in 1920, and in Santa Rosa, where commerce and the very identity of the city were dependent upon thousands of surrounding acres of grapes and hops.[2]

Despite turn-of-the-century "dry" activity in this area, including the formation of a local Anti-Saloon League in 1901 and meetings to praise the efforts of saloon-buster Carry Nation, Sonoma County did not exercise local options

nor did its citizens approve such activities in other areas.[3] The agricultural interests, along with the growing number of mostly Roman Catholic immigrants, repudiated the movement. Neighboring towns voted (Ukiah to remain "wet," Lakeport "dry"). The Sonoma County Labor Council went on record opposing statewide prohibition and asked Congressman William Kent to vote in opposition to a national prohibition. The Bennett Valley Grange took as its slogan, "Protect the Wine Industry" and the county's state representatives, men like State Senator Louis W. Juilliard and Assemblyman Herbert Slater, who were sympathetic to growers, spoke out for local agriculture and against prohibition. There was support for the statewide measure from religious leaders. The Rev. C.F. Clarke was elected president of a new Sonoma County Dry Federation in the spring of 1914, but the November vote was a glorious victory for the "wets" in both Sonoma County and California.

The 1914 vote, however, was the battle, not the war. The wartime measures took effect after the United States' entrance into the European conflict. Congress adopted the 18th Amendment to the Constitution in December of 1917 and submitted it to the states for ratification. Santa Rosans and their grape and hop-growing neighbors had to grit their teeth and prepare for the worst. No whiskey was manufactured after September 1917, no beer after May 1919. After July 1919, it was illegal to sell intoxicating beverages.

Grape growers were frantic. By the fall of 1918, with the Midwest and the "Bible Belt" South rushing to ratify the Prohibition Amendment, they discussed desperate and, in hindsight, impossible means of survival, such as drying grapes by an evaporation process to ship to territories where winemaking was legal. Some winemakers who had been strong supporters of their parishes obtained permits to make wine for sacramental purposes. Laws allowing the manufacture of wine for medicinal purposes, to be sold by physicians' prescription were welcomed. Still, in January of 1920, according to the *Press Democrat*, there were three

There was noisy opposition to any prohibition measure, particularly the 18th Amendment, in wine-rich Sonoma County.

million gallons of wine on hand in Sonoma County—presumably unmarketable.

Some had disposed of their wine in expectation of financial disaster. Italian Swiss Colony at Asti, the largest wine producer in the county, sold a million dollars' worth (84,000 dozen bottles) of Golden State champagne to Japan in September of 1918, announcing that the sale was predicated on the "dismal outlook" for the California wine business. Italian Swiss Colony's founder, Andrea Sbarbaro, had seen the bad times coming. Sbarbaro waged a twenty-year crusade to remove the stigma of alcoholism from the consumption of wine. He lobbied Congress, lectured, quoted scriptures, and pointed to the gustatory habits of highly civilized European nations to teach Americans to regard wine as a temperance beverage. As did so many Italian-Americans, Sbarbaro considered Prohibition a personal as well as an economic affront.[4]

Legislators led by the U.S. Senator from San Francisco, James D. Phelan, and the First District's new Congressman, Clarence F. Lea, fought in vain to prevent the inevitable. In July of 1919, Lea rose in the House of Representatives to remind Prohibition supporters of their promise to give the country a year to "adjust ourselves" between wartime prohibition laws and the Constitutional Amendment. In an impassioned plea, he spoke of the large grape crop then on the vines in California and declared, "If legislation [to enforce the 18th Amendment] robbed the farmers of California of the fruits of their labor, it would be one of the greatest legislative outrages in the history of the country.

"There are double-dealing politicians in power in this country who have the idea they can traffic in the question of prohibition and politically sell out the legitimate rights of the grape growers of California and thereby advance their own political fortunes. I want to say this cannot be pulled off without my standing here and branding it as the political pandering it is.

"Today the sons of grape growers lie sleeping the eternal sleep in the soil of France. It is unworthy of the

—*Press Democrat Collection*

American Congress today under the pretense of war prohibition, under only a color of right, to rob the parents of these boys of what their industry has legitimately earned."

Sonoma County hop growers and vineyardists could be excused their pessimism. Sonoma County was the second-largest hop-producing county in the nation, shipping more than two million pounds of dried and baled hops annually to beer producers. The law prohibiting the manufacture and sale of beer would literally halt all U.S. trade in that single-use commodity.

The California wine industry, meanwhile, was just beginning to hold its own among connoisseurs, and Sonoma County was the undisputed leader with two-thirds more wine production in 1920 than neighboring Napa County. The new law loomed as potential devastation. California historian Kevin Starr couched it in dramatic terms. "Prohibition," he wrote, "descended like a long dark night."[5]

The lights did not blink out all at once. The United States went "dry" with more of a whimper than a bang. The wartime liquor laws were ignored in many quarters, including Sonoma County. As the deadline for a total cessation in the sale of alcoholic beverages approached, there were previews of the scofflaw approach the citizens would take. In the fall of 1919, knowing that a permanent ban would take effect the following January, many Santa Rosa saloonkeepers were taking advantage of the transition from wartime laws to circumvent the Volstead Act. They also were not taking the ban too seriously, as this newspaper account indicates:

"Is Santa Rosa dry?

"The law says it is but there are some doubters. Rumor has it that despite the wartime prohibition on all forms of liquors, whisky is being sold openly at several saloons.

"Of course, the question of the legality of 2.75 percent beer is being threshed out in the courts and it is openly acknowledged by the salesmen and city authorities that beer containing that percentage of alcohol can be obtained in any saloon. The city has even licensed dealers to sell this beer, pending federal decision.

"But the hard stuff—the distilled spirit of the rye and corn—whisky; which was supposed to have been everlastingly knocked out by the wartime prohibition solar plexus blow, rumor declares is still on a more or less open sale.

"In some saloons, it is said, you have to cock your left eyebrow and ask for ginger ale while in others you ask for whisky and get it.

"City and county officials seem to have adopted a policy of hands off, in view of the fact that selling of intoxicating liquor is a federal offense, and thus far no federal officers have gotten as far as Santa Rosa in their raids on whisky-selling saloons. Several arrests, however, have been made in San Francisco."[6]

One of the victims of this business style was the city treasury. If liquor was to continue to be sold after Prohibition took effect, it would not be legal and therefore could not be licensed. The resulting loss of revenue to city government would be substantial. In January of 1920 the City Council levied a new $1 a month tax on city water meters as the first means of "covering" the revenues lost with the cessation of city liquor licenses. The prospect of taxing bootleggers, however improbable, must have crossed the minds of the city officials. But the "dry" vote had to be considered. There was a vocal temperance group in Santa Rosa strongly supportive of Prohibition, although there seems little doubt that the majority of Sonoma County citizens either opposed Prohibition openly or dismissed it as a bad idea that probably wouldn't work.

Prevailing attitudes, a sparse population, a rugged and remote coastline, and a surplus of wine grapes would combine to make the dozen years the 18th Amendment was law very exciting years in Sonoma County. It wasn't beer that made it exciting. Commercial brewing, with its huge vats and rooms filled with complex bottling machinery, could not be a clandestine process. Grace Brothers Brewery, which ranked right up there with Acme and Buffalo as one of

A *grappa* distillery at Geyser Peak in the days when the manufacture of distilled spirits was legal. During Prohibition, *grappa* became known as "jackass brandy."

—*Geyser Peak Winery*

Northern California's leading beers, simply closed its doors for the duration. The brothers, Joe and Frank Grace, converted to carbonated beverages, concentrated on their butter and ice cream business, and expanded the ice house they owned along the railroad tracks. So, generally, Sonoma County's contributions to lawbreaking in the '20s and early '30s came from three camps—the backyard winemakers, the manufacturers of bootleg liquor, and the "rumrunners" who used the coves and dogholes along the coast to transfer Canadian whiskey for the San Francisco market.

Ironically, grape growers did not all suffer immediately as they feared they would. The law allowed family winemaking, up to 200 gallons per person, and the rush to basement crushers took all the grapes the growers could supply and left buyers begging for more to meet the demand from eastern cities. Grape production actually increased in the first years of Prohibition. The effects of the dry laws on the grape industry would be felt in later and lingering change. But in the summer of '20, the outlook was surprisingly rosy. The *Press Democrat* quoted a story from the *San Francisco Chronicle* suggesting that Prohibition was proving a "real benefit to the grape industry." Wine grapes were in such demand, said the San Francisco paper, that "raisins may be in short supply." In addition to the basement winemakers, there were winery owners with licenses to make sacramental wine and medicinal wine who prospered under the dry laws. Kunde Brothers, whose Wildwood Vineyards in Kenwood had been one of the most successful pre-Prohibition wineries, actually expanded in 1920, remodeling the old Franco-American Wine Company in Ukiah, to make sacramental wine—and livestock feed and fertilizer from the by-products. Perelli-Minetti Winery in the Sonoma Valley made $600,000 in profits in three years producing wine for medical and ecclesiastical purposes. Martini Winery on Laguna Road also stayed in full production to make sacramental wine. The increased use of wine for medicinal purposes became, predictably, a source

of humor. In the fall of 1920, the *Press Democrat* reported that many people in Santa Rosa have sore throats and are asking for prescriptions to make "hot claret wine gargle."[7]

Many home winemakers took advantage of the law, selling barrels of "basement wine" to hotels and restaurants whose owners elected to take the risk. The risks were not frightening. One justice of the peace summed it up: Prohibition in Sonoma County was "more of a game than the law of the land."[8]

If the ratification of the 18th Amendment did not stop winemaking in Sonoma County, neither did the Volstead Act stop the sale and consumption of alcoholic beverages in Santa Rosa. Italian immigrants, particularly, had a difficult time understanding how a function so commonplace to the business of living could be considered a crime. And wine was still available. Small family wineries in rural Sonoma County had vats of wine, perhaps 10,000 gallons or more, "sealed" by government inspectors at the start of Prohibition. They continued to sell it. Many simply made more to replace it; others used rocks for their displacement properties to make the tanks sound full to a federal agent's knock and look full when he insisted on a look over the rim. Sons and grandsons of immigrants remember that wine made for family use sometimes mysteriously found its way outside the household. Even urban families made wine, sometimes using their own winemaking equipment, sometimes leasing a neighbor's crusher for their grapes.

The agents who had ignored Sonoma County in 1919 discovered what was going on. Newspaper reporters could no longer gloat that Santa Rosa liquor sellers were getting away with it. Agents made surprise visits to the Italian hotels along Santa Rosa's Northwestern Pacific railroad tracks, where there was always a barrel outside the back door and a meal wasn't complete without a glass of classic Sonoma County red wine. The Battaglia Hotel, Hotel D'Italia Unita, the Toscano, La Rose, the Western, and the Torino all took their turn.

The raids were more predetermined than sporadic, and there is evidence the hotel owners and saloonkeepers knew when the agents were coming. Local officials seemed loath to prosecute. The charges usually were reduced before the cases came to court, and the fines were not excessive. Some compared the money spent to paying dues or buying a business license. Often, the seller would be back in business long before his case came up on the docket.

At the Battaglia Hotel, for example, alcoholic beverages rarely ceased to flow. In addition to the wine the proprietor made at his home nearby, there was always a spare room with enough bootleg liquor to keep the bar running. If federal agents "knocked over" the place and sealed one room for ninety days, there was another to sell from until the seals came off.

News stories about the "raids" in the Santa Rosa newspapers served to assure the temperance workers the

County Detective John Pemberton, right, shown with federal agents in the act of raiding a still, was noted for his zeal in the enforcement of Prohibition in Sonoma County.

—Jimmie FitzGerald Collection

laws were being enforced and let customers know which of their favorite innkeeps had been taken in to be booked and fingerprinted. Justice, such as it was, was usually swift. On March 18, 1920, for example, just two months after the law went into effect, the owners of both the Battaglia and the neighboring Hotel D'Italia Unita were arrested when both whiskey and wine were found on their premises. On April 27, D'Italia owner Louis Franchetti pleaded guilty and was fined $300. Franchetti was a frequent target, as were the owners of the Battaglia, including Olinto Battaglia's daughter, Lena Battaglia Bonfigli.

Lena was arrested at her residence in 1924, when federal agents from San Francisco came to town with seventy warrants based on sales made to undercover agents two months earlier; and again at the hotel in 1930, when fourteen agents swept through the area between lower Fourth Street and Santa Rosa Creek reporters called "the waterfront." It was one of very few surprises, apparently.

The newspaper report said that "although ordinarily word that federal raiders are in town spreads quickly through the 'wet' spots along the 'waterfront,' the Prohibition agents struck so suddenly that all places named in their search warrants were caught completely unawares. This was considered newsworthy."[9]

Ten men also were arrested in that raid including the proprietors of the Roma Hotel, a pool hall, and several soft drink parlors near Fourth and Wilson streets. Linda Brovelli, who lived on West Third Street, was one of several who established "equal rights" for women. Mrs. Brovelli, described by the newspaper as "wealthy," was arrested at least three times for misuse of her backyard winery, once in connection with an insurance claim filed after the winery burned.

It is important to remember that not all the criminal activity associated with Prohibition was reported in the press. It is also important, in keeping the events of that period in perspective, to remember that the journalistic ethics of the time left something to be desired and some of the omissions were undoubtedly purposeful. If the preponderance of European names in the lists of those prosecuted for violation of the dry laws seems unfair, it is undoubtedly because the reporting was unfair. "Uptown" hotel problems were less apt to appear in print. Also, newspapers did not always follow through with reports on the plea or the outcome of the raids.

To the reader who keeps these factors in mind, a survey of the Santa Rosa newspapers of the time still indicates a high level of activity deemed criminal under the new law, and an increasing level of federal interest in the area with mounting pressure on local lawmen to enforce the Volstead Act. In a speech to the Women's Christian Temperance Union in Healdsburg in 1923, Assemblyman T.M. Wright of Santa Clara County, whose Wright Act was California's Prohibition enforcement law, told his audience that Sonoma and Napa counties were the greatest bootlegging counties in the state and reiterated the

The bar at the Battaglia Hotel is pictured in "happier times," when it was open and legal. The Battaglia's Prohibition-era speakeasy was in the alley behind the Adams Street establishment.

—Paul Chiotti Collection

accusation in an interview with a reporter, calling those two counties the highest in the "moist column" of counties.[10]

From the beginning, there was pressure on law enforcement officials to see that the town obeyed the temperance laws. In 1921, City Council members acted on a petition brought to them by Mrs. D.R. Gale, wife of a Santa Rosa attorney. The petition, signed by 600 residents, asked for protection of the youth of the city. The council adopted the Dry Enforcing Law and, within twenty-four hours, officers conducted raids on Louis Gnesa's Fourth Street saloon and Tom Gemetti's Third Street establishment. At both places the police found something called "wine of pepsin" and bitters. At the Hotel D'Italia Unita, they found wine and homemade brandy.

When city police and federal agents raided a dozen Santa Rosa "places" in November of 1921, the pattern was established. Eleven people were arrested of which, according to the newspaper, most took it in their stride. Several walked into the police station smiling, "paid their 'bit' and walked out, still smiling."

One man was compelled to wait at the station house from noon to 5:30 p.m. for a friend to come with the necessary $600 for his release. When finally his friend arrived with the amount of the fine, he handed it over with a shrug, saying: "Well, it's all in a day's work." But the well-publicized raid, the largest to date in the county, brought 1,000 people to a meeting at the First Presbyterian Church to show support for the raids, which they credited to the "get tough" policies of Mayor William Rutherford.[11]

The raids and the nonchalance of the lawbreakers continued, albeit sporadically. A year later another group of citizens interested in law enforcement, this time the WCTU led by Lillis (Mrs. Hollis) LeBaron, met to ask Mayor Lawrence Pressley to remove the police chief, George Matthews, from office for failure to do his duty. That same evening, Chief Matthews and his men swooped down on

—Gemetti Family Collection

three soft drink establishments, arresting the owners for selling liquor.

Part of the game was knowing what was happening in advance. It was standard procedure for sellers of illegal liquor to be given about four hours notice that the federal agents were coming. They would take their liquor supply to a neighbor's to hide it in the shed, carefully keeping about a pint on the premises so the agents would have something to show for their trouble. They would be taken in, booked, pay their fine, and be back in business, sometimes, one suspects, with the very officers who warned them of the raid as customers.[12]

Newspaper reporters learned to play the Prohibition "game," adding new words to their lexicon, new headline shorthand like "Legs" for bootleggers, "Rum" for any illegal liquor, "Drys" for federal agents and "Speaks" for speakeasies—the newest of American English slang terms

The Melitta Band pays a visit to Tom Gemetti's Third Street saloon. Gemetti's was raided but never closed during Prohibition and Tom counted both police officers and judges among his faithful clients.

for drinking places, derived from the hushed tones patrons spoke in to avoid detection. A "resort" was anywhere people went for fun. And when they didn't know what else to call the illicit business it was simply a "place," as in "Frati's place," "Cassasa's place," or "Ariasi's place." Many of the raids yielded a liquor called "jackass brandy," which was the term for *grappa*, a potent clear liquor made from grapes, sometimes infused with burnt sugar to give it the color of brandy. Officers, under pressure to let the citizens know they were doing their duty, were pleased to invite reporters to accompany them on their raids, and the newspapers were filled with high drama.

A reporter was along to record the scene when Santa Rosa patrolmen Albert Schmitt, Charlie O'Neal, and James Birch, and traffic officer F. J. Bennett entered a "resort" at 809 Ripley Street, where they found a wash-boiler filled with hops boiling on a gas stove in the shed at the rear of the house. In the shed they found fifty-three boxes of beer, each containing four dozen pint bottles. While they were on the premises the policemen also grabbed three bottles of jackass brandy, three wooden vats, a cooler, a gas plate and the wash boiler, five packages of hops, and a fifty-gallon barrel of hop syrup. The 2,544 bottles of beer were valued at $636. Lawrence Mora, who police said was the proprietor of the resort, was arrested, along with the attendant, G. Heinman. "It was the sixth raid," said the newspaper, "conducted by Santa Rosa police within two weeks."[13]

Raiders sometimes found more than they were seeking, as was the case with a Kenwood resort owner named Bertino who found himself in double trouble with the law when a couple of "drys" stopped in for lunch and were served "polenta a la Italiano and a cold bottle." The polenta sauce contained robins and the bottle contained near beer which was too "near" to please the law. Game warden Henry Lencioni was notified and found songbird traps in Bertino's kitchen. He was fined $75 and immediately re-arrested for violating liquor laws with his brand of beer.

There were times when the raiders found the tables turned. A Johnny Pemberton adventure, told by E. J. "Nin" Guidotti, a longtime county supervisor, is a story of one such time. "Pemberton was an enforcement officer for the district attorney and he found out that these brothers had a still on their ranch near Occidental, down in a canyon with a creek in it. Somebody must have tipped them off because when Pemberton went to knock it over, they were up on a sidehill watching him from behind some bushes. He hung around awhile, waiting for them to come back; and while he was waiting, he noticed a big steelhead in the creek, coming up to spawn.

"Pemberton, the DA's man, couldn't resist. He pointed his shotgun at the fish and blew it out of the water. One of the brothers up on the hillside scooted over the ridge to a neighbor's house and called the game warden. Pemberton was an awful nice guy, a member of the Elks Club, I remember. He pleaded guilty and I'll tell you it was hell for anybody who tried to rib him about it for years afterward."[14]

———

By spring of 1931, a Sonoma County Civic League had organized with the expressed purpose of promoting temperance and the enforcement of Prohibition laws. Before the ink was dry on the new organization's bylaws, District Attorney Emmett Donohue had announced his campaign to "clean up the dirty corners" of Sonoma County.

Moreover, he said, he did not intend to stop with bootleggers and rumrunners but was targeting "operators of gambling places and habitues of disorderly houses of all kinds." Donohue made the announcement to the press in April after his five undercover investigators had been working for a month. As a result of this "crime survey," he boasted, "I know the location of every illegal slot machine, every disorderly house and gambling place, and practically every 'open' bootlegger."[15]

"Nin" Guidotti, a former justice of the peace and county supervisor, liked to tell tales of Prohibition days.

Those he couldn't go to would come to him. On the same day he announced his plans, the press had the results of what must have been the most creative "sting" in Sonoma County's Prohibition years. With a pressing political need to win one of the battles in this war against crime, Donohue had hired a freelance undercover agent to set a trap for rumrunners in what the newspapers nicknamed the "Carnival Ring."

Using the pseudonym Charles Hartford, the agent, whose real name was believed to be Crowell or Kroll, came to town with a plan to lure booze-peddlers. Posing as the advance man for a carnival called the Decker Amusement Company, Hartford rented an empty lot owned by Edwin Hoag at the corner of Bennett and Hendley. After signing the agreement he hired men to cut the grass, dig postholes, and hang huge banners on the property announcing that the carnival was coming to town. There were promises of the usual wonders. Signs on the city bus and placards in store windows promised "Six Great Days of Fun and Amusement featuring Stella in the Dive of Death, King Zula Lupa from the wilds of Africa and his Eight Ebony Dancers, and many other new and original features staged for the first time in the West. Hot off the iron."

Hartford, described by the newspaper as "genial and convivial" soon gained access to "many places where the palate might be moistened with illegal stuff." He put out the word that the carnival people were interested in purchasing a substantial amount of "stuff" for their personal use during the "Six Great Days of Fun and Amusement." In preparation, he rented a vacant auto wrecking plant on lower Santa Rosa Avenue and gave bartenders and saloon patrons the address and the time deliveries would be accepted, cash on arrival.

At the appointed time, as carloads of illegal liquor came wheeling in, Sheriff Mike Flohr and Deputies Harry Patteson, Herbert Mothern, and Stuart Rich were waiting. Nine men were arrested, seven of them from Santa Rosa. There was no estimate of how many deliverymen escaped.

Paris Night Club Visit Nets Raiders 1 Pint Rum

Newest Resort in County With Exclusive Member List, Very Quiet, is Officer's Report

John Pemberton, county detective, was among the most successful of the agents. When he and two deputies, Phil Varner and W.H. Rochester, knocked over the Paris Club, a mile north of Santa Rosa, on Russell Avenue, it was just one of many visits to illegal premises in a full work week. The Paris Club was the county's fanciest. It had membership lists, admission cards, and entertainers. When it was raided, agents found only a pint of jackass brandy. The newspaper story about the raid speculated that officers may have "called on an off night," for there were no members on the premises.

It was hard to know just which club was the swankiest. When officers raided James MacKaye's establishment in Fetters Springs the night before, they came away describing it as "the swellest place in the county." MacKaye paid a $350 fine on a liquor possession charge. Peter Braga of Valley Ford, whose "soft drink" place was raided the same night, pleaded not guilty. His case was set for trial. That same day they went to Green Valley with a search warrant to seize a cache of white wine they'd spotted earlier. They found the wine barrels empty and most of the 1,200 gallons trickling down a canyon. The owner, having heard of their visit, had knocked the bottoms out of the barrels and disappeared.[16]

Press Democrat editor Ernest Finley, never a hard-liner on Volstead enforcement, kept his good humor in the matter of Prohibition. In the winter of 1923, when snow fell on the mountains around Santa Rosa, the newspaper's "weather ear," a little box in the upper left-hand corner of the front page which usually contained a weather prediction, read: "Snowflakes or no snowflakes, about the only winter sports we can boast of around here are bootleggers."[17]

And, in 1931, Finley fixed his editorial eye on the activities of politicians casting about to solve the thorny problems the 18th Amendment had created. Liberalization of the policy on medicinal liquor, in which prescription-writing privileges for alcohol were extended beyond physicians to include "dentists, veterinarians, optometrists, osteopaths, chiropodists, spineologists and others," drew these comments:

"In the case of the veterinarian, this new order is no doubt a humanitarian gesture. To a Missouri mule who has nothing in particular the matter with him, a good shot of 'jackass brandy' would no doubt be a quick relief for that tired, run-down feeling. The dentist, now permitted to use liquor in his business, may find it more economical than gas. There are no doubt many patients who would prefer 'hooch' as an anesthetic. If given a liberal alcoholic anesthetic at frequent intervals there are some patients who would probably insist on having all their teeth removed, one at a time....

"It is not apparent why the government should stop with veterinarians and dentists and other professions named. With the automobile crowding the horse from the highway, the liquor privilege might be given to garage operators as well...[and] extended to stock salesmen, editorial writers and others engaged in painful and exhaustive occupations."[18]

The newspaper reported that "some of the delivery men apparently 'smelled something wrong' and failed to show up." One driver, according to reports, drove up to the place, sensed trouble, and drove away.

The "sting" was expensive—about $160 per arrest. But by the time word got around town that payments to the phony carnival man had cost the county $1,455 and angry taxpayers were threatening suit, the genial "Hartford" had left town, presumably to stage similar stings in other places. And Donohue, greatly pleased with the initiation of his cleanup campaign, promised reporters that the carnival trap "isn't anything to what will follow." It was called the "most spectacular" liquor raid in Santa Rosa.[19]

What followed for Donohue was a tragic death, unrelated to his fight against Prohibition violaters. Within two weeks of his declaration of war on bootleggers and other errant citizens, Emmett Donohue, the crusading District Attorney, was dead, killed in an automobile accident near Agua Caliente while he was on his way to Sacramento to confer with Sonoma County's legislators.

Not all the criminals were bootleggers. The "loose money" floating around the county must have been sorely tempting. In September of 1922 two Prohibition agents, Hal Emery and Harry Meyer, were arrested for their part in a bribery plot. The men allegedly accepted a bribe of $10,000 to allow several truckloads of wine to be sent from Santa Rosa to San Francisco without interference. Two weeks later, charges were filed against Meyer, Waldo Curtis, George Crawford, and several other "drys" who were accused of extorting $100,000 from Sonoma County winery owners. Part of the charges stated that the agents arrested elderly people, frightening them and subjecting them to unecessarily harsh treatment, until their relatives were willing to pay any amount to secure immunity.[20]

For local law enforcement, total prohibition was an impossibility. Harry Patteson, who would earn a reputation as the last of Sonoma County's fearless frontier sheriffs, worked as a deputy to Sheriff Mike Flohr all through the

In the photo at left, Ernest Finley, the *Press Democrat* editor who kept his sense of humor during the "dry" period, consults with his circulation manager Kenneth Brown, at left.

—Money Family Collection

"lawless" years and followed Flohr in the county's top law
enforcement job in 1934. Tom Money served as deputy to
both Flohr and Patteson before being made undersheriff.
Money long recalled his occupational frustration in those
years: "Sure, we knew what was going on," he said. "But we
didn't have a lot to do with it. It was enforced more by the
federals. They called us for assistance. We just didn't have
the personnel. There were only twelve of us in the whole
county. There were so many of them. We didn't have enough
men to do anything. We had one man at the River, one in
Sonoma, that was two. We had two jailers, night and day, that
was four. There was the sheriff and undersheriff, that was
six, a matron was seven, the telephone operator was eight
and there were four deputies. We knew where lots of 'em
were but we couldn't get out and get the evidence."[21]

If illegal wineries were as commonplace as dairies,
stills were big business in Sonoma County. Federal agents
seemed to be more serious about prosecuting the
bootleggers than they were about winemakers. The
locations were hardly secret. Five-ton trucks loaded with
sugar (a main ingredient) bounced up Kawana Springs Road
south of Santa Rosa, in full view of the neighbors. They were
bound for the old resort, which was raided by federal
agents in 1927 and named as the largest still north of San
Francisco and one of the principal suppliers to Bay Area
bootleggers, producing 1,400 gallons per day. Agents
arrested George Darnell, who said he was a steamfitter
from San Francisco who was in the process of dismantling
the distillery. Agents didn't believe him. The stately old
White Sulphur Springs Hotel, one of the important spas of
the 19th century, had been gutted by the bootleggers and
contained nothing but a two-story still. The resort owner,
Zana Taylor Weaver, daughter of White Sulphur Springs
founder John Taylor, was horrified to learn what the lessees
had done to the family resort. She ordered the hotel
building demolished.[22]

Hikers and teenagers on picnics who strayed across
the wrong field might be met, in the best backwoods

tradition, by men wearing overalls and carrying shotguns,
ordering them out of the area. There were stills in the Dry
Creek Valley, a large still in Windsor, and, probably the
largest of the "homeowned" operations, on the Garayalde
dairy beside the Laguna de Santa Rosa, off Guerneville
Road. Money recalled a raid on that still—"on the lagoon
over there, just this side of Sebastopol"—in which the feds
got "about 200 cans full of good alcohol, good stuff. It would
go around 195 proof. We walked in on them just when they
had this big truck ready to load." That dairy/still, it was said,
produced the highest-quality liquor, because the
bootleggers used fresh cow manure to bury and age the
barrels of "hooch." Santa Rosa residents who were children
during Prohibition remember being paid a quarter apiece to
go with a resort proprietor to sit atop the empty barrels in
the back seat of his car on the way to Garayalde's to have
them filled, lending the bootlegger an air of a respectable
family man on an errand with the children.

Money's firsthand accounts of Prohibition also
included recollections of raids on a still, "another big one"
on the Foote Ranch in Alexander Valley. "Three people,"
said Money, "spent time in jail over that one." He also

remembered the untimely death of Lena's husband, Alviso Bonfigli, in 1929 and his funeral, after which the police were invited to join the mourners in "a couple of drinks."

There were few true speakeasies in Sonoma County. Those were primarily big-city establishments, special places, often in basements, sometimes with entertainment, some run by mobsters. Sonoma County residents did their illegal drinking in less-sophisticated surroundings. They drank in roadhouses, big old country houses converted for the purpose. "Stopping places" is what Raford Leggett called them. "Stopping to water the horses," he recalled, was an accepted euphemism for imbibing and the roadhouses usually had a watering trough in front."[23]

The Stone House on the Sonoma highway was described as "a well-known resort" when it was raided by Sheriff John Boyes in 1923. The patrons at the time of the raid included "members of the socially elite of Santa Rosa,"

but no liquor was found. The sheriff theorized that it had been poured down the sink as officers came through the door.[24] Other popular "places" included Giacomini's Corners at the big bend in Sebastopol Road, Laloie's, east of Santa Rosa, and Smith's Corners, west of town, to name some of the closest and most familiar. But drinkers didn't need to go to the country. Many of the town's saloons, Gnesa's on Fourth Street, Jake Luppold's saloon on Main Street, and the Oberon downtown, did business (almost) as usual.

So did Tom Gemetti. Listed in the 1924 directory as a "Soft Drink Parlor, " Gemetti's Saloon on Third Street had been opened at the turn of the century by a Swiss-Italian immigrant who began with a bakery shop and switched to stronger stuff. Gemetti's sold liquor to Santa Rosans and to the farmers when they were in town before, during and after Prohibition, said family members. What was unique

—Galeazzi Family Collection

The Stone House on the Sonoma highway was one of the "stopping places" raided occasionally by officers, as were many of the roadhouses on the edges of the town.

Sister Clara is in the driver's seat while Dewey Baldocchi peddles bootleg liquor to a regular customer. Dewey and his brother Romeo improvised when Prohibition shut down the family's Piner District winery.

about this estabishment was that Gemetti's was never closed down—not by local authorities and not by the federal agents. Tom Gemetti, said his family, was extremely proud of the fact that, although "raiders" hit his place on occasion, "there was never any trouble at Gemetti's." He was proud that all the members of the Santa Rosa police force were his friends and that judges and lawyers were among his best customers.[25]

Newspaper headlines from the '20s and early '30s are indicators of the changes Prohibition made in Sonoma County life: "Rum Plant Raided in Windsor," "Laguna Still Demolished," "Poison Rum Kills Three," "'Baby-Face' Aide Arrested." Tales of Prohibition took their place in Sonoma County lore—bragging tales of the high quality of Sonoma County grappa, grandiose tales of the amount of money made by bootleggers, and rumrunner stories. These were often the accounts of sights seen and adventures participated in by fishermen and abalone hunters who happened upon an exchange from a launch anchored in an ocean cove and the parties waiting on the shore. Many an innocent man descended a cliff trail on a foggy morning to find a gun stuck in his ribs and a pointed suggestion made that he turn right around and climb back up. Others, not so innocent, picked up substantial sums of money for loading their cars with cases of Canadian whiskey and delivering it to a San Francisco address. Wes Caughey, in a letter written nearly fifty years later from his home in Iowa, recalled his surprise when, "I bought a used 1928 Chrysler roadster from a used-car lot on Santa Rosa Avenue. It had a false trunk bottom, overload springs, oversized tires and it was one of the fastest cars on the road." Caughey never knew its former owner. But he knew what it had been outfitted to do. There were mechanics in Santa Rosa who made good livings doing just that, customizing automobiles for the illegal liquor trade.[26]

Undersheriff Money's account is classic. He tells of the day he and a deputy were driving west on River Road in a sheriff's department Model A. "Along about Rio Nido, we

—*Baldocchi Collection*

passed a bakery truck from a San Francisco bakery, one of those delivery trucks with the name of the North Beach business painted on the side. We didn't think much of it since lots of San Francisco people had summer places on the River. But a few miles further on we passed another delivery truck from the same bakery. When we passed the third one, the light dawned." The deputies wheeled their Ford around and chased the trucks, catching only the last one. It was full of Canadian whiskey.

Despite the proliferation of firearms and the threats, there was comparatively little violence in Sonoma County. The rumrunners, most likely to have criminal connections, were just passing through the county with only an occasional highjacking or gunfight. One of the more colorful characters who passed through was Joseph "Fatso" Negri, who served six months in the Sonoma County Jail for rumrunning and was later arrested on a conspiracy charge for his part in the flight from justice of one of Prohibition's most-wanted gangsters, the infamous Baby-Face Nelson. Negri, whose real name was Joe Passerino, was accused of being Nelson's driver. He turned state's evidence and was released.[27] There was an incident at Bodega Bay in 1926 in which rumrunners opened fire on federal agents with machine guns. But that was rare, the kind of adventure reserved for big cities—or towns on the outskirts of Chicago.

The bootleggers, with some notable exceptions, such as the "steamfitter" owners of the Kawana Springs still, were neighbors, sometimes even old friends. They weren't apt to shoot. And the winemakers didn't consider the problem serious enough to arm themselves.

Less-than-law-abiding citizens endured the rigors of search and seizure. Home vintners had their barrels overturned and their wine dumped into field and stream. A Santa Rosa mortician gained a place in history by tipping over his hearse on the way back from the coast with a load of "imported" liquor. Home brewers often lost their product to federal agents who pierced each beer cap with an ice pick. Those in the medical profession, who could write prescriptions for alcohol for their patients, were carefully watched. Early in the 1930s, as the Great Experiment was drawing to a close, a group of Santa Rosa physicians—"all but three," one recalled—were indicted by a federal judge for selling medicinal liquor prescriptions to pharmacists who would sell the "good" liquor to favored customers. One druggist overplayed his hand, cut the prescription liquor and shipped it to San Francisco for a profitable resale. The "drys" moved in and the town's most respectable physicians were caught in the fallout. They each paid a fine of about $50. The druggist went to jail.[28]

Despite the frenetic enforcement activity, by the early 1930s change was in the wind. Wineries, long sealed, began to test the quality of what was in storage. Grape prices picked up as vintners produced grape concentrate and grape "bricks" to be used when it was over. Large wineries, such as Napa Valley's Greystone Cellars, were purchased by large corporations such as California Vineyards Company. Everyone seemed to know that Prohibition had run its course, that there was a shift in sentiment about the legal consumption of alcohol all across the country.

The newspapers published humorous editorials about the futile efforts to keep the nation on the straight and narrow path. In 1921 there were thirty-five Santa Rosa members in a national organization called The Sanity League of America, dedicated to the legalization of light wine and beer. Even the clergy, eventually, was willing to admit defeat. A Congregationalist minister, addressing a convention in Santa Rosa in the early '30s, told his audience, "You can't dry up Sonoma County for Sonoma County is very, very wet."[29]

In the spring of 1932 the Santa Rosa City Council voted four to one to support the repeal of the 18th Amendment. They drew the wrath of the WCTU and its president, Maria Helena (Mrs. H.M) Reeves, who said she spoke for 108 homes in Santa Rosa, but were heartily applauded by the Sonoma County Grape and Hop Growers, who responded that they represented 15,000 voters. In March of 1933 beer became legal and Congressman Lea was leading the fight to see wine follow suit, as quickly as possible. In May the drugstores put their old liquor and wine on sale without prescription. Some of it, the newspaper reported with undisguised glee, contained as much as 22 percent alcohol.

The vote on Repeal came in June. Californians voted for it, three to one. In Santa Rosa the vote to nullify Prohibition was a whopping six to one. December 5, 1933, Utah became the thirty-sixth state to ratify Repeal and the United States was, officially, "wet" once more. Sonoma County wineries had been gearing up, getting equipment ready. Two weeks after Repeal there were seventy wineries operating in the county, and Italian Swiss Colony threw a grand party at Asti to celebrate the first shipment of legal wine—fifteen express cars filled with 45,000 gallons. By the

A case of Korbel champagne from the Guerneville cellars was among the many thank-you gifts shipped to the White House from California's winemakers to celebrate the repeal of Prohibition.

Franklin Delano Roosevelt
White House
Washington, D.C.

Bubbling Sunshine from Grateful Californians

KORBEL'S VINEYARD

SONOMA COUNTY, CAL.

KORBEL SEC.

rbel & Bros ......San Francisco, Cal.

end of 1933, Santa Rosa's speakeasies closed. Saloon-keepers paid their government stamps and bought their liquor licenses. By the start of 1935, there were twenty-five restaurants in Santa Rosa serving "hard liquor by the drink."[30]

There was some consternation when the cities lost control of liquor licenses to a new State Board of Equalization, which would enforce liquor laws by district. But, in 1937, when the City Treasurer received a check for $9,819.41 for Santa Rosa's share of 1936 Board of Equalization funds, the outlook seemed brighter.

Governor James Rolph, early in the Repeal campaign, had pardoned at least 1,000 Californians who had criminal records as a result of Prohibition laws. In Santa Rosa, bootlegger and customer alike returned to business as usual. Fortunes had been made. That was an accepted fact. And arrests, even jail terms, were put behind. While there was no great honor in being caught bootlegging, there was no great shame either. The shame, as any businessman or farmer would have said, was Prohibition's immediate effect on the hop market and the long-range effect on the wine industry. The 256 wineries in the county had been reduced to seventy by 1933.

The 42,000 acres of vineyards that prospered in Sonoma County before World War I were reduced to less than 10,000 acres by 1940. And, what was worse, Prohibition changed America's drinking habits. There was a new trend toward lighter-tasting beer, using less hops. The high-quality California wine grapes had been uprooted when grape growers discovered that delicate, thin-skinned Chardonnays and Cabernet Sauvignon grapes could not survive the rail trip to East Coast home winemakers. They were supplanted by the tougher, harsher Alicante Bouchets and Carignanes, which produced a rougher, less palatable wine. Also, Americans, including women, caught up in the excitement of the bootleg era, had learned to drink hard liquor. The resulting changes this made in Sonoma County agriculture would alter the patterns on the land for half a century. ❧

Frontier Justice

The lynching of George Boyd, Terry Fitts, and Spanish Charley Valento in Santa Rosa in December of 1920 was the next to the last lynching in the west.[1] Dramatic accounts of the event created widespread notoriety for the town. In some respects, it was the defining event of the Prohibition era in Sonoma County, although the circumstances had little or nothing to do with liquor laws. Illustrated by a chilling photograph, which was widely circulated, the "Santa Rosa necktie party" quickly passed into folklore. The truth about who was involved in the lynching and how it came about would not be reported for sixty-five years.[2]

Santa Rosa was not the logical setting for this ultimate act of violence. Certainly, the town seemed peaceable enough at the start of the 20th century. The municipal crime report for 1901 listed five arrests for use of vulgar language, 146 arrests for drunkenness, twenty-two citations for riding bicycles on the sidewalk, and one fine for "fast driving."

There was no hint, even in the years following the earthquake, when everyone worked so hard, that before the half-century mark, Santa Rosa would be known throughout the state as a tough, frontier town. And Sonoma County would be synonymous with the "Wild West" to many, particularly those with concerns about civil liberties and due process.

The events leading up to the hangings are well-documented. Spanish Charley Valento was a member of Spud Murphy's Howard Street Gang, a collection of San Francisco toughs known throughout the state for their violent acts. Terry Fitts was from Santa Rosa, recently released from the penitentiary and well-acquainted with Murphy's gang. George Boyd was another San Francisco hoodlum who accompanied Fitts and Valento to Santa Rosa to hide out from police. The men were being sought by San Francisco police for questioning about the gang rape of two young women, one of them the daughter of a Petaluma Salvation Army captain, in Valento's Howard Street shack.[3]

Fitts knew his way around Santa Rosa and had taken his friends to Pete Guidotti's house on Seventh Street, trying to borrow money. Guidotti refused. They wheedled some soup from Guidotti's wife and were seated in the living room, eating, when Sonoma County Sheriff Jim Petray and two San Francisco police officers, Detective Lester Dohrman and Sergeant Miles Jackson, came through the front door. The officers had been searching Santa Rosa's west end hotels and speakeasies after a tip that the trio had come in on the up train.

Fitts, the only one of the three who was armed, had laid his revolver on an end table and when the men came through the door, Boyd reached for the gun and emptied it at the three officers. Detective Dohrman lived a couple of hours and died at Mary Jesse Hospital on Fifth Street. Sergeant Jackson and Sheriff Petray died there on the living room floor.

Deputies, who had surrounded the house before the three officers went in, easily captured the three men. Boyd, seriously wounded by a shot from Jackson as he fell, was taken with his companions to the Sonoma County Jail.

Crowds gathered at the jail every night until Petray was buried, shouting and waving their fists in anger at the men inside, threatening mob violence. On the night of Petray's funeral, his widow came to the jail and spoke to the crowd, urging them to go home and let justice take its course. But on the fifth night after the murders, the men were lynched—taken from the jail by force and hanged from a tree in the cemetery.

Reporters wrote that the "mob" of 200 or more armed masked men who "overpowered" jail guards and seized the three men were "probably San Francisco policemen," colleagues of Jackson and Dohrman. They wrote that masked men wore uniform coats turned inside out to conceal the identifying insignias. There were published reports of a caravan of automobiles passing through Cotati, heading south after the lynching. The "out of town" theory prevailed. The following day, when the grand

The macabre photograph at right, the work of an unknown photographer, established the 1920 Santa Rosa lynching as part of western lore.

jury met, jurors returned a verdict within minutes of "death by persons unknown." No investigation was made. No charges were filed.

In truth, it was not a mob at all but a disciplined band of vigilantes with leadership and several days of intense training. They did not "overpower" guards; the keys were handed to them. And they were not San Franciscans but volunteers from in and around the town of Healdsburg, all friends of the popular sheriff known as "Sunny Jim" Petray.[4]

The full story of the lynching came to light sixty-five years later, told by a man who was the youngest member of the vigilante group. His confession would validate the story many people had known but not talked about, and it would cast the newspapers in an accomplice's role for their attempts to shift blame out of Sonoma County. Only Petaluma's *Argus*, of all the area's newspapers, had carried a small story reporting that the lynchers had come from Healdsburg.

The formation of the vigilante group was a carefully selective process. There were no more than thirty men in all, chosen from one hundred or more ranchers and businessmen who offered to participate. Petray was from a pioneer Healdsburg family and these men were his neighbors. The leader, or "captain" as they called him—in deference to his service as a World War I officer and pilot—chose carefully, making certain that each man had a specific assignment. He wanted to avoid, he told his "troops," anyone who was going to get trigger-happy and blow the plan.

The decision to lynch the men responsible for Petray's death was made the night of the day he was shot. Two days later the group was organized enough to begin training. They drilled for three nights—practiced their assignments and stations—in a room in back of the Standard Machine Works in Healdsburg. On the night of December 10, they met there and set out for Santa Rosa and the jail.

The captain spoke to the men before they left. "If any one of you wants to back out," he is reported to have said, "this is the time. Do it now. There won't be one word said. Nobody will think you're a coward. But if you stay, from now on, we're all one."[5]

The men came down from Healdsburg in twelve to fifteen cars, not as a caravan, but separately. When they approached the center of Santa Rosa, they spread out, parking close to the jail on different streets. All were masked with cowboy-style bandanas, red or blue.

Inside the jail, no deputies moved to stop them. Several men carried cutting torches to cut the locks if the keys were not easily surrendered. But officers handed them over without protest, and the men moved to the cells where the three were being held. Valento and Fitts were in cells upstairs. Boyd, who was injured, was downstairs, his wounds bound with a bandage around his mid-section, blood staining the suit of long underwear he was wearing.

It was very dark—December weather, cold and damp but no rain—when the cars which were now formed in a caravan moved toward the Rural Cemetery on Franklin Avenue. The drivers parked them in a semi-circle with their lights on. A couple of vehicles had spotlights which they trained on a big locust tree about fifty yards from the street.[6] There, beside the new, cannonball-ringed monument to war veterans, they hanged the three men with the nooses they had brought with them.

The captain held his men until he was certain the three were dead, then they returned to Healdsburg—some on the highway, some by rural roads like Coffey Lane. A news story in Petaluma's *Argus* that week told of how a crowd of Healdsburg residents, both men and women, were waiting in the plaza to cheer the men as they returned, horns blaring in triumph. According to the same *Argus* story, there were many bandanas found next morning along the Healdsburg road.[7]

They met once more at the Standard Machine Works and the captain took roll. According to accounts from one who was present, he outlined the procedure: "If you are questioned keep quiet; answer simple questions only but do not name any of your companions. If you are taken into custody," he promised them, "the rest of us will come and get you." Then the men returned home to their wives and mothers, most of whom had known of the plans since the inception. The event was

The funeral of Sheriff Jim Petray, whose death precipitated one of the last lynchings in the western United States.

—*Healdsburg Museum*

rarely discussed among them in their lifetimes, even in the most oblique terms.[8]

If the 1920 lynching was not a conversation topic for the participants, it certainly was for other residents of Santa Rosa and Sonoma County. The events of that December midnight were told and retold, although the moral of the story was unclear. While some Santa Rosans continued to point to the lynching as a message to lawbreakers that they should avoid this area, others were ashamed and embarrassed at the town's association with so primitive and violent an act.

The ropes, taken from the men's necks, were cut into small pieces, until only the nooses remained intact. The bits of rope, some no longer than a frayed inch, were labeled and kept as treasured souvenirs. The locust tree where the men were hanged became a tourist attraction. So many chips were whittled from its limbs and trunk by souvenir seekers that it became unsightly, and the Santa Rosa City Council ordered the entire tree removed. Members of the Saturday Afternoon Club, an exclusive women's organization, praised the decision.[9] The motivation was beyond aesthetics. There was a distinct attempt to expunge history in the governmental decision.

At the end of Prohibition, in 1933, when speakeasies and other "resorts" were still thriving businesses in Sonoma County, a private security officer, hired by businessmen to patrol their premises, was shot and killed outside a west Santa Rosa "speak" by hold-up men intent on robbing the illegal establishment.

The officer was Carlos Rolland Carrick, sixty, a sixteen-year veteran of the Oakland Police Department, known as "Bill" to his friends. Carrick, who had operated a merchants' patrol in Santa Rosa for eleven years, was killed when he exchanged shots with a gang of robbers. The shooting took place in an alley adjoining the Buon Gusto, the new name Lena Battaglia Bonfigli had chosen for her

THE WEATHER—

THE PRESS DEMOCRAT
SONOMA COUNTY'S LEADING NEWSPAPER

—JUST 14 DAYS—

VOL. XLVIII   SANTA ROSA, CALIFORNIA, FRIDAY, DECEMBER 10, 1920 —EIGHT PAGES   NO. 139

GANGSTERS LYNCHED!
Armed Mob Takes Boyd, Valento and Fitts
From Jail; Hangs Them on Cemetery Tree

family's old Battaglia Hotel at Sixth and Adams streets.[10]

Police followed a trail of blood to a West Eighth Street apartment where they found and arrested a notorious San Francisco gangland character, Andrew "Doctor" Mareck, twenty-nine, who had been tried but acquitted on murder charges in San Francisco the previous year. The actual killer of Carrick, however, had escaped. Identified by police as another gangland operative, twenty-eight-year-old Frank J. "Slim" Hoyt, he eluded detectives for eighteen months before he was arrested in Sacramento and returned to Santa Rosa to stand trial. An accomplice, George Jones, was arrested five months after the shooting.

The shooting ended a carefully laid plot by Mareck's San Francisco gang to "knock over" prosperous resorts in the Santa Rosa area. Working with two Santa Rosa men who had been employed as printers at the *Press Democrat*, the bandits went first to a brothel south of Santa Rosa, between Petaluma Hill Road and Redwood Highway South, popularly known as 101 Ranch. There they robbed the owner, Dorothy Leonard, at gunpoint, tied her up, along with three of her female employees and their customers, and left, warning them not to try to get loose for half an hour. The men and women worked loose from their bonds immediately and ran to their cars, attempting to follow the bandits, but found the gang had not only cut telephone wires to the house but had also removed the distributor heads from the cars.

From the 101 Ranch, the bandits went directly to the speakeasy at the rear of the Buon Gusto. There they robbed the cash box and the three slot machines, took what money the employees and customers had on them, and went out. Carrick, who was inspecting a light that had gone out in the alley, spotted them and was killed. Evidence indicated an execution-style killing, since Carrick was shot through the roof of his mouth and through the temple at very close range, as well as in the chest.

Mareck and printer Ralph Thatcher were arrested in Santa Rosa. Mareck's wife Thelma and two other accomplices, printer Frank Gingg and another "character" well known to San Francisco police, Tony Cardinelli, were picked up at the Mareck's San Francisco home where they had driven immediately after the shooting.

There were threats of lynching by friends of Carrick, who was a popular member of the Santa Rosa Elks Club. When a mob of 200 gathered outside the jail, Sheriff Mike Flohr elected to remove all the prisoners to San Francisco for safekeeping. Mareck, as the "brains" of the bandit gang, was brought to trial in May for the murder of Carrick, found guilty, and sentenced to life imprisonment, as was George Jones. "Slim" Hoyt, the one that got away, was apprehended in September of the following year (1934) in Sacramento. Hoyt, whose real name turned out to be Bernard Felts, stood trial in Santa Rosa and was given a life sentence.[11]

Violence was a recurring theme in the counties north of San Francisco Bay in 1935. In January of that year, four San Quentin convicts seized the members of the State Parole Board, who were meeting at the Marin County prison. The inmates battered the prison warden, James B. Holohan, to near death and commandeered the warden's car and driver. Led by robber Rudolph Straight, they headed the big Studebaker touring car north.

In Santa Rosa, Sheriff Harry Patteson was in the office when word of the escape came in over the state police telegraph. He immediately gathered available deputies and a handful of highway patrolmen who happened to be in the office and organized a posse, which deployed in four cars. Patteson sent two cars toward the coast, the other two south toward Marin. Patteson himself drove a big Dodge sedan, the model they called "The Ram." With him were Deputy Bill Cook and Jim Shanks of the highway patrol. Patteson's chief criminal deputy, a tall young man not long off the Santa Clara University football team's front line, the future Santa Rosa police chief Melvin (Dutch) Flohr was driving a Buick. With Flohr was Deputy (later to be sheriff) Johnny Ellis and another highway patrolman, Ernie Roberts.

The only information they had was the bulletin received in the sheriff's office before they left. At Bodega Corners, the cars stopped and Flohr ran into a house to telephone the undersheriff, Tom Money, who had been left to monitor the telegraph. Money told Flohr they were headed for Tomales, so the two carloads of armed men headed for the Two Rock road. There, coming the other way, was the carload of convicts and their hostages. The highway patrolmen, Shanks and Roberts, jumped out of the cars and shot the rear tires out on the Studebaker. It went out of control, regained the road, and kept going. The swerving Studebaker and its pursuers went through the town of Tomales where the Sonoma County lawmen slowed enough to allow Marin District Attorney Al Bagshaw and Constable John Bones, who had been at a district court hearing in Tomales when they heard the news, to jump in. With Patteson and Cook in the lead, they continued the chase, heading for the coastal community of Valley Ford, back in Sonoma County.

The chase through Valley Ford was like a scene from a gangster movie. The telephone operator in Tomales had just reached the Valley Ford operator, Grace Cunninghame,

Santa Rosa Police Chief Charlie O'Neal was shot dead by rancher Al Chamberlain in 1935.

—American Legion Collection

Charlie O'Neal. With Patteson in command, they surrounded the creamery. Outlaw Straight, attempting to slip out the rear door and slide along the wall, came face to face with District Attorney Bagshaw, who shot him with a sawed-off shotgun, wounding him fatally. Another convict's attempt to go out the front door met a hail of gunfire from Deputy Ellis. The convicts surrendered.

How did the Santa Rosa lawmen know where to go? Flohr credited Sheriff Patteson. "Harry had a theory about escapes," Flohr said in an interview many years later. "He just figured they'd always head up the coast. He pointed us that way instinctively. And he was right."[12]

The summer of '35 was an uncomfortable one in Sonoma County. Tempers rose with the temperatures as labor unrest and radical politics posed threats of drastic changes. There were several acts of violence in that summer but none sadder than the killing of Santa Rosa Police Chief Charlie O'Neal.

Al Chamberlain was seventy-seven years old that summer, when he went on his shooting spree, gunned down a man on his Alpine Valley ranch, reloaded his big cowboy pistols, came to town, and shot the chief. He was on his way to shoot the sheriff when his plan went awry—a plan that called for him to be lynched, western-style, like the men who had been hanged fifteen years before.[13]

Chamberlain was a real honest-to-God cowboy. He had been one all his life. He was the last of a cattle-raising family that owned hundreds of acres of range land around Santa Rosa. Until 1930 he owned a horse corral on Sonoma Avenue, along the creek, near the site that would one day hold the City Hall. He acted as a guide and packmaster for hunting expeditions into the hills, gave town children free horseback rides, and "commuted" to his ranch on St. Helena Road on horseback.

Some townspeople teased Chamberlain. The horse, after all, had been replaced by the automobile for more

who had a switchboard in her garage, to tell her that the chase was headed her way, when Cunninghame heard the gunshots outside. Deputy Cook was spraying bullets from his submachine gun across the rear of the Studebaker, which was still swerving, only marginally in control due to the flat rear tires. Heading north on Highway 1, they turned left on the Dillon Beach Road. On a turn by the Valley Ford Creamery, the fleeing prisoners finally lost control of the damaged Studebaker. It crashed through a fence and smashed into a shack used as living quarters by the creamery.

The convicts had forced the parole board to don prison garb before they left San Quentin. Flohr would recall: "They jumped out of the car and we didn't know who to shoot. They were all dressed alike." Herding hostages ahead of them, the escapees ran into the creamery, firing as they ran. Inside, they shoved employees into a big walk-in ice box and slammed the door.

Reinforcements arrived from the Petaluma and Santa Rosa police departments, including Santa Rosa's Chief

than two decades. It was said that some members of the police department taunted Chamberlain, called him the "cavalry frontiersman."[14] And city officials, who heard complaints about the smell and the flies generated by his "downtown" horse corral, ordered him to close down. It was Chief O'Neal who signed the final notice telling Chamberlain he had three days to get out before the city

destroyed his corral. That was in 1930. Later, Chamberlain would set that as the date when his mind began to go.

Chamberlain's frustrations with the automobile were well known to the people of Santa Rosa. Young boys shared their fathers' bemusement at Chamberlain's antic attempts to learn to drive, pulling back on the steering wheel and yelling "Whoa!" when he tried to stop his old Chevrolet touring car. If the curb didn't stop him, witnesses said, he'd run up on the sidewalk.[15] Chief O'Neal warned him that he had to get his vehicle under control, that if he couldn't learn to drive, he'd have to stay out of town. But Chamberlain did neither.

On one of these trips to the sidewalk when the car wouldn't "Whoa!" Chamberlain's Chevrolet struck a woman pedestrian and knocked her down. By Chamberlain's account, she was unhurt and even laughed as she brushed herself off. But Chief O'Neal was unamused and brought Chamberlain into court on a charge of reckless driving. He was fined $100 and sentenced to spend a month in jail. Adding insult to injury, O'Neal reportedly taunted him in the courtroom, teasingly suggesting that the judge raise the fine.

For Chamberlain, the stay in jail changed his life; but not in the way O'Neal had intended. He still drove his bucking motorcar, but he became a genuine eccentric. He dressed old-fashioned in flannel shirts reminiscent of the '49ers, big cowboy hats, and boots. He had cards printed that read "Alfred F. (Two-Gun Al) Chamberlain, Santa Rosa Outlaw and Jailbird" and handed them to people he met on the street.[16]

Meanwhile, his financial state worsened. He sold most of his ranch to a man named John McCabe and lost the rest in a tax sale (also to McCabe) in 1935. Later, he would say that this news brought him to his decision to "clean the slate." By his own admission, he planned to kill McCabe, Chief O'Neal, Sheriff Patteson, and his insurance agent Harold Jones, who, he felt, had betrayed him in the loss of his land. Then, he reasoned, a mob would come and lynch him, putting a genuine Wild West ending to the life of Two-Gun Al.

On July 15, a Monday morning, Chamberlain loaded three guns, climbed into his dented roadster, and drove to his old home ranch where McCabe now lived. He waited for him in the shadow of the barn door and when he arrived, told him to put the horses up, that he wanted to talk to him. He shot John McCabe eight times, climbed back into his roadster, and drove to town, stopping at the top of Calistoga grade to reload.

He walked into the police station on Hinton Avenue and found O'Neal alone. He shot him three times, turned, and headed out to find Patteson. The sheriff was next door at the jail. He heard the shots and saw Chamberlain coming. The old cowboy had a .44 in one hand, a nickel-plated .45 in

At left, "Two-Gun Al" Chamberlain tells his story to Sheriff Harry Patteson after the shooting of Chief O'Neal. Above, Sheriff Patteson displays the weapons Chamberlain used.

The sensational trial of Dr. Willard Burke, above, with District Attorney Clarence Lea, upper right, as prosecutor, resulted in a prison sentence for attempted murder for the well-known Santa Rosa physician in 1911.

the other. The guns were pointing downward. Patteson, who was unarmed, started walking toward Chamberlain and just kept walking. Chamberlain asked him, "Are you Harry Patteson?" and the sheriff said, "Hell, no, I'm not Patteson. What do you want with Patteson?" Both men kept walking.

As recognition came to Chamberlain's face, he raised his arms and fired once. Patteson hit him, hurling his body toward the old man in a football-style block, and the bullet nicked a corner of the Grand Garage, across Third Street. Chamberlain went down and two men who had been watching from the service station between the police station and the jail—station owner Joe Schurman and merchant Burnette Dibble—came running, each grabbing a gun from the fallen man's hands. The old cowboy was only halfway through his schedule. But it was over.[17]

Chief O'Neal died two days later. John McCabe rallied and recovered from his multiple wounds. Sheriff Patteson had Al Chamberlain moved to San Quentin that same night to discourage any talk of mob action. Chamberlain went to trial in September and was sentenced to life in San Quentin, where he died.

———

Earlier crimes of the 20th century seemed gentle in comparison to the frontier violence of the '20s and '30s. But the century was no more than ten years gone in Sonoma County when the first "crime of passion" captured the attention of the entire Bay Area.

The famous Dr. Burke, known for his "cures" of nearly every condition that plagued mankind, was the accused. As owner of Burke's Sanitarium on Mark West Springs Road, which brought hundreds of people from the Bay Area annually to avail themselves of his well-publicized regimen for better health, Dr. Willard Burke had been a respected member of the community for some thirty years. Thus, his involvement in a celebrated "crime of passion" was widely reported.

Early in 1910, a young woman named Lu Etta Smith, who was living in a cottage on Burke's property with her infant son, was injured in a blast that destroyed her cabin. Burke was arrested for attempted murder based on allegations that Smith was his mistress, that he was the father of her child, and that he had planted the charge of Hercules powder that caused the explosion. Further, the evidence showed, he then treated Miss Smith's wounds with a salve containing arsenic.

Dr. Burke first engaged the well-known attorney Hiram Johnson to act in his defense. Johnson and Sonoma County's thirty-five-year-old district attorney, Clarence Lea, met at the grand jury hearing on the matter, even as Johnson was canvassing the state to assess his chances in a campaign for governor. Lea came from the grand jury convinced that an in-depth investigation of the dynamiting incident was necessary.

Before the trial began, Johnson had made his decision to make his successful run for governor and Santa Rosa attorney J. Rollo Leppo had taken over the defense. Lea used every courtroom maneuver available to him to

155

convict Burke. At one stage, he invited the jury outside the courtroom where he had constructed a tent-house with a charge of dynamite on the outside and a cardboard facsimile of Lu Etta on the bed. A match was struck. The dynamite went off. Piece by piece the remains of the tent-house were presented as evidence to the jury. The defense based its case on the sanity of Lu Etta, as she believed that her baby, reportedly fathered by Burke, had been born of "astral conception" and that the baby was the new Christ. Judge Emmet Seawell ruled that the jury would observe the baby to see if it resembled Dr. Burke.[18]

Burke was convicted on January 28, 1911, and sent to prison. Paroled in 1915, he was granted a full pardon in January of 1916 by his former defense attorney, Governor Hiram Johnson. The petition for pardon was signed by the trial judge, Emmet Seawell, prosecutor Lea, the members of the jury that had convicted him, the state treasurer and future governor, Friend Richardson, and former state Senator Louis Juilliard.[19]

There was a second sensational trial in 1910, that of Willard Thomas and his wife Mary, accused of cutting the throat of their infant daughter and tossing her body in the creek. The twenty-nine-year-old father confessed. A religious man who sang in his church choir, Thomas told police the baby had been born just four days after he and his wife had wed and he feared disgrace. He was sentenced to life in prison. The baby's nineteen-year-old mother was tried twice. The first trial ended in a hung jury, the second in a verdict of not guilty.

At the end of the summer of 1910, an editorial in the *Press Democrat* praised Lea for handling the largest number of criminal cases in the history of the county with only one acquittal—the young mother, Mary Thomas. Lea's courtroom successes became a springboard to a long political career. He was elected to Congress in 1916 and served for more than thirty years.

The other sensational murder of 1910 was the Kendall Family slaying in Cazadero. The bodies of Enoch and Eura Kendall and their son, Thomas, were hacked to pieces and scattered over the ranch property and burned in the ranch house stove. The family was leasing the Lion's Head Ranch on Austin Creek from its East Bay owners, prominent architect Henry Starbuck and his wife Margaret. The murder came to light when Mrs. Starbuck called Oakland police to say that Henry Yamiguchi, a laborer on the ranch, had come to her home in Oakland and confessed the bloody deeds. Before police arrived, the laborer left. He was never seen again.

Suspicious Cazadero residents, who liked and respected the Kendall family and thought Mrs. Starbuck "odd," remembered the lawsuit filed by the Starbucks against the Kendalls the previous year to attempt to break their lease. Mrs. Starbuck wanted to turn the property into a Japanese art colony. But, while neighbors suspected her, authorities continued to pursue Yamiguchi, to no avail. He was never captured and no charges were ever filed.[20]

Immigrant murders were not uncommon in Sonoma County as new Americans, generally at the bottom of the economic ladder, reacted with violence to the alienation of life in a foreign culture. In 1917 Hom Hong, a Chinese laborer on the Harrison Finley hop ranch on Mark West Road, was murdered, leading police to a San Francisco "tong" with members in both Petaluma and Santa Rosa. Investigation led to the arrest and deportation of six Chinese immigrants.

The following year a Japanese farmworker named Morisawa killed two of his fellow immigrants in a lodging house at the foot of D Street in the tiny Japantown section of Santa Rosa's creekside Chinatown. Exactly two months after the crime was committed, Morisawa was sentenced by Judge Emmet Seawell to "hang by the neck until dead." The following year, at San Quentin, he was executed in that fashion. In 1923, an Afghan immigrant, Ullah Mohanned was hanged at the prison for the murder of a fellow Afghan in Petaluma.[21]

For forty years, the statistical list of homicides in Sonoma County was topped with the name of Polcercarpio Pio, who murdered four people in one bloody evening in 1949. Pio, a Filipino hop worker on the Wohler Ranch west of Santa Rosa, used a shotgun to kill his former sweetheart, her new husband, and her sister, and then walked to the adjoining Grace Ranch to kill a fellow immigrant whom, he said later, had once threatened to kill him. Pio pleaded guilty and did not stand trial. The crimes occurred on the first of November. In mid-December he was sentenced to life in prison. On December 31 he was taken to San Quentin. [22]

Many crimes received sensational treatment in the local and Bay Area newspapers in mid-century, including the bludgeoning deaths of two Sonoma State Hospital employees who were killed with a stone pestle while they slept in their home in the mountains above the Sonoma Valley in 1949. Their killer, an acquaintance named Henry Gulbrandsen, contributed to his own notoriety by confessing the next day, in Eureka, to a newspaper reporter for the *Humboldt Times*. The newsman won a prize offered by a popular radio show of the time, the *Pall Mall Big Story* award, for his reporting on Gulbrandsen's surrender. This guaranteed that the crime would receive national exposure as a radio dramatization. Gulbrandsen was executed in the gas chamber at San Quentin.

The last Sonoma County criminal to die in the gas chamber for at least forty years was a well-known real estate man named Joseph (Jack) Daugherty. At his trial in 1952, defense attorneys attempted to prove Daugherty insane when he stabbed his ex-wife Florena to death the day after he was granted a divorce from her. The murder occurred in February in the garden of the Daughertys' Linwood Avenue home, as two of their five children looked on. But a jury rejected the insanity plea and Daugherty was sentenced to die at San Quentin. The execution was carried out in 1954. [23]

The rural character of Sonoma County often attracted fugitives from justice looking for hiding places. In 1916, socialists Tom Mooney and William Billings hid out in a Guerneville campground after a bomb exploded at San Francisco's Preparedness Day parade, killing ten and injuring forty. Police arrested Mooney at the camp five days after the bombing. Billings escaped but was later captured. [24]

Prohibition, when crime got organized, resulted in a migration of professional criminals from urban areas into rural Sonoma County, where they hoped to go unnoticed. Recurring rumors of mob connections to Sonoma Valley resorts in the Roaring '20s meant that cautious residents kept their eyes open and their mouths shut. There were suggestions, unproven, that the mob owned the Sonoma Mission Inn for a time. Two brothers, owners of a "hot spot" in Agua Caliente called the Lark Club, were shot in a San Francisco bootleg war. Reports that the infamous gangster Baby-Face Nelson had worked in "protection" in the Sonoma Valley for a time lent local interest to the news stories when the law finally ran him down. Santa Rosa newspapermen of the time would later recall that Baby-Face rode shotgun on bootleg liquor deliveries for the Parente gang, operating out of Fetters Springs. [25]

Later, in the summer of 1934, Nelson moved up to Public Enemy Number One with the shooting of John Dillinger. Federal authorities came looking for him, fruitlessly, in Sonoma County when he was reported in hiding at "an El Verano inn" with his driver. The driver, a thug named Joe (Fatso) Negri, was arrested in 1935 as a rumrunner, smuggling liquor at Salt Point, and served a term in the Sonoma County Jail. He was later freed as a government witness.

Rural stills, producing bootleg whiskey, were attended regularly by men who dressed their parts, in dark suits and hats pulled low over their eyes, arriving in long black cars. Chicago was not so far away from Sonoma County, so it seemed.

It was fifteen years after Prohibition ended that Chicago's gangster image was literally visited upon post-World War II Santa Rosa, still a relatively innocent small city

— Press Democrat Collection

A crowd of San Francisco police and press gather around as the body of mobster Nick DeJohn, shown in a Chicago police photo at right, is removed from an automobile trunk after his gangland murder in 1947. DeJohn had been living in Santa Rosa with his family under an assumed name.

When San Francisco police found the Chrysler abandoned in North Beach and investigated, they found the keys were still in the ignition and the tail of a man's overcoat was sticking out of the trunk. The overcoat was on the garroted body of Vincent Rossi. He had been strangled with a piece of piano wire.

Within hours, police knew that Vincent Rossi of Bryden Lane, Santa Rosa, was in fact Nick DeJohn of Chicago, Illinois—gambler, hoodlum, muscleman, and former associate of gangster Al Capone. DeJohn had departed his hometown in haste in '46, after the gangland killing of his relative and employer, Vincent "The Don" Benevento, a well-established Mafioso known as "The Cheese King" of Chicago. When the story was published, neighbors finally had an explanation for the many unusual friends who visited the Rossi family regularly—men in expensive shirts and silk suits who gave lavish tips to the astonished bellhops at the Occidental Hotel.

The DeJohn case occupied the newspapers for months.[26] Headlines linked DeJohn to "a nationwide dope ring." San Francisco police questioned people called Loud Mouth Levine, Big Nose Charlie, and Big Al. DeJohn's movements were traced through his last days. He was placed in "an El Verano resort" in the company of a known Mafia triggerman two days before his death. The three men he dined and drank with in San Francisco clubs the night of his death were arrested. Lena "Rossi" DeJohn retained the famed San Francisco defense lawyer Vincent Hallinan to represent her at the inquest.

The star witness at the trial was Anita Venza, well known to San Francisco police as an abortionist (she was, in fact, convicted in 1955 of running an "abortion mill" in Glen Ellen), who claimed to have overheard the men plotting to kill DeJohn. But, after the trial began, San Francisco's district attorney, Edmund G. "Pat" Brown, determined that Venza was a pathological liar.[27] He asked the judge to grant a mistrial, seeing any case he might have had against the accused men vanish. The case was never reopened.

of 15,000. The main character in the 1947 drama was a man named Vincent Rossi. At least, that's what he told his Santa Rosa neighbors. Rossi told people he was a retired (at age thirty-nine) furniture dealer from the Midwest. He had plenty of money and, with his wife Lena and their four children, lived comfortably in a house they purchased in 1946 on Bryden Lane in the Proctor Terrace area.

Rossi spent much of his day in his garden or in the porch swing, idly watching the world go by. Lena, a frail woman, was considered very religious by the women in the neighborhood, who commented to each other on how often her car was parked outside St. Rose Church. The car was an attention-getter, a racy red Chrysler Town & Country sports coupe, which the young men of Santa Rosa carefully noted when the Rossi family drove downtown in the evening to order ice cream sodas and play the jukebox at a Fourth Street fountain.

Vernon Silvershield was Sonoma County Coroner from 1942 until his death in 1958. In the first six years he was in office, "Silver," as he was known to friends, was also the police reporter and photographer for Santa Rosa's daily newspapers.

In 1939 Sheriff Al Wilkie's entire department numbered eleven, counting the jail cook, who is shown at far left, back row. Also in the back row, from left, Deputy Early, Primo Rocco, William Barnett, Paul Noonan, and an unidentified officer. Front row, from left, matron Grace Bixby, called "Lady Grace" by her colleagues, an unidentified deputy, Sheriff Wilkie, Stuart Rich, and future sheriff John Ellis.

Theories about the DeJohn case abound.[28] Ten years later the Senate Rackets Committee linked the DeJohn murder to a Chicago attempt to take over Texas labor rackets. Others said it was DeJohn's misuse of gambling funds that was the cause.[29]

Gambling money was also offered as an answer to the question that puzzled Santa Rosa residents: why did this Chicago mobster choose Santa Rosa as the new home for the "Rossi family?" There were attempts to prove that DeJohn was connected to a group of suspicious businessmen, led by San Francisco nightclub owner Jack Kent, who were constructing what they said was a resort but appeared to be a gambling casino and brothel on the site of an old French family resort called Villa Chanticleer on Fitch Mountain in Healdsburg.

Kent was called to testify in the inquiry that followed DeJohn's slaying but denied any knowledge of the murder or the man. The attention that was focused on the Healdsburg project, however, stopped construction work. Kent and his partners abandoned the enterprise, leaving

—Press Democrat Collection

*H*arry Patteson wore the sheriff's star for twenty-one years, longer than any in Sonoma County's history. He was something of a hero sheriff in the days when being sheriff also meant wearing a white hat and riding a horse at the head of the mounted posse in every parade in the county.

The path he followed to the county's top law enforcement job was the traditional one. He was a deputy, a city policeman, a small-town police chief, and a chief criminal deputy. Like the other hero sheriff, the slain Jim Petray, Patteson came from a Healdsburg-area ranch family—with political interests. His father C.L. "Ned" Patteson had been county supervisor from the northern district.

Harry began his career within a year after Petray's death and the subsequent lynching, signing on as a deputy to Sheriff Boyes. He left to work for Santa Rosa's Chief George Matthews as a police officer but returned to the sheriff's office when Sonoma resident Joseph Ryan was elected sheriff. Ryan's death in office involved Patteson in the intense politics of county law enforcement. When Supervisor Joseph McMinn was appointed by his colleagues on the board to fill Ryan's term, Patteson, who had openly opposed the appointment, left to rejoin the Santa Rosa police department.

In 1926, he ran for sheriff but was eclipsed in the voting by both Mike Flohr, Petaluma's police chief, and the winner, E. Douglas Bills. The difference between Bills and Flohr was a scant sixteen votes. In 1930, Flohr, backed by Patteson, defeated Bills and appointed Patteson his chief criminal deputy. When Flohr died in 1934, Patteson was appointed to serve the final months of his term. In August of 1934, he won his first election. But in 1938, he lost to a county forest ranger, Andrew "Al" Wilkie.

He retreated to the family ranch, but raising prunes was not his life's work. He became Healdsburg's police chief in 1940, succeeding the young man who had been his chief deputy when he was sheriff, Melvin F. "Dutch" Flohr. In 1942 he ran against Wilkie and beat him in a close election. In 1946 he beat Wilkie again. In 1950 he was re-elected, but not before he encountered a barrage of opposition from the *Press Democrat*.

The *Press Democrat*'s new general manager, a feisty journalist named William Townes, waded into the campaign, charging in front-page editorials that Patteson had failed to stop the growth of organized crime in Sonoma County. He cited the presence of mobster Nick DeJohn in Santa Rosa and the Mafia links to Villa Chanticleer. Townes also editorialized about the increasing number of what he called "Bay Area hoodlums" who disturbed weekenders and vacationers at Russian River resorts.

The term "juvenile delinquent" was new, coined in the post-World War II era to describe wild teenagers who were products of wartime departure from the traditional American family and home. Townes used it to attack Patteson, citing the spread of "delinquency." A vote against Patteson, Townes told his readers, would be a vote against "big city gamblers, procurers, white slave syndicates and other racketeers."

In one editorial, Townes went so far as to warn readers that Patteson had "himself been a destructive influence on the youth of Sonoma County." It was no secret that Harry had been known to take a drink. The voters were not as worried as Townes. Patteson defeated his opponent, retired Navy Commander John Poshepny of Kenwood, by a wide margin. When he ran for his fifth and final term in 1954, Townes had moved on to the *Miami Herald* and the *Press Democrat* grudgingly endorsed him.30

the Villa Chanticleer to sit empty and deserted for ten years, until the City of Healdsburg bought it for use as a recreation center.

———

Law enforcement's continuing problem with prostitution resulted in a turn-of-the-century experiment with legalization of the existing brothels in Santa Rosa. Several establishments in the vicinity of First and D streets were granted permits to operate under city rules, in exchange for a fee. Women did business in rented houses, many of them owned by the town's leading "capitalists." One of the most successful, known as the Chicken Coop, offered shaves in addition to other services. 31

The system seemed to work too well. Business was so good at the "Coop" and its neighbors that, in 1903, an enterprising businessman named Daniel Behmer built the first house in Santa Rosa designed expressly for the purpose of prostitution. Sadie McLean leased the two-story structure at 720 First Street which was soon very busy. Late summer and early fall were the heavy seasons. The horse races were running at the fairgrounds and men would line up for entrance to all the houses, including McLean's. It was not unusual for fifty waiting customers to form a line along the fences opposite the brothels. McLean and two of her girls, she boasted to reporters, could handle twenty-five customers per hour on a busy horse-race night.

It was the fence-leaners who ultimately caused McLean problems. Schoolteacher Louise Farmer lived at 732 Second Street. The fence opposite Sadie McLean's house and Mrs. Lowery's Chicken Coop was Miss Farmer's back fence. This church-going "schoolmarm" was offended by the boisterous men who drank whiskey and cursed and engaged in loud, lewd conversation while they waited their turns. Moreover, if she looked from her back window, Miss Farmer had a clear view of the patrons of McLean's in the upstairs windows, in varying postures and degrees of dishabille.

KEEP

HARRY L.

PATTESON

SHERIFF

Primary Election
Tuesday, June 8, 1954

1

In 1907, Farmer filed suit against landlord Behmer, charging public nuisance and depreciation of value to her property. The judge ruled that Behmer had to pay because he had built the house specifically as a whorehouse. The civil case filled the courtroom and created widespread debate about the city's practice of licensing brothels. City fathers argued that with licensing they could require medical examinations and control sanitary conditions. Before this decision, the practice had been to arrest the madams each month and collect a fine for selling liquor without a license. The $45 a month licensing fee, they said, was a better system. But the decision in favor of Farmer cooled the city's enthusiasm for legalized sin. Eventually, the First Street bordellos closed and Santa Rosa's "tenderloin" re-established itself in other parts of town.

Prohibition proved to be a willing companion for prostitution, and several of the "resorts" of that era were also whorehouses, including the well-known 101 Ranch, where the gang that shot security officer Bill Carrick had begun its Sonoma County robberies. For many years, Roberts Avenue was the hub of activity, an address for at least two long-term establishments. When one closed, business was done from a bar up the street known as Mick's, where there were cabins available on the creekbank. A 1940 survey reported three houses in Santa Rosa, employing a total of seven women. A raid by the sheriff in 1939 had closed all three, but they were open again within a month.[32] During World War II, when the town was filled with soldiers and sailors, the military acknowledged the lure of Roberts Avenue and posted military policemen at each end of the street to keep it off limits to military personnel.

There were other establishments, less organized, both inside and outside the Santa Rosa city limits. An old farmhouse at 471 West College Avenue apparently owed its WWII success to the presence of MPs at the entrances to Roberts Avenue. Twenty years after the war ended, the owner of a concrete casting firm that used the old house as its office was visited by former customers, stationed in

In 1921, two of Santa Rosa's most prominent women, Minnie Thompson, wife of Judge Rolfe Thompson, and Clara Leppo, wife of dentist David Leppo, approached the Chamber of Commerce with a suggestion that the Santa Rosa Police Department add a woman officer to its ranks. A policewoman, they said, would be of material assistance in those crimes applying to younger people and to the women of the city. Chief George Matthews was willing. Policewomen had been successful in larger cities, he told the City Council. In February, Maria Helena Reeves, who had been a leader in the Santa Rosa chapter of the Women's Christian Temperance Union, was appointed to the police force.

In June she was discharged, Chief Matthews and the council citing budgetary constraints as the reason for the cutback. When 235 people signed a petition asking that she be returned to duty, Mrs. Reeves went back to work, paid with contributions from citizens who supported her. But in December, with funding still a problem, Mrs. Reeves was once again discharged. The enforcement of law in Santa Rosa would remain a man's job until after World War II.

Santa Rosa in the military during the war. They had come, they told the owner, to pay their respects.

In the 1920s there was a brief revival of a sinister custom from the county's post-Civil War days—the gathering of members of the Ku Klux Klan. The best explanation for renewed Klan activity, which occurred all over the United States in this period, may be found in historian Walton Bean's suggestion that the release of D. W. Griffith's racist film, *The Birth of a Nation*, based on an inflammatory novel entitled *The Klansmen*, stirred up ethnic and religious hatreds.[33]

The first announcement to the public that the Klan was active again in Sonoma County came October 19 of 1923 when members gathered for an outdoor meeting at McDonald's reservoir, known as Lake Ralphine. Two days later, at a ceremony in Napa County, with a cross burning in the background, 104 new members were inducted into the Klan.

The next initiation rite, in 1923, was in Santa Rosa. The site was a field on the Julius Ort ranch off Petaluma Hill

Above, the Sonoma County Jail at Third Street and Hinton Avenue, on the east side of the courthouse. At right, the main corridor of the sheriff's offices, looking from the jail entrance toward the front door.

Road, rented for the occasion from the owner. Attendance was by invitation only. The *Press Democrat* warned its readers before the event that cards would be required for entry. Klansmen were coming from Solano and Napa counties and, according to the newspaper, "Directions will be given from an American flag-draped auto at the junction of Santa Rosa Avenue and the Petaluma Highway."

An estimated 2,000 persons gathered at the field three miles from town. A large cross burned on the hillside on the east side of the road. In the field, dozens of automobiles parked in a circle. Within the illumination of their headlights, more than 100 white-robed men formed a square. At each corner was an American flag. Outside the square, a larger flag was stretched between two poles and in the center of the square, there was still another flag.

Around the square were the smaller crosses, which prompted the *Republican* reporter to write about the eerie scene "in the glow of a fifty-foot blazing cross."[34]

There were 1,000 masked Klansmen and ninety-four initiates, four of them in the uniform of the U. S. Navy, and another 1,000 spectators who stood on the outer fringes of the parking area, stretching on tiptoe to see the proceedings. Without the invitation card, the *Republican* reported, the curious could get no closer than "the fourth row of machines."

At 10:10 p.m., the officers assumed positions on wooden boxes and "into the circle rode a horseman bearing a lighted cross. Both man and horse wore white robes with the KKK insignia in red letters. The horseman announced that citizens were outside seeking admittance to the

'Invisible Empire.' The inductees were led into the square where they knelt at each post for the rites. The entire unholy rigamarole took about an hour."[35]

There were other such ceremonies the following year in Petaluma, across from General Vallejo's Old Adobe. "The fiery cross," wrote an observer from the Petaluma *Argus*, "shone through the mists of the night and its rays were seen from the elevated portions of this city and the sight impressed all those who noticed it." Klan speakers addressed audiences at Petaluma High School's auditorium in 1924 and at the First Christian Church in Petaluma in '25.

There was another outdoor ceremony in Santa Rosa in '25, in a field south of the Barham Avenue triangle. There were meetings of 300 Klansmen in the IOOF Hall in Santa Rosa and in El Verano. That same year, a state traffic squad captain from Napa was buried with a Klan funeral, his body escorted by six pallbearers in white robes and hoods.[37] But after this three-year flurry of activity, the Klan disappeared

Sonoma County's motorcycle patrol officers were still required to purchase their own motorcycles when this photograph was made beside the courthouse in 1925. Eventually, this group became the first county contingent of the California Highway Patrol. Third from left is Jack Shryver, Petaluma. Second from right is Jim Shands, Sebastopol.

—*Sonoma County Museum*

At left, the Santa Rosa Police Department, circa 1930.

At right, the Santa Rosa Police Department, 1952. Front row center, fifth from left, is Chief Flohr, flanked by Capt. Jack Spaulding on his left and former chief Watt Maxwell on his right.

from the news columns. The descriptions of the meetings, however, had been widely circulated. Later, during the labor troubles of the 1930s, Sonoma County's reputation as a hot-bed of Klan activity would be remembered.

———

In spite of an apparently cavalier attitude toward law and order, Sonoma County's justice system functioned with just two superior court judges at a time for the first half of the century. Two of these judges, Emmet Seawell and Rolfe Thompson, were jurists of merit who won appointments to the state supreme court. Seawell, who worked his way through Pacific Methodist College as a printer and writer for the *Sonoma Democrat*, was admitted to the bar in 1890 and elected Sonoma County district attorney in 1892. He sat in Sonoma County Superior Court for twenty-one years before becoming an associate justice of the state's highest court.

Thompson received his appointment from Governor Young to the state supreme court after nine years as a superior court judge in Sonoma County. He had begun his Santa Rosa law practice in association with his father James Thompson in the 1890s. He had also been employed as assistant cashier of the First National Bank of Santa Rosa, a deputy county clerk, and a deputy district attorney. He had been a member of the Santa Rosa Board of Education, president of the Santa Rosa Public Library Board of Trustees, and an active member of the Republican party, serving as a presidential elector for Herbert Hoover.

Other superior court judges in the first two decades of the 1900s were Albert Burnett (1896-1906), Thomas Denny (1906-1920), and Ross Campbell (1923-1930). Campbell took the bench at the time of Seawell's appointment to the state court. He had been Santa Rosa's city attorney and an assistant district attorney. He had received his law education at Harvard after graduation from Pacific Methodist College in Santa Rosa. Campbell died in office.[39]

Melvin F. Flohr, known to everyone but his wife Wilma as "Dutch," was police chief in Santa Rosa for thirty-four years. A nephew of former sheriff Mike Flohr, he was a young man with just six years experience in law enforcement when he assumed office. He had spent five years as a deputy for Sheriff Harry Patteson and a year as police chief in Healdsburg.

A big man—six-foot, four-inches tall and 250 pounds—he had been a football star at Petaluma High School and a varsity tackle and basketball center at Santa Clara University. As a police officer, he exuded confidence. He walked with the gait of a western marshal and carried with him the certainty that whatever the situation was, he had it under control. Dutch saw "his" town, for that was how he regarded it, advance from the era of lynchings and tar parties to more sophisticated—and far more complex—law enforcement problems. Despite the crowds of servicemen that World War II brought to central Sonoma County and the post-war growth, there were no murders in Santa Rosa during Dutch's first eleven years as chief.[38]

Dutch initiated preventative law enforcement. He spent many hours with children and teenagers in the community. It is not surprising that for two generations of Santa Rosans, he was a definitive figure of their youth. He personally organized the school traffic patrols, worked in the junior boxing league, spoke to student groups. Dutch's career spanned the middle years of the 20th century and, in some respects, he presided over the last of the innocent years, before drugs and street gangs and increased litigation, when a police chief's job was to be a paternalistic figure and keep the peace.

—John LeBaron, Press Democrat Collection

—Sonoma County Law Library

Thompson's replacement, in 1929, was Hilliard Comstock, the leader of Company E in World War I and president of the Santa Rosa Board of Education. Comstock had "read the law" in the offices of the pioneer Santa Rosa attorney James Oates in preparation for admittance to the California bar. He would serve in the superior court of Sonoma County for a record thirty-five years.

When Judge Campbell died, his seat at the bench was taken by Donald Geary, a member of a distinguished Santa Rosa firm, and the son of the 19th century congressman Thomas Geary. Donald Geary was also a World War I veteran, a pilot, and like Comstock, an officer. For more than a quarter of the century, Comstock and Geary together represented justice in Sonoma County.

Judges were giants in the community in those years. Young lawyers stood aside in deference as they passed. Comstock, impeccably dressed, strolled down Mendocino Avenue from his home at the corner of Benton Street to the courthouse every morning, returning the greetings of his fellow citizens with an almost-regal air. There was rumor, never verified, that prospective candidates for county office

were wise to call upon Comstock for his blessing before spending the first dollar on campaign posters. An accomplished orator, Comstock was in great demand as an after-dinner speaker and his presence was generally considered to lend dignity and credibility to public events.

Geary was more irascible. He was a stern taskmaster for the lawyers who came before him and conducted a career-long war with the press, limiting access to his courtroom when he deemed it necessary and couching his decision in such legal terms that he was upheld on appeal when challenged by irate editors and publishers. Outside the courtroom, however, Geary was known for a sense of humor that extended to an occasional water fight with his bailiff in the marble halls of the courthouse or other pranks which belied his courtroom demeanor. He was also known as a kindly man who was considered a mentor by many younger members of the Sonoma County bar.

Sonoma County gained a third superior court in 1951 and Charles McGoldrick, the district attorney, received the governor's appointment as judge. McGoldrick brought three distinctions to the bench that were departures from the earlier years. He was the first World War II veteran to sit in superior court in the county. His reputation was that of an aggressive prosecutor. And his private practice, before he was elected district attorney, had been in Petaluma, not Santa Rosa. 40

Santa Rosa attorney Lincoln F. Mahan was the county's first municipal court judge, appointed in 1955; he then succeeded Donald Geary to superior court. He was re-elected without opposition until his retirement twenty-one years later. Contests for judgeships were rare. One notable exception to the no-opposition custom was the election year 1950, when J.N. "Nick" DeMeo ran against Judge Geary. DeMeo, the scrappy son of an Italian shoemaker from Santa Rosa's west end, saw the contest as

—Finley Collection

Upper left, Judge Rolfe Thompson, who was named to the state supreme court in 1929 after nine years on the Sonoma County Superior Court bench, Above, Judge Thomas Denny, who served as superior court judge from 1906 to 1920. Below, Judge Emmett Seawell, who served twenty-one years in Sonoma County Superior Court before his appointment to the state supreme court in 1923.

—Finley Collection

class warfare. He ran against the domination of the courts by what he called "old Santa Rosa." Judge Geary won in a landslide.

Judges are the traditional heroes of the legal profession, but it is also traditional that lawyers elect their own heroes from their ranks. They select the lawyers who are acknowledged in their time with a variety of flattering adjectives—best, brightest, quickest legal mind, brilliant in the courtroom, hardest worker. These are the ones veteran lawyers choose to tell about when they are introducing new lawyers to the legal history of the region.

In Sonoma County there are many oft-repeated names: the young Clarence Lea, whose prowess in the courtroom carried him to a record sixteen terms in Congress; J. Rollo Leppo, the Santa Rosa defense lawyer of the '20s and '30s, noted for his small-town approach to the law; Bryce Swartfager, who could be counted on when minorities needed representation; Clarendon Anderson, who was known throughout his life as "The Judge," although he never was one—it was an appellation awarded him by his colleagues as a tribute to his vast knowledge of the law; Carlton Spridgen, who was so thorough and precise in his professional dissertations that the verb to be "Spridgenized" became a synonym for having looked at all sides of an issue; George Murphy, the dapper bachelor who always wore a gray fedora, had his suits tailor-made in San Francisco, and loved baseball so much he talked in game terms—"I fielded your message on the first bounce and I'm tossing it right back"; Lewis (Duke) DeCastle, whose reputation in criminal defense was equaled only by his casual attitude toward business (as public defender, he had no office, but put his hat on a bench in the courthouse and invited clients and other lawyers to leave messages in it).

Leroy Lounibos was considered to be the finest trial lawyer of his time. He and his brother John, who began practicing together in Petaluma in 1934, were a good team, combining Leroy's courtroom abilities with John's research skills. Judges and colleagues both paid tribute to the

The first Sonoma County Superior Court jury to include women sat in 1922 on the case of Firmin Candelot's trespass lawsuit against the city of Healdsburg. First row, left to right, Laura Coltrin, Marnella Trosper, Bertha Agnew, Sophie Hammell, Alberta Lichau, Walter Leroux. Back row, left to right, Conrad Peters, Fred Hefty, Frank Joseph, George Morken, Arthur Neistrath, Albert Jacobsen.

Sonoma County's judges were all men. There was only one brief lapse in the male domination of justice in the first part of the century. That came in 1917 when attorney Frances McGaughey Martin, described by the newspaper as "the well-known woman lawyer," apparently took the bench in Judge Denny's court to grant an interlocutory decree of divorce, to a Sebastopol farm wife.[41]

Thus, acting-judge Martin, according to the newspaper account, became the first woman in the United States to ascend to a superior court bench, even temporarily, and the first woman to "grant" a divorce decree, although court records show it was Judge Denny who signed the official document.

Martin was an appropriate choice for a gender statement. A leader in woman suffrage causes, she was one of the three McGaughey sisters—Dr. Anabel McG. Stuart was a physician, and Elizabeth McG. Bennett was a pharmacist—who put Santa Rosa at the forefront in women's rights at the turn of the century.

discipline which enabled Leroy to handle tremendous case loads, coming into court with seven or eight cases in a day and doing justice to each client. Young lawyers, in awe of his workload, made teasing reference to the weekly court docket as the "Lounibitian Calendar."[42]

Nick DeMeo, the attorney who challenged Judge Geary, would earn his legal laurels with his contributions to the profession. Nick was famous throughout the state in the field of continuing law education, setting up procedural guides and checklists, and revising court forms for uniformity. He spoke often and wrote books and articles on legal economics, office practice, and discovery procedures.

Nick was part of another brother team. He and his brother Charles started practice at the height of the Depression. Initially, they went to work for separate firms because they couldn't afford to rent an office of their own. Nick would later recall that times were "so tough I tried case after case pro bono while becoming indigent myself." He financed his law practice for several years by playing his banjo with dance bands in the Bay Area.[43]

Finlaw Geary was another trial lawyer, considered a master at reading the attitudes and feelings of witnesses, as well as judge and jury. Finlaw was also the son of the congressman, brother of the superior court judge. The Geary firm did most of the railroad legal work in the area north of San Francisco, and Finlaw became an expert at insurance defense. Judges considered him to be among the best cross-examination lawyers in the profession.

Unlike his more conservative brother, Finlaw Geary was a bachelor and something of a bon vivant. He was a regular at the Elks Club rooms, for cards and conviviality, and was Santa Rosa's number one sports fan. His "Quarterback Club" was a select group of men who gathered for late lunches after sporting events in town. Finlaw also devoted considerable energy to alumni activities at Stanford University, where he had played varsity tennis. When Santa Rosa Junior College began, Geary focused his attention on building a sports program. In 1925, he brought into the family law partnership a former Stanford athlete, Clarence J. "Red" Tauzer, who became coach of SRJC's new

Superior court judges, left to right, Hilliard Comstock, Donald Geary, Charles McGoldrick, and Lincoln Mahan.

football team and a member of the college's first board of trustees. In the 1940s, when Tauzer served in the Navy, Geary sat in his place on the board. Geary Hall, the second building on the campus, was named for him in recognition of his support of the new institution.[44]

There was a distinct aura of energy and importance emanating from the marble halls of the courthouse in the center of Santa Rosa's busy downtown. The courthouse crowd included lawyers from the smaller towns, where specializing was unknown and attorneys were called upon for a wide range of legal matters. Healdsburg's Francis Passalacqua was just one of many who practiced this type of "family law" in mid-century. Born in Healdsburg to Italian immigrant parents, Passalacqua was educated at St. Mary's College in Moraga and Santa Clara's law school. He opened his law offices in his hometown in 1939, practicing alone; and in the years that followed represented clients in everything from wills, partnerships, and tax cases to defense on first-degree murder charges.

These lawyers appeared in the justice courts as often as superior courts. California's original justice court system, based on townships, was the forerunner of the municipal court system. These courts remained in effect throughout the county until 1955, when Santa Rosa's was changed to a municipal court.[45] Justices of the peace, as they were known, were not required to be lawyers. Some, like Mahan, Ray Grinstead of Sonoma, and Albert Schiedecker of Sebastopol, were practicing attorneys, but, in fact, most were not. E.J. "Nin" Guidotti, a real estate man by profession who later served as a county supervisor, started his political career as a JP in the Guerneville court. Petaluma's justice of the peace for many years was Rolland Webb, a colorful character whose true occupation was that of a mortician. One of these justices of the peace was the first woman to sit as an official judge in the county. Ellen Fleming was appointed to fill the term of her husband, Lee, when he joined the Marines in World War II. It would be forty years or more

Santa Rosa attorneys, left to right, Rollo Leppo, Nick DeMeo, and Finlaw Geary.

—Finley Collection

—John LeBaron, Press Democrat Collection

—LeBaron Collection

170

before there would be another woman on the bench in Sonoma County.[46]

In 1943, the California Youth Authority purchased land on Sonoma Highway at the foot of Hood Mountain to build a state institution for delinquent girls. The site included the original buildings from the Los Guilucos Rancho and had been the country estate of a U.S. senator from Utah, Thomas Kearns, and a retirement home for members of the Knights of Pythias lodge. For a name the CYA went to the historical beginnings. Los Guilucos School for Girls lasted nearly thirty years, with as many as 270 teenage girls at a time living there after being remanded to the CYA by the court system.

Los Guilucos was considered a model institution by juvenile authorities and very successful by state standards. Problems were generally limited to an occasional runaway and the rate of recidivism was very low. There was just one incidence of violence there, but it had considerable effect on the attitudes of the community toward the "bad girls" at Los Guilucos.

For four days in March of 1953, with the population of the school at 159, the girls rioted. The director, Julia Combs, placed the blame on a core of six girls who had been sent to the school together, from Los Angeles. The violence began in the dining hall. Led by a fourteen-year-old, a band of girls ranged across the campus, breaking windows and smashing furniture and equipment. The rioting continued through the night. When the first wave subsided the following afternoon, thirty girls had been injured. The sheriff's department, Santa Rosa police, the Sonoma County unit of the California Highway Patrol, and the security force from Sonoma State Hospital in Glen Ellen worked to put down the disturbance. Six of the girls were taken to the county jail, six more to Napa State Hospital, which had lock-up facilities. Some twenty girls escaped the grounds. Half were recaptured immediately, the other half were found later.

The Los Guilucos riots of 1953 was the first Sonoma County occurrence of a new kind of violence that would become all too familiar in the second half of the 20th century.

They had broken into a Kenwood market and were drunk on stolen beer. Sonoma Valley residents became increasingly alarmed at the news from the school.

On the fourth day, police seized thirty-eight girls, including those identified as the ringleaders, and took them to the Sonoma County Jail. The rioting ended. The violence caused many injuries and thousands of dollars in damage to the school. Nervousness over the school and its occupants plagued neighbors. The riots cost the superintendent her job. Combs resigned and was replaced by a CYA parole officer named Beatrice Dolan, who would, in short order, change the atmosphere of the school and, eventually, through a citizens' advisory committee, calm the fears of the community.

"Mama Dolan," as her charges called her, established a state school curriculum and a therapy program and brought community volunteers to the school to teach classes in practical skills such as waitress training and cosmetology. She called the students "my kids" and treated them with respect. Dolan's work at Los Guilucos, and later at the CYA school for girls at Ventura, earned her professional recognition and an appointment to the National Council on Crime and Delinquency.[47]

Technological advances in both transportation and communication had considerable impact on law enforcement at mid-century. The good-old, bad-old days of the 1920s, when twelve deputies covered the entire county, would be replaced by an organized, uniformed force of officers in constant communication with both office and each other. It may even be symbolic that Harry Patteson, whose final term began in 1954, was the last sheriff of Sonoma County to wear a ten-gallon hat. The lynching, the trials of Al Chamberlain, the rumrunners, and the sporting houses, the Wild West were things of the past. The new system would be more sophisticated—to deal with more sophisticated crimes. ❧

Hard Times

At Christmas in 1931, the combined charities of Santa Rosa fed 1,221 needy people holiday dinner and supplied gift baskets for families. The American Legion members marched into the depths of the hobo jungles on the edge of town to dish a hearty Mulligan stew for transients. The Salvation Army had already instituted its "woodpile" system, which offered homeless men an opportunity to work for a meal. But it was "Dad" Burchell's soup kitchen, more than any of the organized effort, that would become the symbol of Santa Rosa's response to the financial crisis of the 1930s.

The kitchen was not a kitchen at all, but an empty lot on First Street where the elderly man and his wife fed the hungry every day. He was William E. Burchell who, with his wife Eva, had worked with the Salvation Army in their native England. In 1927, they came to Santa Rosa from Canada. When the need arose, the Burchells resumed their care of the homeless and hungry.

Soon after their arrival, the couple set up a "giving stand" on Fourth Street to collect money to provide Christmas dinner for the poor. When the collapse of the American economy multiplied the need, they expanded their charitable work accordingly. They opened a welfare store on Second Street where they distributed donated clothing and established their open-air kitchen.

The Burchells were not alone in their good work. Dairyman E. J. Ferguson of Ludwig Avenue gave ten gallons of milk every day for "the children." The butcher shops furnished soup bones. The grocers rallied 'round the soup pot, providing potatoes and onions and carrots and "anything that would make good soup," as Paul Mancini would remember in later years. "We used to get those small potatoes in 100-pound sacks," Mancini said. "Dad would come around with his model A Ford or whatever it was—a little truck—and we'd throw the sacks up there and make the truck shake."

Paul and his brother Reno ran the Court Market at Third and Main streets in the early '30s. They were among the many market owners and butchers in town who supplied the Burchells with the ingredients for their soup, made fresh every morning in a huge cauldron over an open fire. The market owners' good work was unofficial and they left no permanent record or statistics on the amount of meat and vegetables donated, the quantities of soup consumed, or the number of hungry people who dined in the empty lot.

The grocers "were all in the same boat," Mancini recalled. "We sold carrots for 1 cent a bunch; bananas, 10 cents a dozen. If we had two people working for us and we didn't need them and they had families, what we did was divide their time and keep both on a part-time basis. I believe most of the businesses tried to do the same thing."[1]

The Burchells' work continued throughout the hard times. When Dad died in 1937, at the age of eighty-one, Eva Burchell carried on, assisted by the community, until shortly before her own death in 1940.

———

Dad Burchell's patrons were the hobos—or the more colloquial "bindlestiffs" or mock-heroic "knights of the road"—who provided the most visible evidence of the Depression. "I'd say there were fifty, sixty, seventy-five people fed at the pot every day," Mancini said. "They came into the towns whatever way they could travel. They used to go down to the depot for the night, or under the bridge. If they were passersby, transients. Then, of course, they'd go on to try to get a freight ride. One would tell the other about the soup kitchen."

In March of 1931, the newspaper reported that the "tramp population" had doubled in recent months. The usual 800 who traveled along the Northwestern Pacific Railroad's route, the story said, had increased to 2,000.[2] There were hobo "jungles" wherever there were railroad tracks—the largest campsites being at Fulton, where the NWP rail line to the Russian River met the main north-south

———

Mrs. Lennie Huskey buys groceries from Paul Mancini, left, and his brother Reno in their Court Market in 1934. The Mancini brothers were among the many Santa Rosa grocers who contributed to a soup kitchen for the hungry and homeless during the Depression years.

line. In East Petaluma, patrols were set up by railroad detectives and sheriff's deputies after a "jungle killer" murdered a man for his shoes and his blanket.

Generally, railroad agents were lenient about the hobo jungles, leaving the transients to their own devices so long as they didn't set fire to the tall grass or raid chicken houses on neighboring farms. Santa Rosa's favorite stopping place was a warehouse owned by the Petaluma & Santa Rosa Railroad on Sebastopol Avenue. Used as a fruit terminal during the harvest season and a storage shed the rest of the year, the warehouse became a flophouse as soon as the work day ended and the sun set. The covered loading dock made a sheltered bunkhouse.

P&SR officials did object to this unauthorized use of the premises. The hobos were tearing off the crossbracing on the building's underpinnings to use for firewood and weakening the foundation of the structure, they said. As fast as railroad workers replaced the braces, the hobos ripped them off. Santa Rosa police officers began regular patrols. They were responding not only to P&SR complaints, but to the laments of Roseland poultry farmers who blamed the increase in thefts—eggs stolen from hens' nests and fryer pens raided—on the temporary residents. The hobos, to avoid police patrols, abandoned the loading dock and crawled under the building itself for shelter on wet nights.

There were several dozen homeless men—and several women, according to reports—sleeping beneath the building on a night in the wet winter of 1939 when the warehouse collapsed. The building was filled to the ceiling with sacks of dried prunes. The weight of the fruit and the lack of bracing took its toll. Eleven men died in the heap of fallen beams and flooring and fruit sacks.[3]

"Poison rum," as the newspaper stories of the time called it, was responsible for many more hobo deaths than the collapsed warehouse. The "travelin' men" drank in the name of forgetfulness, of camaraderie, and even of warmth. Before the repeal of Prohibition, with no cheap wine available, they drank a concoction they called "butter-milk,"

Stock Crash Takes Mind Off Politics

By SENATOR H. W. SLATER

—Press Democrat Collection

a mixture of denatured alcohol and water, which took on a milky aspect. Bad alcohol, pneumonia, rail accidents, and murder were common by-products of the hobo society of the '30s.

Even veteran politicians like Herbert Slater failed to heed warnings of the impending economic disaster. The column that accompanied this headline was written in the week following the stock market crash of 1929.

The Great Depression was late in reaching the Pacific Coast and, to some degree, the agrarian nature of Sonoma County served to shield it from the hardships experienced in the nation's cities. There was, in fact, a distinct air of bravado in Sonoma County at the first news of the stock market crash of late October 1929. The leading political columnist, who was also the state senator from Sonoma County, Herbert Slater, made light of the news of financial disaster, protesting humorously in his *Press Democrat* column of October 31 that "It was no easy task to dish up...daily political gossip. People were taking stock of stocks and not of politics.... But yesterday the sun shone. The north wind went down and the stocks went up." Expressing confident hope in "sane business," Slater left the topic and went on to speculate about the re-election of Governor Clement Young.

In an editorial written for the New Year's edition of the *Press Democrat*, 1929 was described as "a banner year" with "all forms of industry showing decided gains over the preceding years. In spite of stock crashes, short crops, and other forms of impending disaster, we came through unharmed and happy."

This optimism continued for a short time. According to newspaper reports, 1931 was actually a "boom" year, the biggest year for construction in Santa Rosa since the building boom of 1921-22. In April, the timber industry heralded the "largest trainload of redwood in the history of the industry" being shipped out of Mendocino County. Santa Rosa lumbermen, according to the *Press Democrat*, were gathering at the railroad station to help celebrate this fifty-car shipment.

It was inevitable that a county already damaged by the effects of Prohibition on vineyard, hopyard, winery, and brewery would be dealt a second blow by the general economic collapse. Sonoma County's pockets, already empty when the crash came, could only become emptier.

Sonoma County in 1930 had a population of 62,222, of which 25,186 were classified as rural farm residents, 18,155 as rural non-farm, and 18,881 as urban. Santa Rosa had 10,636 people; Petaluma, 8,245; Healdsburg; 2,296; and Sebastopol, 1,762. Sonoma's population was less than 1,000. Sonoma County was distinctly a county of small farms and orchards, most of them (5,100 of 7,000) less than fifty acres.[4]

Even the diversity and relative prosperity of the small family farm, however, could not stave off the effects of the Great Depression. While the first to suffer hardship were the workers who lived in the towns, where they had no means of raising their own food, the farmers themselves were soon impacted. And, because of Santa Rosa's dependence on agriculture, the economic shock waves traveled quickly through the community.

Before it ended, the Depression would lower farm income dramatically. The scarcity of cash, the loss of buying power, had a disastrous effect on the business community in the urban areas. In 1930 there were 1,948 retail stores in the county. By 1935 there were 1,298. Some 650 businesses had failed. The number of people employed in the county decreased by 865 from 1930 to 1933 and the average annual wage shrunk from $1,509 to $1,001 in the same three-year period.[5] The statistics were repeated all over the nation. In '33, first lady Eleanor Roosevelt warned women of "an inevitable reduction in income" and exhorted them to "be brave and without panic."[6]

The blow must have fallen abruptly. In August of 1930, the Chamber of Commerce was reporting that Santa Rosa had no unemployment problem. "Santa Rosa, for the first time in months, is without a single unemployed person and there are more jobs available than there are workers to fill

The largest trainload of redwood in the history of the North Coast timber industry was shipped from Mendocino County in the spring of 1931. Overly optimistic Santa Rosa businessmen gathered at the depot to watch it pass through, heralding it as a sign that economic woes were at an end.

—*Sonoma County Museum*

—Press Democrat Collection

It would prove difficult to convince people who had no money to keep spending it, but the business community tried—with ads such as this one which appeared in the *Press Democrat* in November of 1932.

The county had eight overworked social workers. The city of Santa Rosa's one social worker was also the corporation yard superintendent and his social work consisted largely of supervising the city's woodyard. The Red Cross helped distribute flour provided by the federal government in 1933 and the Salvation Army continued to feed and clothe multitudes.

In the fall of 1932, Santa Rosa began a survey of unemployment preparatory to the establishment of a winter relief program. City Manager Charles Dunbar asked all jobless men to appear at City Hall—ironically, the office of the tax collector—to register with the city's new social service commission. A total of sixty-eight men registered on the first day.

The main thrust of the city's relief efforts in 1933 hinged on a ballot measure in which citizens approved an expenditure of $10,000 from the city's sewer bond fund for relieving the needy unemployed. The money was used by the social service commission to put the jobless men to work, as had been done on a lesser scale in 1931, on community projects.

Government projects would provide salvation for many. In October of 1932, a delegation of Sonoma County leaders—Supervisor Thomas Ferguson; George Bauer, business agent for the Carpenters' Union; G. Lansing Hurd and J.A. Tedford, secretary and president of the Santa Rosa Chamber of Commerce; and publisher Ernest Finley—called on contractors building Hamilton Field, a "bombing base" in Marin County, to include Sonoma County laborers in their work force.

Innovative ideas such as a "share-the-work" plan were proposed by the newspaper. This called for five men working six days each week to drop a day apiece in order to allow a sixth worker five days of paid work. Such emergency measures were more optimistic than practical as wages continued to plummet and even those who had work found themselves struggling to support their families.

By January of 1933 there were 668 needy men on the

them."7 By December, the *Press Democrat* had opened a Relief Store at the newspaper office, collecting groceries and warm clothing from the local merchants so poor people could "shop" for what they needed. The business community had discovered what Dad and Eva had known for quite a while. Some 225 families and fifty-five single men took food and warm clothes from the Relief Store that winter.

The Salvation Army's "woodpile" was a balm to the consciences of the righteous who saw the system as a way, as one told a newspaper editor, "to see that Santa Rosa becomes unpopular with professional beggars." Later, City Relief adopted the woodpile concept, requiring the able-bodied to chop wood for needy families in exchange for meal chits. Transients could sleep one night in the City Hall, which had space for a dozen and was always filled.

rolls of Santa Rosa's social service commission. One eighteen-page edition of the *Press Democrat* contained ten pages of names on the delinquent tax rolls. The newspaper was filled with "Situation Wanted" ads, but no "Help Wanted." There were sad little stories of pets deserted by their owners, many of them transients, because they couldn't feed them. In rural areas this caused more problems for ranchers as untended dogs began to run livestock and kill sheep.

Santa Rosa's banks closed on President Roosevelt's national order March 6, 1933, but were quickly declared solvent by bank examiners and were ready to open eight days later on a limited basis. They would cash paychecks but until the national situation was clarified, withdrawals would be limited to $10.

With the election of Franklin Roosevelt in 1932, the New Deal relief measures began to translate to public works jobs throughout the nation. Former President Herbert Hoover's relief bills of 1930, totaling $150 billion, including $116 billion for public works which had never been implemented, were tapped by FDR's emergency measures.

Agencies known by their initials—WPA for the Work Projects (originally Progress, but soon changed) Administration, PWA for Public Works Administration, CWA for Civil Works Administration, FERA for Federal Emergency Relief Act (SERA was the state equivalent), NYA for National Youth Administration, and CCC for Civilian Conservation Corps—were known scornfully as "Democratic alphabet soup" by critics of the New Deal. But they put people to work.

The WPA administrator in Sonoma County was W.C. "Cap" Woodward. His work would prove to be very important. His job was to provide funds for wages, as the PWA provided funds for materials. The benefits to the communities went well beyond food on dinner tables. In the last half of the 1930s, money from these agencies for materials and labor gave Santa Rosa, all of Sonoma County, in fact, a face lift.

—Sonoma County Museum

The "blue eagle" banner of the National Recovery Act draped public buildings, such as the Sonoma County courthouse below, during the Depression. President Roosevelt's work projects provided thousands with wages in the troubled 1930s.

—LeBaron Collection

—LeBaron Collection

The new Sonoma County Hospital on Chanate Road was just one of many public facilities constructed with government funds in the Depression years. Note the sign at left, crediting assistance from the Public Works Administration. PWA provided materials. The WPA, or Works Projects Adminstration, paid the laborers.

WPA money paid eighty men for eight months at the Santa Rosa Municipal Airport, grading, installing a drainage system, constructing three eight-inch-thick all-weather runways. They built new fences, fixed the old ones, painted airport markers and the hangar roof, and paved the entrance and the parking area.

The new County Hospital building kept fifty-two men working for six months, not only in new construction, but in the refitting of the old hospital building for a tuberculosis sanitarium. At Santa Rosa Junior College, WPA workers built the theater arts building and the Bailey Field bleachers. They built Analy High School, Cloverdale High School, and large parts of Healdsburg and Sonoma Valley high schools.

Playing field improvements at Brush School on Santa Rosa's eastern edge, Park Side in Sebastopol, and Jonive near Freestone kept twenty men employed for three years. At Waugh School on Corona Road north of Petaluma, the one-room schoolhouse had settled and warped and was threatened with condemnation. The WPA workers built a new foundation, reinforced the framework, stuccoed the exterior, reroofed, repainted, improved the playground, and presented the rural district with a new school. The project kept nineteen men working for a full year.

In Sebastopol, workers paid with government money (part city, part state, and part WPA) demolished the old wood-frame City Hall and built a new one of reinforced concrete, as well as a new fire station. They also installed water mains and constructed a warehouse and corporation yard for the municipal water system. The reservoir got a new roof. Cloverdale's City Hall and fire station were built with state and WPA funds. In Petaluma, WPA money painted seven schools, installed storm drains, and improved the streets. In Sonoma, workers landscaped the plaza and built an outdoor theater in the center.

Several hundred workers benefited from these municipal projects as did the communities. Under the supervision of contractors and skilled labor, the WPA workers resurfaced 112 miles of county roads, installed 448 culverts, built twenty-nine wooden bridges, three masonry bridges and one steel bridge, and installed 35,000 linear feet of curbs and gutters and 26,000 feet of sidewalk in the years between 1935 and 1938.[8] Private contractors who were in charge of the projects were praised for treating the job "as if the money were from their own pockets."[9]

The money went a very long way. Project supervisors were proficient at scrounging and scavenging materials to save as much as possible for wages, the local economy being the primary concern. In Santa Rosa's Juilliard Park, for example, workers built walkways, a redwood pergola, a drinking fountain, spray fountain, and bridge, all of stone, and a complete irrigation system. Years later, when city workers replaced the sprinkler system, they found it had been constructed of mismatched and odd-sized pipe and fittings, made to work by the ingenuity and determination of men whose priorities were to spend what money they had on people, not parts.

The bridge into Doyle Park was built of old basalt paving blocks salvaged from street work, basalt curbing, and old street railway rails for reenforcement. The gravel for the concrete came from Spring Creek, below the bridge. The only purchased materials were the metal part-circle culvert and the Portland cement.

Nowhere was the make-do attitude more apparent than in the WPA Women's Project. Finding that women were becoming "fearful of the future, despondent from weary hours of job hunting, and careless of their appearance," WPA officials put them to work, too. The government took over an overalls factory on Sebastopol Road that had been idle since the start of the Depression. The factory's fifty-eight power sewing machines were used to make clothing for the poor while training the women to sew for their families. With scraps of material left over, they made quilts, pillow covers, rugs, and stuffed toys. The sixty-seven Santa Rosa women made 92,000 garments and, according to the

government report, "improved their physical, mental and cosmetic well-being." They made new clothes for themselves and were treated to free permanent waves by students at the beauty school.[10]

WPA money was spent on wages for professionals and clerical workers who transcribed data on handicapped students for the school districts and worked in the public libraries, cataloging, indexing, and repairing and binding books—a project long-neglected for lack of funds. Skilled and specialized workers from the relief rolls built exhibit space for a museum at the junior college and classified, labeled, and cataloged the Indian artifacts, rock specimens, and examples of flora and fauna. Nine families of white collar-workers lived on the wages of this project for a year. In addition, the first-ever WPA archaeological dig was funded at the behest of Santa Rosa Junior College instructor Jesse Peter. Peter received a grant of $10,000 a year for the excavation and research necessary to "unravel the entire history of prehistoric civilization in Sonoma, Napa, and Marin counties."[11]

The WPA and the NYA were largely responsible for the birth of public recreation in Sonoma County. Like the hot lunches for school children, which the WPA also instituted, the credit for making recreation an accepted government service belongs to the Depression-era agencies. In 1937, WPA manager Woodward assigned four recreation leaders to Santa Rosa, four to Petaluma, two to Healdsburg, and one to Cotati. In the summer months, he sent fourteen recreation leaders, after lifeguard training, to the Russian River beaches. The leaders came from the relief rolls and were taught to organize sports and games and handicrafts and to guard the safety of the youngsters who enrolled in their programs. The WPA also built a tennis court in Santa Rosa and made vast improvements at Healdsburg's Tayman Park Golf Course.

The NYA provided funds to high schools and the junior college to employ students as an incentive to stay in school and out of the labor market. SRHS employed fifty students on campus; SRJC, 124. In addition, the NYA program for young people who were not in school trained eighty people for clerical work, automotive trades, and gardening.

The CCC was a more comprehensive plan to "save" the young people of the Depression era. One of the most successful of FDR's agencies, it also saved the county's natural resources. There were two CCC camps in Sonoma County—Camp Sebastopol at the eastern foot of O'Farrell Hill housed 1,119 young men between 1935 and 1942. Camp Armstrong, established in Armstrong Woods State Park in 1933, had 817 residents. Camp Sebastopol's population was from Louisiana, Georgia, Florida, Alabama, and Missouri. Camp Armstrong's residents were almost all Californians.

Camp Sebastopol was operated for the Gold Ridge Soil Conservation District. The young men laid miles of concrete drainage pipe, which they manufactured at a pipe plant on the creek that ran through the camp. They drilled wells and built check dams, contoured orchards, trenched and ditched for the drainage systems, planted shrubs and trees for slide prevention, and built stone retaining walls. Walt Adams was the engineer in charge.

The Armstrong Woods camp had a dual identity. As Camp Armstrong, it was managed by the California Division of Beaches and Parks, for which the men built roads, campsites, picnic areas, fences, and all the original buildings in the park. As Camp Armstrong Woods, it was under the authority of the California Division of Forestry, doing stream clearance and trail construction in the Austin Creek watershed. Camp Armstrong Woods men also built the fire lookout tower atop Mount Jackson.

Several of these projects were accomplished jointly with other government agencies. A crew of WPA workers, supervised by a Sonoma County resident James W. Keegan, former owner of Mirabel Resort, worked with the CCC crews on the amphitheater and other buildings at Armstrong Grove. Other joint projects with the WPA included: the ranger's residence at the Forestry's head-quarters on West College Avenue in Santa Rosa; the restoration of General Vallejo's Home in Sonoma for the state park system; and the construction of trails and pit toilets and drinking water systems at Salmon Creek, Portuguese Beach, Schoolhouse Beach, Wright's Beach, and Goat Rock on the Sonoma Coast.

The wages the "CCC boys" earned were sent directly to their families, except for $5 a month which financed their social lives—a day at the Russian River beaches, a dance at the hall over the post office in Sebastopol, or a weekend trip to San Francisco, which could cost them as much as $2.[12]

In addition, the State Emergency Relief Administration (SERA) distributed surplus commodities and contributed to at least twenty smaller projects in the Santa Rosa district, putting the unemployed to work replacing sidewalks, curbs, and gutters in Santa Rosa, painting the interior of Santa Rosa's schools, building bleachers and three bus stop shelters for the high school, building a playground at Howarth Park on A Street, cleaning sewer mains, and making improvements to Santa Rosa's Municipal Sewer Farm. Women were paid by SERA for making and remodeling garments for Red Cross distribution to the poor, and for housekeeping in homes where care was needed.

In the early years of federal aid, CWA money was spent on Santa Rosa projects, including the widening of Mendocino Avenue, improvement of Reservoir Road, concrete septic tanks for the sewer farm, painting of City Hall and the removal of the old streetcar tracks from Fourth Street, renovation of the swimming tank, and improvement of the fire department building. CWA paid wages to 1,130 men.[13]

One measure of effects of the Depression can be found in a unique document with the cumbersome title of: *Sonoma County, A Preliminary Study by Members of a Study Group in The School of Social Studies, 1940.* The study was part of a San Francisco project led by sociologist Myer

Cohen who came to the county in January of 1939. With a grant from the Rosenberg Foundation of San Francisco, a fund set up by Santa Rosa's leading merchant family, Cohen conducted a two-year project in adult education. The idea captured the interest of the more liberal segment of the community. Discussion and study groups were established in Petaluma, Sebastopol, Healdsburg, Windsor, and Santa Rosa. In the spring, the Santa Rosa group—nine men and ten women from diverse professions—read Helen and Robert Lynd's pioneer sociological work, *Middletown in Transition*, and decided to do a similar survey of Sonoma County.

The makeup of the Santa Rosa group was, in some ways, almost as interesting as the study. Five of them were teachers; four were housewives. There were two social workers, one physician, one lawyer, one minister, one real estate and insurance broker, one merchant, one "coffee pedlar," one pharmacist, and one farmer.

Cohen, writing of the results of the survey, cautioned that it was not to be compared to the work of trained scientific investigators, nor was it to be considered a finished work but rather "an instrument for continued study."

However misleading it might be, the picture of the community that emerges from the 1940 report was one of a town that had glimmers of promise. For one thing, home building was increasing. The construction industry had all but vanished five years earlier. There were nine construction loans in all of Sonoma County in 1935, the study found, totalling $27,200. The single-family homes, surrounded by their own yards, housed fully 98 percent of the residents in 1930. By the late '30s they gave way to multiple dwelling units. The shift was not yet as dramatic as that which World War II would bring, but it was significant nonetheless. The conversion of many of the large old homes to apartments and the demand for apartment buildings or "flats" began to put the carpenters, masons, and laborers back to work.

It is not surprising that 2,000 of the county's 7,000 farm owners worked at jobs away from their land by 1940, a number that had increased at least 10 percent since the Depression began. Nor is it surprising that any enforcement of strict mortgage policies would meet with resentment from farmers and, in some cases, outrage.

Salvation for Sonoma County's small farmers came from the paternalistic attitudes of some community leaders, notably editor Ernest Finley of the *Press Democrat* and banker Frank Doyle. Finley's editorials in support of mortgage relief for the small farmer were beacon lights of hope for worried readers. The Exchange Bank's Doyle was noted for a mortgage policy his customers called "understanding" and in years to come he would be credited with saving many a small farmer's land.

Still, when mortgage protests reached the Pacific Coast, it was Sonoma County that was selected as the site for the first farmers' rally against foreclosure held in the west. In the summer of 1933, some 3,000 farmers, called together by Wilford H. Howard, the Graton rancher who was president of the Farmers Protective League, and J. Stitt Wilson, the Berkeley activist, gathered on the steps and lawn of the courthouse in Santa Rosa for a demonstration which turned the attention of the nation to the plight of the small California fruit grower.

The elderly rancher who was the focus of the protest was James L. Case, a seventy-year-old apple and cherry rancher from Forestville. Case was a retired Methodist minister. He had owned his fifty-acre ranch on Mirabel Road for twenty-two years and had planted his fruit trees himself. It was an exemplary orchard, well cared for. Case and his family—he had young children despite his age—lived in an eleven-room house he had built himself. "The showplace of Forestville," newspaper accounts called the ranch.

In 1932 crop prices dropped. Case paid his taxes but could not make the payment on his $14,000 mortgage. In the summer of 1933, the Analy Savings Bank foreclosed. A sale of the ranch and all the "chattels" was set for July 14. The first call, from Farmers Protective League president Howard, was for a mass meeting at the Case ranch on the Sunday before the sale. Wilson, the former Socialist mayor of Berkeley, called upon the farmers to "Rally to the banner of humanity" as he spoke from Case's front porch, which had been draped with American flags. The rally attracted the attention of the national press.

Editor Finley was writing daily, calling for a stay on foreclosure, outlining plans for mediation. Sebastopol's

BANKER PRESENTS PROPOSITION

—Press Democrat Collection

Catholic priest, the Rev. Charles Phillips, made it a moral issue, asking why Case could not "be given a chance to harvest his apple crop that is now ripening on his trees." Through Finley's political connections, word of the Case situation reached Washington, D.C. National leaders, already highly sensitive to the plight of the American farmer, tried to intervene with the bank. Bank president Arthur Swain received a message from President Franklin D. Roosevelt himself, as well as Henry Morganthau, head of the Farm Credit Association. Governor James Rolph telephoned the banker to ask for leniency for Case. Congressman Clarence Lea added his plea, as did Assemblyman F. Presley Abshire, himself a prune rancher, and state Sen. Herbert Slater. But bank directors met and decided that no change in policy was justified. The sale would go on.

The families on both sides of the issue suffered through the protests. Case's daughter, who was a sophomore in high school that year, would later recall her embarrassment over the publicity. Swain's daughter, who questioned the casting of her father in the role of the villain, remembered the episode as "dreadful." Her father was threatened with lynching, she recalled, and there were threats to kidnap her and her twin brother.[14]

On the day of the sale, farmers from all over Northern California, along with a substantial number of newspaper and wire service representatives, crowded into Santa Rosa to rally at the courthouse. Howard, the Farmers Protective League president, had set the tone in a statement to the press the day before the sale. The gathering would be, he said, "A meeting of such significance, that the tired eyes of the nation will be focused and action taken there will...reach to the four corners of the land, giving hope and encouragement to thousands of home and ranch owners deprived of their life savings and turned out in the evening of their lives...."[15]

The ending was dramatic and, at least temporarily, a happy one. As the town clock struck ten, the appointed time

When the apple orchard of Forestville minister James Case was threatened with foreclosure in 1933, farmers from all over the state rallied to his cause. At left, Arthur Swain of the Sebastopol National Bank confers with editor Ernest Finley, seated, who intervened on behalf of Case.

PEN STROKE HALTS EVICTION AS THOUSANDS JOIN IN PROTEST

The newspaper reported a "rolling roar of cheers" as the crowd of farmers gathered in front of the courthouse heard J. Stitt Wilson, facing the crowd at far left in the above photo, announce that an injunction had halted the foreclosure sale. At right, Judge Hilliard Comstock, seated, signs the injunction as rancher Case watches.

—Press Democrat Collection

for the sale, a man elbowed his way through the crowd to the steps and whispered to Berkeley's J. Stitt Wilson. Wilson raised his arms over his head. Superior Court Judge Hilliard Comstock had returned from a trip in time to issue an injunction to halt the sale. The press noted the "rolling roar of cheers." Finley's mediation plans went into effect. Case was given three months to make his payments. Within that period the Jones Act, a state mortgage moratorium, went into effect. The farmers had won the fight.

But they had not won the war. Between August of 1933 and April of 1934, Sonoma County farmers required $1,572,800 in cash farm loans from the federal government. Nearly all the loans were made on property that was heavily mortgaged and facing foreclosure.[16] Some of the farmers in the crowd on the courthouse steps that day in '33, joining in the singing of "John Brown's Body" in celebration of victory, would lose their own farms before the war economy brought new prosperity.

The Depression was a bleak chapter in history, although Americans would acquire a kind of pride in their ability to cope with hardship and to help each other. Businessmen strived for optimism, even when there was little to build on. Stockbrokers, particularly, were challenged. But, as always in a free enterprise system, there was money to be made. Broker Leonard Talbot, who was working in Sonoma County for a Chicago brokerage firm in 1929, would decline, for the rest of his life, to discuss the negative effects of the October crash. "The prices went down," he would tell an insistent interviewer nearly seventy years later, "until there was a very great opportunity to buy."[17]

For the working class, however, the Depression was the greatest economic challenge of the century. It changed the country's politics and created an awareness of human needs. And it added a new term to the American lexicon—"Depression mentality"—which would be used to describe a certain cautious attitude in financial affairs for generations to come. ❧

Hard Work

Placed in the context of the troubled Depression years, the events of Santa Rosa's summer of 1935 are just one more episode in the violent history of California labor. The intensity of emotion that exploded in what historian Carey McWilliams has called "a saturnalia of rioting, intimidation and violence" was to mark Santa Rosa for the half-century to follow as a dwelling place of political conservatives, a town where reformers needed to proceed with caution.[1]

Silva M.A. "Jack" Green, a Santa Rosa sign painter, and Solomon Nitzberg, a chicken rancher at Two Rock, were stripped to the waist, covered with tar and feathers, and instructed to get out of Sonoma County and never return. The two men were part of a group of labor organizers who had been taken forcibly from their homes by an organized band of "night riders," brought to a hop warehouse on Santa Rosa's Third Street, and ordered to kiss the American flag and swear they would cease organizing activity. When Green and Nitzberg refused to comply, the buckets of tar and sacks of feathers were brought forth to perform this gesture of ignominy.

The night of August 21 was the culmination of years of fear and anger. These men had, indeed, been actively working to organize apple pickers in the county. Sonoma County farmers depended on a migrant labor force of thousands of pickers who came every harvest to work for about 25 cents an hour. Farmers were frightened by the wholesale failure of agriculture in the midwest, and they saw the march of the more militant urban unions into the orchards and fields as a threat to the future of the family farm, an institution on which the county's very lifestyle depended.

The action of the mob that resulted in two men injured and painted with tar and coated with chicken feathers was neither sudden nor spontaneous. Four years

Sonoma County's violent summer of 1935 was capped by a wild night in August when vigilantes tarred and feathered labor organizers in Santa Rosa. The incident gained international attention. The same photograph of Jack Green and Sol Nitzberg which appeared in the *Press Democrat*, left, also appeared in publications throughout the world. At right, the photo is the cover of a workers' daily newspaper titled *AIZ*, published in Czechoslovakia with an international circulation of 300,000.

of name-calling and escalating violence preceded the event. The organization of a radical union called the Cannery and Agricultural Workers Industrial Union (CAWIU) engendered a militant statewide group known as the Associated Farmers of California. With the backing of law enforcement officials, frightened farmers warned, threatened, and sometimes terrorized workers to halt the ruralization of the union activity they feared would break the back of a Depression-weighted agriculture.

In the parlance of the time the union organizers, most of whom were members of the American League Against War and Fascism, were all considered "Commies" or "reds," and the farmers all "Fascists." The labor organizers passed petitions, marched on Sacramento, and talked strike talk to groups of workers. The farmers lobbied for anti-picketing and anti-riot laws, burned crosses outside labor camps, and organized quasi-military forces.[2]

In Sonoma County, the name-calling escalated to confrontation level in 1932 when Thomas Bertino, passing a petition attempting to certify the Communist Party for the county election ballot, was jailed, prompting an anonymous threat that "blood will be shed" if he were not freed. When a signer, John Felciano, protested to authorities that he had been misled about the intent of the petition, Bertino was arrested and charged with "falsifying." Both witnesses and spectators at Bertino's court hearing were thoroughly (some said roughly) searched and a rally of support had to be canceled when the carpenters' union hall suddenly became unavailable.[3]

In 1933, a "jobless march" on Sacramento united local police, sheriff's deputies, traffic officers, and members of the American Legion, a group whose members had become vocal supporters of the Associated Farmers throughout the state. They gathered in Santa Rosa ready to deal with some 200 marchers who were expected to pass through on their way to the state capitol to attend a rally asking for increased welfare benefits. The armed men announced their intention to see that the marchers were

Nummer 38   19. September 1935

—Pamela Dornfeld Collection

185

refused both food and shelter. The worried citizens were overreacting. Only twelve marchers showed up in Santa Rosa and, after a few speeches on the courthouse steps, walked on to Cotati to spend the night.

Santa Rosa's National Guard was mobilized to help on the San Francisco waterfront when longshoremen struck at all Pacific Coast ports in 1934. The bloody San Francisco dock strike became a citywide general strike. Customers from San Francisco came to Santa Rosa to buy supplies when the strike paralyzed San Francisco commerce. Among farmers, fears of the spread of labor unrest escalated. Apple growers, whose annual Sonoma County production figures were more than 50,000 tons of fruit, were particularly uneasy. The Farm Bureau asked the Board of Supervisors for a county ordinance forbidding labor riots. The board declined to pass such a law, but the decision could scarcely be considered a victory for the unions. Violence spread across the countryside. On July 14, the night before the general strike began, nine maritime workers from San Francisco, called "terrorists" in the *Press Democrat* headlines, were arrested for attempting to interfere with truck traffic on the Redwood Highway. Four of the men were accused of firing on a produce truck driver near Cloverdale. The other five were suspected of attempting to set fire to trucks and were picked up by highway patrolmen near Petaluma. Fearing further disruption of trucking, the sheriff and CHP formed armed convoys, specifically to escort the county's apple crop to market. Sheriff Harry Patteson deputized more than 150 men as an "Army of Peace" that same summer.

Meanwhile, a leader emerged for the workers in the person of Vernon Healy, a labor organizer who helped form a chapter of the Public Works and Unemployed Union in the county. Healy had been a candidate for state senate on the Communist ticket in the last election and was representative of the forces the farmers feared most.4 So was Louis Lagomarsino, an elderly rancher from the Monroe district on the western edge of Santa Rosa.

Lagomarsino was the Communist candidate for assembly in 1934. Both had county ties, Healy being a former Cotati blacksmith who now worked as a foreman for the State Emergency Relief Administration (SERA). Still, it was these two, plus Bertino, *Press Democrat* editor Ernest Finley pointed at when he wrote calling for a "housecleaning" to remove outside agitators from the county.5

In the spring of 1935, as the well-organized Associated Farmers of California was assuring its members that it had successfully ended labor organizing in the state, things turned ugly in Sonoma County. Trouble began when two men were arrested for handing out pamphlets calling for a "May Day United Front." Lagomarsino posted their bail. An American Civil Liberties Union lawyer came from San Francisco to meet with city attorney Edward Koford and charges were subsequently dropped. But it was apparent to the citizens of the county that the "red menace" was still a threat, despite disavowal by Sonoma County unions of Healy's radical PWUU.

At the end of the month a large group of apple pickers and packing shed workers, estimated by the *Press Democrat* as between 400 and 500 in number, heard speeches by Healy and Lagomarsino and voted to strike for an increase in wages from 25 cents to 40 cents per hour. Growers met and agreed they could not afford to increase the labor cost of the harvest. The strike was on.6

The optimistic news for the growers was that the 500 strikers were only a small part of the thousands of pickers who came to work in the Sonoma County harvest every year. Sheriff Patteson's "Army of Peace" swelled to 500 special deputies and he promised growers his office had a stockpile of "tear bombs, nauseating gas and other modern equipment" in case of riots in the orchards or packing sheds.7

Growers went to San Francisco to emergency camps run by the State Emergency Relief Administration and brought truckloads of pickers to their orchards. Vigilantes surrounded the strike camp near Sebastopol,

Sheriff Takes Poke At Red

Chief Floors Another In Short Battle

No Sir, No Cowards In S. R.

SHERIFF HARRY PATTESON had bruised knuckles of his right hand wrapped in adhesive tape and a belligerent delegate of "The American League Against War and Fascism" gingerly rubbed a tender jaw as the main casual-

patroling the camp boundaries. Talk of "necktie parties" presented a real threat in Santa Rosa, where the highly-publicized lynching of three men had occurred just fifteen years earlier. Sheriff Patteson refused to offer protection to the frightened strikers unless their leaders left the county. Healy and Lagomarsino complied. But they did not stay away.

Four days into the strike the leaders returned to Santa Rosa for a meeting at Germania Hall on Third Street. Although the meeting was advertised as a United Front rally against war and Fascism, growers knew it was attended by several hundred striking apple workers.[8] While the meeting was in progress, a band of 250 vigilantes stormed up the stairs and into the hall, seized Lagomarsino and kicked him down the steps, and beat a man identified in the newspaper only as "one Marcus, operator of a Cotati service station." Marcus, said the *Press Democrat*, was believed to be the official organizer for the Communist party. The mob, described by the newspaper as "orderly and well-organized," set on Vernon Healy with billy clubs, leaving him bleeding from scalp wounds that required hospital treatment.

Before they left the hall, the vigilantes addressed the workers. One apple grower, unidentified in the newspaper accounts, spoke to the workers of the ruin that ranchers would face if the Gravenstein strike were permitted to continue. He appealed to them to return to their jobs. Another speaker, also unidentified, warned that a continuation of the strike would occasion a vigilante visit to the Handy's Grove fruit camp, scene of the first mass meetings to discuss wage demands.

The message was received. Loud and clear. Convinced the strike could not safely continue in the violent climate, packinghouse employees signed an agreement with the packers and shippers and reported for work on schedule the next morning. But no such agreement was made with the growers, and the pickers remained on strike. Representatives for the apple and hop ranchers met with District Attorney William Cowan, Senator Herbert Slater, and members of SERA, asking for a "no-work, no-eat" policy. They wanted SERA to declare that able-bodied workers could not receive relief if there was work available. When state officials balked, the growers sought a court order. Growers issued an ultimatum to the relief agencies.[9] Both the WPA and SERA were warned that all radicals must be purged from their ranks in Sonoma County within forty-eight hours. District WPA director F.M. Holley responded the following week with an assurance that his government agency would not tolerate "interference" by agitators with the federal work program.

The county's acknowledged agitator, Communist party member Healy, added fuel to the fires when, on August 9, he filed suit in superior court against federal, state, and city law enforcement agencies, listing twenty-eight men in his accusation against those who had beaten him in the vigilante action at Germania Hall on August 2.[10] He named CHP officers and a *Press Democrat* reporter, along with Assemblyman Hubert Scudder; the mayor of Santa Rosa, George Cadan; and the secretary of the Healdsburg Chamber of Commerce, Fred Cairns. The Healdsburg chamber, not intimidated, passed a resolution calling for a loyalty oath from every person on relief rolls in California. The *Press Democrat* editorial writer favored such a requirement.

Meanwhile, as growers' attempts at legal sanctions against striking workers failed, tempers were flaring. When a representative from the American League against War and Fascism came to the sheriff's office to present copies of a resolution denouncing the vigilante activity at the Germania Hall meeting, Sheriff Patteson punched one of the spokesmen in the face. Santa Rosa Police Chief Emil Biavaschi punched another. Then they ran the visitors out of the office.[11]

Labor organizers, eager for more confrontation, then aimed at the most vulnerable spot in Sonoma County agriculture, the hop harvest. Faced with a two-week season in which the hops had to be picked and processed, the growers of the county's most perishable and economically volatile crop were the targets. On August 21, the day before the hop harvest was to begin, labor organizers secretly distributed leaflets calling for a strike in the hop yards as well as the orchards. It was, the growers would say later, the last straw.

A group of 300 men, mustered by the American Legion—the organization which had been at the forefront, statewide, in the ongoing protests of labor activity as "Un-American"—met that same night. They gathered at two locations, at Depot Park and at Third and A streets, because they had heard there was to be a labor meeting. Finding no meeting at either place, they broke into small groups and went out on a night-rider mission, seeking those they believed were causing the labor problems.[12]

They seized sign painter Jack Green as he was leaving his studio in the Dougherty-Shea Building and, according to court testimony later, brought him before "the boss," Fred Cairns, who was waiting in the nearby Native Sons Hall. Using Green as bait to get the others, they drove him first to the Bertino residence and then to the Lagomarsino ranch, but found no one home. They went next to Two Rock to the home of Sol Nitzberg. They sent Green to the door to call Nitzberg out, but Green bolted, ran inside, and joined Nitzberg, who had a shotgun and announced his intention to protect his wife and children, who were also in the house.

After a brief siege outside the Nitzberg home, a canister of tear gas was lobbed into the house and the Nitzberg family and Green emerged, coughing and gasping. The two men were taken back to Santa Rosa, where other bands of vigilantes had arrived with their own captives. There were Charles Mayer and George W. Ford from Cotati and Ed Wolff, who was dragged from his hiding place at the home of Beulah B. Heaney, on Walker Avenue in Santa Rosa.

The five men were taken to a warehouse on Sebastopol Road and warned to cease any further interference in the harvest. All the men were beaten. An American flag was produced and they were ordered to kiss it. Mayer, Ford, and Wolff did so, leaving their bloodstains on the banner. Green and Nitzberg refused. The crowd, according to the *Press Democrat* account, "howled with rage." The pair were beaten until they complied, stripped of their clothing, covered with crank oil and hot tar and feathers, and dumped from a car at the edge of town. They were picked up by William Heaney, Beulah's son, who was looking for them. They were taken to the Heaney home on Walker Avenue and then returned to their homes. Both sought medical attention, Nitzberg in San Francisco, where he took sanctuary at the home of a relative, and Green in Santa Rosa.

It was October of 1936, fourteen months after the incident, before the charges of assault, kidnapping, and conspiracy, brought by victim Jack Green, reached a Sonoma County courtroom. The state attorney general's office, yielding to Green's persistent claims that he could identify men in the band that seized him, served as prosecutor when the Sonoma County District Attorney's office declined to bring charges.

Charges against eleven of the twenty-three men identified by Green—including *Press Democrat* reporters

Herbert Waters Jr. and Julian Mayar—were dismissed at the preliminary hearing.[13] A dozen men were remanded for trial, but, at the outset of the trial a visiting judge dismissed charges against three ranchers and a businessman, all Healdsburg-area residents, for lack of evidence.

Those who stood before the bar of justice in the four-day trial were also mostly from Healdsburg. Fred Cairns, secretary of the Healdsburg Chamber of Commerce, was named by prosecutors as the "captain" of the vigilantes. Arthur Meese was president of the Healdsburg chamber. William Casselberry was identified as a former city editor of the *Healdsburg Tribune*. B.H. Madison was a Healdsburg fruit buyer; William Maher, a Healdsburg businessman. John Barries was a rancher, Sidney Elphick was a Cotati resident, and Thomas Campion, the lone Santa Rosan charged, was a cigar store clerk, later to become a court bailiff.

The defense attorneys for the accused were the best Sonoma County could offer—Finlaw Geary, whose courtroom skills were celebrated, and Clarence J. "Red" Tauzer, later to be state senator from Sonoma County. From the attorney general's office, E.B. Power was chief prosecutor.

The trial attracted statewide attention from the press. "The Tar Party" had become a cause championed by the American Civil Liberties Union, whose efforts kept it alive in the minds of the general public. It may be safe to conclude that the trial, as well as the event itself, generated more interest outside than within Sonoma County. The *Press Democrat*, whose reporters were in the thick of the fray, made no pretense of objectivity, and those who recall the times would later express surprise at the importance historians attached to the events of that summer and the trial that followed. Herb Waters, who was a twenty-three-year-old reporter then, recalled the trial in later years: "There were people involved from the sheriff's office, from the police department. They were all in the courtroom and nobody knew anybody," Waters said.

It took four days to present the evidence. On the last day the judge dismissed charges against Madison and Campion. The day before the cases of the remaining six defendants went to the jury, news came that the United States attorney had banned the American League Against War and Fascism from using public schools. This was good news for the defense. Attorneys Geary and Tauzer predicted the ban would help their clients. The verdict came back in sixteen minutes—not guilty on all counts.[14]

The list of members of the jury indicates a predominance of ranchers and their wives—eight of the twelve. The jury foreman was Roy Daniels, a retired Santa Rosa piano dealer. Gus J. Wright, a Guernewood Park realtor, was a jury member. So were Healdsburg housewives Rena Belli and Myrtle Brown. The remainder were all involved with agriculture: Joseph McDonough, an Alexander Valley rancher; Nellie Teavis, wife of a Healdsburg rancher; Catherine Sprauer, wife of a Roblar District rancher; F. Presley Abshire, a Geyserville rancher who later succeeded Red Tauzer in the state senate; Conrad Peters, a Penngrove rancher; Carolyn Kennedy, a Sebastopol apple orchard owner; LaVerne Furman, a rancher from Freestone; and George Foote, a rancher from Geyserville.

Herb Waters, his own charges dismissed at the preliminaries, covered the trial for the *Press Democrat*. His account of defense attorney Tauzer's presentation to the jury is indicative of the tone the hometown newspaper chose to record the event.

"Tauzer pulled a small, silken American Flag from his pocket," Waters wrote, "which he placed on the railing before the jurors. Tears dimmed the eyes of the jurors, courtroom staff members, the six defendants and half-dozen newspapermen as Tauzer paid tribute to the Stars and Stripes and praised the defendants for protecting the flag from those who sought to tear it down."[15]

An ACLU reporter, writing for the organization's San Francisco newspaper, saw it differently. "Of course," he wrote, "no one expected convictions in mob-ruled Sonoma County."[16]

The messages delivered in the wake of the widely publicized violence of Santa Rosa's "saturnalia" summer indicate some ambivalence on the part of the citizens of Sonoma County. Jack Green experienced enormous difficulties in his attempt to bring his attackers to justice. Sheriff Harry Patteson, seen by some as the hero of the summer for his "Army of Peace" action and his "walk-down" of murderer Al Chamberlain three weeks earlier, nonetheless was defeated in his attempt at re-election the following year. It was the only defeat he suffered in the six times he stood for the county's top law enforcement position.

In a time when politics often seemed to be a choice of two extremes, the labor press and more liberal newspapers, such as the *San Francisco News*, viewed Santa Rosa's long, hot summer as a milestone in the "rising tide of potential Fascism in California"[17] while conservative editors hailed the vigilantism fostered by the Associated Farmers as Sonoma County's "direct answer to the red strike fomenters."

The liberal *News*, of course, was gleeful in reporting the subsequent difficulty experienced by farmers in inducing farmworkers to come and work in Sonoma County.[18] Even the wire services saw the news value in this turn of events in 1936. "The mob action of the vigilantes," reported the United Press wire service, "has frightened away from the county so many workers that the county is 20 percent under the number of pickers needed."[19]

It's true that strikebreaking and widely reported violence did backfire on the farmers. In August of 1936, the manager of the National Reemployment Service admitted to his advisory board that hop growers were willing to pay higher wages than the previous year and provide transportation to the hop yards. The *Press Democrat* failed to comment on the irony. But even an offer of higher wages was not enough inducement to bring migrant pickers back to Sonoma County, and local growers, complaining of the labor shortage, were forced to plead for help to save the crop.

Historian McWilliams dubbed this situation "the Santa Rosa technique," in his book *Factories in the Field*,

calling it "the short-sightedness of employer violence." In the harvest season of 1937, according to McWilliams, "Sonoma County flooded Los Angeles County officials with telegrams demanding that 20,000 workers be detached from relief rolls and sent north to work in the orchards."[20]

A Los Angeles reporter, Tom O'Connor of the *Evening News*, came to Sonoma County to report that there was no labor shortage, that growers were unwilling to pay a decent wage, and that migrant workers in this area were "destitute." He blamed state officials for cooperating with the influential growers. The fact that the WPA shut down in Sonoma County in August of 1936 so as to provide farm harvest workers, halting work on twelve government-financed projects employing 250 men, lends credibility to reporter O'Connor's claims that state officials were cooperating with growers.[21] Apple pickers, however, were paid an average of $56 per month, while WPA workers were making $44.[22]

Historically, agriculture had been king in Sonoma County. Farmers, particularly the growers around Santa Rosa and Healdsburg, were the power elite. They owned substantial acreage, often lived in big houses in town, and controlled the politics and social life of their communities. Until the labor movement of the 1930s, their will was never seriously opposed. Their labor force had consisted of a series of immigrant groups, each new one joyfully replacing the previous, eager to begin a new life in America.

The Chinese who worked the fields in the 1870s and 1880s had been replaced by the substantial numbers of northern Italians who came to California, starting before the turn of the century. As the Italians moved from field work to other endeavors and to farms of their own, growers found Japanese contract laborers, offered by "bosses" similar to those who had supplied Hawaii's plantation owners with workers, eager to bring crews to Sonoma County in the harvest seasons.

In the fiscal year 1907-08, according to statistics from the Bureau of Labor Statistics, there were 3,035 workers employed on Sonoma County farms. Of that number, 642 were permanent employees, 2,393 were temporary. Nearly half of the temporaries—1,182 workers—were Asians. Many Japanese, like the Italians, were quick to leave the fields for orchards and chicken ranches of their own. Their well-known independence, in fact, caused farmers to consider them less satisfactory than the Chinese. Employers said they forced higher wages than they could afford to pay.[23]

Japanese farmers were the first Asians to challenge California's Alien Land Law of 1913 which denied them property rights. The Kawaoka family of Penngrove challenged the law in 1923 when the father filed letters of guardianship to hold property—a chicken ranch—for his three children, all of whom were born in the United States. Superior Court Judge Rolfe Thompson ruled against the Kawaokas, in language indicative of the existing attitudes toward Japanese.

"The purpose of the Alien Land Law," Judge Thompson wrote, "...is to protect our rapidly vanishing fertile soil against the invading horde of brown men who come here and shatter our standards of living and citizenship; who substitute their philosophy of politeness and cunning for 'golden rule,' who bring to us their Oriental ideas and religion. Over 5,000 of them were born in California last year.... They monopolize our richest fields.... Little wonder our legislators in their wisdom have found it necessary to defend our schools, our homes, and our lands against this unwelcome and unscrupulous invasion by every legislative means within their power."[24]

T. Fujita and his family fared better five years later when he filed letters of guardianship for his children, who were legal owners of his Penngrove chicken ranch. Charges of fraudulence for attempting to evade the land law were denied by a visiting judge and the decision was upheld in a subsequent appeal. Most Japanese immigrants planted

Asian workers comprised a substantial percentage of the agricultural work force in the 1920s and 1930s. Japanese Harry Otani, left, with a Filipino worker named Cortez at the Sherwood Seed Farm near Cotati. Otani later owned an open air farm market on a Farmers Lane corner that became Montgomery Village.

—*Otani Family Collection*

orchards and raised chickens on leased or rented land until their American-born children reached a majority and could legally own property. It was 1952, after the relocation camps of World War II, before Japanese immigrants were allowed to apply for United States citizenship.[25]

Filipino laborers were also contract workers who came by way of Hawaii, but not until the late 1920s. Joe Rivera was among the first to come to Sonoma County. His job was at the seed farm in the Cotati Valley, where he worked with "lots of Filipinos and lots of Japanese" who were generally isolated from Sonoma County society. Lucas Benigno was one of another group of pioneer Filipino workers in Sonoma County. Benigno's group came directly from the Philippines on their own. They were very young and very poor, having spent their savings for a $96 one-way passage to California. They earned reputations as hard-working field hands. Their wives, who came to join them in the late '30s, worked as domestics in Santa Rosa.[26]

The Filipinos, newly arrived in the United States, did not escape the labor unrest and violence of the '30s. There were bitter incidents in labor camps around Sebastopol when white workers formed vigilante groups to run the Filipinos out of the county, accusing them of taking jobs from Depression-poor white workers. The Filipinos could expect no help from the law. A story passed to subsequent generations in the Filipino community tells of a worker who went to the sheriff of Sonoma County to report threats made on his life. The sheriff is said to have told the worker: "If you don't want trouble, get out of town."[27]

World War I brought labor shortages to the county, but no serious crop loss occurred. Women and children worked in place of men who had gone to war. To be sure that there were plenty of workers in the apple packing houses, school was two weeks late opening.[28] The few times there were not sufficient numbers of harvest workers, boys and girls from San Francisco orphanages were brought in to pick berries and prunes, comparatively easy crops for children.

The workers designated by Depression-era researchers as "tramps" were always part of the agricultural labor force in Sonoma County. Frank Speth, in his thesis on farm labor here, describes them: "These men tramp the roads of the country with their blankets on their backs, begging for food; at times they work for short periods, moving on as soon as they have a couple of dollars in their pockets. They are restless and not dependable as laborers...during the harvest season their numbers increase. They come in hopes of securing work and, as one farmer expressed it, 'afraid that someone might offer them a job.' Where they are used, there is an evident shortage of labor."[29]

The Wheatland Riot of 1913 is generally regarded as the first indication of farm labor problems in California. The riot occurred when the Industrial Workers of the World protested the living and working conditions of some 2,800 hop pickers on the Durst Ranch in Wheatland in the Sacramento Valley. There were five deaths in the Wheatland riot, including the district attorney, a deputy sheriff, and several workers. The National Guard was called to stop the violence. The growers responded by hiring Burns Detective Agency security guards to effect a sweep of "Wobblies" in California agriculture.

Shock waves from the Wheatfield Riot swept through the hop fields of the state, including Sonoma County. The following summer, migrant hop pickers posted demands throughout the county asking that growers assure them free tents, free drinking water, one toilet for every fifty persons, and separate toilets for women. They also asked that men be available to help women and children lift sacks into the wagons. They asked a minimum wage of $1.25 per 100 pounds picked.[30]

In 1935, with Sonoma County ranking tenth in the nation in agricultural production, the labor force required at the

Ranchers supplied the labor camps but the workers made their own entertainment. This impromptu camp show took place on an outdoor platform on a ranch off Eastside Road in 1955.

peak of the harvest season was 20,000 workers, a number exceeding the population of Santa Rosa by some 5,000 people.[31] About one-third of these workers were migrants.

The migrant workers of the 1930s, armies of unemployed men and women from the cities, and dust bowl migrants forced off their own land in Arkansas, Oklahoma, and the Texas panhandle by the drought, were a different kind of farm labor. Driven to the fields by desperation, their circumstances seemed a far cry from the glorious hopefulness of the immigrant American.

The automobile changed the pattern of migrant workers. Entire families were packed into a car or truck to follow the California crops. The majority of these "Depression drifters" found work in California's Central Valley, but many also found their way north to Sonoma County. It is estimated there were more than 1,000 dust bowl migrant families in the county after 1935. Although they came to be known by the generic (and too-often derisive) term "Okie," they were from any of a half-dozen states on the southern plains where the wind had blown the farms away, the development of the tractor had phased out the sharecropper, and the Depression had made a marginal existence impossible.

Many of these migrant families found living conditions in California as tenuous as the life they had left behind. By the time the migration reached Sonoma County, the federal government had stepped in, building a series of farm labor camps in the Central and Salinas valleys where the families were guaranteed sanitation, hot showers, and a tent cabin for shelter. In 1938, two years after the dust bowl migration to California had reached its peak, long enough for a substantial number of workers to have pushed north, the Farm Security Administration proposed to build a labor camp in Sonoma County.

As was the case in previous farm labor disputes, the Sonoma County controversy came after much of the state felt the issue had been settled. In an editorial on January 5, 1938, the *San Francisco News* summed it up: "Opposition to

—John LeBaron, Press Democrat Collection

Federal camps for migratory farm laborers and their families has pretty well subsided as their benefits are realized. But it cropped up again recently in Sonoma County after the Farm Security Administration announced purchase of land for a new camp at Windsor near Healdsburg."

The camp proposal had met immediate opposition. Farmers, still raw from the apple strike of '35, viewed any labor camp as a dangerously fertile ground for union organizers. Santa Rosa attorney C.J. "Red" Tauzer, chairman of the National Re-employment Service's county advisory committee, reacted as early as 1936 to the earliest reports of labor camps in the Central Valley, expressing fears that the government was creating what he termed "a radical hotbed."[32] The Associated Farmers of Sonoma County, joined by the county's chambers of commerce, organized a vigorous campaign against the plan. When Farm Security

Administration officials failed to heed their protests and selected a site for the camp on Windsor River Road, convenient to both hops and prunes, they asked for a conference with Jonathan Garst, FSA regional director, who came to Sonoma County in January of '38 for the confrontation. At the Santa Rosa meeting, opponents presented their six points:

1. The camp would not provide enough housing. The government promised quarters for 250 families while 12,000 workers were needed each harvest season.
2. The location was poor.
3. Sonoma County's short harvest season did not justify such an expenditure of federal funds (a $617,000 grant from the FSA).
4. Sonoma County would have to provide schooling, medical care, hospitalization, and, possibly, direct relief for the camp residents.
5. Camp residents could refuse to admit newcomers who might become radical labor organizers.
6. Local peace officers would have no jurisdiction on federal property.[33]

The protests fell on deaf ears. Government camps had been successful in other agricultural areas of California. "If 75 percent of the agricultural employers employing 98 percent of the migratory farm labor in this county were to testify that there was no necessity for such a camp, couldn't it change your views?" Garst was asked. He answered that such testimony would not change the government plans. The interests of the migrant farm worker would be considered over the wishes of the farmers, he told them. Nor did he yield to requests for three or four seasonal camps in place of a permanent one at Windsor. The Farm Security Administration paid $8,000 to Harold Calhoun for nearly sixty-seven acres on a wooded knoll about two miles west of the Redwood Highway. The project was put out to bid in mid-February 1938.[34]

Wilford Howard was vocal in his support of Camp

The Crownover brothers and their families came from Calumet, Oklahoma to Camp Windsor in the late 1930s, working as pickers along the way. This photo of the Hyrum Crownover family was taken at Camp Windsor in 1939. In the back row, left to right, are Ann, Jessie, Hyrum, and Glen. Vel and Bill are in the front row.

—Crownover Family Collection

Windsor. Howard was a member of the State Farm Debt Adjustment Commission and Sonoma County chairman of the advisory committee on rural rehabilitation set up by the federal government to determine who would get farm loans. He had stepped to the forefront as a progressive agricultural leader in the mortgage protest focused on Forestville apple rancher James Case. Now, he responded to the Associated Farmers' objections in a statement to the press citing conditions in the hop and fruit districts of Sonoma County that "are a menace to health and an insult to decency." The federal camp, Howard said, would fulfill "a New Deal pledge by the President of the United States to improve the living conditions of the ill-housed, ill-fed, and ill-clothed of the nation."[35]

The outcome of the Camp Windsor controversy—the camp, when built, proved to be a dependable labor source for the very growers who had opposed it—was very different from earlier confrontations between labor and growers in Sonoma County. With the Depression waning and the Red Scare diminishing, none of the dire predictions of the farmers came true.

Camp Windsor, with its wood and canvas dwelling units, health clinic, laundry room, and dance hall for Saturday nights, looked like heaven to the road-weary migrant workers. It was the first Sonoma County home for at least 1,000 people, most of whom stayed for a summer and then found steady jobs and "a place of our own." The residents of Camp Windsor had a nickname for the place. They called it "Little Quanah," after a town in north Texas where many of the migrants had lived. The Rev. Charles Coates, a Healdsburg minister, was one of the transplanted Texans. He arrived at Camp Windsor, he liked to say in later years, to find there were "more people from Quanah in Windsor than there were in Quanah."

The prosperity that came with World War II extended to the migrant workers. Coates summed it up. "After the war come on," he said, "we could look at the jobs we'd been doing and know we didn't have to do that anymore."[39]

"**M**y father hadn't planned to be a migrant," said Opal Garrett Young, who was one of the first from Oklahoma to arrive in Sonoma County after the drought created the dust bowl and the Crash of '29 created the Great Depression. Remembering the childhood experience fifty years later, she spoke the words in a direct manner, intending them not for poignancy but for pure fact. "He'd planned on having a home and raising his family. There were lots of people like us who were uprooted by what happened in the '30s."[36]

It was the hop harvest of 1932 that brought them, ten-year-old Opal and her family. "My father always said when he was a little boy in Missouri he used to dream about how heaven looked and when he got to Sonoma County, he figured he'd found it."

The Garretts almost didn't make it to Sonoma County. "When we came across San Francisco Bay on the ferry, we had no money. None. My father had to borrow $2 from another traveler to get us to the hop fields. We came in an old Chevrolet. We didn't have a mattress on top of the car, we had a chicken coop. With chickens. When we stopped my mother would get out and gather eggs. The car's radiator went bad in the desert, but fortunately it rained just ahead of us all the way so we could keep filling it up. When we came to the mountains and the car couldn't make it over the steep parts, my two big brothers would hop out and give it a shove."

While Opal's family was in the first wave of migrants, who had to fend for themselves, Joe Young is representative of the later dust bowl refugees. Joe, in fact, claimed responsibility for starting the Quanah "connection" in Sonoma County. He heard about Camp Windsor from a friend and wrote "the folks. I didn't mean to start the whole gang out this way, but I guess I did," he said.[37]

The camp was not exclusively Texan. It was the first Sonoma County home for the Crownover family of Calumet, Oklahoma, who came by way of the cotton fields of Arizona and pea fields of the Imperial Valley. Glen Crownover, ten years old when his family left Oklahoma, remembered Camp Windsor—and getting there. "We almost starved to death," said Crownover. "Dad picked cotton. I picked and my sister Ann picked. Dad had $10 when we got to Buckeye [Arizona]. In a week or two we were down to $1. They didn't pay us in money. They gave us scrip to buy food, but we couldn't make enough to live on."[38]

Because of the drama of the Tar Party and the events that led up to it, and the opposition to Camp Windsor, albeit unsuccessful, it may seem that the story of the working class in Sonoma County in the first half of the 20th century is more a history of organized opposition than organized labor. In truth, trade unions fared reasonably well through this difficult period of Sonoma County's working class history, seemingly standing aloof from the troubles of the farm workers, which attracted more attention. The union movement was strong in the county and had been since its beginnings in the 1870s with the militant Workingmen's Party activity. The Santa Rosa Labor Council had organized in 1902. In 1909, the State Building Trades Council of California chose Santa Rosa for its eighth annual convention, an event attended by high praise for Santa Rosa as a union town.[40] By 1922, when the first Sonoma County Labor Journal was published, unions were well established in the county.

The noisiest of the group, perhaps, was the Sonoma County Building Trades Council, which included the carpenters', masons', and the laborers' unions. On their behalf, the council protested all efforts by the city and, to some extent, the county, to make street and civic building improvements at less than union scale wages. Although persistent, the building trades' unions were neither the most demanding nor the most effective of the labor organizations. In 1917, when the building trades' council petitioned the City Council to pay all employees assigned to curb and gutter work at union wage of $3 a day, their cause was successful. But, at the same time, painters in Santa Rosa were striking for $4.50 a day.[41]

The presence of the Industrial Workers of the World, or "Wobblies," resulted in increased awareness in all areas of union activity. Labor felt the need for support organizations. The Santa Rosa Labor Council welcomed a new union of laundry workers in 1914. The Painters Union also affiliated with the council that year. Bartenders Union, Local 770, organized in 1915. But opposition to union activity

was also solidified. The Santa Rosa Chamber of Commerce endorsed the statewide farmers' fight against a proposed eight-hour day. The issue was soundly defeated by the voters. Companies such as Mead Clark Lumber played on anti-union sentiment with ads promising that more than 95 percent of the flooring used in California had no union stamp on it.[42]

Yet Assemblyman Ralph Salisbury and Mayor Charles Lee joined Congressman William Kent of Marin County and his wife, a representative of the National Woman Suffrage Movement, in welcoming speeches to the California Federation of Labor at its convention in Santa Rosa in 1915. The state labor group promised that there was "no room in the federation" for the Industrial Workers of the World, but raised another politically explosive issue by welcoming two Japanese delegates, albeit without votes. The convention renewed its pledge to fight Asiatic labor. In 1915, laundry workers paid for an ad asking all union people to use Hughes and Hollister Wet Wash, the only union laundry in Santa Rosa, after Pioneer Laundry refused to fire employees who wouldn't pay union dues.[43] All forty-five members of the Boot & Shoe Workers Union employed by the Santa Rosa Shoe Manufacturing Company staged a two-day strike in 1915 to protest cuts in wages and the dismissal of a member.

In 1918, telephone operators and electrical wire workers staged a strike that stopped telephone service in the community, and labor unrest continued in that profession for a year or more.[44] Hours were as much a consideration as wages. In spite of the defeat of the Universal Eight Hour Law, limiting the work day, workers at Levin's Tannery organized a brief and successful strike which shortened their work day from nine hours to eight. The following year, in a rare show of unity, Santa Rosa's unions and the Merchants Association requested and got from the City Council the town's first "Sunday Law" requiring all stores, work shops, barbershops, factories, banks, and offices to close on the Sabbath. Restaurants, hospitals, drug stores, ice cream parlors, and filling stations were exempt.[45]

Organized labor prospered through the 'teens and '20s without serious opposition. In 1920, a nine-week strike of Petaluma millworkers who made chicken feed gained support from Santa Rosa union members who voted to boycott that city's Egg Day Parade. There was also a countywide move to stop eating and buying eggs until the millworkers gained their demands, but the economic sanctions were scarcely felt by the poultry industry, which was enjoying a national market. There was a Bay Area rail strike that same year which stopped all Santa Rosa freight trains. It was supported by the county's unions. The labor climate seemed comfortable enough for Santa Rosa's school teachers to talk of organizing for higher wages.

Organized labor may have reached its peak of strength in the '20s. Santa Rosa unionists built bleachers for 10,000 to celebrate the Golden Jubilee of Labor. Pathe News movie cameramen came to Santa Rosa to film the parade, a visit that was regarded as an honor by the local press.

The building trades' unions flexed their political muscles in the '20s. Carpenters and electricians walked off the building site for St. Rose Catholic Church's new parish house. Carpenters struck again while building the new high school and a new Fremont School on the old high school property on Humboldt Street in 1924. The strike lasted nearly three months and angered the community. Public sentiment was that the union problems were disrupting the education of Santa Rosa's children.[46] The labor dispute took a nasty turn when non-union workers, brought in to finish the job, were beaten by union men wielding steel pipes. The community outrage was expressed in the statements of civic leaders and letters to the editor of the newspaper.[47]

A potentially dramatic labor incident was avoided when, in 1929, a tear gas bomb placed in a Santa Rosa theater during a musicians' and projectionists' union dispute failed to detonate. Again in 1929, unionists turned out for the Labor Day celebration in great numbers,

apparently coming from all over the Bay Area as the newspapers reported that southbound ferries were unable to handle the crowds going home.

A shortage of farm labor was, once again, the central problem of the World War II years. Union organizing attempts were curtailed, not only by wartime patriotism but by the desperate shortage caused when men marched off to join the armed forces. In California in general and Sonoma

Braceros pose in an orchard near Windsor in the 1940s.

County specifically, the shortage was exacerbated by the relocation of the Japanese to camps far from the Pacific Coast. Japanese crews had supplied much of the seasonal labor in hops and orchards in the 1930s.

In the fall of 1942, Sonoma County schools delayed opening for several weeks to allow young people to work in the harvest. Even urban schools in the Bay Area closed to allow youth organizations to travel to rural counties to assist in the farm labor. The first of these "city kids" to report to Sonoma County came in groups of fifty from San Francisco high schools. They camped along the Russian River and were assigned to prune ranches and hop yards. Urban organizations also participated. The San Francisco Hiking Club sent 150 members. They came with their own commissary of food, bedding, and supplies. They were given shelter at Healdsburg High School.[48]

Women and teenagers answered the growers' pleas, but defense work took many of the women and their help was only a stopgap. Growers imported Jamaicans to pick the orchard crops and found them startlingly unsatisfactory from the outset. Walt Tischer, who managed both hop and apple harvests, recalled the Jamaican "experiment" in later years. "They didn't like it here one bit," said Tischer. "They said, 'We are British subjects. We can't live in tents.' And they hated hops."[49]

The most dramatic effect on labor in Sonoma County that resulted from World War II came with the *bracero* program. After the near-disaster of the 1942 harvest, the federal government scrambled to put in place a program to bring Mexican *campesinos*, or field workers, to the United States as temporary farm labor. The first group of Mexican workers to come as contract labor under the new program—labeled *bracero* (meaning strong-armed worker)—worked for Talmage "Babe" Wood at his parents' ranch on River Road in the summer of 1943.

When the Japanese family that had picked Wood's hops, prunes, pears, and apples was sent to relocation camp, Wood had been caught short-handed in the harvest of '42. He learned of the new Mexican National program and he enlisted immediately. "The government had opened an office on the fifth floor of the Rosenberg Building, "he would recall. "I contracted for 125 workers for the harvest of '43."

They came in special buses from the border. Most were between the ages of sixteen and twenty-five and came from Mexican farms. A few were from Mexico City. They carried with them little but the straw hats that were their trademark. Unlike the family-style harvest labor to which Sonoma County growers had become accustomed, these workers were not in a position to bring their own tents and camping gear for a gypsy-style summer of work.

"Our agreement with the government said we had to provide food, housing, and medical care," Wood said. "We put up tents with cots and blankets, built a community kitchen and a place to eat. We had a big cook stove and a cook who fixed three meals a day. It was a shaded campground. We drilled a well. And when they wanted to swim, we dammed Mark West Creek."

"When the harvest was over," said Wood, "they all wanted to stay in this country. But the contract was only for that season. I picked fifteen to stay the full year. I taught them pruning—we had vineyard and forty or fifty acres of apples. They worked out just fine."[50]

Benny Carranza might have been on that bus from the border. He had already achieved a measure of success as a professional basketball player in the Mexican league of the 1940s. He came to the *bracero* program in '43 as a kind of adventure and, by late summer, was picking hops on the I.D. Wood ranch (no relation to Babe Wood) on Brittain Lane west of Santa Rosa.

Benny, described by his friends as "the best dancer in Sonoma County," remembers that first summer as a time of high spirits among the men who felt very lucky to be earning U.S. dollars to send home to their families. "A beautiful time," Carranza would later recall. "On Sunday people would come from all over. There were lots of girls from the city and it was like a carnival, a fiesta, on the ranch."

Carranza, who knew English, supplemented his field labor pay with part-time work for Don Mills, the Sonoma County contractor who had signed with the federal program to import Mexican laborers. Because he could interpret, Benny assisted the growers in choosing workers from the men Mills brought from the border. Not all of his memories are as happy as those of the Sunday fiestas. "You'd be surprised," Carranza said, "how growers would treat the men. They even opened their mouths and looked at their teeth—like a horse. We felt degraded. We suffered, our people did, in those first years."

Like many *braceros*, Carranza was in and out of the United States in the 1940s. He worked at the Wood ranch. He worked for the Mills agency. He went home to Mexico to play the basketball season. "I even came back as a tourist one season," he said. He was not typical of the Mexican worker. His job with Mills gave him status in the Mexican community. "Benny was *el patron*," friend Rafael Morales remembered. "No matter what went wrong, they would come to Benny. 'Please, can you get me an extension? Please, Benny, they treat me bad.' You can hear lots of history from Benny," said Morales.

Morales, a foreman for a Windsor vineyard for more than thirty years, first came to the United States as an illegal alien in the '40s. With other young men from his native Oaxaca he made his way to a border town, hoping to find a labor contractor. But there were far more available workers than there were spaces on the contractors' buses. Word of the money to be made in the American fields had spread through the Mexican countryside, and workers, impatient with the Mexican government's system for issuing the "green cards" which identified workers as official members of the *bracero* program, simply crossed the border illegally. There they might find a renegade contractor who would place them, or a rancher, eager to circumvent government rules and minimum wages, who would give them day work.

The ones who could not find a contractor or did not trust the ones they found, sometimes struck out on their own. Morales spent three years shuffling back and forth across the border, working the farms of the Imperial Valley—Brawley, Calapatria, Westmoreland, where the heat was 110 degrees. Morales recalls hiding by daylight, traveling at night, working a day here and a day there for 35 cents an hour.

Finally, in 1951, he came to Sonoma County as a contract laborer and went to work for Harold McClish on his Westside Road ranch. For seven years he worked and saved money and waited for the all-important papers that would allow him to become a permanent resident. He sent for his wife and children. Their family home became the foreman's house on the McClish ranch, where he began his legal residence in the United States.

Lolita and Tony Tamayo went through their time as illegal aliens together. Tamayo left a grocery business in Guadalajara to join the *bracero* program in 1943, to make

"My life in Healdsburg," Rafael Morales wrote of these workers' tent cabins in 1952.

—Rafael Morales Collection

money to buy the building that housed his store. Like many Mexican workers he recognized the opportunities available in the United States. He returned to Guadalajara and married Lolita. They came to the United States, to Sonoma County, as illegals.

"We were wetbacks," Lolita Tamayo recalled, telling how she hid in a creek on a Sebastopol ranch, eight months pregnant with her first child, crying and praying that the men from Immigration would walk on past.

The stories told by Sonoma County residents who came, both legally and illegally, in the first years of Mexican labor, are stories like Lolita Tamayo's and Rafael Morales's. They tell of hiding, "making a nest like a rabbit" in hay stacks, of cooking on the ground, washing clothes in apple boxes, of hoeing rows a mile long with no water until the end, of subsisting for weeks on stolen fruit from the orchards, of crowded holding cells and more-crowded buses carrying them back to Mexico—where they would start all over again.[51]

While there was never again a season like the summer of '35 when organizers would be tarred and feathered in Sonoma County, agricultural workers would once more be the focus of organizing activity in the 1950s. In August of '55, William Grami, an organizer for the Teamsters Union, reported to sheriff's deputies that he had been kidnapped at gunpoint and beaten and robbed. Grami could not identify his assailants but told of threats from apple processing plant managers during labor negotiations. Cannery owners charged that Grami's abduction was staged by the union to gain public sympathy for its cause.

At the time of Grami's report, four of the six apple processing plants in Sebastopol were being picketed by Teamsters, who had begun attempts to organize apple workers several years earlier. In elections called under the auspices of the National Labor Relations Board in several of the plants, the union failed to gain representation. Charges of unfair labor practices against the plant managers went unproven.[52]

Santa Rosa and Sonoma County, as well as state and federal agencies, continued to make a sharp distinction between agricultural workers and the community labor market. A 1952 survey of labor in Santa Rosa, conducted by the State Department of Employment, reported 16,480 persons employed and 800 unemployed, being careful to label the statistics as "nonagricultural employment."

The survey showed that 6,300 of the persons employed in Santa Rosa (and 500 of the unemployed) were women; that there was a seasonal fluctuation in the labor market of about 2,500 persons, based largely on forestry and construction work. Wholesale and retail trade accounted for the highest number of wage earners, 5,500, nearly one-third of the market. Service-related jobs, 3,400, manufacturing, 1,760, the building trades, 1,700, transportation and utilities, 1,590, and government work, 1,390, comprised the remainder.

Wages in 1952 ranged from $60 a week for a skilled manufacturing worker (in this case a sewing machine operator at the shoe factory) to 85 cents an hour for a cannery worker. Stenographers made $50 weekly; typists, $45 dollars. Electricians could expect to be paid $3 an hour, butchers and machinists, $2.08, and laborers, $1.85— all of these being union scale.

Despite its proximity to the San Francisco Bay Area, where labor issues were at the top of the political agenda, Santa Rosa and Sonoma County remained provincial in these matters through the first half of the century. The agrarian character of the county set it squarely in opposition to all attempts to organize farm labor. And, despite some significant support for the trade unions in the town itself, to most wage earners, Santa Rosa was not considered a "union town." ❧

Workers in a Sebastopol apple processing plant, circa 1950.

Who's in Charge

The whoop-and-holler frontier politics of the Missouri-Confederate-Democrats who settled most of Sonoma County had been left behind in the 19th century. Representation still leaned heavily toward the democratic side of both the Congress and the state legislature. But great change lay ahead. The woman suffrage movement was being taken seriously—at least in local elections. Minorities were beginning to be heard. And two men who would dominate the county's political scene at the state and national level were just emerging as leaders.

In 1955, Charles J. Hagerty, longtime assistant secretary of state for California and a keen observer and chronicler of the state's politics, proposed a mythical California Political Hall of Fame. Although Hagerty had been closely associated with some 50,000 politicians in his forty years in the state capitol, he chose only ten for this honor.

—Finley Collection

There were seven Republicans on Hagerty's list, inluding Earl Warren and Hiram Johnson. The three Democrats selected were James D. Phelan, a state senator and mayor of San Francisco, and Clarence Lea and Herbert Slater, both of Santa Rosa.

The two men were contemporaries. While Slater represented Sonoma County's interests at the state level for much of the half-century, Clarence Lea was working on behalf of the North Coast in the House of Representatives for almost the same period of time.

For thirty-two years, from 1916 to 1948, Lea represented Sonoma County and ten other Northern California counties in Congress, his sixteen terms a record for the First Congressional District.

Lea, who came to the office from his position as a highly successful and popular district attorney of Sonoma County, ran—mostly unopposed—in a district that comprised Marin, Lake, Mendocino, Humboldt, Napa, Glenn, Colusa, Yuba, Sutter, and Butte counties, as well as his Sonoma County home. At a time when cross-filing was allowed on the California ballot, Democrat Lea won both his own party's and the Republicans' primaries in all but two elections. The first time he stood for the office he was opposed by Republican Edward Hart. Twenty years later the Republicans put up Nelson Van Matre of Healdsburg, but Lea polled 53 percent of the vote in the general election. In 1934, he was opposed by Allen Gifford, a Socialist candidate, and in 1940 and 1942 by Communist Party candidate Albert (Mickey) Lima, but he outpolled his minority candidate opponents in each instance with 93 percent of the vote. His toughest minority challenge came in 1938 from Ernest Mitchell of the Townsend party, the followers of Dr. Francis Townsend, a Long Beach physician with a pension plan proposal that drew thousands of elderly Californians to "Townsend Clubs" all over the state.

Lea served in Congress under six presidents and was in Washington longer than any other California congressman. As a new congressman he devoted himself to

Congressman Clarence F. Lea, at left, served a record sixteen terms from the First District, representing Sonoma County and ten other Northern California counties in Washington for thirty-two years.

the concerns of his constituents. He authored the California Indians Claims Bill and was instrumental in the establishment of a Sacramento Valley flood control district. Later, his bills aided Pacific Coast ship building. Harbors at Crescent City, Humboldt Bay, and several other California coastal towns were made possible by his legislation, and he worked vigorously for the establishment of Hamilton Air Force Base in Marin County. He was proud of his conservation record, which included the acquisition of some 50,000 acres of wilderness in Lake and Mendocino counties as national forest.

He served on the committee that wrote the legislation that would ultimately build Hoover Dam. He was an early advocate of veterans' relief and active in establishing a system of veterans' hospitals. He served on numerous agricultural subcommittees and actively supported the government's rural electrification projects.

His interest in public health, specifically research for disease prevention and safeguards to protect the public, was well known. Arguably, his most important single piece of legislation was the Lea-Copeland Pure Food and Drug Act.

Sonoma County's political leaders greet U.S. Senator William Gibbs McAdoo on a visit to Santa Rosa in the 1930s. From left to right are Ernest L. Finley, Congressman Lea, Senator McAdoo, and Santa Rosa City Manager Charles O. Dunbar.

—*Finley Collection*

State Senator Herbert Slater, below, represented Sonoma County in the Legislature for thirty-seven years. Hubert Scudder, at left, was a Sebastopol resident who served fifteen years as assemblyman before being elected to Congress, where he served five terms.

—John LeBaron, Press Democrat Collection

He was also vitally concerned with interstate and foreign commerce and served on that House committee for twenty-seven years. In 1937, after a long Republican tenure, Texas Democrat Sam Rayburn became Speaker of the House, and Lea became chairman of the committee.

In 1932, Lea was the only California Democrat serving in the House of Representatives. And he was never, in his thirty-two years in Congress, busier than he was that year. He authored the Natural Gas Act, served on the committee that wrote the Securities Act, and, on March 7, introduced—and had passed—twenty-one bills in a single day.

Another of Lea's great interests—perhaps fostered by the fact that he represented the westernmost district in the nation at the time—was aviation. He was responsible for the Air Commerce Act of 1926, which was the first federal control of air traffic. It served as the cornerstone for the development of commercial aviation. The Lea-McCarran Civil Aeronautics Act of 1938 established the Air Safety Board and the first central agency to regulate airports. It is still the base for regulatory air laws. The Lea Civilian Air Pilot Training Act provided the first government standards and training for young pilots and would prove invaluable to the Army Air Corps during World War II. His pre-war legislation, the Lea Transportation Act of 1940, coordinating all transportation agencies in the nation, was also to prove farsighted.[1]

Thanks to Lea's tenacious hold on the office, there were only five other congressmen from Santa Rosa's district in the first half of the century. Frank Coombs, a Napa Republican, was elected in 1900 and served one term, being unseated by a Napa Democrat, Theodore Bell. Bell, too, was a one-term congressman, being displaced in 1904 by Duncan McKinlay, a Santa Rosa paint store owner. McKinlay, a Republican with a gift for oratory, held the office for three terms, retiring in 1910 when William Kent, the Marin County conservationist, ran and was elected on the Hiram Johnson-inspired Progressive ticket. Kent, too, served three terms, retiring as Lea began his long congressional career.[2]

—Sonoma County Museum

Herbert W. Slater was Lea's counterpart in state politics. First elected to the state legislature as an assemblyman in 1910, he served two terms, then, in 1914, ran for and was elected to the office of state senator, a position he held until his death in 1947. During his ten terms in public office, he continued his work as a journalist, holding the title of "advisory news editor" and writing a daily political column as well as a hunting and fishing column for the Santa Rosa newspapers.

Slater, a native of England and the son of a Church of England rector, had come to Sonoma County by way of New York, New Orleans, and Monterey, to work on a ranch near Fulton in the 1890s. In 1892 he took a job turning the crank on the press for the *Press Democrat* and, in 1894, both he and his friend Charley Reindollar were hired as writers for the newspaper on the same day.[3]

Slater was a likeable man who soon became a regular in the company of "bon vivants" who enjoyed regular tours of Sonoma County's drinking and dining establishments. It was in one of these, the Cicucci Hotel in Sonoma, in 1910, that Slater and his friends made the decision that launched his political career.

Soon after his election to the assembly, cataracts caused him to lose the sight in both eyes. Surgery restored partial vision in one eye, but a minor accident, a blow from a jack handle while changing a tire on one of those tight-springed early automobile wheels, cost him the use of his good eye, too. By 1919, he was blind. As "the blind senator," he became near legend in both Sacramento and Sonoma County for his ability to recognize acquaintances by the sounds of their voices and their footsteps. At home, his blindness was an accepted fact. His columns were dictated. The news of the day was read to him. But in Sacramento, many of his casual acquaintances and even some of his colleagues, were unaware of his blindness.

Slater's popularity among the voters of his district was based on his personal record rather than party affiliation. A friend and confidant of his publisher, Ernest Finley, Slater criss-crossed the aisle in the senate chambers four times in harmony with Finley's endorsement of candidates for governor. Which one influenced the other is an unanswered question. Beginning and ending as a Democrat, he became a Progressive when Hiram Johnson ran for governor, a Republican in the election of Friend Richardson, and then came back to the Democratic side for the administration of Culbert Olson.

He was extremely interested in fish and game regulations, and he authored pioneer legislation on behalf of the handicapped, as well as bills to preserve the Sonoma Mission and Fort Ross as state parks. He was chairman of the senate education committee, and his authorship of public school legislation earned him honors from educators. Santa Rosa's second junior high school bears his name. He was responsible for much of the legislation establishing agricultural fairs in the state, a pet project of publisher Finley's. He was also the author of the "Little Lindbergh Bill" exacting a death penalty for kidnappers.

When Slater died in 1947 he was seventy-two years old. He suffered a heart attack at the corner of Fourth and E streets, on his way to the newspaper office to write his columns. His last political endeavors were meetings with Governor Earl Warren at the Sonoma County Fair and with former President Herbert Hoover at Bohemian Grove, both within the week. His last "Rod & Gun" column, which appeared on the day of his death, was a lively account of a wild pig hunt near Cazadero.

Slater was a lifelong bachelor. His colleagues and his constituents were his family. His body lay in state for three days at Welti's Funeral Home, on the very corner where he died, and his funeral at the Church of the Incarnation was the largest that congregation had witnessed, with people standing on the steps, the sidewalk, and into the street to pay tribute to their legislator and their friend.[4]

Slater's control of the state senate seat was nearly as effective as Lea's tenure in Congress. There were just six other senators serving in the first fifty years of the century:

Democrat J.C. Sims, 1899-1903; Republican and former Santa Rosa mayor Edward Woodward, 1903-07; Republican Walter Price, 1907-11; Santa Rosa attorney and Democrat Louis Juilliard, 1911-15; and, after the death of Slater, Republican attorney Clarence J. "Red" Tauzer, who died in office; and his successor, Geyserville prune grower F. Presley Abshire, a Republican, who finished Tauzer's term and was re-elected twice.

Sonoma County's representation in the state assembly was considerably more confusing, as districts altered often and two or more assemblymen came from districts that included portions of the county. Of the twenty-three assemblymen who looked after the county's interests between 1900 and 1950, fourteen were Republicans. They

Sonoma County was an important cog in California's political machinery in the years before World War II. Below, Ernest L. Finley, center, president of the Redwood Empire Newspaper Publishers' Association, greets former governors Friend W. Richardson, left, and Frank L. Merriam, right, at a publishers' meeting in Cloverdale in 1939.

—Press Democrat Collection

Northern California still dominated state politics in the first half of the century, giving voters of Sonoma County a sense of power and urgency. Slater's place in the legislature was considered important. Governors visited the county routinely. At least one had hometown connections.

Santa Rosa voters were very interested in the gubernatorial election of 1926. Clement C. Young, the Progressive Republican who challenged his party's incumbent, Friend Richardson, was a former Santa Rosa resident and an 1886 graduate of Santa Rosa High School (where he was a classmate of Assemblyman David Anderson). He kicked off his campaign, in fact, with a speech in Sebastopol.[5]

Young had been speaker of the state assembly during the Progressive era and, when he ran against Richardson, was serving as lieutenant governor. He made his Progressive followers uneasy during the election campaign by accepting the support of San Francisco banker A.P. Giannini. In the year after he took office, his newly appointed superintendent of banks, Will C. Wood (who would later be a vice president of Bank of America), revoked the restrictions on branch banks. Before the year was out, Giannini's Bank of Italy had increased its branches from 98 to 289.[6]

There were glimpses of the Progressive philosophy in Young's administration. In 1929 California became the first state to require counties to provide old-age pensions for employees. And political historians would later note that Young's most substantial achievement was a business-like reorganization of the state budget system.[7]

Prohibition was the issue that defeated him—with some behind-the-scenes help from the man he had defeated in 1926. After a disastrous decade, many voters were ready to call the Great Experiment a failure and talk about repealing the 18th Amendment. Young was not one of them. An outspoken "dry," he was challenged in the Republican primary by a high-profile "wet," Mayor "Sunny Jim" Rolph. Richardson, seeking political revenge, encouraged another dry candidate, Buron Fitts, to enter the race, dividing the large dry vote in Protestant Southern California. Rolph won by a narrow margin and went on to win the general election.

The Sonoma County Courthouse, in the center of Santa Rosa, was the wellspring for much of the political activity of the first half of the century.

included Valley Ford banker Harrison M. LeBaron, 1899-1900; F.A. Cromwell, 1901-1906; merchant H.L. Tripp,1905-06; Stanley Collister, 1907-08; Windsor rancher W.A. Weske, 1907-08; W.B. Whitney, 1909-10; James W. Hamilton, 1911-12; Santa Rosa hop broker Robert Madison, 1917-20; Lyman Green, 1917-18; A.F. Stevens, 1919-22; Lucien Fulwider, 1921-24; Emmett Donohue, 1923-24; Hubert Scudder, 1925-40; and Richard McCollister, 1941-60.

Democrats who served in the assembly in those years were former Santa Rosa city attorney William F. Cowan, 1899-1900; Finley's partner Charles O. Dunbar, 1903-04; Juilliard, 1909-10; Slater, 1911-14; G.W. Libby, 1913-14; George Salisbury,1915-16; Knox Bolde, 1915-16; dentist David Anderson, 1925-28; and Frank Luttrell, 1929-30. Salisbury, a sign painter by profession, was a member of the Santa Rosa City Council when he was elected to the assembly and continued to serve as a councilman while in the state legislature.[8]

Hubert Scudder, a Sebastopol insurance man, represented Sonoma County in the assembly for the longest period of time, his fifteen-year tenure spanning the years from 1925 to 1940. As did his predecessors, Scudder followed Slater's lead in legislation affecting the county. His first assembly bill was an accompanying measure to Slater's senate bill to restore Fort Ross as a historic park. Scudder was assemblyman through the Depression years, the time of Sonoma County's labor problems. One of his bills, albeit unsuccessful, was a proposal to allow school boards to determine what groups would be allowed to use school facilities. This came after Lewis School's trustees drew criticism for denying a request for meeting space to the National Farmers Union, which was considered to be a Socialist organization.[9]

Cross-filing, legal in California after 1920, allowed candidates to appear on both parties' primary election ballots. The direct primary law was revised by legislation authored by Clement C. Young, speaker of the assembly. There are no better examples of the benefits of cross-filing than in the careers of Lea and Slater.

Cross-filing often made the general elections quiet events. Financial backers made their commitments early. In 1930, Scudder's financial disclosure revealed he spent $118.25 on his general election campaign. (The same year Congressman Lea, Senator Slater, and Mark West resident

Finley Collection

District Attorney George W. Hoyle

*T*he politics of roadbuilding were also intense. Roads had originally been the province of the individual townships. As political boundaries for supervisorial districts were established, the supervisors were given the authority to appoint their own district road bosses. It was political patronage at ground level. Marshall Wallace, a road department employee through most of the half-century and longtime county engineer, would sum up the situation, whimsically but not without considerable truth, in his oft-stated belief that "the basic unit of politics in Sonoma County is the chuckhole."[10]

As the county's rudimentary road system converted to automobile traffic in the years following World War I, it became apparent that a countywide system would be necessary. But supervisors were loath to relinquish their control. The voters were vitally concerned with the routes, the quality of construction, the road conditions, and, of course, the cost to taxpayers. These were central issues in county elections.

Serious conflict over control of the county roads arose almost immediately after the Better Roads Bonds were passed in 1919. When the grand jury report was filed in January of 1920, County Engineer Lloyd Aldrich drew praise for his work while District Attorney George W. Hoyle and Third District Supervisor William Cunningham of Windsor were criticized for impeding the engineer's progress on road projects. The jury report delineated the "sides" being chosen in a battle that would be waged for the next five years.

Hoyle, according to the grand jury, had created legal obstructions to the Reams Act, the legislative measure, which had passed the previous year placing county roads under the control of a county engineer. In Sonoma County the designated "power" was Aldrich. But neither Hoyle nor Supervisor Cunningham was willing to acknowledge his authority. They were fighting for the old system in which the county surveyor worked closely with supervisors and their appointed district road bosses. Cunningham refused to turn over the inspection and design of roads in his district, which included the area around Santa Rosa, to the office of the county engineer. Hoyle, in his role as the people's attorney, had refused to order the transfer.

Hoyle defended himself, charging that the engineer's surveying crews had put in short hours and that the engineer had advertised the same bids twice. But Hoyle and Cunningham lost the first round in court. Judge Thomas Denny of Sonoma County Superior Court ruled early in 1920 that the Reams Act was constitutional, and that Cunningham's refusal to release his district's roads to countywide control was illegal, and that Hoyle's office should have required the release.[11]

The citizens, particularly residents of the Third District, quickly formed into opposing camps. The Farm Bureau came down on the side of the engineer, voting to censure Hoyle and support the grand jury. In a second superior court opinion, Judge Emmet Seawell again upheld the Reams Act and Aldrich, despite Hoyle's charges that the new road construction was illegal because the necessary cost and quantity estimates had not been filed with the county clerk.

In February there was the hint of settlement with the news that the engineer's office would advertise for new bids and begin the road project again. But the political battle did not subside. In April of 1920, a committee of businessmen including banker Frank Doyle, Rincon Valley rancher Sheridan Baker, and Santa Rosa mayor William Rutherford, started a recall movement against Supervisor Cunningham. At the same time, the Sebastopol Commercial Club pledged the first $300 for a campaign "war chest" to recall District Attorney Hoyle. They were joined by the Taxpayers Association. Hilliard Comstock, the young attorney just home from the war in France, was suggested as Hoyle's replacement.

The recall movement was actually a contest with engineer Aldrich, and he enjoyed some victories in the early rounds. In the spring of 1920, he was elected president of the California County Engineers Association and received high praise from the California Automobile Association after that organization conducted an investigation of the costs for surveying the county roads. The costs ranged from $104 per mile on the road from Valley Ford to Guerneville, via Freestone, to $945 per mile on the rugged terrain into Cazadero. The CAA called these figures "remarkable."[12]

Hoyle and his attorney, William F. Cowan, issued their own report on road building costs, contradicting the CAA figures. Recall committee spokesman Rutherford challenged Cowan's facts and figures. The fight went on into the summer as the Reams Act's constitutionality was appealed to a higher court. Both sides continued the war of words, Hoyle producing letters from contractors criticizing Aldrich; other county engineers, including the head of San Francisco's engineering department, praising Aldrich. The recall of Cunningham was canceled when it became apparent that the recall election would be held in conjuction with the primary election on August 31, when Cunningham would come up for re-election anyway. There would be no need to vote for or against him twice on the same ballot.[13]

But the recall of the district attorney proceeded apace, with Comstock as the committee's candidate. Hoyle, defending himself with further attacks on Aldrich, asked for investigation of highway bridge costs, questioning payment of claims endorsed by Aldrich. Engineers from the State Highway Commission, along with county surveyor R. Press Smith and Joseph Cox, a civil engineer

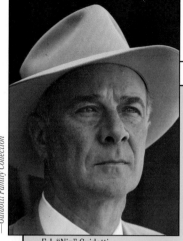

E.J. "Nin" Guidotti

George Kennedy, above, and son William Kennedy, below.

from Healdsburg, were commissioned to inspect the bridges.

Even the inspectors could not agree. At the end of July the assistant state highway engineer, H.E. Warrington, reported that investigation had shown the bridge alterations to be "proper." But county surveyor Smith and engineer Cox disagreed, calling the bridge work "careless construction." The American Federation of Labor came out in support of Hoyle, against the recall, as did, editorially, the *Press Democrat*.[14]

In the election, Hoyle retained his position. The recall was defeated by a vote of 5,979 to 3,304. Santa Rosa voted 610 for the recall, 1,249 against. Supervisor Cunningham was re-elected in the Third District while the veteran supervisor J.H. Weise of Glen Ellen and Oscar Charles of Fort Ross, both supporters of the county engineer, were defeated in the First and Fifth districts. The day after the official election results were announced, Engineer Aldrich resigned, as did most of his department. Surveyor Smith was appointed to the engineer's position.[15]

Within a matter of months, it was apparent that the Better Roads Bonds were inadequate—or that costs were too high. The $300,000 authorized for a highway between Petaluma and Valley Ford had been expended by January 1, 1921, with less than two miles of pavement laid down. In the fall the Reams Act was declared unconstitutional by the state supreme court in an opinion ruling. The ruling was met with regret in Sonoma County, where it was regarded as another obstacle to the completion of an adequate county road system. The exception was Supervisor Cunningham. With the elimination of the office of engineer, Press Smith became county surveyor once again, and all road work was returned to board control. The office of county engineer became an appointed position when Sonoma County became a charter county in 1925.

Eventually the Board of Supervisors accepted the need for an engineer, a position which included the roles of road commissioner and county surveyor. Under the long tenure of Marshall Wallace, the supervisors allowed him to advertise for bids and be in charge of road crews, which was a big step toward transfer of control. Wallace, running against his former employee, Lyle Everett, in 1950, was the last elected county surveyor. During the 1940s, as a result of the Collier-Burns Bill, it was determined that the road commissioner must be a registered civil engineer. This quieted much of the political controversy over county roads.[16]

Road projects were an invitation to controversy. In 1933, First District Supervisor Fred Lowell, a Sonoma resident who had served on the board since 1921, was indicted by the grand jury on eleven felony counts of padding payrolls and misappropriation of funds. Peter Basaglia, a Sonoma cement contractor, testified that he had used the name of a cousin in Switzerland on his payroll for First District road jobs. He turned the cousin's wages, Basaglia admitted, over to Lowell in order to keep his county job.

———

The controversial Cunningham left the board in 1924 and was succeeded by Santa Rosa resident T.J. Ferguson, who would represent the Third District for ten years. By the election of 1936, the board had E.J. "Nin" Guidotti, a Guerneville real estate man and former justice of the peace, who would be involved in the politics of the Fifth District and the county through most of the mid-century, and Joseph Cox, the Healdsburg engineer who served nineteen years from the Fourth District.

In the central Third District, the election of '36 was also a portent of change, albeit distant. For the first time in the county's history, a woman was a candidate for supervisor. She was Ruby Jewel Codding Hall, the granddaughter of Confederate pioneer Tennessee Carter Bishop, who had served as sheriff in the 1880s. Mrs. Hall's platform was a clear call. "It's time to elect a woman," her campaign ads said. "The Board of Supervisors are the housekeepers of your county." [17]

Mrs. Hall's bid was not successful. She was defeated in the primary by Bennett Valley rancher James Jamison. When Jamison died in February, Governor Frank Merriam appointed Santa Rosa Republican Frank Churchill, a commercial seed grower by trade, to the job. Nurseryman Lloyd Cullen was elected in Santa Rosa's Third District in 1940, replacing Churchill. Cullen served through the war years with Guidotti, Cox, Howard Knight from the Sonoma Valley, and George Kennedy, a Sebastopol orchardist who had replaced the veteran Petaluma supervisor Blair Hart as Second District representative in 1938. When Kennedy died in 1950, he was replaced by his son, William Kennedy, who held office until 1954. In 1944, Boyes Springs realtor James Lyttle became supervisor from the First District. Lyttle, who served until 1957, was the dominant force on the board through those years, serving as chairman for a record seven consecutive years.

In 1948, Vic Anderson replaced Cullen as Santa Rosa's representative on the board, the same year that Richard Miller scored an upset victory over three-term incumbent Guidotti in the Fifth District. Miller moved to Arizona after four years in office.[18] Don Richardson of the pioneer Stewart's Point family was appointed to replace him. At the special election in July of '54, Guidotti returned to office and served ten more years, for a total of twenty-two years as a board member. In 1954, Leigh Shoemaker, a Petaluma businessman, replaced William Kennedy in the Second District seat and Everett Lampson, a Geyserville rancher and automobile dealer, succeeded Cox in the Fourth District.[19]

—Doris Kennedy Collection

—Doris Kennedy Collection

William Maddux, a candidate for secretary of state, filed reports indicating they spent no money in the general election. Lea, of course, was successful. Maddux was not.)[20]

When Congressman Lea retired at the age of seventy-four, Republican Scudder was elected to the first of his five terms in Congress. But he had only one cross-filing success in his congressional campaigns, an indication that post-war politics were becoming more sophisticated and contentious in the district.

Scudder defeated Democrat Sterling Norgard in 1948 and Marin County Democrat Roger Kent in 1950. In 1952 he captured both the Republican and Democratic primaries and won easily in the general election over the controversial Santa Rosa builder Carl Sullivan, who ran on the Independent Progressive ticket. In 1954 Scudder beat Max Kortum, a Cotati rancher, and in 1956, Clem Miller, the Democrat from Corte Madera who would win the seat upon Scudder's retirement at the end of the term.

A Sebastopol native, Scudder devoted most of his career to politics. After leaving the assembly in 1941, he served as vice president of the California Republican Central Committee. When he ran for the First District House of Representatives seat in 1948 he was the only Republican in the state to defeat a Democratic opponent in a congressional race.

County government was dominated by rural interests. Roads and bridges, assessments and property tax rates, railroad rights-of-way, the protection of law enforcement, all were issues that struck to the core of an agricultural

The Sonoma County Board of Supervisors. Above left, 1948. From left, Lloyd Cullen, Nin Guidotti, Chairman James Lyttle, Joseph Cox, and George Kennedy. On the 1951 board, left, Chairman Lyttle is flanked by, left to right, Richard Miller, Joseph Cox, Victor Anderson, and William Kennedy.

community. There was no question that country, not city, ruled in the first half of the 20th century.

In spite of the fact that the political power was on the farms, however, the two largest cities in the county, Santa Rosa and Petaluma, did their share to churn county politics. These towns had been rivals since the first vote to bring the county seat to Santa Rosa from Sonoma in 1854—Petalumans siding with Sonoma City in the unsuccessful attempt to keep the county "capital" near the southern border. The bitter days of the Civil War, when Petaluma was a Union town and Santa Rosa the seat of the "Sonoma County Confederacy," left lingering animosities. Twice in the 19th century, Petalumans had led attempts to strip Santa Rosa of the county seat. In 1906, after the earthquake, the south county tried again. Petalumans offered a site—the Hill Plaza in the center of town—on which to rebuild the county courthouse. County supervisors declined.

In 1919 the county's attention was centered on a bill in the state legislature making the division of counties a much less complex process. Petalumans rallied behind it. The editor of the *Petaluma Courier* encouraged a barrage of letters and telegrams to assemblymen, urging its passage. The bill did reach the floor of the assembly in the spring but was defeated 57-7.[21]

South county critics of what had been known in the previous century as the "Santa Rosa Gang" were not ready to concede. In 1920, a group of businessmen from the southwestern corner of the county set boundaries for the new County of Petaluma. It would include, in addition to the Petaluma area townships, the entire Bodega township and part of Redwood township—the towns of Valley Ford, Bodega, Monte Rio, Occidental, and Camp Meeker. The proponents were led by banker C.A. LeBaron of Valley Ford, lumberman A.H. Meeker of Camp Meeker, Bodega dairyman A.L. Tomasi, and R.P. Baker, also from Bodega. This new proposal to divide and conquer created considerable interest in Petaluma; but in November of 1921, the California Supreme Court ruled against the "divisionists," disallowing an election.[22]

Rebuilding from earthquake ruin and refitting for the automobile seem to have been the priorities in the early years of the century. In 1912, with the new courthouse firmly in place in the center of town, Santa Rosa built a new City Hall. The architect was the same as the one who designed the courthouse, J.W. Dolliver, but the building was far less elaborate—a two-story structure with the police station and a small city jail on the ground floor, the council chambers and offices upstairs. It is interesting to note, in the municipal reports of 1917-18, that the city's curbs and gutters were valued at more than $90,000—almost twice as much as the $48,000 City Hall.[23]

The politics of the city, under the strong-mayor, ward-oriented charter, could best be described as "uneven" in the first two decades of the century. Fiscal policy was generally conservative and personalities, personal feuds,

—*Santa Rosa City Hall*

Mayor John P. Overton, above, was mayor at the time of the 1906 earthquake. Below, Santa Rosa's City Hall, center, on Hinton Avenue on the east side of the courthouse.

—*Chamber of Commerce Collection*

and, sometimes, whimsy seemed to be as important in city elections as a desire for good government.

Banker John P. Overton, son of A.P. "Boss" Overton who was mayor, district attorney, judge, and bank president in the '80s and '90s, was in his second term as mayor at the time of the earthquake and led the city through the troubled time. He returned to the council in the 1920s to take up once again the Progressive plan for Santa Rosa that had been stalled by the earthquake and the rebuilding efforts.

Santa Rosa had been governed since 1905 under a freeholders' charter, freeholders being property owners who were eligible to vote, which many felt gave too much power to the mayor. Under the provisions of the charter, the mayor was elected at-large, that is by all city voters. He served with six councilmen who were nominated by the ward system, which divided the city for district representation, but were also elected at-large at two-year intervals. The daily business of the city was accomplished

THE SUFFRAGE RALLY LAST NIGHT A GREAT SUCCESS

There was a large and enthusiastic audience at the Columbia theatre last night at the rally under the auspices of the Santa Rosa Political Equality Club.

splendid achievements of the movement in another hemisphere. Mr. Connolly advanced logical argument in support of his contentions and made an able address.

He was followed by Senator Louis W.

by a city clerk, a city engineer, a police chief, and a street commissioner, whose job was almost as political as the road commissioner's had been in Sonoma County's formative years.

In 1908 the mayor was James H. Gray, whose office was in the Chamber of Commerce office. Councilmen were L.W. Burris, Aubrey Barham, Eugene Bronson, Charles Forgett, Robert L. Johnston, and Fred Steiner. The election of 1908 was acrimonious. In an editorial in his *Press Democrat* in 1910, editor Finley recalled the campaign. "Neighbor was arrayed against neighbor, friend against friend, personalities and uncalled for insinuations were indulged in to an extent never before known in the history of local affairs."[24]

The election of 1910, it was decreed, would be different. Mayor Gray had declined to run for re-election. "Conference committees" of Democrats, Republicans, and the Municipal League (Louis Juilliard and Charles Dunbar represented the Democrats, Frank Muther and Samuel Bogle, the Republicans; Robert L. Thompson, David P. Anderson and George Reading, the Municipal League.) met and agreed upon a slate of candidates. All three contributing groups agreed on the candidacy of banker James R. Edwards for mayor. He was elected by the largest majority given a candidate thus far.

That election was a triumph for consensus or committee politics. The next mayoral election was also a triumph—for another new political force. On January 2, 1912, a landmark event in Santa Rosa's history took place. Jennie Colvin, who owned a rooming house called the Alpha on B Street, walked out her front door, accompanied by her husband Paul, went directly to the county courthouse in the center of town, and registered to vote. She was the first woman in Sonoma County to do so.

Three months earlier, in October of 1911, women had won their suffrage in the state of California by a narrow 2,000-vote margin and in Sonoma County by even less—186 votes. The heroines of this tenuous victory were two Santa Rosa women whose talents were well known and who had earned the respect of both sexes. One was Frances McGaughey Martin, the women's attorney with an oratorical bent, who was the natural choice to be the leader of the

Fred Steiner served Santa Rosa as councilman and city manager.

John Rinner lost his bid to be mayor to a woman suffrage candidate.

Political Equity Association of Sonoma County when the suffrage campaign was organized in 1910.

Her "second" in the organization was Sarah Latimer Finley, also a widow. She was older than Fannie and had spent her life, not in classroom or courtroom, but in her gracious home on McDonald Avenue where she lived with her husband, a minister and educator, and raised her future journalist son Ernest. Knowing this, readers of the *Press Democrat* were not surprised when it was one of the first newspapers in the state to endorse Constitutional Amendment No. 3, giving women their franchise.

In the weeks preceding the special election, the Political Equality Association staged a rally at the Columbia Theater at which a former consul to New Zealand, John Connolly, retired and living in Occidental, testified to the "splendid achievements" of voting women in that country, and young Master Wesley Templeton read a poem entitled "Ma Can't Vote."

California's popular reform governor, Hiram Johnson, spoke to a crowd at the Rink Pavilion on the need to amend the state's constitution, with particular emphasis on giving women the right to vote. Editor Finley promised that voting rights would make women "brighter and more intelligent" and scorned, in his front page editorial, the opposition's argument that suffrage would "remove woman from her rightful sphere, take her from the home and make her bold and unwomanly."[25]

It was a close call. It was three days after the vote was taken before the last precincts (Cazadero, Kellogg, and Marin, west of Petaluma) came in and the Political Equality Association members knew they had triumphed.

Santa Rosa approved the amendment, 497 to 376. Sebastopol and Cloverdale were also in favor. Sonoma led the towns that were against women voting with ninety-four opposed to fifty-seven in favor. Healdsburg turned the amendment down by eighteen votes and Petaluma by four votes. Statewide, the margin was 2,069. But that was enough for Jennie Colvin.

Many women followed Jennie to the county clerk's office to register. In April of 1912, they voted in a Santa Rosa city election for the first time. The *Press Democrat* recorded the event for posterity: "For the first time in the history of Santa Rosa today, women will cast their votes along with the sterner sex for their choice of mayor, councilmen, city recorder, clerk and assessor. Consequently, it will be unique in this particular and it is an occasion of much interest. There are several hundred women registered to vote and as stated they will visit the polling places for the first time armed with the dignity of full citizenship."[26]

The first women to their polling places in Santa Rosa were Cora Boyes, wife of the chief of police; Julia Hankel, a dressmaker; Sara Gore, a widow; Mary Alice Rafferty, a telephone operator; Clothilde Rozas, wife of an employee of the Petaluma & Santa Rosa Railroad; and Mary Blanche Mallory, whose husband was a physician.

These women led a parade that did, as the suffragettes had promised, "make a difference." The favored candidate for mayor, optometrist John Rinner, had been endorsed by the newspaper and approved by the incumbent City Council, and he offered a record of public service.

But Rinner was perceived as opposed to woman suffrage, although he had denied the allegation. On election night, crowds gathered around the traditional bonfire in the street outside the *Press Democrat* office to be serenaded by the Italian band and await the latest returns, delivered to the newspaper office by a corps of boys on bicycles enlisted for the purpose. It soon became apparent that an upset was in progress. A traveling salesman by the name of John Mercier, a write-in candidate, the first in the history of California, had upset Rinner and the status quo.[27]

After that election, women at the polls was not considered remarkable in Santa Rosa. In 1914, they voted for state office for the first time, although they failed to elect the county's first woman candidate for state office,

J.C. PARSONS FOR COUNTY SURVEYOR

Emily Skoe of Petaluma, who ran for the state assembly. In 1920, under the protection of the 19th Amendment to the U.S. Constitution, women voted in their first national election.

Full rights, however, were a long way from accomplished. It was 1922 before a Sonoma County Superior Court seated women on a jury. The first women on a justice court jury were seated in 1916 in a Healdsburg Justice Court trial. It was, in fact, an all-female jury that found a man not guilty of shooting a killdeer, a protected songbird, near Skaggs Springs. The newspaper marveled at their leniency toward a male scofflaw and commented on the gallantry displayed by Justice George Phillips. It was, said the report, "the first time an assistant district attorney has said, 'May it please the court and ladies of the jury.'"[28]

In Santa Rosa's city government, the first direct involvement of women came in 1950, when Madeline Noonan was named to the planning commission and Anna Ronk to the park and recreation commission.[29]

In 1914 a committee of freeholders was appointed to write amendments that would revise the city charter. The committee members included banker Frank Brush, hardware merchant James C. Mailer, farm implement merchant Alfred Trembley, and former mayor John P. Overton. The changes the committee proposed included decreasing the number of councilmen from six to four, elected by ward rather than just nominated by ward. It called for four-year terms of office rather than two-year, $1,000 a year salary for the mayor and $25 dollars a month for each councilman, and gave the citizens power for initiative, referendum, and recall. Both Overton and Trembley voted against the proposed charter changes. In the September election, the new charter proposals lost by seventy-two votes. It was a lackluster turnout. Voters exhibited little interest in the proposed changes; in fact, they seemed more interested in who was on the committee than what it proposed.

As the automobile increased in importance, the condition of city streets became a central issue. The municipal reports of 1912 clearly show a city in transition. In March, the city accepted a bid to lay 9,000 square feet of asphalt on Fourth Street where the streetcar tracks had been removed. In June, city engineer John C. Parsons was authorized to provide hitching posts for "people coming in from the county" and to improve the Ridgway Lot at the corner of Third and B streets for the tethering of horses. At the same time, Parsons was putting contractors to work widening, paving, and installing cement curbs and gutters along the downtown streets.

Press Smith, appointed city engineer in 1914 by Mayor Charles E. Lee, set grade and line stakes on a dozen or more streets that year and prepared specifications for curbs, gutters, and paving. But despite the construction projects, improvements were not coming fast enough to suit the citizens. There was public discussion in the winter of 1914-15 about the condition of the streets as yet unpaved. Second, Third, and Spring streets were called "mudholes,"

John C. Parsons, whose campaign poster for county office is shown at left, was the city engineer who oversaw the paving of downtown streets in 1912.

William E. Rutherford's term as mayor was marked by political in-fighting.

portions of Fourth Street were "a disgrace," and North Street was a "lake." Hardware merchant James C. Mailer filed a complaint with the city attorney against the condition of Third Street between E and F streets, saying that he had broken three springs on his automobile in the chuckholes.

There was constant experimentation with new paving material—hot mix, water-bound macadam, and Willite. Some worked better than others. There were complaints, in 1915, of "auto speed burners" who were "wearing out" College Avenue, hitting between a forty and sixty mile per hour clip." Santa Rosa Avenue (which had been Main Street since the 1800s) was partially paved, intersections only. Curbs and gutters were ordered for Benton, Davis, Ellis, Chinn, Cherry, Fourth, Ninth, Second, Tupper, and Tenth streets that year. Citizens who did not do the work themselves or have it done would be levied for city installation.

Still, the access to downtown Santa Rosa from the south must have been tenuous. A contingent of Cotati citizens presented themselves at the Santa Rosa City Council session in August. They were members of the Cotati State Highway Club, and they pleaded for a bridge over Santa Rosa Creek at A Street. They suggested that Santa Rosa merchants were losing $150,000 a year because the roads from the south were impassable five months of the year. But Santa Rosa residents, who couldn't pay for the curbs and gutters for which the city had billed them as part of the ongoing paving projects, brought suit to test the city's authority to assess them.[30] The election of 1916 may have been an expression of dissatisfaction about the street work. Hardware merchant Mailer, who had complained about chuckholes, defeated Mayor Lee by 196 votes.

Mailer, who served just one term, disagreed with the council on several matters, including the city's purchase of Southside Park. Mailer used his veto power to stop the purchase and apparently his political influence to change the minds of some councilmen, for the council then sustained his veto.

By 1917, Santa Rosa was anxious to show off what eleven years of concentrated effort could accomplish in an earthquake-damaged town. City officials played hosts to the annual convention of the California League of Municipalities. The most important order of business was the endorsement of planning commissions in member cities. It was September and the weather was "unbearably hot" for the social portion of the agenda, which included a barbecue at Italian Swiss Colony at Asti, a street dance, and a visit to Sebastopol by the delegates' wives.[31]

The brief tenure (1920-22) of Mayor William E. Rutherford, a pharmacist by profession, proved to be the harbinger of change in city government. Rutherford's governmental path was rocky from the start—the council denied approval to his first appointees and open warfare soon broke out between him and the street commissioner, Daniel "Doc" Cozad, who was also charged with maintaining the city's water system.

Within the first months of Rutherford's administration, city officials leveled criticism at Cozad's performance, particularly at his care of the water system. According to the mayor, sediment was "to the top of a man's knee boots" in the storage tanks. When Dr. Jackson Temple, the city's health officer, charged the city's water supply was not clean and Cozad was responsible, Cozad attacked the physician physically, striking him in the face. Mayor Rutherford labeled the assault as "lowbrow gang politics," and Cozad was charged with assault, his case concluding twenty days later in a hung jury, with Cozad claiming he was acting in self-defense. Another complaint, that he used the city farm, at the sewer plant, as free pasturage for his horses, was added to the list of dissatisfactions. Rutherford vowed to see him removed from office.[32]

Early in 1921, Cozad resigned, accusing Rutherford of pushing him out of his job. Rutherford appointed Henry H. Elliott to the position. But four of the councilmen refused to approve Elliott's appointment and Cozad withdrew his resignation. Councilmen Frank Blanchard and Alfred Trembley, who had backed Rutherford, changed their minds and voted against Elliott. Rutherford accused them of "going back on their word." Councilmen wanted Cozad, Rutherford charged, because he "does their work." Rutherford accused Cozad, also, with failure to report a cave-in in the water systems which, according to City Engineer L.L. Mills, was potentially disastrous. But a petition from the business community, signed, according to the newspaper, by "the biggest taxpayers in Santa Rosa," was offered in support of Cozad and he remained in office. However, after the election of April 1922, Rutherford did not.

Cozad's problems did not end with the election. The following month he was accused along with Councilman Fred Oliva of taking free water from the city. Officials charged that neighbors reported Cozad's and Oliva's water meters had not been read in more than a year. The new mayor replaced Cozad, adding the job of street commissioner to that of city engineer Mills and the council approved the change. Cozad was out. He remained in the fray, however, joining with his Howard Street neighbors Ora Parrish, J.I. "Ike" Parsons, and Dr. Sam Bogle in a suit against the council in March of 1927 in an attempt to stop the city from paving streets with Willite rather than concrete.

In 1922 the new mayor was Lawrence A. Pressley, an officer in the Exchange Bank. One of Pressley's first acts as "chief executive" was to set in place the mechanism for a new city charter. A committee of freeholders, that is resident property owners eligible to vote, was elected—with banker Frank P. Doyle, to no one's surprise, receiving the highest vote. The freeholders were charged with writing a new city charter.

The document they presented to the voters took away the powers given to the mayor in the old system and established the city manager form of government in Santa Rosa. It was approved by the voters and approved by the legislature the following year.[33] In the new charter the ward system was phased out. Five council members would be elected at-large to four-year terms and would receive no compensation, except when they sat as a board of equalization, for which they were paid $5.

The next task was the selection of a city manager. There were ten candidates for the job. The "boom" was for Abner Hitchcock, an attorney and the former mayor of Mitchell, South Dakota. Hitchcock was selected for the $4,000-a-year job in 1923, but his tenure was short. The change to the manager system had made economy-minded citizens uneasy. The council election of 1924 was considered to be a kind of referendum on the question, since three of the candidates were running as a slate in opposition.

That election marked the entrance to city government of Charles O. Dunbar, a political power in the county and the state since the turn of the century. Dunbar, who may have been the central figure in early-century city politics, was elected to the council in '24 and promptly elected mayor, replacing Newton Kinley, who was filling the unexpired term of Mayor Pressley, who died in office in February of '24.

The first mayor without executive powers, Dunbar had run and won on a slate which included the owner of the Pioneer Laundry, Dominick P. Mack, and attorney William Vallandigham. With their victory, Hitchcock submitted his resignation and the council, exploring new definitions for the manager's position, appointed a civil engineer, John E. Williams, as manager. L.L. Mills, the former engineer and street commissioner, was his assistant.

The first order of business for Dunbar was the new sewer plant. Lawsuits had been filed against the city the previous year, reviving an old dispute over alleged danger to the health of people living downstream from the city's

—Santa Rosa City Hall

Charles O. Dunbar was postmaster, mayor, and city manager, a political force in the community.

sewer farm. The Peterson family's complaints about creek pollution had begun two generations earlier—in the 1880s—when the city of Santa Rosa installed a single septic tank to treat its effluent. The tank was located in the Wright District on the banks of the creek, about a mile upstream from the hop ranch of Martha Ames Peterson. In 1897, the widow Peterson's suit against the city went all the way to the state supreme court and resulted in a permanent injunction, enjoining Santa Rosa from polluting the creek.

In 1902, the city had "re-perfected" its sewer system with the use of bacteria to break down sludge. The County Atlas of 1909 credited Santa Rosa with "a septic system second to none." But, by 1923, the compliments ran out. Elmer Peterson filed suit, charging that the city was violating the injuction won by his mother twenty-seven years earlier. Polluted water was once again flowing from the sewer farm into Santa Rosa Creek, he charged in two separate suits. In one, he sought a new injunction, in the other he asked $12,000 in damages, contending that his children's typhoid fever and diphtheria had resulted from creek pollution.[34]

The city's health officer, Dr. Jackson Temple, expressed concern that rapid growth (from approximately 6,000 in the mid-'90s to nearly 9,000 in 1923) had overtaxed the system. In addition, an order from the State Board of Health declared the city in violation of a new state law prohibiting the disposal of sewage in a running stream. Council action was needed. The council set a bond election for the following March, meanwhile exploring ways to solve the disposal problem. Councilmen proposed increased irrigation on the city farm and on surrounding land. They heard but rejected a proposal by manager-engineer Williams to join with Healdsburg and a contingent of Russian River resort owners in building a "closed sewer" to the Pacific Ocean. The plan the voters of Santa Rosa approved, in March of '24, a month before the municipal election, was for an all-new sludge and sewer treatment plant. Voters passed a $142,500 bond issue for the project.

Mayor Dunbar and the new council proposed a different plan. Improvements to the existing septic system with the addition of chlorination, they agreed, would accomplish the clean-up at greatly reduced cost. Williams was placed in charge of the project. The revamped system, known as an Activated Sludge Sewage Disposal Plant, was completed and running within three months—at the cost of $3,000.

It wasn't enough for state health regulators. In the fall of '24, the state board ruled that the improvements had not abated the pollution. Santa Rosa was still in violation of state law. The council, at Dunbar's behest, then hired an "expert," an employee of a San Francisco chlorine company, to supervise the installation of a dry chlorinator on the creek bank through which the water would pass on its way from the septic system to the running stream.

The council was assured that the chlorination process, which was new, would guarantee wastewater "without disease, germs or odor of any kind."[35] To oversee the task, the Board of Public Utilities (BPU) was established. The mayor was a member, along with city manager Williams, and two former councilmen—former banker and manager of the McDonald water system George Cadan and foundry owner Fred Steiner. For two years the BPU heard chemists hired by the city and chemists hired by Elmer Peterson argue about the quality of the wastewater. A committee of Santa Rosa physicians—Thurlow, Bonar, Clark, and Fleissner—found "almost a total absence of odor." They called for further testing, at the point where the water entered the creek.

In 1925, with the BPU securely in place, the council voted to decrease manager William's salary by one-quarter. With the BPU lessening his duties, the manager would be paid $3,000 per year instead of $4,000. The elderly Williams resigned in 1926 pleading "ill health." The State Health Department issued a permit for Santa Rosa's new system, including two additional wooden septic tanks, six additional small holding ponds, and a dry-feed chlorinator. A duplicate settling tank and chlorine tank for cleaning and repair purposes, and for emergencies, also was built. The law suits were withdrawn. The $158,000 remaining from the sewer bond issue would be used for other civic improvements.

———————

Dunbar's first term was a trial by fire. The council in-fighting over how much power the mayor and the manager should be allowed continued. Mayor Dunbar was making some sweeping decisions. And, when Dominick Mack died after nine months in office, the minority opposition on the council—contractor William J. Meeker and Newton Kinley—resigned, intending to force a special election which would bring them a third vote. But Mayor Dunbar, citing as his authority a section of the city charter which gave the mayor full powers in times of "extraordinary emergencies," appointed a former mayor and ally, John P. Overton, to fill Mack's seat. The quorum of three promptly accepted the resignations of Meeker and Kinley and chose BPU members Cadan and Steiner to fill their unexpired terms.

Meeker enlisted attorneys Hilliard Comstock and Roe Barrett to bring suit against the city to force a special election, a suit which the newspaper deemed frivolous since the incumbent councilmen would "probably be candidates and their services are praised." Nonetheless, the issue went to the state supreme court before it was decided in favor of Dunbar and his council.

In 1926, Dunbar was endorsed by voters, who returned him to office for a second two-year term. A force in state politics, he was also the Democratic candidate for lieutenant governor that year, but was not elected. Three weeks after the municipal election, he resigned to become the city manager, succeeding Williams.[36]

Dunbar developed the concept of an administrator as manager rather than attorney or engineer. At the start of the Depression, he asked the council to cut his salary, which had crept to $4,200, back to $3,800. He held the post for seven years, until he resigned to accept a federal position—as Collector of Customs for the Port of San Francisco.

Born in Glen Ellen and trained in the printing profession, Dunbar learned the art of politics early and used it effectively throughout his career. He was described by his friend and former partner Ernest Finley as a "self-made man" who "progressed no farther in his schooling than the grammar grades."[37]

He was regarded as progressive— serving on the first park commission. But he was also a fiscal conservative, which was a popular position in 1920s Santa Rosa. His successful renovation of the sewer system had cost just $7,000. With the remaining funds, Dunbar's administration built four concrete bridges over Santa Rosa's creeks, bought a new fire engine, rehabilitated the fire house, spent $80,000 for benefits for the unemployed in the winter of '32 and '33, and had money remaining in the treasury when he left the city for the Port of San Francisco.

Dunbar's seven years as manager was the most progressive period of the young century. Just two years after he became manager, in a speech at the dedication of two of the new bridges built with sewer bond money (one on Main Street, the other on Sonoma Avenue), Dunbar summed up the achievements of the city in the four years since he became mayor and then manager—four years of achievements that may have surpassed all that had been done within the city in the previous two decades. In addition to the bridges, there had been an extension of the water and sewer system, he told the crowd, $500,000 worth of paving, 150 new light standards, the purchase of Fremont School site on Fourth Street for a city park, the construction of a municipal swimming pool on King Street, the acquisition of Burbank's gardens by the junior college. Two decades after the devastating earthquake, Santa Rosa had left recovery behind and was looking ahead.[38]

The borders, if not the official limits, of Santa Rosa crept outward slowly through the first half of the century. After the earthquake, the population had dropped by nearly 1,000 (from 8,700 in 1900 to 7,817 in 1910). By 1918 the estimate was 11,000, living in two square miles.[39] In 1910 there was some small expansion eastward with the annexation of Dorothy Farmer's land along a new street off Sonoma Avenue called Sotoyome Drive. But Santa Rosans were conservative. In 1920, an unsuccessful election was called to extend the city boundaries north to Steele Lane and Lewis School, south to McMinn Avenue, including the race track, west to the Monroe School district line, and east to Hoen and Sonoma avenues.

By the 1920s, however, with a new charter and an aggressive council and city manager, Santa Rosa looked toward expansion. The Chamber of Commerce and the newspaper discussed future growth as the happiest of prospects. On New Year's Day of 1925, a story in the *Press Democrat* trumpeted the joy of Sonoma County merchants over the news that the Wendover cut-off was ready for traffic. This stretch of new highway in the Nevada desert may have seemed remote to some but, according to the newspaper, it would be a means to divert tourists and subsequent new Californians from Los Angeles to the north.

"It means as much to Sonoma County and the whole of Northern California as any piece of improvement to be carried out in many years.... Reliable figures have been gathered which show that the majority of tourists coming to California pour into Salt Lake City from the north and the south as through a tunnel.... Nearly all of these tourists expressed a desire to come straight across to S.F. but on account of terribly bad roads...90 percent of them went down over paved roads to Los Angeles. Now there are good roads straight from Salt Lake City to S.F...and when they (the eastern tourists) see this country how many people do you suppose will settle in Los Angeles?"[40]

This was a prosperous time in Sonoma County. Agricultural production was near its peak and Santa Rosa, as the market and shipping center, basked in the glow of prosperity. How many of those tourists from the east actually visited and decided to stay is questionable. But the city was attracting new businessmen, new lawyers, new doctors, and even the longtime residents were becoming upwardly mobile, building bigger homes on property along Sonoma Avenue and the Sonoma Road.

In 1923, building permit totals exceeded a million dollars for the first time in the city's history. Contractor Walter Proctor, who had built bridges for state highways and office buildings, including Santa Rosa's Pacific Gas & Electric Company office on Third Street, subdivided open land that reached all the way to Franklin Lane, a street that would be renamed Bryden Lane. He advertised it as Santa Rosa's "choicest and only restricted residential

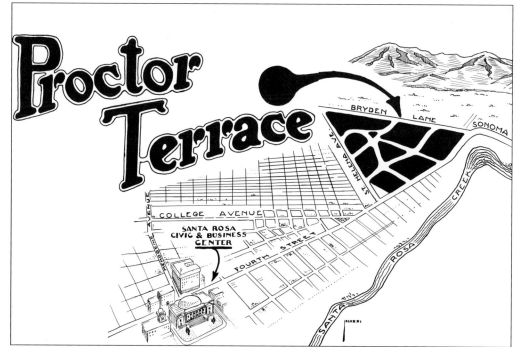

—*Finley Collection*

neighborhood." On new streets called Proctor Drive, Austin Way, and Morley Way, Proctor and real estate agent Raford Leggett began selling building lots in early 1924. On the opening day of sales, in March, a band concert and an aerial circus drew large crowds to the new "Proctor Terrace" section, referred to by the Exchange Bank as "Santa Rosa's first addition." No such real estate hoopla had been seen in Santa Rosa since the land auctions in South Park and the Pierce Addition in the late 1880s.

In the next four years, Proctor would build twenty-seven new homes, most of them large, two-story English cottage-style structures. The homes were considered upper-class—a 20th century extension of McDonald Avenue elegance—although the promised "entrance columns of attractive design with ornamental monuments at the four corners" never materialized.[41] The city's residential district now extended to the edge of what had been Franklintown, the 1850 settlement that predated Santa Rosa. The new town was about to eclipse its history.

In far less dramatic fashion, the town was expanding in other directions. A pair of small subdivisions, Avalon off Sebastopol Road (twenty-four lots filed by Vittona and C.R. Cavallero, Ada and A.M. Tomasi, and Minnie and Hume Bunyan) and Bell's subdivision near Walker Avenue were added in 1929 to the city limits. Graycourt Subdivision continued the eastward movement along Sonoma Avenue in 1928, eighteen lots on a new street called Gray Court developed by Mae and W.S. Gray. The southern boundary expanded in 1930 with the Hindringer subdivision, a block of lots bordered by Frazier, Pressley, DeTurk, and Temple streets, land owned by Louisa Hindringer.

While the Depression effectively halted development in the early 1930s, Santa Rosa was already in recovery before the World War II economy took hold. In 1936, Genevieve Talbot received permission for an extensive subdivision east of town and south of Santa Rosa Creek, adding Leonard, Raegan, and Parker streets (all named for Talbot sons) to Talbot Avenue and extending Doyle Park Drive. One of the first houses built in the new subdivision was the home of Leonard Talbot, appropriately at the corner of the two streets bearing his names. In 1938 the Talbot subdivision was annexed to the city.

To the south, developer Carl Sullivan built Walnut Court, from Sonoma Avenue to Matanzas Creek, in 1937. Thelma and William Rapp hooked on to the Talbot subdivision with ten lots at California and Leonard in '39. In 1940 Alderbrook and Bay streets became part of the city. Across the creek, Edward Brigham and Fred Cross divided twelve lots known as the Brookside Addition in 1939. Vallejo Street and Flower Avenue were added to the city map in 1940. The Sunset subdivision in the Roseland district, including homes on McMinn and Burbank avenues, were developed in 1940 by Archie Fenton.

Expansion went farther east when Marion and Thomas Proctor (no relation to developer Walter Proctor) laid out streets and sold lots on Proctor Heights in 1936, streets with romantic names like Sunrise and Sunset, Del Rosa and Osage. At the foot of the Proctor Hill, Rae and Joseph Giusto developed Easthaven Acres in 1938. William Grahn added Montecito Villas, from Montecito Avenue to Grahn Drive to Norte Way, in 1939.

In 1937 Charles Neale and Francis Carrington filed the Joyce subdivision which added Neale Drive and an extension of Beaver Street from Spencer Avenue to the railroad spur track. Abby and Glenn Murdock whose home was on the hillside above Lewis Road split the family property in partnership with Thomas Daniels in '39.

In 1940 realtor Harry B. Fetch subdivided land north of Sonoma Avenue, naming his streets Oriole, Oriental, and Roosevelt avenues. Oriole was changed to Talbot to match the street on the other side of the railroad right-of-way. Oriental would become Macklyn when the U.S. went to war with Japan, and Roosevelt, which had apparently been named for Teddy, became the less-political Rosedale.

The Santa Rosa Fire Department photos at right were both taken in 1940. Top is the new Benton Street Station which opened in July of that year. The engine is a 1940 American LaFrance pumper. The firefighters, left to right, are Jack Wright, Captain Fred Pette, Lloyd Bowman, Bob Dixon, Hall Caine, and Grady Nix. Below is the Headquarters Station on A Street. The engines are a 1939 American LaFrance pumper, 1928 Dodge squad truck, 1920 American LaFrance pumper, and a 1928 American LaFrance quad. Firefighters, left to right, are Eugene Duignan, who was later fire chief; Bert Yaeger, Captain Percy Eckhart, Joe Barretto, Joe Potts, Hall Caine, and Charles Ingham.

—Santa Rosa Fire Department

In 1940, the Santa Rosa Fire Department moved into two new homes—the main station in the 400 block of A Street, where there were two engine companies, and the Benton Street station, which was the first substation. The department had sold its last four fire horses in 1926, and the firemen (ten paid and seven more who were known as "callmen") had to make do with an old Victory Dodge and one pumper until 1928 when Chief William Muenter took delivery of an American La France engine, which was the department's pride. The horse-drawn pumpers continued in use through the 1930s, being pulled by trucks or loaded on flatbeds to reach fire locations. Firemen's duties were varied. In the '30s and '40s they were routinely assigned to direct traffic at busy intersections. Muenter was chief until 1938, and Lloyd Rhoades was chief until 1943, succeeded by George Magee who would serve for eighteen years.[42]

—Santa Rosa Fire Department

221

The Grace Tract was the largest subdivision of 1940, making residential lots of the Frank Grace family property northwest of Bryden Lane. Streets were named for family members of the Grace and Geary families—Finlaw, Thomas, Patricia, Pamela, Julianne—and when sons and daughters ran out, family holdings such as the Mendota cotton ranch and the Delevan rice ranch in the Central Valley. Howard Rogers' Addition—Rogers Way, Siesta Lane—was subdivided in 1941.

The town now extended east to Farmers Lane, moving back toward the Carrillo Adobe—the remains of which were being used as a prune dryer by the Hoen family—where it began 100 years before.[43]

Santa Rosa's predominant governmental philosophy in the pre-WWII years was paternalism. Dunbar had been replaced on the City Council by hop broker Robert Madison. But it was George Cadan who would assume a ten-year mantle of mayoral leadership as the city entered the last spurt of civic improvement before the Depression years. Two of his council colleagues also served for many years. John Overton served a total of eighteen years, and Steiner sixteen years.It was apparent that in troubled times, Santa Rosa residents trusted these leaders. In 1930 Cadan, Overton, and Steiner were elected to four-year terms on the council without opposition and without a single dissenting vote.[44]

When Dunbar left, his job as city manager was filled by Councilman Steiner, a twenty-five-year veteran of city politics. Steiner served until his death in 1936, when city engineer Arthur P. Noyes was appointed to succeed him. Noyes resigned in 1938 and Joseph Berry was named to the job. He served until 1942, when John A. Tedford was appointed. In the next eight years there were three city managers: Joseph Ladner, Ross Miller, and Edgar Blom.

The time from the late '20s through World War II was a period of unusual stability in city government. Political observers of the period would say that the community had worked out a balance between two controlling elements— the Masonic Lodge and the Roman Catholic Church. In early years, there was no question that the Masons were an important force. The Masonic Hall had been one of the first buildings constructed on the town plaza in 1854 and most of the early civic leaders were members of Lodge 57, Free and Accepted Masons. But the Irish Catholic community was influential also. And by the 1920s it was not unusual to find that city councils, schools boards, and other governing bodies included members of both groups. It was an unspoken—at least, unwritten—rule. But it prevailed.

George Cadan's terms as mayor, from 1928 to 1938, took the city through much of the Great Depression, including municipal welfare and public works projects and

At lower left, Mayor Robert F. Madison buys tickets to a benefit baseball game from Austin Sullivan. Above, George Cadan was mayor of Santa Rosa for ten years. Obert Pedersen, below, was the "clean sweep" mayor of the postwar years.

the disbursement of federal and state funds. Upon the resignation of Steiner in 1933, shoe store owner William E. Healey Jr. was appointed to fill his unexpired term and was re-elected to a four-year term of his own in 1934.

Robert F. Madison, whose father had been a councilman from 1926 to 1936, took his turns as mayor from 1938 to 1942 and from '44 to '46. Madison was probably the central political figure of the early '40s, although city politics, like county and state politics, took a far back seat to federal business in the war years.

Ward von Tillow, who owned a dry cleaning establishment, was elected to the council in 1938 and served one term. He would return ten years later. Realtor Ernest Eymann served as mayor from '42 to '44. Furniture dealer Obert Pedersen, who was elected to the council in '44, was mayor from '46 to '48. Other council members in that period were contractor William Rapp, who was elected in '42 and resigned in '45, and Phil Pyke who was appointed to fill the remainder of his term. Ray Brazil, elected in '44, resigned in August of '46 and automobile dealer Robert L. Bishop was appointed to fill his term. Bishop was then elected for a full term, leaving the council in 1952.

Pedersen was mayor during the "clean sweep" election year of 1946, which brought a slate of three businessmen, title company owner J. Mervyn Daw, Jess Gantt, and lumber dealer Steve Yaeger, to office. The campaign and the sweeping changes in city government that followed gave impetus to Santa Rosa's proud boast of the next twenty years—that it was "The City Designed for Living."45

With a new council and a new city manager Ross Miller, plans were drawn to relieve traffic congestion by opening the many dead-end streets in the downtown area, to solve sewer and water system deficiencies, to install traffic signals and off-street parking, and to expand the city park system. To finance this, the council proposed a 1 percent sales tax and an increased business license tax.

To sell the proposal to voters, the council and a citizens committee put together a public relations campaign that included speeches at service clubs, newspaper interviews, radio talks, and a doorbell-ringing information blitz. The tax measures were approved and the improvements begun. In addition, under manager Miller, the council drafted a new zoning ordinance as a plan for future growth; a citizens committee was formed to campaign for a new hospital, and such dreams as a new City Hall and the improvement of Santa Rosa Creek were included in five and ten-year programs.

This plan of action attracted statewide and even national attention. Santa Rosa's municipal improvements became the subject of a pamphlet entitled *The People Design the City*, published in 1947 by the State Reconstruction and Reemployment Commission. In the fall of 1947, Mayor Pedersen sent copies of the booklet to Santa Rosa civic leaders, pointing out that the publication "has made Santa Rosa one of the most publicized cities in the nation." His letter included comments from the editorial pages of several newspapers about *The People Design the City*:

San Francisco News—"The point is that Santa Rosans not only analyzed their troubles, but DID something constructive about them. And they inspired the whole community to get the job done."

New York Times—"...an energetic attack on the basic problems and foresighted planning will gradually bring into realization a Santa Rosa 'designed for living.'"

San Francisco Examiner—"Democracy is working among neighbors—as it always works best."

Christian Science Monitor—"Santa Rosa has a plan that has made it the talk of California. Santa Rosa is a town that saw its own weaknesses and did something about it."

Ward von Tillow came back to the council in 1948. Mayor Daw served that year only and stepped back to a councilman's role, setting a precedent for mayor to be a largely honorary position circulated yearly among the

Ward von Tillow, above, came back to the City Council after ten years. Larry Zuur, below, was part of a 1952 election ticket.

—Santa Rosa City Hall

—Santa Rosa City Hall

—John LeBaron, Press Democrat Collection

Left to Right, Jerome Kushins was elected to the council in 1950, Karl Stolting in 1954, and Sam Hood was named city manager in 1950.

council. Bishop was mayor from '49 to '50 and von Tillow from '50 to '51.

In 1950 shoe manufacturer Jerome Kushins and real estate broker Alex McCluskey were elected, replacing Gantt and Yaeger. In 1952, Lawrence Zuur, a wholesale grocer, and Leon Reynaud, an auto dealer, ran as a team for the seats vacated by Bishop and von Tillow. Reynaud resigned in 1954. Zuur served until 1956.[46]

For the first time growth was the central issue. Orderly growth, that is. Zuur's report to his fellow councilmen on the meeting of the League of California Cities in San Diego in 1952 should have served notice that Santa Rosa and Sonoma County were not in this alone. The most important business of the league meeting was a resolution asking the state legislature to set up building requirements for urban unincorporated areas to comply with the codes of the cities. Legislators were asked, also, to examine county building codes and bring them closer to city standards.

Sam Hood, the city manager whose tenure oversaw the greatest changes in Santa Rosa since the '06 earthquake, was named to the manager's office in 1950. Hood had no public administration experience. He had come to Santa Rosa as manager of the Montgomery Ward store, having served in various management capacities with that retail and catalog chain since 1928. In 1949 he resigned to become executive director of the Sonoma County Taxpayers' Association. The next year he took the manager's position.

He came to the job as post-WWII demographic changes were mounting to the pitch of a population boom. In the ten years Hood was city manager, the population nearly doubled, the assessed valuation tripled, and the city quadrupled in area. His role was to provide the leadership and vision as the city changed from a small, self-contained community to an expanding mid-sized city preparing for more growth that was certain to come.

A forceful man who was beloved by his staff, Hood

Politics was a community activity in the first half of Santa Rosa's 20th century. When there were speeches to be heard, as in this 1930s event photographed by Vernon Silvershield, adults and children alike flocked to the courthouse to listen and cheer.

was noted for his ever-present cigar, his running battle with developers over the direction and quality of the "new" city, and his gruff public persona. In his administration, under the supervision of his good friend and city engineer Robert Van Guelpen, the master plan to sewer the Santa Rosa plain was compiled, and an annexation plan was adopted.

In 1954, a three-man slate consisting of electrical contractor Karl Stolting, retired van and storage owner H.A. "Art" Jensen, and real estate man Vincent Rafanelli ran together for the seats being vacated by Daw, McCluskey, and Kushins, all of whom announced that they would not seek re-election. Water and parking, the new councilmen agreed, were all vital issues, but the most vital at this point in the city's development, they identified as "annexation."

Circumstances changed the politics of the county and the city after World War II. Paternalism in government was waning. There would be more progressiveness. And, perhaps, less stability. While the county supervisors still "ruled" in many ways, increased urbanization would lend more weight to city decisions. And the wave of new residents would lap over town boundaries into rural areas, creating land use issues that would not be resolved before the century's end. ❧

Lessons Learned

The most important innovation in Sonoma County's educational system in the first half of the 20th century was the founding of Santa Rosa Junior College.

It seems impossible to tell the story of Santa Rosa Junior College without recalling the words of its first dean, Dr. Clyde Wolfe, a mathematics instructor who spent just one year as an administrator. Wolfe's resignation and departure from Santa Rosa was accompanied by his prediction that Santa Rosa Junior College was destined to be "no more than a bump on the top side of the high school."[1]

Rather, the junior college became the focus of both community energy and community pride in the first half of the 20th century, for its athletic endeavors as well as its scholastic achievements. The concept of a two-year institution of higher learning in Santa Rosa was first proposed at a 1917 meeting of the Federated Home and School Association, an organization dedicated to the improvement of schools. The fourteen-member association was headed by Mrs. George Reading. Speaking in favor of the proposal were Thomas F. Brownscombe, superintendent of Santa Rosa schools, and Dewitt Montgomery, Santa Rosa High School principal. The recommendation was taken to the school board, where trustees John Rinner, Finlaw Geary, May Payne, Eugene Farmer, and Henry Noonan voted to establish the institution, the eighteenth junior college in California, the following year.[2]

The fall of 1918 was not an ideal time to launch an academic endeavor. World War I had not yet ended, and the Spanish influenza forced a five-week suspension of classes just a month after they had begun. The financial picture was equally bleak. The Caminetti Act of 1907, which was the enabling legislation for the establishment of junior colleges, provided for neither fixed academic standards nor financing. The schools were deemed as public education and could charge no tuition, but these "post-graduate" courses were not allowed to share the high school appropriations from the state. It is not surprising that six of SRJC's seventeen predecessors had closed by 1921.

The junior college, meeting in the high school building, being taught by high school teachers in borrowed quarters, with borrowed equipment and borrowed books, survived. The JC's thirty-two students were displaced along with high school students by the fire of 1921. They moved into Fremont Elementary School, which they promptly nicknamed "Fremont University." In 1925, with 168 students, the college moved into the new high school building. Dean Wolfe had resigned in 1920, replaced by Dean Richard Brost, who also served a single year. In 1921 science teacher Floyd P. Bailey was named dean, beginning a tenure of leadership at SRJC that lasted thirty-six years.

Athletics were a big part of the junior college program from the beginning. The football team had lost its equipment in the high school fire, but the town was anxious to support a "college eleven." Fans joined in providing financial assistance for the "Bear Cubs," a name chosen in deference to the University of California Golden Bears, although the school colors, red and blue, walked the middle line between Cal's blue and Stanford University's cardinal.

Dean Bailey gave much of the credit for the early success of the athletic program to a volunteer coach, the young attorney Clarence "Red" Tauzer, who took on both the football and basketball teams in 1923. The teams played against Sonoma County high school teams and Bay Area state colleges, as well as other junior colleges. In 1926, Tauzer's Bear Cub football team defeated San Jose State Teachers College, a triumph for a school with no campus and an enrollment of less than 200. The score was 12-6.

In 1927 Santa Rosa voters established a separate junior college district. In 1928, Analy High School District joined the district. Although Healdsburg, Sonoma, and Petaluma voters declined to join in an election in 1929, students from those schools continued to transfer to the junior college. In 1930 the junior college became independent of the Santa Rosa Board of Education and elected its own governing board. The board of trustees, nominees selected by committees of the Santa Rosa and Sebastopol chambers of commerce for the 1930 election included Clarence "Red" Tauzer; William Shuhaw, district manager for PG&E, who had been a supporter and adviser in the establishment of the college's engineering program; Sheridan Baker, the Rincon Valley farmer, representing the rural interests; mill operator John Bridgeford, Sebastopol; and banker George Bech, from Guerneville. Bech would establish a record for service to the junior college. He served until 1957 as a board member and resigned to become the college's first business manager.

At the end of the 1920s, the junior college student body numbered 300 and was creating an overcrowding problem at the high school. It was time for a home of its own. Immediately to the north of the SRHS campus, on the other side of the railroad spur track, there were forty acres of oaks and wildflowers. The property had been one of the favorite spots of the famous plant breeder Luther Burbank and he had used the grounds for many experiments requiring native plants. Ownership of the land was shared by the City of Santa Rosa and the Santa Rosa Chamber of Commerce. The joint purchase had been made shortly after Burbank's death in 1926, with the announced intention of establishing a park in his memory, to be known as Burbank Creation Gardens. But financing had been difficult and the start of the Great Depression in 1929 had made it all but impossible. Two restrooms and a few walkways were the only improvements when, in 1930, the SRJC Board of Trustees made a proposal to use the land as its campus.

With the permission of Burbank's widow, Elizabeth, and the cooperation of the owners, the transfer was negotiated by Red Tauzer, with the stipulation that the eastern edge of the parcel, fronting on Mendocino Avenue, would not be building sites, but would remain parklike, for the enjoyment of the public as well as the students. That decision, according to campus folklore, was a matter of

—Santa Rosa Junior College Collection

When Floyd Bailey retired in 1957 he had taken Santa Rosa Junior College from a student body of thirty-two to more than 2,000 full-time students. He had built a campus envied by larger, richer colleges. He had assembled an outstanding faculty. His school had received the highest accreditation rating a two-year college could receive.[3]

Floyd Bailey was not an administrator; he was a father figure. The college was his life and he knew what was best for it. He didn't always appoint a committee. He didn't always ask the board's permission. Bailey's confidence and independence are evident in the anecdotes and memories of him compiled by his successor, Dr. Randolph Newman.[4] His faculty remembered Bailey—"always Mr. Bailey, never Floyd"—with affection. They tell the "Bailey stories" that have become campus legend:

How he refused to let the campus maintenance crew lay the brick walkways between the new buildings until the students had worn a pathway between them. That was where the walkways would go, he told his staff, because that's where the students would walk anyway.

How, one day after World War II, he stood at an upstairs window in Analy Hall, looking out over a campus Brawl Day activity. The campus was crowded with returning GIs and Bailey, watching the students with pleasure, responded to a faculty member's concern that the scrimmage going on around the flagpole would ruin the grass in the quad. "Grass can grow back," Bailey said.

How he worried about community scrutiny, advising teachers who had an afternoon off not to be seen around town, in order to avoid criticism. But he was likewise quick to defend. When a businessman who was also a member of the college's board of trustees telephoned to say he had seen a faculty member downtown during class hours and wanted to know if Bailey knew what the teacher was doing off-campus, Bailey reportedly answered to the satisfaction of the businessman. "He's spending money," he said.

How he kept the students at the top of his priority list. The manager of the student union, known as "The Coop," was told when he was hired by Bailey that the school would rather the student cafeteria lose $1,000 than make $1,000.

How he never forgot his responsibility to his faculty and his staff. When two longtime teachers grew old and ill and were unable to teach, before the days of teachers' unions and mandated sick leave, Bailey simply ordered that they be kept on the payroll. "He didn't recommend it," Newman recalled. "He just did it."

Red Tauzer was from Willits, but he took Santa Rosa as his home and Santa Rosa Junior College as an important part of his life as soon as he completed his own education. He was a graduate of Stanford University, where he was student body president and captain of the basketball team. He had completed Stanford Law School and served in the military in World War I when he arrived in Santa Rosa to enter law practice in the Geary & Geary firm. Dean Bailey promptly offered him the unpaid job of coach. Urged on by Finlaw Geary, a senior partner in his law firm whose dedication as a sports fan was legendary, Tauzer took to the task with enthusiasm. He stayed on as coach, spending much of his spare time with the teams, until 1930 when the first professional coach, Richard Blewett, was hired.

Blewett was another SRJC zealot who served on the college faculty for more than three decades, coaching several sports, sometimes concurrently. In his later years as athletic director, liked to tell of the days when he ran between innings from the baseball dugout to the track to set up the hurdles for the next race.

Tauzer's service to SRJC only began with athletics, it didn't end there. He became the young college's chief advocate in the community, chairing the Chamber of Commerce's Junior College Committee, speaking for the college at service clubs and women's groups, lending his muscle as well as his leadership ability to work projects. As commander of the American Legion and a founder of the Santa Rosa Kiwanis Club, he quickly became a respected civic leader. In 1947 he was elected state senator from Sonoma County. Santa Rosa Junior College was always at the top of his agenda.

In 1930, after the junior college district was formed, with a board of trustees to be selected, the committee met to nominate a slate. The first name mentioned, the first person agreed upon was Red Tauzer. He was, as President Bailey would later recall, "a natural."

contention between Ernest Finley, editor of the *Press Democrat*, who felt it wasteful not to use the land for buildings, and President Bailey, who stoutly maintained the original agreement, as would his successors.

When the property issues were settled, a campus building program, achieved at the height of the Depression, created the permanent nucleus of the SRJC campus. Pioneer Hall, the campus's first building, was ready for occupancy in the spring of 1931. Geary Hall, the science building, was next. By 1940 Tauzer Gymnasium, Garcia Hall, Analy Hall, Bussman Hall, and Luther Burbank Auditorium were in place, as well as Bailey Field and the school's landmark arched gate, donated by the American Legion (again, through the offices of Red Tauzer) and the student athlete society.

Some of the construction work was accomplished with the aid of federal matching funds and Depression-era work projects. Federal Works Administration and Public Works Administration funds were used in the buildings. Works Progress Administration funds provided the labor for drainage and the campus walkway system. In 1940, 100 benches and ground light standards were installed on campus, purchased from the World's Fair on Treasure Island.

There was only one bond issue, for $138,000 in matching funds, for construction of a campus that would be compared to the wooded campuses of elite eastern colleges and would be considered among the most beautiful of all the junior colleges in the state.

In 1900 there were three public elementary schools in town—Fremont (which was the new name for the original Fourth Street School), Lincoln School on Davis Street, and Luther Burbank School on South A Street. The district was still the Court House District, the Santa Rosa name having been pre-empted by Bennett Valley farmers for their school way back in 1852.

—Santa Rosa Junior College Collection

In 1910 both Roseland and South Park School were annexed to the Court House District, but in 1919, Roseland parents petitioned for withdrawal, starting a court fight that lasted two years and ended with a ruling from the state attorney general dissolving the Court House district. Roseland had ongoing financial and legal problems based on a low assessed valuation and low student population. Trouble piled on trouble. The new five-room school building burned in April of 1921 before it was occupied and had to be rebuilt. It opened in April of 1922. South Park, where assessed valuation was so low there was no chance for independence, stayed in the district.

Santa Rosa was required to re-form its district. Once again, Bennett Valley residents were urged to give up the name Santa Rosa, which they, once again, refused to do, so the district was renamed the City of Santa Rosa School District. The elections of 1922 set up an elementary school district and a high school district under one admin-

At right, Pioneer Hall, the original building on the Santa Rosa Junior College campus. Above, Analy Hall under construction.

—Santa Rosa Junior College Collection

—LeBaron Collection

Santa Rosa Junior College was built on a site intended originally as a park in memory of Luther Burbank.

Nowhere are the rewards of the carefully nurtured friendship between the Santa Rosa Junior College and the community more evident than in the last will and testament of Frank P. Doyle.

The Exchange Bank president's interest in the betterment of Santa Rosa and Sonoma County was well known. He had been instrumental in saving large portions of the Sonoma Coast from private development to provide public access to the beaches he had loved all his life. He had a particular fondness for children. He and his wife Polly O'Meara Doyle had one son, Frank O'Meara Doyle, who died in 1921 at the age of thirteen, and, two years later, Doyle established a park in the boy's memory.

As Doyle entered his eighth decade, his concerns were for the welfare of his community, particularly the young people, and for the future of his financial institution. Firmly committed to the concept of a "hometown bank," he came up with a plan that would insure that his bank remained independent and locally owned and would shower his blessings on the young people of his community—beyond his imagination.

He placed his shares of Exchange Bank common stock—a controlling interest—in a perpetual trust. When he died in 1948, it was revealed that the Doyle Trust was simple and straightforward. From the dividends on his stock, the trust would pay $2,000 annually for the improvement and maintenance of Doyle Park. The rest was to be awarded to Santa Rosa Junior College to be distributed, as the Frank P. and Polly O'Meara Doyle Scholarship Fund, to "worthy young men and women" attending the college.

The value of the stock at the time of his death was more than $600,000. The first distribution of scholarship funds totaled $21,000. In the ensuing years, as local banks became increasingly rare, the Exchange Bank was not a candidate for merger or buy-out. It remained locally owned. Three trustees appointed by the bank directors from their ranks administered the fund. As the value of the stock increased, the dividends increased accordingly. Hundreds, eventually thousands, of students would attend the college aided by funds from the Doyle Trust. The gift made Santa Rosa Junior College unique among two-year institutions. Some believe it to be the best endowed two-year college in the western United States.[5]

istrator—the first being the distinguished Dr. Jerome O. Cross, versed in both Greek and Latin, respected by all as a scholar and a gentleman. Because of a state attorney general's ruling, the reorganization began with two boards, elected separately although they shared three of the same members. Attorney Hilliard Comstock, physician R.M. Bonar, and housewife and civic leader Sara Hatch were elected to both boards. Along with them on the elementary school board were shoe store owner Ross Moodey and electrical contractor Clark Van Fleet. Rural interests were represented on the high school board by Sheridan Baker of the Brush School District and Milo Baker, who was not related to Sheridan, from the Dunbar District. Sheridan Baker was the Rincon farmer. Milo Baker, who lived on Adobe Canyon Road near Kenwood, was a well-known botanist and future teacher at Santa Rosa Junior College.[6]

After 1924 the membership of the two boards was always the same, the result of a state court ruling that high school districts could take rural elementary school districts into their system without direct representation.[7] The name confusion was solved when in 1942 Bennett Valley finally agreed to become Bennett Valley School District and Santa Rosa's elementary and high school district became Santa Rosa City Schools.[8]

Lewis School, established on the Healdsburg road in 1867, was one of the oldest districts in the Santa Rosa area. Although it was within the city's purview, it remained independent until 1948. Proctor Terrace, the first "new" school in the district, was opened the same year, a year in which the elementary school system increased by one-half. Proctor Terrace was built on Bryden Lane and Fourth Street, on long-forgotten borders of the old town of Franklin, which was born and faded in the early 1850s, preceding the organization of Santa Rosa as a community. Monroe School, another existing district west of Santa

Luther Burbank School on South A Street was one of the three public elementary schools in Santa Rosa at the turn of the century.

There was a spate of "women's politics" in the election of 1922 when Louise Clark ran for and won a seat as county superintendent of schools, defeating incumbent Ben Ballard. Clark, who ran on a "woman's ticket," was successful despite opposition from teachers and trustees alike.

Clark's use of the phrase "came out of the kitchen" to question the competency of a Glen Ellen teacher caused something of an uproar in the general election. Teachers, most of whom were women, were so irate they ran a write-in campaign for Ballard, although Clark had beaten him in the primary. Ballard had received the endorsement of the trustees of 106 of the county's school districts. But Clark still won. In 1926 she was defeated by Oscar F. "Doc" Staton of Sebastopol, whose wife Mary served as assistant superintendent for three years of his tenure.[9]

—Finley Collection

Rosa, was annexed in 1950. Two schools, Steele Lane and Doyle Park, were opened in 1953, the first and second of several which would be necessary to accommodate the "Baby Boomers" and the rapid growth of post-war Santa Rosa.

The reorganization of 1942 sent the city district's seventh and eighth graders to a newly established junior high school in the old annex building on Humboldt Street. In 1950, ninth graders were added and Santa Rosa Junior High switched buildings with Fremont Elementary School, moving to its permanent home on College Avenue and King Street, the 19th century site of Pacific Methodist College. The district's second junior high school, Herbert Slater Junior High, opened in 1954 in east Santa Rosa.

In 1921 Santa Rosa High School, built in 1895 at Humboldt and Benton streets, burned to the ground. The cause of the fire would remain mysterious. Several possible causes were suggested: faulty wiring in the belfry, a cigarette or match tossed carelessly into the oiled sawdust the custodian used to clean the wood floors, a cigarette that found its way into the leaves raked from the grounds daily in the fall (the fire was in mid-November), or towels thrown over gas heaters in the locker room by a visiting basketball team that had played there. All were considered by the school board, which ordered the removal of gas heaters from school buildings and wiring inspections of all schools in the district. The cigarettes were a societal problem. Smoking had become popular after World War I. And witnesses recalled that there were smokers among faculty, staff, and basketball fans, including students, at the school the night of the fire.[10]

Whatever the cause, the loss was total and the inconvenience to education great. It was January of 1925

At left, an impromptu "car show" for photographer Ted Nelson at the new high school, circa 1930. Above, the 1929 SRHS football squad with coach Carleton "Dummy" Wells, a University of California football star, in the back row, second from left.

before a new school building was open for classes. For six semesters, the 700 high school students "met around," a housing solution remembered as both a hardship and a lark. Classes were taught all over town: at the library, in the old Congregational Church, in the upstairs hall above Mailer-Frey Hardware, in the Labor Temple, the Masonic Temple, the Chamber of Commerce office, Mailer's warehouse, a courtroom, and the high school annex, which consisted of adjunct buildings on the campus which had not burned.

The delay of the new high school building was due, in part, to a disagreement over the location. The site selected was on Mendocino Avenue adjacent to the Northwestern Pacific's crosstown spur line. It was part of the old Ridgway property and the Leppo tract and contained a house owned by the Todd family. Residents of the southern and southwest parts of town protested, lobbying for a site downtown.

One influential property owner, Sampson B. Wright, obtained an injunction against the district to prevent the sale of the bonds that would finance the new building. District Attorney George Hoyle represented the school district, arguing that Wright, as a resident of the Wright District, which was not part of the high school district, could not legally bring action. Wright, who did file suit, was roundly castigated for his action. The Saturday Afternoon Club passed a resolution condemning the suit because it delayed the proper education of the town's youth. Carpenters Union Local 751 also condemned Wright for the delay. In hindsight, there was some irony in this action, since the carpenters would, themselves, incur the wrath of the community for a three-month strike in mid-construction. Wright's suit was, as Hoyle had predicted, ruled illegal, and construction began in the spring of 1923. The new building, designed by W.H. Weeks of San Francisco and his Santa Rosa associate William Herbert, was considered a showplace.[12]

—Wood Family Collection

Dr. Lloyd K. Wood

*J*erome O. Cross succeeded Thomas F. Brownscombe as superintendent of Santa Rosa schools in 1921 and served twenty years, through many important changes in the district's makeup. Given to discourses on his philosophy of education, Cross was regarded as the community's resident intellectual. When he resigned in 1942, Lloyd K. Wood who had been principal of SRHS became superintendent. Wood would run the district, winning praises from a 1950s' national report on secondary education, until his death twenty-six years later.[11]

The high school principals in the early part of the century were E. Morris Cox, Charles Search, Dewitt Montgomery, I.D. Steele, and Gardiner Spring. Walter C. Patchett followed Spring and served until 1938. After Wood became superintendent the job was given to Thornton H. Battelle, who was in charge of SRHS during the war years; Frederick Duey was named principal in 1946 and held the job for twenty-four years.

Santa Rosa High School's early-century faculty was comprised of dedicated and beloved teachers, none more dedicated or beloved than Frances Louise O'Meara. Miss O'Meara was a tiny woman who liked to say that her initials, FLO'M, stood for "Funny Little Old Maid." In her fifty years of teaching in Sonoma County schools she acquired a reputation much larger than her stature. "Mighty" is an adjective often used by students recalling Miss O'Meara and her discipline methods. Her English classes were the largest classes in Santa Rosa High School and there was seldom even a whisper when she stood to teach.

Martha Erwin, who was her student and later her colleague in the SRHS English department, remembered her as "a classicist who schooled us in the Greek myths, in Homer's *Iliad* and *Odyssey,* and made it all so vivid that eventually I had to go to Troy to see for myself. She saturated us with poetry and filled every day with lively

Among the earliest Montessori schools in the state was the kindergarten established on Humboldt Street before 1920 by May Marshman Payne. The divorced mother of four daughters, Payne became interested in the educational philosophy of the Italian physician Maria Montessori and preached its doctrine to public and private school administrators alike.

In 1917, backed by the Parent-Teachers Association and the Saturday Afternoon Club, Payne was elected to the Santa Rosa Board of Education, where she served for nearly a decade. At the same time, into the early 1920s, she operated her private Montessori kindergarten and lectured on Montessori principles to teachers and parents. Luther Burbank, who employed her oldest daughter, Adelia Payne (later Keegan), as a secretary and stenographer, became interested in Payne's work and presented her with "didactic apparatus" for her Montessori work.[15]

imagination.... She had a magnificent Irish sense of humor, a very solemn sense of humor. But there was a sparkle, a gleam, in her eye."[13]

By 19th century standards, Frances O'Meara got a late start at teaching. She was twenty-four years old, with a purely Santa Rosa education from Miss Chase's Seminary, when she went to teach in the tiny Madrona School near Cazadero in 1889. From there she worked her way back to town, moving to Spring Hill School west of Sebastopol and finally to Santa Rosa, where she taught for forty-five years.

She was born in Oregon and came to Santa Rosa as a child. Her father, James O'Meara, was a writer and newspaperman who worked for a time as the editor of the Santa Rosa *Republican*. Her sister, Polly O'Meara, married the town's leading citizen, Frank Doyle of the Exchange Bank.

Miss O'Meara retired in 1939 and died soon after. The class of '39, with some understanding that they were

bearing witness to the end of a remarkable period of education in Santa Rosa, dedicated the yearbook to her with these words: "You have left us so many worthy things...."[14]

Orbin Walter Fortier coached basketball and baseball at SRHS for twenty-five years before becoming dean of boys and finally vice principal of both Santa Rosa Junior High and Herbert Slater Junior High. His Class A or varsity teams won thirteen championships in eighteen years, his B teams, nine in thirteen. They beat Lowell High of San Francisco—a team considered unbeatable—two years in a row. They beat the Stanford freshmen. They beat SRJC and College of Marin.

But Fortier's contribution to Santa Rosa education was more than athletic. In response to principal Gardiner Spring's request that he "fire up the student body," Fortier wrote a school song to the tune of his home state's "On Wisconsin," changed the school colors from black and lemon yellow to black and burnt orange, and designated the teams as the Santa Rosa Panthers—his legacy to generations of rally committees. He was the adviser to the student newspaper and yearbooks in his early years. (He taught a journalism class at SRJC when the college was still sharing a building with the high school.)

Fortier was also an important link between the school and the community. He was an active Mason and president of Scottish Rite and the Kiwanis Club. His well-known "Poker Club," a penny-ante social group of educators, was rumored to be the power organization in the school system.

The political "division" of Santa Rosa between Masons and Roman Catholic Church extended to the school board, which almost always had a Mason and a Catholic among its five members, as well as a businessman, a lawyer, and a woman. The Masonic-Catholic balance was evident in school athletic programs as well. Fortier represented the Masonic side, football coach James Underhill, whose teams were equally successful, the Catholic contingent. They vied for funding and favors from the board; both were granted, since school athletics were very important to the community.

The most powerful subdivision of Santa Rosa High School, however, was the music department. The music faculty consisted of dance instructor Mildred Hahman Turner, a granddaughter of Santa Rosa's pioneer merchant family, choral director Helen Cochrane, and instrumental music instructor Josef Walter. Several of Walter's students became successful professional musicians, including oboeist Laila Storch Friedmann, conductor Corrick Brown, and composer-arranger Pete Rugulo. The music department was treated very well by the administration and the board. A measure of its success: for many years SRHS was one of the few high schools in the state of California with a separate building for music studies.

The free night school of the 1920s was a popular service offered by the Santa Rosa school district. In 1920, there were 125 students enrolled, arriving at classes from the trains in a bus provided by the district. Working people remained enthusiastic about this educational opportunity. Classes were held in the new high school building when it opened in '25, as well as in the annex on Humboldt Street. School officials anticipated an enrollment of 250 students in the spring semester of that year.

An institution for the Roman Catholic education of young women, under the direction of the Sisters of St. Ursula, had been established in Santa Rosa in 1880. In 1901, the Ursuline Academy was granted a charter as a liberal arts college and continued, until 1936, to offer degrees. When

Ursuline Academy, to the rear of St. Rose Church on B Street, was chartered as a college in 1901 and offered degrees in liberal arts until 1936.

—*LeBaron Collection*

—Press Democrat Collection

Ursuline moved to a new school off Mark West Springs Road in 1957, the high school enrollment included sixty-nine resident students and 150 day students.

The Ursuline nuns had made several attempts at establishing a parochial elementary school around the turn of the century and, in 1910, opened a school for boys known as St. Charles' Preparatory Academy, which had as many as sixty students before it was discontinued at the start of World War I. It was not until the Rev. Henry Raters became pastor of St. Rose parish that St. Rose Elementary School was organized. The three-story structure at Ninth and A streets, behind the church and adjacent to the Ursuline College, was dedicated in September of 1931 and opened with an enrollment of 235 students and a faculty supplied by the Ursuline order.[16]

In 1953, after a second Catholic parish was established in east Santa Rosa, St. Eugene's School opened. The faculty was from the Sisters of St. Joseph of Orange, a nursing and teaching order that had come to Santa Rosa to establish Memorial Hospital.

Many private schools began and ended in the unsettled financial climate of the first fifty years of the century. Santa Rosa Normal School, which had been preparing students for teaching for thirty-eight years, closed in 1918. Prof. A.C. McMeans announced in July that he would not reopen in the fall. But the same year the Santa Rosa School of Languages opened, where Prof. Vincent G. Nicoletti taught Italian, French, Spanish and English for foreigners in his Cherry Street home. Bent Conservatory of Music was on Sonoma Avenue. Dean Edwin W. Bent taught piano, organ, composition, sight singing, and vocal repetoire; and his instructors offered classes in violin, cello, mandolin, guitar, horns, and woodwinds. Sidney Tilden Dakin, a well-known San Francisco painter who was in much demand as a decorator by San Francisco society matrons, moved to Santa Rosa and opened an art school after the '06 earthquake destroyed his San Francisco studio. Dakin also taught at the Ursuline College.

St. Rose Elementary School on NInth Street had 235 students when it opened in 1931.

*E*very morning, before the start of classes in typewriting, accounting, shorthand, banking procedures, and the Palmer method of penmanship, the students of Sweet's Business College gathered for the morning song. More often than not, the song was "Smiles." Professor Sweet was a positive thinker. And he taught his students to be the same.

The young people who came to Prof. James S. Sweet's Santa Rosa Business College in the first four decades of the century were mostly the sons and daughters of immigrants—from northern Italy, Switzerland, Germany, the isle of Foehr in the North Sea, the island of Sao Jorge or Pico in the Azores—people whose English was minimal, who took great pride in the business skills their children learned.

About three-quarters of the student body were female, and for these first-generation Americans, a Sweet's certificate was a passport out of the cannery. Prof. Sweet and his nephew, Clyde Sweet, who later took over the administration of the school, were able to find jobs for most of their graduates, even at the height of the Depression. But many of the men and women who took Sweet's business training went back to the farm, using their bookkeeping and banking skills for the business of agriculture.

Students came to the school on Ross Street by bicycle, by horse and buggy, on foot, and on the train. Students from Petaluma came by way of Sebastopol, stopping at Woodworth and Orchard and every whistlestop where the farm kids parked their bicycles. The fare was a nickel. It was an hour's trip to the Santa Rosa courthouse and two blocks on the run to Sweet's. Train students from Petaluma and the west county were generally ten minutes late.

Many of Sweet's students boarded in Santa Rosa to attend classes, some at Hattie Ward's boardinghouse around the corner on Mendocino Avenue, some with Minnie Coulter, the superintendent of county schools who took in students from outlying schools at her house on Cleveland Avenue, and some with Prof. Sweet and his wife Julia at their home on Cherry Street.

Prof. Sweet was a man of many accomplishments. He was an educator with a national reputation; a politician who represented Santa Rosa at the state level during his years as mayor, 1898 to 1902; and a writer of romantic songs. He took his songwriting and his civic service seriously, but his true mission was that of a teacher. His personal interest in his students is well documented. He loaned them money and helped them through family crises. If they were sick, he visited them in the hospital.

The business course was a short one. Most students completed Sweet's in nine months. But they remembered it with the same nostalgia university students have for their campus days. Many credit their success in life to the education they received there. Many met their spouses at Sweet's. It changed their lives.[17]

Luther Burbank College of Commerce opened in 1933 in the fourteen-room house Burbank had built on Sonoma and Santa Rosa avenues before the earthquake. His widow was a member of the board of directors. The "garden campus," the college advertised, was a living memorial to the Santa Rosa horticulturist.

There were three elementary school districts in Rincon Valley before World War II. Rincon School dated back to a schoolhouse on Middle Rincon Road opened in the 1860s. In 1880, the school moved to a hillside location on Sonoma Highway, still in one room. In 1905, a second classroom was added and, in 1913, a third, making it one of the larger country schools in the area. Wallace School started in 1871 at the east end of the valley. Brush School, on Brush Creek Road, was the newcomer, organizing as a district in 1917.

Into the 1920s, these were schools with hitching posts, since there was still an occasional student who rode a horse from a distant farm. Ted Gambogi drove a unique sort of school bus for Brush School—an old carriage once used by the Overton Hotel to meet the trains. Gambogi drove the carriage, pulled by a team of horses, around the valley, picking up children for school in the morning and returning them home in the afternoon.[18]

The Rincon Valley schools were near the city, but it was a straitlaced farming community. In 1922 three Rincon trustees resigned in a disagreement over the length of the principal's skirt. The administrator in question, Mrs. Thornsberry, had been under close scrutiny from the board for most of the year as a result of reports that her choice of reading material was not proper. The students were reading the novels of Zane Grey and Rex Beach's adventure story, *The Iron Trail.* No action was instituted against the principal. The county superintendent appointed three more trustees.

After several unsuccessful attempts to merge the districts, the citizens got down to serious business in 1946.

The Rincon Valley Grange held a series of public meetings and, in December, the voters approved a consolidation plan. In April, they passed a bond issue for a new school. It wasn't opened until 1950. In the meantime, the expanded district continued to hold one class at Brush School, one at Wallace, and the rest at the old Rincon School.[19]

The Rincon District would be the rapid-growth district of the 1950s and 1960s. Village School, the first of a series of schools built to accommodate children from the new east Santa Rosa subdivisions opened in 1952.

———

Rincon was only one of the great number of rural school districts for which Sonoma County was well known. At the turn of the century, the county superintendent, Carl H. Nelson, wrote: "It is a fact known to such persons only as have taken the trouble to inform themselves, that Sonoma County has more school districts than any other county in the state of California. Schoolhouses are scattered in the hills and valleys the entire length and breadth of the county; no corner too remote that it has its 'little red schoolhouse.'"[20]

There were 180 school districts in the county in pre-unification days, many of them one-room schools that were a district unto themselves, governed by property owners whose ancestors had built them with volunteer labor and donated materials. The disappearance of these schools was an indication of the changes in education in the first half of the 19th century. Some 144 Sonoma County school names have been "retired" as a result of unification, improved transportation, and urbanization. Many of those names have the ring of history to them— names like Alpine and Jonive (pronounced Hoe-neeve, with the Spanish J), Kidd Creek and Tarwater and Tan Bark and Bliss and Felta and Miriam and Oriental and Scotta and Grape. Some, like Table Mountain and Double Pine and Creighton Ridge, were remote even by turn-of-the-century standards.

In addition to the close-in school districts such as Wright, Hall, Mt. Olivet, Piner, Todd, and Hearn, there were many one-room'ers in central Sonoma County, clustered around the county seat. Alpine was one, high up on the Calistoga grade on St. Helena Road. Strawberry School was on Sonoma Mountain Road above Bennett Valley. Tarwater was near Mark West Creek. And there was Riebli, a good example of the birth and death of a rural school.[21]

John Riebli was a Swiss immigrant who bought land in 1905 on Mark West Creek, not far east of where it stretches out across the Santa Rosa plain. He had both vineyard and orchard and raised cattle and Angora goats. There were six children in the Riebli family. The nearest school was Wallace in upper Rincon Valley, several miles south, across the ridge. Mark West School, on Barnes Road on the plain,

The schools that would become the Rincon Valley School District. At far left, above, Mr. Pye and his students at Brush School, 1927. At left, below, students pose outside the original Wallace School, circa 1915. The school was built by Pleasant Wells on land he donated in the 1880s. Below, the Rincon School on the Sonoma Road.

—Beth Winter Photo

239

Riebli School, built on land along Mark West Creek donated in the first decade of the century by farmer John Riebli, is a good example of the one-room country school.

—*LeBaron Collection*

Photos on the page at left represent four of the many rural schools surrounding Santa Rosa in the early years of the 20th century. At upper left, Piner School. At upper right, the primary grades of Hearn School, 1922. At lower left, Strawberry School on the eastern slope of Sonoma Mountain. At lower right, Wright District School.

was even farther; Tarwater was a long uphill climb. So Riebli and his neighbors formed a school district. He donated the land for the schoolhouse and schoolyard and the school took his name.

It opened with twenty-seven students in one room, including the six Rieblis. The first teacher, Harriett Burnett, boarded at the Riebli home, which was standard educational practice in country schools. A later teacher, Lulu Helman, drove out from town every day in a horse and buggy. Elma Dakin Goodman, one of the first students to graduate from Riebli, went off to normal school and came back to teach there, scarcely older than her oldest student.

By 1943 improved transportation made it easier to attend Mark West School. There were just sixteen students in Riebli School so it closed, and the district disbanded. The property reverted to the family. Ed Riebli, one of the original students, tore the schoolhouse down and built a residence on the site, leaving a rose bush that had been planted on opening day, winding forty feet toward the top of a schoolyard pine tree, as the only reminder of what had been.[22]

The one-room schoolhouse, which disappeared with increasing frequency after 1940, was one of the aspects of the early century that residents would come to regard with nostalgia. As the tempo of daily life increased, the memory of being driven home in an old carriage, behind a team of plodding horses, would become a thing to cherish, as would so many memories of the simpler life in Santa Rosa "before the war." ❧

Between Wars

Santa Rosa in the 1920s and 1930s is described as a peaceful town to grow up in. "We spent much of our time in the streets and they remain in my memory," a resident would recall. "The hot asphalt of College Avenue on a summer's day, outer Mendocino on the way to school, Second Street by the tannery and the creek. On the Fourth of July the veterans of the Great War, with still a few from the Spanish American War, would parade up McDonald Avenue under the trees, stopping at Soldiers Park to hear speeches and 'Taps' played against the echo bugle in the Odd Fellows Cemetery. The dust hung in the warm still air after they passed and we boys would march along behind, wondering what it was like to be in a war." This is the way Robert Herbert, a retired naval architect who spent his boyhood in Santa Rosa, remembers the town.[1]

Family life in the early part of the 20th century was pretty much the stuff of Thornton Wilder's America—a kind of Grovers Corners in California. The boys went skinny-dipping in the creek downstream from the railroad bridge, little girls practiced their piano lessons in Victorian homes on tree-lined streets, the Western Union boy delivered telegrams on his bicycle, and the merchants and bankers walked home for lunch.

To the residents of outlying Sonoma County towns, Santa Rosa may have seemed, as one gentleman who grew up in Guerneville termed it, "a socially-incestuous, self-satisfied village of...the world's best people."[2] It's true that Santa Rosa's insularity, exhibited clearly by its Old West politics and farm town self-reliance, was beyond doubt. But to the lucky people who lived in it, Santa Rosa would have seemed charmed. Putting the politics aside—as, indeed, most residents did—life in Santa Rosa between the Great Earthquake and the Second World War could best be described as idyllic, small-city America.

Burgess Titus, who grew up in that Santa Rosa, in a household where his mother stayed home to mind the family, gives us a peek into family life in the personal reminiscences he titled "I Remember When." He remembers the Saturday night bath as "quite an undertaking. Mom would start about supper time to heat the water in the teakettles and pots and pans, on the wood cook stove. Later the galvanized wash tub was set on the floor in the kitchen. I don't remember if the cold water was poured in first or the hot water first. I don't remember if I got in first because I was the oldest of the three brothers, or if the youngest got in first because he had to go to bed first."

The Titus family lived in several different houses while the family was growing up. "Our little house on Barnett Street, next to Olive Street was too small and Pop put up two tents on platforms with side boards about three feet high for our bedrooms.... There was only one better place to sleep on a rainy night and that was in the attic, under the shingled roof of the Sebastopol Avenue house. The Barnett Street house had a 'modern' outhouse. It was built up against the end of the house so that from the street it looked like part of the house."

The Titus house on South Davis Street had gas jet lamps on the walls and kerosene lamps on the tables. "When Pop got one of the new Rayo kerosene lamps with the round wick, it brightened up the parlor so we could sometimes see to read. This house had an out-back two-holer privy and covered pots in each bedroom."[3]

The Tituses were neighbors of Luther Burbank and Burgess was one of the many children who visited with him when he was tending plants near the fence. "He would stop and talk with us," Titus remembered. "I especially remember the time we schoolchildren went to see him in front of his big house on the north side of Tupper Street when Henry Ford, Thomas Edison and Harvey Firestone, and a few political dignitaries were there to visit him."

Luther Burbank remained Santa Rosa's favorite citizen. But his fame, based largely on his work in the 1890s, became a burden to him in the 1900s. The unscientific press overstated his accomplishments. His worldwide importance

Much of the social life of the young people of Santa Rosa seemed to center around sporting events. Claude Sanborn, a young man who worked as a cement and brick contractor and served as captain of Company E of the National Guard, was an enthusiastic amateur photographer who made a scrapbook of the sporting events he captured with his camera. Sanborn's notes in the scrapbook tell us these are, top row, left to right: a walking advertisement for a baseball game, boating on the Russian River, and a pole vaulter named Hitchcock going over the top. Second row, left to right: the Santa Rosa "nine," a diver showing off at the Russian River (The row boat advertises a Santa Rosa drug store), and a game of "auto polo" at the fairgrounds. Bottom row, left to right: snow in Santa Rosa, a runner at a track meet at the fairgrounds track, and the Santa Rosa High School alumni football team.

created a backlash from his fellow hybridizers, some of whom became quite vocal in their attempts to discredit him.[4] But his public image, that of a gentle, white-haired man who worked magic in his garden, persisted with the general public and he remained one of the great American heroes of his time.

In his 1930 novel The *42nd Parallel*, which was part of his *USA* trilogy, author John Dos Passos chose Burbank as one of nine Americans (with Thomas Edison, Charles Proteus Steinmetz, Andrew Carnegie, William Jennings Bryan, Eugene Debs, Minor Keith, Robert LaFollette, and Big Bill Haywood) to profile. In his prose-poem titled "The Plant Wizard," Dos Passos writes:

Young man go west;
Luther Burbank went to Santa Rosa
full of his dream of green grass in winter everblooming flowers ever-
bearing berries; Luther Burbank
...carried his apocalyptic dream of green grass in
winter

and seedless berries and stoneless plums and
thornless roses brambles cactus—
...out to sunny Santa Rosa;
he was a sunny old man
where roses bloomed all year
everblooming everbearing
hybrids.

Biographer Peter Dreyer, in the preface to *A Gardener Touched with Genius*, calls Burbank "an immensely intricate character" who "possessed a mysterious charisma that drew sycophants and eulogists like bees to nectar...." He was, says Dreyer, "never able to resist playing to their adulation."

People flocked to see him. Jack London came often from his home in Glen Ellen, writing in the guest book his thanks for "an intellectual hour." Burbank's many visitors included William Jennings Bryan, Helen Keller, Ignace Paderewski, and Sir Harry Lauder. In 1924, the Paramahansa Yogananda, newly arrived from India, came to teach Burbank the technique of Kriya Yoga, a method the Swami would introduce with great success in the western world.

As Burbank grew older he went out less and less, and his reclusiveness became part of the Burbank legend. He traveled between his Santa Rosa gardens and his Sebastopol experimental farm—but not much farther. A Santa Rosa man, it was said, once met Mr. Burbank on the train on his way to San Francisco. He was bound for Stanford University to deliver a lecture, he told him, and he loathed the thought. Before the train arrived at its destination, Burbank reportedly offered to pay the man if he would go in his place and deliver the lecture. While it was probably intended as a joke, it was not repeated as one.

He was almost a mythic figure. He became whatever special interest groups wanted him to be: the nurseries, who were his eager customers after his "New Creations in Fruits and Flowers" was published in 1893, created Burbank the magician, a gardener who could make new plants spring from the earth; the Santa Rosa Chamber of Commerce

Luther Burbank's Santa Rosa gardens with his greenhouse, home, and carriage house in the background.

—*Chamber of Commerce Collection*

created Burbank the tourist attraction, photographed from every angle, "at home" to all visitors.

Both images caused him difficulties. His early success, blown out of proportion by the advertising claims of nurserymen selling his products, caused other hybridizers to doubt his claims. He was, after all, just one of them. They, too, were improving plants as part of their regular workday. In 1909, the *Pacific Rural Press* told the story of the resolution passed by the Pasadena Gardeners Association condemning "the faking methods and exploitations of alleged but false creations by Luther Burbank."

The *Rural Press* writer was not surprised. "The most sensational agricultural event of the week is the arraignment of Mr. Luther Burbank at the bar of horticultural judgment. We have apprehended its coming for a long time. We have not hesitated to state in these columns that the extravagant exaltation of the man and his achievements by those who really did not know either one or the other was, in our view, the most serious menace to his career, because it caused him to be misjudged and his work to be misunderstood."[5]

The following year, in an interview with the *San Francisco Chronicle*, Burbank outlined his problem: "The extravagant estimates of my work have been the bane of my existence. There has been much written about me by sensational writers who know nothing either of me or my work. I am not responsible for all these things and anyone with any knowledge of horticulture could discern at once that much of the stuff sent is nothing but space-writer's chaff."

Santa Rosa's eagerness to promote the area through him proved bothersome also. He was hounded by curiosity seekers, until one day, in exasperation, he posted a sign in his garden saying "My Time is Worth $20 a Minute."[6]

In 1912 Burbank entered into an agreement with an Oakland banker and San Francisco stockbroker. The Luther Burbank Company was formed to market his seeds and plants, with most of the stock held by Bay Area

—*Chamber of Commerce Collection*

At left, Burbank entertains Scottish singer and comic Sir Harry Lauder who was among many celebrities who came to visit the Santa Rosa gardens. Below, Burbank confers with Santa Rosa civic leaders in front of his new house on Santa Rosa Avenue. Left to right: Harold K. Wiedenfeld, Elmer Mobley, an unidentified man, John Rinner, Roe M. Barrett, and Carl Barnard.

—*Press Democrat Collection*

businessmen. Burbank, they promised, would never have to worry his head about business matters again. It would all be taken care of for him. Three years later, when it became clear the marketing promoters were overstating the nature of the company's plants and seeds, the corporation was in bankruptcy and Burbank was filing suit for money owed him from the sale of his work.

The Luther Burbank Press and Luther Burbank Society, which proposed to publish twelve volumes of his

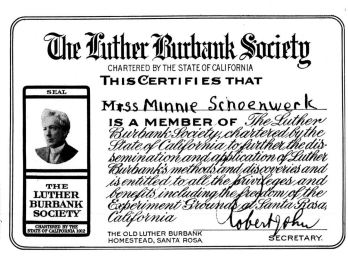

The Luther Burbank Society

CHARTERED BY THE STATE OF CALIFORNIA

THIS CERTIFIES THAT

Mrss Minnie Schoenwerk

IS A MEMBER OF The Luther Burbank Society, chartered by the State of California to further the dissemination and application of Luther Burbank's methods and discoveries and is entitled to all the privileges and benefits, including the freedom of the Experiment Grounds at Santa Rosa, California

Robert John

THE OLD LUTHER BURBANK HOMESTEAD, SANTA ROSA.

SECRETARY.

SEAL

THE LUTHER BURBANK SOCIETY

CHARTERED BY THE STATE OF CALIFORNIA 1912

history and life's work, were also organized in 1912. Much like the National Geographic Society, members would be apprised of his new work and receive the books at a nominal cost. World headquarters was in the old Burbank home. He had moved to his new house across Tupper Street six years earlier. In 1915 world headquarters moved to New York City, and, within months, the society was defunct. The society and press did manage to complete the publishing effort, and the result (although ghost-written and padded with extraneous commentary) was a truly handsome twelve-volume set. Sold in a choice of bindings and enhanced by numerous four-color photographs—one of the earliest

uses of such technology in book production—the sets would become collectors' items and would continue to offer insights to researchers and historians.

Divorced in 1896 after six years of apparent turmoil with the shrewish Helen Coleman Burbank, whom he had met on a train trip east and married in 1890, Burbank lived as a bachelor until his sixty-fifth year. In 1916, he married for a second time. His bride was Elizabeth Jane Waters. She was in her late twenties and had been his secretary for two years. She would remain his staunchest supporter for more than fifty years after his death.

Burbank always had his critics. People were shocked that he would "dare to interfere with the handiwork of God."[7] But children loved him, and he them. He entertained them when he could, making them laugh by turning somersaults on his grass. They came from Burbank School to see him on his birthday, and to sing for him. He was a frequent inspirational speaker at schools in Santa Rosa and Sebastopol, exhorting the students to hard work.

Occasionally, there were reports of Burbank assuming a kind of messianic posture. He is reputed to have confided in one friend that the world had "experienced many Christs" and hinted that he might be one of them.[8] People ascribed miracles to him. There were many who believed he "taught" his plants to grow properly. Others believed he could cure illness by "laying on of hands."

Reporters asked his opinion of everything. They called him "The Wisest Man in the West." While he might have disputed the title, he did not refuse to answer. Asked about jazz music, for example, he delivered a diatribe, saying, "I hate the very word and as for the thing itself and all it stands for, I can't bear even to think of it." The headline in the *San Francisco Examiner* read: "Spirit of Jazz Will Drag Race to Level of Savages, Says Sage."[9]

Burbank's tragic mistake came on a much more serious topic. And it was really his old friend Henry Ford who started it all. In the February 1926 issue of *Cosmopolitan* magazine this mechanical genius's ideas on afterlife were set forth and an enterprising editor decided it would be a story to learn Burbank's views on the same subject.

The interview that appeared in the *San Francisco Bulletin* on January 23 set bells jangling on every news telegraph in the United States and Europe. Burbank told reporter Edgar Waite he believed in some sort of force that controlled the universe—but he declined to give it a name. He suggested that organized religion was faltering. He said he was an infidel. Then, in a second statement attempting to explain to the legion of Christians who rose up in wrath, he said that he did believe in a Supreme Being and was an infidel only as "every great reformer has been a disbeliever in some of the accepted tenets or opinions of people in general. In that light Christ and all other reformers have been infidels, not accepting the current opinions of the times." People were misunderstanding him, he told a *Press Democrat* reporter the next day. "Infidel" and "atheist" were not interchangeable terms, he said. But what his critics heard was that he was not only calling himself an

infidel, he was calling Jesus Christ one as well.[10]

Santa Rosa's ministers joined the denouncers. The Rev. Fred Keast of the First Methodist Church led off, with the Rev. Elmer Ingram of First Presbyterian and Dr. Julian Blodgett of First Baptist close behind. The Church of the Incarnation pastor, Dr. William Short, declined to comment. And Father John Cassin, at St. Rose, attempted perspective by telling a reporter, "The old Church goes right along in spite of these things." Burbank's chief defender in Santa Rosa was Ernest Finley. The *Press Democrat* editor, himself the son of a minister, treated the issue in his down-home style in an editorial headlined "Let Mr. Burbank Alone." "There is nothing much the matter with Mr. Burbank," wrote Finley. "He may differ with certain people on theories concerning the hereafter but there are many such theories and the world is not yet through with them by any means."

Burbank biographers Ken and Pat Kraft suggest Burbank picked the wrong word. "He had the whole English language to choose from, and he picked a word that carried

Josef Walter's student orchestra pays Burbank a visit on the occasion of his 77th—and last—birthday in March of 1926, a month before he died.

—*Press Democrat Collection*

247

haunting, hazy, subconscious tremors of savagery, of medieval blood and hatreds," they wrote.[11] But the purest definition of the word—"a person who does not believe in the prevailing religion"—seemed to be exactly what he meant. Satan didn't concern him, he would explain when invited to expand on his views from the pulpit of the First Congregational Church of San Francisco. He did not believe in damnation. He suggested mankind "have one world at a time" and "read the Bible without the ill-fitting colored spectacles of theology."[12]

His visit to the San Francisco church followed the firestorm of criticism engendered by the newspaper interview. He had been alternately denounced and prayed for by the Christian faithful all over the globe. In Santa Rosa, the Sonoma County Women's Christian Temperance Union, which had previously honored him with a life membership, invited him to a mass meeting to pray for his soul. He politely declined. Abusive letters demanding he retract his statements piled up. When the invitation to speak in San Francisco was offered, he accepted.

The speech was eloquent. His friend Frederick Clampett, who knew how he hated public appearances, was there to report on how nervous Burbank seemed, how thin and frail he looked on the pulpit, and how gloriously he rose to the occasion.

The sermon, for the most part, made things worse for Burbank. Religion was a current national topic. William Jennings Bryan's fire-and-brimstone castigation of John Scopes, a Tennessee schoolteacher arrested the previous year for teaching evolution to his students, was still ringing in the ears of God-fearing Americans. So, while the Santa Rosa gardener did receive some touching statements of support—one from a Baptist minister in Kansas City who was cast out of his church for endorsing Burbank's statements—much of the reaction was hostile. "A poor, deluded dupe of the Devil," one critic called him.[13]

"Burbank," writes biographer Dreyer, "had anticipated that 1926 would be a good year." Several new strains of gladioli, Shasta daisies, and roses, which he had been perfecting for several years, would be ready for release. In an interview with *Popular Science Monthly* before his seventy-fifth birthday, he had told the writer he looked forward to five more years of productivity.[14] But it was not to be. On March 24, 1926, two months after the controversy over his faith arose, Burbank suffered a heart attack. The prescription was rest and quiet, and he seemed to be responding. Six days after the attack he was seized with unremitting hiccups. He lived only twelve more days. On April 10, weary from lack of sleep, unable to eat, wracked with the ceaseless spasms, he lapsed into a final coma. He died Sunday, April 11, shortly after midnight.

His funeral was held in Doyle Park, where he had often strolled. The Rev. Caleb Dutton, a Unitarian pastor from San Francisco who had married the Burbanks, performed the funeral services. Burbank's old friend Sen. Herbert Slater introduced the speakers. A crowd estimated at 5,000 heard a speech by Judge Ben Lindsey, the freethinking jurist who had come from his Denver home to keep a promise he had made to Burbank many years before. Wilbur Hall, who had written Burbank's history, read the famous eulogy which Robert G. Ingersoll had spoken at his own brother's funeral in 1879. Burbank was buried at the edge of his gardens under a Cedar of Lebanon he had planted thirty years earlier. He had often told friends and family it would be his only grave marker.

Luther Burbank's fame would live long after his death. His final controversy would continue to be debated for the remainder of the century. The contrast of the freethinker in the farmtown setting, among his Christian friends and neighbors, was hard for writers to resist. When *Los Angeles Times* columnist Lee Shippey visited Santa Rosa in 1942, he wrote about the town's most famous resident and those well-publicized views on religion. Burbank's criticism of Christianity, wrote Shippey, came "at the time all the residents of Santa Rosa walked down the shady streets which led to church every Sunday morning with their Bibles in their hands...."

———

The major religious groups had been well established in Santa Rosa before the turn of the century. The Protestant community, founded in the southern traditions of the early settlers, prospered in the settled, farmtown atmosphere. Some ministers, like the Rev. Elmer E. Ingram at the Gothic-spired First Presbyterian Church at the corner of Humboldt and Johnson streets, stayed many years. Ingram came to the church in 1919 and stayed until his death in 1942. In 1921, a grateful congregation presented him with a Buick touring car as a Christmas and New Year's gift. Ingram was succeeded by his assistant, Graydon McClellan, who served—with time out for service as an Army chaplain—until 1953. His successor was David Barnett.

The town's second Presbyterian church, the Church of the Roses, was built with a flourish in 1952. Located in the new Montgomery Village area, it was constructed as a publicity stunt between 7:09 a.m. and 12:25 p.m. in a single Saturday. Developer Hugh Codding donated the six-lot site and the building materials and provided the 200 workers. The Rev. William Bowen held services in the new church next morning.

Bethlehem Lutheran Church had two long-term pastors to guide the congregation through the better part of its first fifty years. Pastor George Shurson served twenty-five years, from 1917 to 1942, at the church on Tupper Street. Pastor Julius Hansen came in 1943 to serve for nineteen years.

St. Luke's, the Missouri Synod Lutheran Congregation, lost its forty-eight-year-old church building on Seventh Street between Washington and Davis streets in 1947. It was in the path of the new Highway 101 bypass. The old parish hall, moved to the new church site on Mendocino Avenue at Denton Way, was used for services while a new church building was constructed. E. F. Heise, a member of the congregation, served as contractor on a cost basis and other members worked as volunteers. The new building was dedicated in 1949. The tower and the parish hall were added in 1953.

Other denominations changed spiritual leaders regularly. The First Baptist Church and The First Congregational Church each had fourteen pastors between 1905 and 1955. The Baptists worshipped in a redwood frame church building on B Street which enjoyed a modicum of fame, having been drawn and described by cartoonist Robert Ripley as "The Church Built from One Tree" in his nationally syndicated "Believe it or Not!" feature. Ripley

—Ripley Museum

249

was right about the church. It had been constructed in 1873 from lumber carefully set aside by Guerneville mill owner Rufus Murphy who wanted to see the structure made from one tree only, both as a curiosity and as a promotional statement about the California redwood.

Six members of Santa Rosa's black community met with the Rev. Washington Boyce in 1951 to organize the Community Baptist Church. The congregation met at the Native Sons Hall until a church building was constructed on Grand Avenue in the South Park Neighborhood in 1954. By the early '50s, there were several Baptist churches in Santa Rosa. The Village Baptists and the College Avenue Baptists gave up some members in 1951 when the Rev. Don Frazier formed a Baptist mission which became the West Santa Rosa Baptist Church, opened on Easter Sunday, 1954. Grace Baptist, which had been meeting in the Saturday Afternoon Club House for two years, also chose Easter, this time in 1955, for the inaugural service in its church building on Petaluma Hill Road.

The First Congregational Church was located on E Street at the time of the 1906 earthquake, and the pastor was the Rev. Arthur Patton who had come to Santa Rosa from a church in South Hadley, Massachusetts. When news of the earthquake damage to the Rev. Patton's western church reached his former parishioners, they took up a collection and sent the money to make the necessary repairs, including the replacement of the stained glass windows broken in the quake.

The Santa Rosa Congregationalists joined with members of the First Presbyterian Church for worship during World War II. The call for ministers to serve as chaplains produced a shortage of clergy which was answered in this manner by many Protestant churches. The old Congregational church building was deemed inadequate after the war and, in 1953, a new First Congregational Church was dedicated at the corner of Humboldt and Silva streets.

The Episcopalians' Church of the Incarnation added a parish house to its Mendocino Avenue complex during the rectorship of the Rev. William Short in 1925. In 1935, the Rev. Arthur G. Farlander, for whom the church's parish hall is named, became rector, a position he would hold until his death in 1952. The Rev. Percy G. Hall, who was chosen rector in 1954, was a retired colonel who had served as Third Chaplain under General George Patton. Hall served the Church of the Incarnation for eleven years. During the Hall years there was a proposal to move the church from its downtown location to a Bennett Valley site, but the move was voted down by the congregation.

The First Methodist Church congregation, which had worshiped for fifty years at a solid structure constructed of quarried basalt on Fourth Street near E Street, federated with the Methodist Episcopal South congregation in 1925 and in 1951 moved into a new church building across Santa Rosa Creek on Montgomery Drive.

Another landmark stone church was the Christian Church on Ross Street, which was dedicated in 1896. The structure remained standing, as did most of the town's churches, through the 1906 earthquake. It was, in fact, used as a morgue for earthquake victims. An annex and a parsonage were added to the church in the mid-1920s, but in the Depression years the parsonage was sold to pay the mortgage. Howard G. Stansbery became pastor in 1947 and was leading the congregation when the first unit of the new church was constructed on Pacific Avenue in 1953.

Santa Rosa's Seventh-day Adventists built the first Adventist church west of the Rocky Mountains at Second and B streets in 1869; moved to a new church on Orchard Street between Seventh and Cherry streets in 1912; and, outgrowing that facility, moved into the former First Presbyterian Church when that congregation moved to Pacific Avenue in 1949.[15]

The Salvation Army's soldiers arrived in Santa Rosa in a horse-drawn chariot in 1889 and quickly became known for their good work with the hungry and homeless. The Army was an important charitable force during the Depression years when its meetings and religious services were held at the pink stucco house Luther Burbank had built for himself on Santa Rosa Avenue. There the soldiers operated a daycare center and served as a depot to distribute food and clothing to the needy.

Mormons made an early entry into Sonoma County. Church records show that Sam Brannan, the colorful founder of Calistoga, led a group of Mormon settlers to the area around Skaggs Springs before 1850, and Mormon elders were conducting occasional services in Santa Rosa in the 19th century. But it was 1933 before the first Santa Rosa branch of the Church of Jesus Christ of Latter-Day Saints was made official. Services were held at lodge halls until 1948 when a new building was constructed at the corner of Johnson and Beaver streets.

Sonoma County's branch of the Reorganized Church of Jesus Christ of Latter-Day Saints formed in 1886 in Petaluma. The first Santa Rosa church was built on Fifth Street between A and B streets in 1895. In the early part of the century, the congregation sold the church building and met at Germania Hall until 1937 when, with volunteer labor and donated materials, members remodeled a house on Tupper Street which would be their meeting place for twenty years.[16]

The Christian Missionary Church organized in Santa Rosa in 1885. Soon after the turn of the century, the congregation affiliated with an international missionary movement known as Christian and Missionary Alliance. For the first half of the 20th century, the group met in a church in the 500 block of Humboldt Street. In 1955 the congregation headed by the Rev. Linden Heath purchased land for a new church on Sonoma and Hoen avenues.

Many new churches were organized in the first half of the century. First Church of Christ Scientist began in 1904 with the establishment of a Christian Science Reading Room in Santa Rosa. The first church was a converted residence at Third and E streets, which had both worship space and a reading room. It opened in 1912. The site for a new church building at North and Fifth streets was purchased in 1950.[17]

The Church of Christ in Santa Rosa was organized in 1908 and met in a rented hall until 1917 when the members constructed a church building at First and E streets. The Church of the Nazarene began with just eight members in 1912 and built a church on Ellis Street in 1917. Foursquare Gospel Church bought the building in 1946 when the Nazarenes moved to a site on College Avenue. Jehovah's Witnesses organized its first unit in Santa Rosa in 1932.

Santa Rosa's first Assembly of God congregation was formed in 1927 and met in rented halls until 1940 when they moved to their new church building at Davis and Earl streets. Twenty years later they would build a large church on Steele Lane.[18] Santa Rosa Bible Church's first meeting was on Easter Sunday in 1936. In 1942, the congregation bought the old German Methodist Church at Cherry and Orchard streets, where they worshiped for twenty years.

Roman Catholics, their numbers increased by the steady flow of Italian immigration, filled St. Rose Church on B Street. Father John Cassin, who had come to St. Rose in 1890 and ordered the construction of the stone church in 1900, stayed on as pastor until 1932. Cassin was an ecumenical force in the community, working with the Protestant ministers in common causes. He earned the respect of *Press Democrat* editor Ernest Finley, among others. Cassin, in demand as a public speaker for both religious and civic events, was, in Finley's words, "a man of liberal views and was in no way averse to mingling with the Protestant ministers of the town, which was an innovation.... Father Cassin was known to almost everyone in the community and was a welcome guest anywhere."[19]

Father Cassin was succeeded as pastor by the Rev. Henry Raters, a German-born, Swiss-educated scholar who spoke seven languages. Raters had come first to St. Rose in 1922 as assistant pastor to Cassin. He served for several years at St. Joseph's in Cotati and in Novato before being called back to Santa Rosa.

Raters, who had a reputation for a "crusty" exterior and a warm heart, served in Santa Rosa for thirty years, in a

At left, Father Henry Raters, the scholar-pastor of Santa Rosa's Roman Catholics for three decades. Below, St. Rose Church on B Street.

period when the population increased enough to warrant a second parish. In 1950, a boundary line through the town was agreed upon and a new church was planned for east Santa Rosa.[20]

St. Eugene's, which would later become the cathedral of the new Santa Rosa diocese, was built in a corner of the Hahman prune orchard at the southern end of the rickety bridge where Farmers Lane crossed Santa Rosa Creek. The first pastor of St. Eugene's was the Rev. Erwin J. Becker, an energetic German with a background as a youth pastor. His baseball teams had been the pride of San Francisco's Mission Dolores and he stepped into the Santa Rosa lineup with the same enthusiasm. Celebrating his first Mass with his new congregation at the Native Sons Hall, Becker marshaled a legion of volunteer laborers to construct the church and landscape the church grounds. It would soon be on the edge of a busy shopping center. Within two years the site of the Otani family's open-air farm market across the old railroad right-of-way from St. Eugene's became Montgomery Village shopping center.

Santa Rosa's Jewish community, which had met in private homes and halls since the 1860s, celebrated the opening of its first synagogue with the wedding of Bess Brand and Frank Arian in September of 1922.[21] The synagogue was located at the eastern end of Third Street on land donated by tannery owner Nathan Levin, who was so proprietary about the building and its use that members of the congregation referred to it as "Levin's shul." It remained a traditional shul, with the men on one side and the women on the other, until the congregation moved to new quarters on Orchard Street in 1946.

Congregation Beth Ami organized in 1941. The first meeting was in Irving Klein's home. Fred Rosenberg was the first president. The building they purchased on Orchard Street between Cherry and Johnson streets had been the Seventh-day Adventist Church. The congregation met until the early '50s without a rabbi, led mainly by laymen Michael Sugarman, who owned a plumbing supply shop, and Louis

Shapiro, a woolbroker, with a visiting rabbi for high holidays. In the early '50s, Rabbi Leo Trepp, who also worked as an instructor at Santa Rosa Junior College, came to be the first official rabbi for the congregation.[22]

When the Chicago World's Fair ended in 1932 a building constructed for the South Manchurian Railway exhibit was donated to the Buddhist Church of America. It was a fine building, an authentic representation of the Kamakura period of the 13th century, constructed of Japanese woods and decorated with hand-carved ornamentation. Church officials, knowing that the Sonoma County Buddhists had a new priest but no temple, gave the building to the Sebastopol congregation. Money was donated to send a member to Chicago to supervise the dismantling. Railroad cars carrying the temple pulled into Sebastopol on January 26, 1934. Ground was broken on property the congregation had purchased at Gravenstein Highway and Elphick Road. And the reassembling began. With careful volunteer labor, the temple was ready for dedication in April. It was given the name Enmanji, which means, given the versatility of the Japanese written characters, both "Sonoma Temple" and "Peace and Harmony Temple."

Russians who fled the revolution, coming to the United States by way of Harbin, in Manchuria, and Shanghai and San Francisco, founded an Orthodox Church on Mountain View Avenue south of Santa Rosa in the 1930s. Many of the Russian families, including at least one member of the Russian royal family, Alexei Kropotkin, came to Sonoma County during the "chicken boom" of the pre-World War II years. Kropotkin's daughter and son-in-law, Maria and Eugene Bilkevich, were among them, running a store in Fallon, in Marin County, and a small chicken and hog ranch near Cotati.

By 1934, there were enough members of the Russian Orthodox Church in Sonoma County to meet as a congregation, each with stories of escapes from the Bolsheviks. The Rayburns had been a merchant family in a town near Moscow, escaping to Latvia hidden in boxcars. Alex Sokol, who married Madeline Rayburn, had come to the United States through China, going to the YMCA in Shanghai to ask, "Do the American people need us?" There were fifteen Russian families in all. When they began planning for the church, they were joined by several Greek and Serbian families who shared the common bond of Orthodoxy. St. Mary's Orthodox Church, dedicated to the Protection of the Holy Virgin, was constructed in 1936 on land donated by the Rayburns.

European immigration had laid clear patterns on Sonoma County and Santa Rosa before the turn of the century. In the 1880s and 1890s the area which contributed the most new residents to Santa Rosa was the northern provinces of Italy, and this continued to be true in the first three decades of the 1900s. Natives of Tuscany and Liguria

The Rincon Hotel, commonly known as the Stone House on the Sonoma road, was built from basalt blocks by owner Massimo Galeazzi. It was a boarding house for Italian immigrants who worked in the basalt quarries in Annadel.

—*Michael Malvino Collection*

253

—*LeBaron Collection*

led the parade of new Santa Rosans. Many, particularly those from the Massa Carrara region of Tuscany, where the famous marble is quarried, found work in the basalt quarries.

Daniele Catalani was one of the blockmakers. His son, Joe, remembered his work and the pride he took in it. "I remember some Irish blockmakers and couple of Swedes," said Catalani, "but most of them were Italians. Lots of them, like my father, had worked in the marble pits in Carrara. Each one of the blockmakers was his own boss up there in the quarries. There were quarrymen and muckers, helpers, you know, but the blockmakers did their own drilling and blasting. And most of them, like my dad, made their own tools, too. They had a community forge in Kenwood, and a sharpening shop."[23]

Anselmo Baldi also began his life in Sonoma County as a blockmaker. He was sixteen when he came to Santa Rosa from Tuscany in 1905 and worked in the quarries for

—*Michael Franchetti Collection*

—*Doris Bradley Collection*

Below, right, an Italian family and friends gather for a summer dinner under a grape arbor on Santa Rosa's westside.

The barroom was an important facet of the Italian hotels that were clustered near the NWP railroad depot. Trio on the page at left includes, in the top photo, Jack Fumasoli serving customers at the Western Hotel; in the photo at bottom left, Luigi Franchetti behind the bar in 1915, one of the several years he leased the Battaglia Hotel, and bottom right, Bert Guidotti in his remodeled Toscano Hotel in 1935.

five years, until he was injured in a blasting accident. In 1910 he opened a grocery and feed store at Melitta Station, where the ore cars carrying paving blocks came down the tracks from the quarries in Annadel to meet the railroad. He became a naturalized citizen in 1912 and, in 1921, turned the Melitta store over to his brother-in-law, Ted Gambogi, another refugee from the quarries. Baldi opened a larger grocery in Rincon Valley, at the corner of Sonoma Highway and Middle Rincon Road. This store prospered as the gathering place of the Rincon Valley farming community for nearly fifty years.

Some of the blockmakers worked for themselves. They sold their stones to one of their countrymen, Natale Bacigalupi, who represented them as a broker to the San Francisco markets. The spolls, or cuttings left when the blocks were shaped, were sold to Southern Pacific to line the banks along the railroad tracks. Some uncut pieces of quarried basalt were used to build the stone fences of Rincon and Bennett valleys. And many quarrymen cut large stones for building blocks.

Massimo Galeazzi's stone building on Sonoma Road, constructed from the stones he quarried himself from the hill on his property at the confluence of Santa Rosa Creek and Brush Creek, became a kind of Santa Rosa headquarters for the blockmakers. Most of the blockmakers were single men, newly arrived in the United States. Working hard to save money to send for their families, to marry, or to buy their own land, they lived in boardinghouses and hotels, many of which, like Galeazzi's, were built of the stone the men quarried each day.

The Stone House, as it came to be known, was built in 1909 as a boardinghouse, tavern, and grocery store called the Rincon Hotel. There were other, smaller boarding-houses at Kenwood and Melitta and at Annadel Station, but Galeazzi's, with never fewer than twenty-five blockmakers sitting down to Mama Galeazzi's ample dinners, was the largest. When fire destroyed the wood frame second story of his stone hotel in 1912, Galeazzi added another story of

stone and connected it to the original dwelling with an archway. He added his trademark, a white stone engraved with M. Galeazzi, and the date, 1912, that would identify the landmark structure through several "lives," including at least three saloons and a conversion to office space.

Galeazzi was one of four Italian immigrants who became master masons using the basalt blocks. Peter Maroni, Angelo Sodini, Natale Forni, and Galeazzi, together and separately, were responsible for the construction of the Western Hotel, LaRose Hotel, the railroad depot and adjoining buildings, St. Rose Church, and the celebrated Wolf House of writer Jack London, built by Forni, which burned before its famous owner could occupy it.

All of the hotels around the railroad depot at the end of Fourth Street were Italian-owned. The Battaglia, the

—*Bonfigli Family Collection*

—*Song Borbeau Collection*

At right, Song Wong and her San Francisco cousins pose for a family photograph on Second Street, circa 1928. Below, the last of Santa Rosa's Chinatown buildings in a photograph made on Second Street about 1950. The buildings were stores and restaurants downstairs, living quarters upstairs and each took its turn as the site for the lottery. The building at right had been On Chong, where Chinese youngsters bought noodles for 10 cents a bowl.

—*Chamber of Commerce Collection*

Torino, the Hotel D'Italia Unita, and the Toscano were all on Adams Street, immediately west of the railroad track. These hotels were the first U.S. addresses for the immigrants. In the early '20s, when Lena Battaglia and her husband Alviso Bonfigli took over the operation of her father's hotel, families would get off the train and come directly there, her family would later recall. There would be six or eight kids sleeping upstairs in one room, sleeping on the floor, until they could find a place of their own. There was a family dining room in the back, where the newcomers ate.

If this immigrant community seemed to be a sharp contrast to the peaceful, Victorian town a few blocks east, it didn't bother the young inhabitants, once they settled in. "We lived in an Italian ghetto," recalled Lena's son Dan Bonfigli, making it sound like a wonderful memory. "We weren't exposed to the rest of Santa Rosa at all." Italian children who grew up on Santa Rosa's west side were sometimes eight or ten years old before they saw the courthouse or the town's central plaza. It was like traveling to another city. Their world was between St. Rose Church, the first Lincoln School on Davis Street, and Santa Rosa Creek, where they swam in the summer months.[24]

They did go uptown, of course, although much of their lives was centered in the west side. It was a big day for the Italian community in 1926 when General Pepino Garibaldi, grandson of the Italian hero, came to Santa Rosa. He received a tumultuous welcome, met Luther Burbank, gave a talk to schoolchildren in his excellent English, and marched in a parade, led by L'Indipendenza band, with the state commander of the American Legion.[25]

Blacks and Asians did not find Santa Rosa a welcoming community in the first half of the century. As in all of California, indeed the entire West Coast, equality under the law was non-existent. Owners of city lots with titles dating back to the 1920s may still find a conditional paragraph on the original deed providing that "no person of

African, Japanese, Chinese, or any of Mongolian descent shall be allowed to purchase, own, lease, or occupy said real property or any part thereof."

Minority groups may have received mixed messages. In 1923 Judge Ross Campbell ruled that Sonoma County apartment house owners could refuse to rent to Negroes, reportedly a first-of-its-kind ruling for California. Yet the following year, the same judge held it unconstitutional to forbid aliens to have guns. The case of Kim Hing, charged with possession of a gun, was dismissed by Judge Campbell, who ruled that Hing had been denied his rights of equal protection under the law, which Judge Campbell said was applicable to both foreigners and citizens.[26]

Native Americans, whose families had been rounded up and sent to reservations or pushed northward by the early settlement, generally came into the valley only during harvest season, to work as day laborers in the hopfields or the orchards.

There was a Chinatown—never again as large as it was before the anti-Chinese movement on the Pacific Coast in the 1890s, when Santa Rosans staged an intense, and successful, boycott of Chinese labor in an effort to force the Chinatown population out. And there was an even smaller Japantown—a few businesses catering to the Japanese orchardists and chicken farmers in the rural areas and to the families of Japanese workers who worked in Sonoma County in the harvests. The 200 or more Chinese who lived along Santa Rosa Creek, on First and Second streets east of Main (later Santa Rosa Avenue), until the agricultural economy of the county was changed by World War II were predominately farm workers or domestics. Almost all the residents of Chinatown were bachelors. They had wives and children in China, and they regarded their stay in the United States as a temporary sojourn. They worked on the surrounding ranches picking hops, apples, and prunes and working in the apple driers. They lived in boardinghouses along Second Street, ate in the tiny Chinese restaurants, smoked their habitual opium pipe in the special rooms set aside for that purpose, and kept apart from the rest of the town.

The Wongs were one of the few actual families living in Santa Rosa's Chinatown in the early part of the century. The father, known in Santa Rosa as Tom Wing, was generally regarded as the mayor of Chinatown until his death in 1918. Born in China, he had come to Santa Rosa before 1900 and was soon established as "Boss Man," acting as labor contractor, providing crews of Chinese workers to ranchers on demand. When Santa Rosa's merchant families needed a domestic, they might contact Tom Wing, who would find the right person to serve their household. Wing's family ran the largest of the Chinatown boardinghouses and sold groceries, clothing, and farm implements in their store. Wing was also the banker for the Chinese workers, holding their earnings or lending them money when they needed it.

Wing's wife Lun Wing was one of the few, if not the only, woman in Chinatown in the early days of the century. Her daughter, Song, remembered the meals her mother cooked at the boardinghouse at 640 Second Street to feed the men in the slow season, when they weren't living and working at the ranches. Song's grandfather Jam Kee Poy ran

Japanese and Chinese businessmen mingled in Santa Rosa's Chinatown area. The Market Laundry, at First and Main, was owned by the Iwaoka family. The Nagase family owned a grocery at Second and D streets.

—*LeBaron Collection*

257

a restaurant on Second Street which moved west as Chinatown diminished, first to Main Street and then to Third Street in 1920. When Jam Kee died, Song inherited the restaurant, which remained popular with the entire community long after Chinatown was gone.[27]

Wing's honorary title as Chinatown's mayor was inherited by Charlie Quong Sing, owner of Quong Sing Mercantile Company on Second Street. In 1933, he handed out Chinese candy to children of the community to celebrate his eighty-third birthday.

As in other Chinatowns along the Pacific Coast, Santa Rosa had a Chinese lottery, which, according to some, was the enterprise that kept Chinatown prosperous. Many of the mercantile shops selling tea and curios were barely concealed lottery establishments where the games went on day and night. The cheapest ticket sold for 10 cents. Many Santa Rosa residents were regular customers. Farmers in town for the day played the lottery routinely, as part of their "town business" and checked their tickets weeks later, when they came to town again. The top prize was $1,000 and when someone won a big payoff, the whole county knew about it. As with the opium rooms, police seemed to look the other way. There might have been a raid or two each

year, for appearances, but little more.

There were, however, instances that police could not ignore. In 1920 Kim Lee, "king of the lotteries," was arrested for gambling, paid a $200 fine, and was sent to jail for fifteen days. In 1922, a Santa Rosa police raid netted fifty-seven people at the rear of Wau Tom's store at 643 Second Street—fifty whites and seven Asians. According to the newspaper report, Santa Rosa's "society women" had already left. In '25, Mayor Dunbar declared "open war" on Chinese gambling joints. Chinese opium parlors were also raided periodically through the '20s and '30s. Attorney Bryce Swartfager often defended the Chinese arrested.

There were sinister moments—such as the day in the late 1920s when a San Francisco "tong war" spilled over into Santa Rosa and Chinese newcomers who had come to open a restaurant (later determined to be an excuse for hiding out from San Francisco enemies) were shot down in the street.

But generally, it was a peaceable kingdom in those woodframe buildings along the creek. The Japanese families, who owned the Market Laundry on Main Street and the Sanyo Grocery, and the Wongs were good neighbors. The children played together, shared their rice cakes and almond cookies, and walked to and from the Fourth Street School and Santa Rosa High School together.

While Chinatown was pretty much a world unto itself, Caucasian residents came to Second Street for Chinese New Year's when the storefronts were all decorated with bits of paper in the "lucky colors," red and gold, and the air was filled with the scent of spice and incense, ginger and flowering quince blossoms, and the smoke of a thousand firecrackers, rattling and snapping in the streets. New Year's, for the Chinese, was a time to remember ancient deities, such as the Kitchen God and the Front Door God, and it was the one time in the year the old customs were honored. The white residents of the community came—as tourists—to see the festivities. They came, too, to buy firecrackers for their own Fourth of July celebrations from

A lifeguard demonstrates artificial respiration at the municipal swimming pool on King Street, built in 1925 with money raised by the Playgrounds Association.

the two or three establishments that always had them in stock.

The first twenty years of the century were devoted more to regaining the quality of life enjoyed before the 1906 earthquake. There was little time for civic improvement. In 1918 there were but three public parks: the half-acre Library Park next to the library at Fourth and E streets; South Side Park, which was a three-quarter acre parcel between Orange and Olive streets; and Northwestern Pacific Park at the railroad depot at the end of Fourth Street, owned by NWP.

In 1921, the thirteen-year-old son of banker Frank P. Doyle and his wife, Polly O'Meara Doyle, died. Two years later, to perpetuate the memory of their only child, the Doyles deeded to Sonoma County twenty acres for a park to be named "Frankie Doyle Park." One week later, Elizabeth and Luther Burbank donated $5,000 for development of a playground in the park in memory of young Doyle.

The new park, which as the city expanded would become a municipal park, was an oak-filled glade that formed a kind of triangle, with the point at the spot where Spring and Matanzas creeks joined. The spot had been used by the early residents of the valley as a "matanza," a convenience holding area where cattle could be driven and slaughtered. Later, it had become the property of the Hoen family who allowed the public to picnic there, and it was a favorite place for Santa Rosa families, who knew it as "Hoen's Island."

When Doyle died in 1949, his will specified an annual stipend of $2,000 from the Doyle Trust for the city to improve and maintain the park. Since the amount was specified, the allotment has not increased over the years as it has for the other Doyle Trust benefactor, Santa Rosa Junior College's scholarship program.

In the 1920s, Doyle was a member of a civic group called the Santa Rosa Playgrounds Association which

Leonard Howarth was a British-born industrialist who became a millionaire in paper mills, mining, and lumber in Everett and Tacoma, Washington. Stricken by paralysis in his mid-30s, he came to Santa Rosa in 1906 to seek treatment at Dr. Willard Burke's sanitarium on Mark West Springs Road. In 1908, Howarth built a home described by the newspapers of the time as "palatial" near Mark West Springs Road and Redwood Highway North. He named it The Maples and, for the remaining thirty years of his life, he divided his time between Tacoma and Santa Rosa. He remained confined to his "invalid chair" until his death at age sixty-four, in 1930.

Howarth's residency was a source of great pride to the community. In 1924 the newspaper bragged on the amount of income tax Howarth had paid—the "highest in Northern California" the story said, more than $116,000, "more than Spreckels, Sproule, Fleishhacker, Phelan, Crocker or A.P. Giannini."[28]

Howarth was not only the president of the Everett Paper Mills and the St. Paul and Tacoma Lumber Company, he was also one of the largest stockholders in Pacific Gas & Electric Company at the time of his death. He owned a substantial amount of property in downtown Santa Rosa, including the Occidental Hotel and Santa Rosa Hotel buildings and business property near the corner of Fourth and Mendocino. The Santa Rosa Hotel building, which was originally the Overton Building, was sold to the Rosenberg family in 1934. Howarth's estate was estimated between $7 million and $10 million. In his will he left $300,000 to be divided among Santa Rosa, Tacoma, and Everett. Santa Rosa's share was $75,000.

A group of Santa Rosa businessmen— including editor Finley, banker Ransom Cook (who would become president of Wells Fargo),

Judge Comstock, merchant Fred Rosenberg, and attorney Finlaw Geary—was entrusted with the disposition of these funds.

It established the Santa Rosa Foundation and bought land adjacent to Burbank School on South A Street and built the city's first "modern" playground, including a public tennis court. In 1934, the city limits were extended to take in the school and park site. The new ten-acre park was named for Howarth. The remainder of the Howarth bequest was invested. By the mid-1950s, there was more than $108,000 to help construct the community park around Lake Ralphine. The Howarth Park name was given to the new park and the old Howarth Park was renamed Burbank Park.

planned an expansion of the city's park and recreation system. In 1925, the group used city funds and funds raised by the business community to build a municipal swimming pool on King Street, to replace the old A Street Plunge. Lobbying by the Playgrounds Association resulted in the formation of a city park commission in the mid-'20s. Doyle was the first chairman.

The original site of the town's first public school, the Fourth Street School, later called Fremont School, was acquired from the school district in the late '20s to be developed into a park. In 1929, Oakland landscape architect Howard Gilkey, a former Santa Rosan and student of Luther Burbank, was hired by the park commission to design a park to be called "Fremont Plaza." Gilkey was also commissioned to landscape the tiny triangle-shaped park at Fourth Street and College Avenue.

In 1931, nine acres of land on the site of the elegant home and orchards owned by the Juilliard family from the 1870s, was donated to the city for a park. Juilliard Park was developed in the Depression years as a government project. Its stone bridge and pond and walkway were constructed from ten tons of rock hauled from the Kenwood quarries.

DeMeo Park was built in the late '30s after Nick DeMeo, city attorney, discovered the city owned an acre of undeveloped land on West Seventh Street between Polk and Madison streets and urged its improvement. When the park was dedicated in 1939, westside neighbors asked the City Council to name it for DeMeo. There was some ethnic pride in the request since DeMeo had grown up in that "Italian town" section, where his father was a shoemaker.

In 1952 the city purchased land on Franklin Avenue, the site of a defunct sawmill, for a park site to serve residents of the northern end of the junior college neighborhood and the newer Hillcrest area. Once the land purchase was made, the city ran out of park funds and the old sawmill sat crumbling on the site, presenting a safety hazard, parents thought, for their children.

The Franklin Park Neighborhood Association decided to clear the site and build the park themselves. The association raised money, scrounged materials, and blocked the city's intent to split the park property with an extension of King Street. Members worked every Sunday for thirty-five weeks to remove the sawmill and build a clubhouse—a redwood structure with a stone fireplace in a large meeting room, a kitchen, an office, and two restrooms. The project was dedicated in June of '53, and immediately following the ceremony, association president Fred Daniels handed the keys to the mayor. The hardworking neighbors donated their $20,000 building and all the improvements around it to the city. *The Ladies Home Journal* published a four-page picture story on the Franklin Park project, unique in the history of the community.[29]

John Rosseter was another gentleman rancher whose wealth made him the object of community pride. A friend of Leonard Howarth's, Rosseter owned the Pacific Mail Steamship Company, based in San Francisco, and was president of Sperry Flour Company. He spent much of his

In 1926, Mr. and Mrs. John Rosseter set San Francisco society agog with a birthday party for their prize thoroughbred stallion Disguise at their Wikiup Ranch north of Santa Rosa.

Isabelle Juilliard McDonald, left, lent her home and gardens for charity events like the fashion show Virginia Grace modeled for in the 1940s. In the bottom photo, the members picnic during a work day at the new Santa Rosa Golf & Country Club on Los Alamos Road in the 1920s.

leisure time at his Wikiup Ranch north of Santa Rosa. When his ship the *Golden State* was commissioned in 1921, he invited brewery owner Joe Grace and his family to sail from New York through the Panama Canal on the maiden voyage. Rosseter was very active in the Democratic party and it was not uncommon for candidates for governor and vice president to be entertained at Wikiup.

The ranch was a showplace. Rosseter's Berkshire hogs were housed in a stone and redwood glass-fronted barn with nickel-plated trolleys to carry food to the hogs. The thirty-one-stall horse barn, with a floor of cork and asphalt bricks and silver-plated brass fittings on the doors, was so elegant visitors often mistook it for the main residence.

Rosseter was a sportsman who raced greyhounds— in 1934 his dog, For Freedom, was the fastest greyhound in the world. And his racehorses were even more successful. Wikiup was essentially a horse ranch where Rosseter and his wife raised racing thoroughbreds. In 1920 their horse Inchcape won at Aqueduct and was considered a prospect for the Kentucky Derby until he went lame. But their most treasured possession was the stallion Disguise, who had sired horses that had won more than a million dollars for the Rosseter stables. In 1926, the Rosseters put the social set on its ear with a joint birthday party for Disguise and Tod Sloan, the famous jockey who had ridden the stallion's colts to victory.

The party was written about in newspapers all over the United States and, for a decade or more, was the standard used for social events in the Bay Area. Sloan, wearing the the Rosseter racing colors, burnt orange and white, sat astride the twenty-nine-year-old stallion, who pranced like a two-year-old, his mane curled and beribboned for the festivity. A giant horseshoe-shaped table was set up on the lawn with a "place" for Disguise in the center of the horseshoe. The horse had a birthday cake of grain and mash, decorated with carrot candles. Jockey Sloan had a real cake to share with guests from New York, Los

Jake Luppold, white coat, poses with clients, outside his legendary Senate Saloon on Main Street.

One of the sad things that happened in Santa Rosa between the two wars was the death, in 1922, of Jake Luppold, "The Mayor of Main Street." Luppold had been one of the community's true characters and his Senate Saloon at Second and Main, just south of the courthouse, was among the busiest taverns in the town. There was a remarkable collection of junk in the Senate. The product of the bartender's recent surgery might be on display in a quart jar on the bar. Sometimes it was a mountain lion, shot by one of the clients, hanging from the ceiling until the tip of its tail just touched the floor. And, after the night in 1908 that Jake burned the "hoodoo auto" while the whole county cheered, there was the molten metal remains of a red Dodge touring car hanging from the rafters.

The prank had started with a familiar burst of Luppold bombast. A butcher named Viers had gone south, literally. He had gone to Mexico owing many people money, including Luppold. In exchange for a worthless promissory note, Jake had laid claim to the Dodge, which he then complained about bitterly, as not being worth half the debt.

Among the customers listening on this night in 1908 was Chris Donovan, the hop broker, who had also had a bad financial year. Hop prices had been at rock bottom. Donovan, nicknamed "The Uncrowned King of Ireland" by Luppold, had a few more beers and suggested to the bar owner that the Dodge was a jinx, the cause of the low hop prices, the unsettled economy, and whatever else Luppold wanted to include. What they needed to do, they agreed, was to destroy this jinx and make life safe for honest beer-drinking Santa Rosans once more.

A month before the election in 1908, Luppold applied to the city for permission to burn the car in the middle of Main Street, in front of the Senate Saloon, on election night. Reporter Herbert Slater sensed there was a story here and filed it with the wire services. It was picked up in Chicago and Boston and all over the country. Luppold received more than 100 letters which were about equally divided among those who wanted the car, those who had further instructions on exorcism, and widows who wanted Jake.

On the appointed night, Luppold was in fine form. His candidate, William Howard Taft, was winning. And he was about to be rid of the accursed Dodge. The bonfire itself drew a crowd that filled Main Street for two blocks in either direction. Donovan brought a symbolic bale of hops to toss on the flames. The crowd roared. The metal was still warm when they hoisted the wreckage to the rafters of the saloon. It is said that hop prices soared in the years that followed.

The Dodge's carcass stayed in the saloon until Jake died. When he was gone, his friends began to tell the tales that would have made Jake blush—stories of the Thanksgiving feasts he gave for the poor every year, with the help of Ah Moon, the Elks Club steward; of the orphans he trotted over to McNamara's haberdashery for new clothes; of the stack of IOUs "a foot and a half high" they found on his desk. "The best free lunch in town," Santa Rosa men said of the Senate Saloon. And Jake Luppold? "Well, say now, do you remember the night Jake burned the hoodoo auto?"[30]

Angeles, San Francisco, and Santa Rosa —including Mr. and Mrs. Mark McDonald, Mr. and Mrs. Joseph T. Grace, Mr. and Mrs. Ernest L. Finley, Mr. and Mrs. George Proctor, and Senator Herbert Slater.

Fountaingrove Ranch was another focal point of Santa Rosa's social life. All semblances of Thomas Lake Harris's Brotherhood of the New Life, which had established its "home center" at Fountaingrove in the 1870s, was gone by the early 20th century. But the former Utopian community continued to be a matter of curiosity after Kanaye Nagasawa became proprietor of the 1,500 acres of vineyards and the successful winery. Nagasawa, who had been among the earliest Japanese immigrants to the United States, was known to his Santa Rosa neighbors as "the Baron of Fountaingrove," a reference to his Samurai ancestry.

Nagasawa would become famous in his home city of Kagoshima as one of the "Kagoshima Fifteen," a group of young people sent abroad in the 1860s by the head of the Satsuma clan before Japan was opened to European visitors. Nagasawa, who met cult leader Harris at his community in upstate New York and came with him to Santa Rosa when he bought Fountaingrove, was the only one of the fifteen students who did not return to Japan to be influential in government as that nation took its place in the world. He did, however, act as an unofficial representative of Japan in Northern California and helped set up the Japanese exhibit at the Panama Pacific Exposition of 1915, for which he was awarded his native country's Order of the Rising Sun. At Fountaingrove he was host to a stream of Japanese visitors who considered the ranch a necessary stop on their tours of California.

When he was not entertaining Japanese delegations, he was entertaining his fellow Santa Rosans. He loved to

Kanaye Nagasawa, the "Baron of Fountaingrove," entertained Santa Rosa neighbors and Japanese dignitaries at his hilltop winery.

gather influential townspeople around him and became famous for his lavish dinner parties during Prohibition when he would tap the cellars of Fountaingrove wine and brandy for his doctor, lawyer, and merchant guests.

Nagasawa never married. He brought three nephews and their families from Japan to share his good life. His intention was that their children, born at Fountaingrove, would inherit the ranch property. But after his death in 1934, creditors stepped forward with claims (which Nagasawa's heirs would dispute in coming years) and the land was sold at auction. The buyer was Errol MacBoyle, a Grass Valley gold mine owner. MacBoyle and his wife Glendolyn continued the Nagasawa tradition of entertaining at the ranch. After MacBoyle's death, his widow married German-born Siegfried Becchold, who removed the vineyards to make pasture for his beef cattle, spelling the end of the ranch's seventy-five-year winemaking history.[31]

Traditional social events of the early part of the century covered a wide range of interests: from Laura Cragin's annual Daffodil Tea at the Congregational Church, which drew hundreds of guests every spring; to the riotous Pignelligan, an Elks Club dinner which provided the funds for the Elks' annual Christmas party for poor children at the California Theater. When Santa Rosa Golf and Country Club's new clubhouse was completed in 1922, it immediately became another social center. Country club dances routinely drew one hundred or more of Santa Rosa's "upper crust." The names always made the society columns of the newspaper, and they were all familiar names.

There were still the house parties. Mark and Isabelle McDonald (Isabelle had been a Juilliard) entertained at Mableton, the plantation-style summer home Mark's father had built in the 1870s. The George Proctors and Joe Graces were also known for their parties. Before the country club opened, the Proctors gave the traditional New Year's party at their country home near Kenwood. Often, the entertainments were benefits. In 1934, Mae and Joe Grace invited 200 to their home for bridge and a garden party to raise funds for the Santa Rosa Symphony. Mrs. Anna Love Finlaw was considered to be "the social leader of Sonoma County" in the first thirty years of the century. When Mrs. Finlaw entertained, the newspapers listed not only her guests but her menus of "crab, oysters, claret, and quail."

Not all the parties were exclusive. When the merchants organized a street dance in 1927 to celebrate the new lighting downtown that made Fifth Street and A Street "as bright as Fourth," 5,000 people turned out.

The prosperity and optimism of the '20s produced an outburst of social activity. Lodge rosters were filled. Service clubs, like Rotary and Kiwanis, received their charters—Rotary in 1921, Lions Club in 1923, and Kiwanis in 1925. J.C. Penney came in 1930 to speak to the joint service clubs which then included High 12 and 20-30 along with the other three. The countywide University Club was established in 1923, bringing speakers to talk on intellectual topics. All who had completed two years of college were eligible for membership. Santa Rosa's branch of the American Association of University Women was organized in 1935 with forty members and Miss Miriam Hotle as the first president.

Young people joined social fraternities and sororities. In 1919 the members of Kappa Alpha Pi invited 300 friends for a "social." The fraternity membership included Mervin Finley, Frank and Tom Grace, Kenneth Hudson, Wilson Hall, and Fred Wright. The patrons were Hilliard Comstock and the George Proctors. In 1924, another fraternity, Phi Delta, held a New Year's dance for 200 at the Saturday Afternoon Clubhouse.

The most influential women's group in town, the Saturday Afternoon Club, founded in 1894, was growing large enough that by the early 1930s it had subdivided into special interest sections—garden, drama, literary, and music—while continuing to meet once each month to hear noted lecturers and speakers.

—*Saturday Afternoon Club*

Socialization was not bounded by city limits. The Monroe Clubhouse, described as "the best country clubhouse in the county," was built on West College Avenue in 1922. The Monroe Club had organized seven years earlier when nine women who lived in the Monroe District saw a need for "social and intellectual advancement" in the farming community to the west of town. Money for the clubhouse was raised with card parties—mostly Pedro and Whist—in members' homes, local halls, and even old chicken houses. Through the coming years the clubhouse would be the scene of literally thousands of club plays and socials and a twice-monthly dance to music played by groups like Cappelli's Orchestra, Cliff Dont's Orchestra, the Bavaria Club Orchestra, the Merrymakers, and the original Melody Boys.[32]

The Masonic Lodge, with 442 members in 1930, was, for political as well as fraternal reasons, the most important organization in town. But the Elks Lodge was not far behind it in the ranks and was indisputably more fun. The lodge's clubrooms were the "courthouse annex." Supervisors, county officials, judges, lawyers, and businessmen met there with ranchers from around the county who were in town for the day. Drinking was an undeniable part of business and politics after (and perhaps during) Prohibition and the ritual of "a couple of highballs and lunch at the Elks Club" was a Santa Rosa tradition. The Elks' charities were well known and universally praised. They fed the hungry, gave Christmas toys to the poor

—*Finley Collection*

Above, left, the members of the Saturday Afternoon Club gather in 1908 to break ground for their clubhouse at Tenth and B streets. Bankers declined to lend the women money for their venture but one of the members had a rich aunt who supplied the capital. Officiating at the groundbreaking ceremony were the club's president, Mrs. James Sweet, and the club's founding president, Mrs. Anna Love Finlaw. The men in the photograph, at far right, are architect Brainerd Jones and contractor Victor Durand. Bottom left, the reception room of Elks Lodge 646, a hub of male social activity.

On the page at right, photographer Vernon Silvershield has captured a May Day celebration in front of the courthouse in the early 1930s.

children, funded scholarships, and sponsored scout troops and baseball teams. Their money came from two sources: the Elks Carnival, an annual event attended by literally thousands of Sonoma County men, and the Pignelligan.

The carnival was billed as a Friday night event, but in reality it lasted all weekend. Gambling games, all highly illegal, were moved into the clubrooms for the occasion, and law enforcement simply looked the other way so the Elks could raise their money for charity—and let off a little steam, as the saying went.

The pig feed, fondly known as the Pignelligan, began in 1938 when Maurice Nelligan, a bachelor and clubroom regular, donated several young pigs to be roasted to raise money for the children's Christmas party. The dinner was such a success, it was repeated every year for thirty years, always with the same menu—pork, wild rice, applesauce, and Santa Rosa's Franco American sour French bread.

The fashions and fads of the times didn't bypass Sonoma County. By 1923, Santa Rosa's fashionable young women were wearing knickerbockers and flapper shirts, with their grandmother's shawl to complete the fashion statement. Many young men turned out in raccoon coats, despite the temperate climate. By 1924, the newspaper was asking if it were possible that "milady" would soon wear trousers on the street. The Powder Puff Shoppe, a beauty salon, advertised its operators' skills in both marcelling and bobbing, the two most popular new hairstyles, in 1925. In 1927, a Sonoma County judge, ruling on a case from another town, decreed that girls with bare legs could not be turned away from school. At Santa Rosa High School, dean of women Docia Patchett said most Santa Rosa girls wore stockings, so it was a moot point. That same year a male student organization at Santa Rosa Junior College tried to make it mandatory that all men wear blue jeans on campus. A committee was appointed to enforce the "rule."

The Charleston arrived in Santa Rosa in January of 1926, according to a *Press Democrat* writer who felt the dance's first local appearance, at holiday parties, important enough to warrant comment. Other fads occasioning news stories were chain letters and Ouija boards. When, in 1920, a judge in Yolo County outlawed Ouija boards as dangerous, the newspaper observed that there were many such fortune-telling boards in Sonoma County. The writer did not say "Watch out!" but the implication was clear.

There had not been an agricultural fair in Santa Rosa since 1890 when the fairgrounds was sold to the Pierce

From its inception in 1894, the Rose Festival was the most important social event of the year in Santa Rosa. And the honor of being selected as Rose Festival Queen was the highest accolade paid to a young lady. In 1917 the title went to Irene Baciagalupi, shown in her festival finery in the top photo. Below, Miss Santa Rosa of 1918, Eleanore Rosebraugh, cavorts on the beach at Santa Cruz.

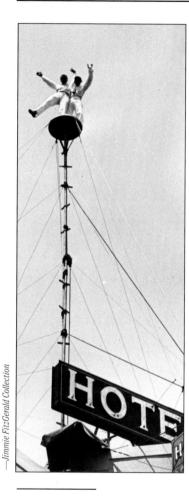

The 1920s and early 1930s were a time for elaborate publicity stunts. Flagpole sitters and tree sitters were instant celebrities. In 1932 flagpole dancers "Betty & Benny" added a new dimension, dancing and doing acrobatic stunts for sixty hours on a thirty-inch disc fifty feet above the Occidental Hotel. When they came down they were taken by ambulance to the Cline Theater where they talked about their ordeal to a packed house.

*T*he first Santa Rosa lad to go off to New York and strike it rich was a buck-toothed, awkward boy from Orchard Street who really wanted to be a big-league baseball player. But he ran head-on into Frances O'Meara, the tiny but determined English teacher at Santa Rosa High School. Her attention to his talents set him on a course for world fame.

Robert Leroy Ripley, known to classmates as "Rip" or "Roy," came to Santa Rosa High School from Lewis School in 1904. He lived in a white frame house at 1117 Orchard Street with his carpenter father David, his mother Lily Belle, his sister Ethel, and his brother Douglas. Until Miss O'Meara took him in hand, Ripley had not done well in school, much preferring to draw pictures when he should be doing his homework. Miss O'Meara may have been the first teacher to take a real look at his pictures. She praised him and encouraged him to illustrate the poetry the class was studying, in place of the essays the other students were assigned. And she put him to drawing cartoons and covers for the student publication, *The Porcupine*.

In 1908, his senior year, his father died, and Ripley took a part-time job with the Kinslow Marble Works, polishing tombstones. It wasn't enough money to help his family, so he dropped out of school before graduation to find full-time work. He took his drawings to San Francisco to an editor of the *Bulletin*, who hired him as an artist. Several years later he moved from San Francisco to the *New York Globe* where, in 1918, he began to draw his cartoons of little known sports facts and general oddities. He called it "Believe It or Not!"

The success of the cartoon is nearly legendary. Ripley became one of the most widely traveled men in the world, crossing deserts in camel caravans, and slogging through trackless jungles in search of oddities for his daily cartoon. Ripley's "Believe It or Not!" became the most widely read feature in the world at the time. He was the star of his own weekly radio show. He lived in the center of the social whirl, being much sought after by New York hostesses. Except for a seven-year marriage to a "Follies girl" which ended in divorce, he spent his life rich and "eligible."

He never forgot the debt he owed Miss O'Meara. In 1932, returning from a trip to Asia, he visited his hometown where the citizens held a reception for him. On the stage of the high school auditorium, he hugged his old friend and teacher and gave her a jade and gold necklace he had brought from the Orient. She, in turn, expressed her pride in her pupil's success and her sadness

at the loss of his early poetry illustrations, which were burned in the old high school fire. After the formal reception, the "boys" he had played baseball with in school repaired with him to The Tavern, a spot north of town (later known as the Paris Inn), for a rollicking luncheon that lasted until suppertime.

Ripley died in 1949. When word came that his body had been sent from New York to be buried in the Rural Cemetery, a group of his friends, including attorneys Charles and Nick DeMeo, were sent by the city of Santa Rosa to Oakland to meet the train and bring him home. His old friends, N.A. Ridley, Larry Walker, Donald Gray, Gus Lee, Galen Lee, and William Lawrence, were his pallbearers. The list of honorary pallbearers read like the "Who's Who" of Santa Rosa.

His "Believe It or Not!" cartoon would continue long after his death. The question of whether all his fame and fortune brought him happiness was raised by an old school friend, poet Nell Griffith Wilson, who kept a letter he had written her of the pressure of his work and his incessant travels: "Thus," he wrote, "one day's work is never done and peace of mind I never have. Never become too ambitious or you will suffer always."[33]

brothers for a stock farm. In 1912, the Donovan brothers, merchant Ney and hop broker Chris, bought the former fairgrounds and, with a support group from the community that included J. Francis O'Connor, Pete Bussman, Sheridan Baker, and Ira Pyle, staged successful fairs in 1913 and 1914, when World War I intervened. The fair revived in 1920 but in '22, with horse racing outlawed by the state, the enthusiasm for the new board auto racing track at Cotati overcame interest in agriculture. The track was open just two seasons. "This venture," wrote Finley of the auto track, "was meteoric in origin and perished just as quickly." But there were no more fairs for eleven years.[34]

The impetus for the modern revival came in 1933 when the legislature approved pari-mutuel betting, and horses were back on the fair circuit. Santa Rosa already had a horse track in place. In 1936, in a whirlwind organizing campaign with the "Big Three" (Doyle, Finley, and Grace) at the forefront, the Sonoma County Fair Association formed. The association merged with Sebastopol's Gravenstein Apple Show, usurped the October dates already set aside for that event, and the city bought the fairgrounds back from Ney Donovan. The first race of the first fair was won by a Sonoma County entry, a mare named Helen Catherine from Jack Millerick's Schellville stable. The first special racing purse was named for John Rosseter. A total of 70,000 people came through the gates in the five days of the fair.

The following year the Board of Supervisors assumed official control of the fair, with Emil Kraft as manager and a board of directors of leading citizens. Joe Grace was the first president. He stayed in that office for twenty years, becoming the "grand old man" of the county fair circuit. When he stepped down in 1955, he was replaced by Petaluma cattle buyer Chris Beck, who was killed the

Joseph T. Grace was generally regarded as the "father" of the modern Sonoma County Fair.

A winner crosses the finish line, in front of the chalkboard that told bettors the pari-mutuel odds, at the first fairs in the late 1930s.

Dagwood Dunn in his diner.

following year in a plane crash along with fair manager Ken Carter and concessionaire Lou Basso.

Other Santa Rosa members of the early fair boards included Finley and Doyle, Fred Rosenberg, Finlaw Geary, and Maurice Nelligan, and, from other parts of the county, Alma deBrettville Spreckels and, later, L. E. "Bud" Castner from the Sonoma Valley; A.H. Meese, Healdsburg; Lee Torr, Monte Rio; and R.E. Oehlmann, Sebastopol.

Growing up in Santa Rosa in the first half of the century was small-town living. Teenagers were a necessary part of the agricultural harvest season and school openings were often delayed until the prune harvest was in. Students earned money for their school clothes picking first hops and then prunes, a back-breaking enterprise since the fruit was first shaken from the trees and then "picked" from off the ground.

Despite a 1920s' concern over "cooing bees" in automobiles, young people's easy access to cars was still years away. The economic constrictures of the '30s and the war shortages of the '40s made most teenagers pedestrians or bus passengers. Most of the places where young people gathered were in the downtown area. Bouk's, an ice cream and candy store on Fourth Street, noted for its frozen milk shakes, was a favorite spot. Owned first by the Bouk family and then by Lou and Bud Pitts, Bouk's employed at least two "dippers" to create the chocolate candies in the glass cases and high school girls to work the fountain. The ice cream was made on the site, using gallons of cream purchased from and delivered by a nearby dairy. Working at Bouk's, for the students, had social as well as economic value. It was the after-school meeting place, the after-movies stop, and, perhaps best of all, was downstairs from the hall where the young men of the National Guard met weekly.[35]

For adults who still enjoyed the conviviality of the sandwich shop, there were the trolley diners. After the Petaluma & Santa Rosa Railroad switched from electric to diesel, abandoning the trolleys that carried passengers around the county, at least three of the cars were converted to diners. One was the Streetcar Cafe in Petaluma. Another was the Pullman Diner, owned by George and Helen Drobnak, on Mendocino Avenue just south of McConnell Avenue. Nicknamed the Ptomaine Trolley—more from collegiate cleverness than culinary criticism—by the SRJC students who frequented it, the Pullman was removed in the mid-'50s to make way for the expansion of Park Auto Market.

The third off-track trolley was on Fourth Street across from Fremont Park. Originally owned by "Slim" Watson, who was better known for the nickel hamburgers he sold at his snack shop near the Roxy Theater, the trolley was purchased by Orville "Red" Cooper and his wife Evelyn and renamed "Red & Evie's Trolley Stop." The Coopers had a faithful clientele of mechanics from Swift's Garage next door and mail carriers working out of the Lea Annex post office at the corner of Fourth and E streets.

Other diners just looked like they were trolley cars. One of these was The Circus, a lunch counter on Third Street near B Street owned by Gene Darnell. This was a home-away-from-home for telephone operators and installers, from Pacific Telephone's offices next door. Chauncey Wolcott owned the original Fifth Street lunch counter, across from the post office, but Till and George Cross's Snack Shack was in the same block for forty-one years, having been opened by Tillie's mother, Josephine Hines, in 1929. On the opposite side of Fifth Street was Dagwood Dunn's, opened by Neta and Pat Dunn in 1948. The Dunns served breakfast and lunch (mostly hamburgers) to loyal customers who stood patiently behind the nine stools waiting for someone to finish so they could be seated.

Movies, as anyone who gasped at the wonder of Technicolor can tell you, were better than ever—every year. The Cline Theater, owned by Dr. John Cline, a physician who lived nearby on B Street, was originally a vaudeville house, described in 1919 as "the finest playhouse north of San Francisco."[36] By the 1930s, it had been rechristened the Roxy and given over exclusively to films. The G&S became the California within five years of its opening. Both of these theaters offered Santa Rosans a touch of the grandeur that moviehouses effected as Hollywood and its extravaganzas began to dominate the entertainment business.

Neither achieved the scale of Sacramento's Alhambra, which was set in a park with reflection pools. But they were smaller-town versions of San Francisco's Fox or Warfield and certainly the finest Sonoma County had to offer. The Cal, as it became known, had a giant Wurlitzer organ which had once provided background music to the silent films. Both had balconies, elaborate chandeliers, and wall murals. But, more important, they were where young Santa Rosans took their dates—each had a snack shop alongside for popcorn or candy, Wolcott's at the Roxy, Townsend's at the Cal. And they were where Depression-

Below, a 1937 crowd lines up down the B street sidewalk to see the latest film at the California Theater. At upper right, the Tower Theater on Fourth Street shows its opening night marquee in 1939. Lower right, a playbill from the Roxy, a converted vaudeville theater at Fifth and B streets.

—Sonoma County Library

—Finley Collection

—LeBaron Collection

era residents could afford an evening of entertainment. Indeed, when it was "Cash Night" or "Bank Night" or a Saturday when patrons received a piece of green glass dinnerware to add to their set, people could scarcely afford not to go to the movies.

The Tower Theater, which was merchant Fred Rosenberg's celebration of the Depression's end and the completion of his splendid new department store, opened in the fall of 1939. The Tower occasioned considerable excitement as the town's "ultra-modern" theater, rivaling, according to the newspapers, "the picture palaces of the major metropolitan centers of the west." It was considered to have the most up-to-date theater equipment in Northern California. The modern design, matching the neighboring department store, looked surprisingly ordinary from the street. But the lobby had terrazzo floors and black walnut paneling. There was also a glass brick wall in the lobby, which was definitely in the style of the times, and a rotunda in the center with an etched-glass mural. The loges at the Tower not only rocked, but slid back and forth, "identical to those installed in fine theaters in New York and Chicago."

The Tower played nothing but first run films through the '40s: such classics as Errol Flynn's *Robin Hood*, Gary Cooper in *The Plainsman*, and the best of Ginger Rogers and Fred Astaire.[37] The content of movies had long been a concern of the citizens. In 1915 the City Council had appointed a Movie Picture Censorship Committee which met with the theater owners of Santa Rosa at the request of Mayor Charles Lee. The owners agreed to eliminate "all suggestive advertising and suggestive language at matinees," with the welfare of the children and young people of the community in mind.[38]

Despite its heritage of frontier justice and rough-and-tumble politics, Santa Rosa considered itself a cultured town. Since the 19th century, when Santa Rosans proudly matched their Athenaeum against Petaluma's Hill Opera House, the town had provided a nurturing climate for artistic endeavor.

The annual summer lecture, concert and drama tour known as the Chautauqua circuit stopped in Santa Rosa, as well as Petaluma, Sebastopol, Healdsburg, and Ukiah, after 1916. In Santa Rosa the traditional Chautauqua tent was pitched on the North Street lot, adjoining the new Fremont School. Crowds flocked to hear the great Metropolitan opera star Ernestine Schumann-Heink and another famous opera singer, Alice Nielsen, who traveled in her own private rail car. The undisputed "star" of Chautauqua was William Jennings Bryan, twice a candidate for president and the greatest orator of his time. Bryan filled the tent when he spoke in 1918, proving his versatility by addressing in one speech such various topics as the Bible, poultry farming, Prohibition, and the history of war.

Chautauqua brought explorers and adventurers, Indian chiefs and ministers, musicians and unique entertainers like ventriloquist Edgar Bergen, who introduced Charlie McCarthy to audiences under the Chautauqua tent. Later Chautauquas were fund-raising opportunities. The Santa Rosa Playgrounds Association sponsored the program in 1921 to raise money for a swimming pool—then built the pool in 1925 on the Chautauqua site. The last year the circuit came to Santa Rosa was 1927, when the speaker was Kentucky's Senator Alben Barkley, who delivered his famous talk on American traditions. Barkley would later serve as vice president under Harry Truman.

From the Great War through the 1930s there was a parade of speakers sponsored by community organizations and churches—popular writers and lecturers like poet Edwin Markham, who was graduated from the Christian College in Santa Rosa in the 1870s, Will Durant, and Rockwell Kent. Helen Keller addressed 1,200 people at the Federated Church in 1925. Hundreds more were turned away. Poet and folksinger Carl Sandburg appeared at the high school, sponsored by Santa Rosa Junior College, in 1934.

Some of the famous just visited. Child star Shirley Temple and her family stopped in Santa Rosa on their way to an Oregon vacation. Writer Peter B. Kyne, creator of the "Cappy Ricks" stories in the *Saturday Evening Post*, was a frequent guest at the Rosseters' Wikiup Ranch. Novelist Gertrude Atherton lived at the Occidental Hotel in 1935, while completing her novel *The Golden Peacock*.

Hometown talent was constantly on display. The early century elocutionists, such as Lorena Hoag, were joined in the '30s by Harriet Parrish Barnes, whose one-woman shows were well-received. Barnes, who would be hostess

—Ann Bean Collection

on a radio interview show for KSRO for many years, performed the Broadway success *Victoria Regina* for Santa Rosa audiences in 1936. The play had been censored in New York. Barnes's version was uncut.

While Jack London, who died at his Glen Ellen ranch in 1916, would remain the most famous of all Sonoma County writers, the county's women poets and writers were greatly celebrated in the '20s and '30s. Their names filled the social pages of the newspaper weekly, either because they were reading or signing their own work or gathering to admire the work of their peers. In 1927, six women formed a Sonoma County branch of the American Pen Women. They were journalist Byrd Weyler Kellogg; poet Eugenia T. Finn; Grace Davis, a Sebastopol teacher and compiler of a manual for teachers; Sarah Hammond Kelly, a writer of children's stories and an occasional adult mystery; Edith Granger Hawkes, the postmaster in Fulton whose "Index to Poetry" was a standard library reference; and the Kenwood poet, Nell Griffith Wilson, whose work celebrated the county's farms, orchards, and harvests. Most of them were also members of the Sonoma County Chapter of the League of Western Writers, which chose the early Depression years for the daunting task of compiling a Sonoma County anthology.

That anthology, *The Singing Years*, was published in 1933. While it featured the work of both men and women, it served as a showcase for the Pen Women and their poet colleagues. All of the Pen Women founders were represented, in addition to well-known Sonoma County writers Ina Draper DeFoe Greathead, Celeste Granice Murphy, Ann Roller Issler, Lillian Burger Slater, and Fidelia Furber Harlow, who was also a painter. Helen Miller Lehman, a member of the Santa Rosa Board of Education, was the first president of the league and her poetry is part of the collection. One of the most interesting poets represented was Joy O'Hara. She was a good poet, recognized nationally and published regularly in magazines like *Good Housekeeping* and poetry journals like *Wings* and

Scripts. She won several important poetry competitions. Joy O'Hara was the pen name of Agnes Stephens (Mrs. Ben) Farquar, Santa Rosa deputy city clerk from 1930 until 1940 and city clerk from 1940 to 1953. Santa Rosa's favorite women's columnist was Nora Noonan Plover, the clever wife of the county probation officer, John Plover. She wrote regularly in the *Press Democrat* in the 1920s.

The trio of county histories produced in the first half of the 20th century followed the "mug book" pattern established in the 1800s, whereby citizens were urged to purchase space in a biographical section to tell their life stories (photos were rare and more expensive). The historical value of the biographies is mitigated by the editorial control of the "clients," who in 19th century versions of these books often included elaborate drawings of their homes or ranches embellished with extra stories, barns, and orchards; but the history portions of these books was a link with Sonoma County's early years.

Much of these histories' text is based upon the work of Robert Thompson, the county clerk and earliest historian. But Thomas Gregory, a Bloomfield native and *Press Democrat* writer, whose history of the county was published in 1911; Honoria Tuomey, from Bodega, whose work was published in two volumes in 1926; and the many writers who compiled Ernest Finley's "Golden Gate Bridge Edition" history of the county in 1937, each added his or her own emphasis and style to the telling of the old stories.

Gregory lavished praise on the pioneers and recounted the natural virtues of the county until it seemed a veritable paradise. Tuomey's work is heavily weighted toward the Sonoma Coast and the Russian sojourn at Fort Ross. Finley's history is more measured. He employed a trio of professional researchers to work with a twenty-six-person advisory board and three of the county's best-known writers, Byrd Weyler Kellogg, Helen Miller Lehman, and Lucile Rood Kelly.

Sonoma County's importance to California artists had been established before the turn of the century. San Francisco landscape painters, many of whom were members of the Bohemian Club, had discovered the beauties of the redwoods along the Russian River. Some artists came and stayed for a while, giving art lessons to support themselves while they painted. One of these was Lorenzo Latimer, who was here, teaching in both Santa Rosa and Healdsburg, until 1910.

Bruner's Art Store was also well established by 1900. Clement Bruner was the agent for many successful North Coast artists including Grace Hudson, the Ukiah painter whose portraits of Pomo Indians were widely praised. Paintings by William Keith and Sidney Tilden Dakin could also be found at Bruner's, along with the sculpture of Julia Briggs Painter, who had done a bust of Burbank before his death.

Elizabeth Hoen, a daughter of pioneer merchant Berthold (Barney) Hoen, gave art classes at "Hoen's Island," the glade between two creeks which in 1923 became Doyle Park. In the 1930s there were more than a dozen Sonoma County artists painting and exhibiting successfully in the Bay Area. Grace Griffith Allison was one of them. She was the sister of poet Nell Griffith Wilson, both being the daughters of the pioneer apple grower, Nathaniel Griffith. Mrs. Griffith Allison, who worked in a studio at her Vine Hill Road home, exhibited at Gump's in San Francisco, galleries in Carmel, and in England in the mid-'30s. Another Santa Rosa native, Ruth Comstock Stratton, was known for her starkly realistic painting done in tempura. Juanita Storch, who worked at Bruner's, painted scenes around her Rincon Valley creekside home which celebrated the simple beauty of the Sonoma County landscape.[39]

Ann Ruggles Johnson, a young Sonoma artist, was enjoying success by the late '30s, as were Perry Jewett, Dr. G. Saddler Pittock, Lucille Poppe, Mabel Allen, Alice Abeel, Leonie Schmidt, Olive Gore, and Lidia Dole. Another Santa Rosa native who was very successful in her chosen art form was Dorothy Wright Liebes whose textiles gained her national recognition.

George Trombley, above, formed the Santa Rosa Symphony Orchestra in 1927. Below, members of the Indipendenza Band, sponsored by an Italian lodge in the 1920s, formed the nucleus of Santa Rosa's municipal band of the 1930s led by conductor Charley Vitale, center.

Perhaps the most accomplished artist living in Sonoma County in the first half of the century was Alphonse Sondag, a Paris-born painter and sculptor, who became well known in the state in the 1920s and 1930s for his paintings of the California missions. He painted other historical sites and buildings in the Mother Lode and returned again and again to Sonoma, which he referred to as the "cradle of California." By 1932, he also had painted Fort Ross, the Bodega area, and Jack London's ranch buildings and was at work on an oil painting of Burbank's Cedar of Lebanon. In '32, he proposed to paint historical murals on the walls of the courthouse, but the supervisors declined his offer. A resident of Kenwood, he worked and lectured in Sonoma County until his death.[40]

Santa Rosans had been humming along to good music ever since the Philharmonic Society organized its musicales in the 1870s. In the 1920s, the widening popularity of both radio and the Victrola set off long and serious debates about the future of live music. Concerts and opera, some thought, were doomed. In Santa Rosa there was no evidence of this. The Cline Theater offered one musical extravaganza after another. In 1923, for example, there was a concert by violinist Efrem Zimbalist, a music revue by Mamie Smith's company of Negro singers and dancers, and a performance of *The Merry Widow* with the New York cast.

Performers from Santa Rosa participated in the national talent searches which were so popular in the 1930s, including the "Major Bowes Hour." In 1936, Mayor George Cadan declared a Major Bowes Day in Santa Rosa when the national winners performed at the California Theater. In 1936, five Sonoma County residents were selected from the 300 who auditioned at the Occidental Hotel for "California's Hour," a Los Angeles radio show. Those selected were Henry Passalacqua, a Healdsburg tenor who had studied in Italy; Gertrude Rosenback, a Santa Rosa mezzo-soprano; violinist Vincent Trombley; tenor Joseph Novelli; and contralto Enola MacKenzie. Santa Rosan Dean McCluskey took the stage name Don Dean and became a "crooner" and orchestra leader who enjoyed a successful South American career as "the Rudy Vallee of the Argentine." He was the son of Nora and Alex McCluskey. In 1919, Dorothy (Mrs. Raegan) Talbot, the opera singer wife of one of the Bennett Valley Talbots, made her debut at a concert at the Mark McDonalds' Mableton.

Music made at home was also a Santa Rosa tradition, ever since the German immigrant merchants organized a brass band in the 1860s. Santa Rosa High School formed a band in 1917. In 1924, Mrs. L.B. McGuire, who ran a dance academy, organized the Santa Rosa Boys Band (fifty pieces), the Brownie Orchestra (twenty pieces), and the Apollo Club, a select group of twelve young musicians. It was a forerunner of the Mickey Mouse Orchestra, a group of young instrumentalists of the 1930s, who played for the "kiddie" matinees on Saturdays at the California Theater.

In the 1920s, the Italian Band, properly known as "L'Indipendenza" for the lodge that was its sponsor, was led by Professor Angelo Capelli, a Florentine immigrant who

owned a music store and recruited Italian youngsters for music lessons and his band. In the 1930s, many of Capelli's musicians joined the Santa Rosa Municipal Band led by Charley Vitale, a one-armed conductor and trumpet player (a painter and paperhanger by profession). Eventually the two bands merged under Vitale. They were union musicians and picked up extra money during the Depression years playing for street fairs and community events.

Serious music in Santa Rosa was pushed to a new dimension in the late 1920s when a dedicated young man from Michigan, seeking a town in need of musical direction, chose Santa Rosa. With his baton under his arm, George Trombley came west from Kalamazoo in 1927 looking for a place to teach music and develop an orchestra. From his enthusiasm, the Santa Rosa Symphony was born. Within months of his arrival, Trombley had a full schedule of pupils and had assembled a group of thirty-two talented amateurs. After fourteen weeks of rehearsal, the orchestra played its first concert in April of 1928 at the Elks Club.

Trombley inspired his musicians and the orchestra gained recognition quickly. In the 1930s, they "played the Palace" (San Francisco's Palace Hotel) for a KGO radio broadcast. The Redwood Empire String Ensemble, a group of orchestra members, were regulars on Santa Rosa's own KSRO radio. The orchestra performed with the San Francisco Ballet at outdoor performances at Armstrong Grove in Guerneville.

When Trombley retired after thirty years, the Santa Rosa Symphony was a sixty-piece orchestra composed entirely of professional musicians. He had conducted 179 concerts and approximately 3,000 rehearsals. He only missed one rehearsal. And, according to the town's musical legend, he didn't so much miss a rehearsal as gain a bassoon. It was an emergency appendectomy that accounted for the lapse in attendance and a chance to meet a young physician named Harding Clegg who confessed to playing the bassoon. Trombley recovered quickly and Clegg brought his bassoon to the woodwind section.

At right, a Santa Rosa tennis player leans into her forehand on the tennis club's court at the Fourth Street end of McDonald Avenue. Below, golfer Jessie Burlington, who, with her husband, owned a Santa Rosa bakery, tees off at the Santa Rosa Golf & Country Club on Los Alamos Road. Watching at far left is the club's women's champion, Fremont school teacher Clara Robertson.

—Chamber of Commerce Collection

—LeBaron Collection

The man the orchestra members called "Mr. T" had his favorite selections. Dvorak's "Slavonic Dance" was apt to appear on the program fairly regularly and he delighted audiences by conducting it *con molto gusto*, stomping his foot on the podium until the dust flew. He earned the affection and respect of the community with his dedication and his attention to young musicians, working many extra hours with them at his home across Mendocino Avenue from Santa Rosa High. He and SRHS instructor Josef Walter inspired Santa Rosa youngsters to musical heights, accounting for a sound professional base for Trombley's orchestra and several distinguished musical careers, among them that of his successor, Corrick Brown.41

The first golf course in Santa Rosa was a small, private club in the Roseland District which did not endure. Its owners, Mr. and Mrs. James Gray, moved here from the east and found that there were no golf links. Reluctant to give up their favorite sport, they built a nine-hole course on their property west of Santa Rosa. They played there with

their eastern friends but, according to the *Press Democrat*'s social columnist of the early century, their new Santa Rosa friends did not take to the game and they soon abandoned the links to "more practical uses."

It was another decade before Santa Rosans awoke to the charms of the game. In 1919 another newcomer, an Englishman named Jim Whittingham who had married a Santa Rosa widow, rallied the citizens to golf. The Santa Rosa Golf Club organized and hired their first pro—before they had a course to play on. The pro, who doubled as greenskeeper, was a Scotsman named Don MacPherson. Talmadge "Babe" Wood, then a teenager, had the honor of hauling the first load of sand for the tee-boxes to the fifty-acre site the club selected on Los Alamos Road. Wood loaded the sand in his REO Speedwagon at Bodega Bay and brought it to town as the first step in the construction of a golf course.

In the spring of 1920 there were 155 members in the Santa Rosa Golf Club. They turned out for work parties to clear the rocks off the fairways and plant the temporary greens. The enthusiasm for the sport was evidenced by hop broker Chris Donovan, who wired his pledge for lifetime membership from a ship at sea, on his way back from Europe in May. By July 4 club members were ready for their first tournament. The clubhouse, designed by noted San Francisco architect Albert Farr, in a style described as "modified English," opened in 1922.

The 1920s was a time of great interest in golf in Northern California. Tayman Park in Healdsburg was built in 1924; the Northwood course, adjacent to Bohemian Grove on the Russian River, was also constructed in the 1920s. But Santa Rosa had the distinction of being the first, and golfers came from all over the county to play.

Like the golf club, the Santa Rosa Tennis Club, with a court at the south end of McDonald Avenue, was social as well as athletic. But baseball was pure sport. And Santa Rosa, historically, was a great baseball town. The first team was organized in 1861 and the town was never without at

Santa Rosa Junior College's "Canadian" ice hockey team of 1939 and 1940 beat the best college teams in the United States.

—Santa Rosa Junior College Collection

*E*rnie Nevers came to Santa Rosa from Wisconsin as a high school student and immediately transformed the SRHS football and basketball teams of the early 1920s into proving grounds for one of the greatest athletic talents of his age.

Nevers, who was the player-coach of the SRJC team for a single season in 1922, went on to All-American glory at Stanford University. As fullback for Pop Warner's undefeated team, he played in the 1925 Rose Bowl and sports writers said "the big, blond fullback from Stanford was the whole show" for Warner's team, which lost to coach Knute Rockne's Notre Dame. Early in his professional career Nevers brought his teammates, the Duluth Eskimos, to Santa Rosa for an exhibition game. His career with the St. Louis Cardinals is well documented, including the game in which the Cardinals whipped the mighty Chicago Bears 40-6 with Nevers scoring all of the forty points—a record that still stands.[42]

All of Santa Rosa eagerly followed Nevers' athletic exploits, but none with more intense interest than his SRHS classmates and the younger boys in his neighborhood. Nevers lived in Rincon Valley with an older sister and her husband in a small white house opposite the brass foundry on Santa Rosa Creek. The "Rincon kids" were privileged to participate in the hayfield football games that were, in reality, a contest between Nevers and all the rest.

Aubrey Brandon was one of those boys, perhaps ten years younger than Nevers. In later years, he remembered his hero: "When any spare moment presented itself, Rincon Valley had a football game. The game was played on any relatively flat field. I seem to remember best Austins' hayfield at the corner of Sonoma Highway and Calistoga Road where, from time to time, we would gather after the hay had been cut.

"The players would form into two groups with Ernie and me (I was a skinny seven-year-old at the time) on one side and ten to fifteen 'big guys' on the other. The game was called 'Stop Ernie!' I would center the ball to him and run as fast as I could to get out of the way while the opposing side would try to stop this tow-headed hurricane. I can still see this mass of humanity moving irresistibly forward with tacklers hanging on for dear life, trying to bring Nevers to earth."[43]

Football great Ernie Nevers, right, played on Santa Rosa High School's first championship team in 1920. Below, top row, left to right, Stacy Lee, Coach Victor Hodge, Joe Dearing, Tom Grace, Ernie Nevers, Al Lucas, and Jerry Griffin. Front row, left to right, Gale Johnson, Roy Penry, Vinton Deter, Woodburn Stocker, Frank Feliz, Bill Cowan, Percy Alexanderson, and Clifton Morrill.

—Grace Family Collection

least one baseball club after that. The Italian boys from the west side added a lot of spark to the Rosebuds and the Elks in the '20s and '30s. Willie Rossi and Norm Maroni one of the five Maroni brothers who played in the '20s and '30s, were each associated with the game for fifty years as players, managers, and, in Rossi's case, as umpire.

A more surprising sports craze of the 1930s, given Santa Rosa's temperate climate, was ice hockey. It was, in a way, a result of Prohibition. While Grace Brothers couldn't make beer, the company operated an ice plant, Union Ice Company. The plant was threatened with competition from another plant in town, one that reportedly planned to build an ice skating rink. To head off that venture, Joe Grace, who was head of the family enterprise, built one first. It was behind the brewery, adjacent to the cooling plant—a large, unlovely, barnlike arena with an ice skating rink.

Grace came up with a plan to create interest in ice skating. He talked Santa Rosa Junior College, and football and baseball coach Clarence "Cook" Sypher, into starting a hockey team. Sypher, who had never seen a hockey puck, met with the ice hockey coach from the University of California and learned the basics of the game. The secret was Canadians—Canadian hockey players who would come to Santa Rosa, play two years for SRJC, and then go on to UC Berkeley's team.

Grace Brothers gave them jobs. Sypher enrolled them in night school and bought a book on how to coach ice hockey. There were just four Americans on the 1939 team and a dozen young Canadians, seventeen and eighteen years old. For two years, until war stopped the fun, the SRJC Bear Cubs hockey teams rolled over opponents and packed Joe Grace's ice arena with spectators. In 1940, they beat the University of Southern California, the University of California at Los Angeles, and Cal, all in a row. The night they played USC there were 2,500 people inside the arena and another 1,000 outside cheering—in the rain. They beat the University of Colorado that year and the University of Illinois. They played Illinois on New Year's Day and beat

them 16-1. And then it ended. Great Britain went to war in 1940 and the Canadians were called home for military service. The glory years of hockey were brief in Santa Rosa. But memorable.[44]

Change was a byword for the medical community in the first half of the century. Dr. R. Lee Zieber, who would be named as the California Medical Association's "Rural Practitioner of the Year" before his long career ended, came to the practice of medicine in a time when his father's medical office had a gasoline-powered, water-cooled X-ray machine.

When Dr. William J. Rudee bought his first medical equipment secondhand from Dr. Alan Thompson, a turn-of-the-century physician in Santa Rosa, he was surprised to find that the house-call bag had a revolver in it.

In the Tanner Hospital, which had been the Mary Jesse Hospital, the power would go out in the operating room when someone pushed the elevator button.

Babies were generally born at home or if the birth was a difficult one at the Mary Jesse/Tanner Hospital. If physicians foresaw serious problems, patients would be transported by train and ferry to San Francisco hospitals.

There were eighteen physicians practicing in Santa Rosa at the time of the 1906 earthquake. By the 1920s their ranks had swelled to twenty-two. There were few specialists. Physicians practiced in their offices and out of their medical bags more often than in hospitals, for hospital care was extremely limited. The County Hospital, where physicians volunteered their time, was for indigents only. Paying patients had to make do with doctors' office surgeries.

The Mary Jesse was a private hospital owned by Dr. James Jesse and named for his late wife. It was a converted two-story house at the corner of Fifth and King streets that was also used for critical care of private patients. In the late '20s, it was purchased by nurse Eliza B. Tanner and continued, as the Tanner Hospital, through the 1940s. There were also tiny nursing hospitals. Some, like the Katherine Sanitarium on McDonald Avenue, were run by a registered nurse but offered surgery facilities to physicians. Others were doctor owned. The Santa Rosa Hospital on Humboldt Street was an enterprise of Dr. Jackson Temple and Dr. J.W. Scamell in the early years of the century. In addition, there were a number of nurses who took patients into their homes for convalescence.

In a community where nearly all the physicians were general practitioners who treated entire families through two and three generations, "beloved" was not an unusual adjective to attach to a doctor's name. But none in Santa Rosa were more beloved than the woman known to her patients as "Doctor Dear." Anabel McGaughey Stuart, a leader in the Santa Rosa medical community in the last decades of the 19th century, practiced in Santa Rosa until her death in 1914, when her patients dedicated a fountain to her memory in the little park next to the library.

Dr. Jesse was another holdover from the previous century who practiced for a time in the 1900s. Dr. Samuel Bogle was county health officer for many years, beginning his tenure in 1904. Dr. Burton Zinnamon became public health officer in 1938.

Among the other physicians practicing here at the time of the earthquake, there were those whose medical practices in Santa Rosa would span several decades: Dr. R. M. Bonar, Dr. Albert Herrick, Dr. Silas Rohr, and Dr. Elizabeth Yates. By the 1920s, they were joined by Dr. Cuthbert Fleissner, Dr. Alfred. A. Thurlow Sr., Dr. Nils Juell, Dr. Ross Hamlin, Dr. William Shipley, and Dr. Joseph Shaw, who was Burbank's physician. Dr. Marguerite Fulmer, with offices in the Rosenberg Building, treated children's diseases and Dr. J.H. McLeod was an eye, ear, nose, and throat specialist. The rest were general practitioners.

The medical community grew as slowly as the population in the early years of the century. Dr. Leighton

Ray came to Santa Rosa in 1926 as the designated physician for railroad employees but he liked to tell in later years how he sat alone in his new office for three weeks before he saw his first patient, which was the Northwestern Pacific depot cat with a rubber band wrapped around its tail. The cat was in great pain and had to be anesthetized. Ray liked to say no cat had ever had such professional medical care from a Harvard graduate. Soon after, Dr. A. Morse Bowles set up his practice, as did Dr. Ralph Harr, and Dr. Waldemar Pleth. Many new doctors entered an established practice for a time before striking out on their own. Dr. Zieber started in the offices of Dr. Hamlin in 1934.

In 1937, when the new County Hospital was opened, the University of California Medical School established a residency program in general practice there. This brought a new kind of "country doctor" to Santa Rosa, now a town of 12,000 with a complement of physicians who had reached retirement age. Many graduates of the residency program stayed in Sonoma County. Dr. Alexis Maximov was in the

Nurse Anna Bossa poses for a photograph in front of the Mary Jesse Hospital on Fifth Street, circa 1919.

—Marie Lauritzen Collection

—Helen Rudee Collection

first class of residents in 1937 and he stayed to practice in Santa Rosa, later specializing in obstetrics and gynecology. Of the six members of County's "Class of '41," a designation they would proudly share through some forty years of practice, four stayed in Sonoma County—Drs. Harding Clegg, William Rudee, and Raimond Clary in Santa Rosa, and Horace Sharrocks in Sebastopol. War interrupted the flow of residents but brought another wave of general practitioners immediately after—including Drs. Frank Norman, Robert Huntington, Martin Hutchinson, Frank Lones, and Ben Barbour. Women physicians were fewer than they had been at the turn of the century. In 1949, however, Dr. Edith Young became Sonoma County's health officer. There were no more than four board certified specialists in the early post-war years—Dr. Katherine Quinlan, radiology, Dr. Wilson Stegeman, urology, Dr. Pearl Konttas, pediatrics, and Dr. Paul Quarry, surgery. The "Age of the Specialist" would not come to Santa Rosa until Memorial Hospital was opened in 1950.

This new breed of country doctor drove cars that were faster than Dr. Jesse's Schelling, and they carried no weapons. They wrote prescriptions for life-saving drugs like penicillin, which would have astonished the gun-toting Dr. Thompson and delighted the helpless physicians of 1918 who had tried in vain to stop the Spanish influenza. But they were still jacks-of-all-medical-trades—delivering babies, removing gall bladders, stitching up wounds, and counseling distraught parents with all the skills of child psychologists.[45]

Among the eighteen dentists practicing in Santa Rosa in the 1920s were: Dr. Ralph Nelson, who had practiced in the 1800s; Dr. David Leppo, who was one of the first presidents of the California Dental Association; Dr. David P. Anderson, called "D.P." by patients and friends, who was political on a broader scope, serving in both city government and the state assembly, and Dr. Ovid Tuttle, who began his forty-nine years of practice in Santa Rosa in 1913.[46]

When 1918 was designated nationally as "The Child's Year," Santa Rosa joined in by allotting city funds for child welfare clinics. The need was clear. In 1919 a countywide Red Cross committee on public health nursing was formed to recruit eligible nurses to take the new public health course offered by the University of California. Myrtle Sacry was the first Santa Rosan to make application and was awarded a scholarship by the committee.

While Miss Sacry was completing her course, the Red Cross offered classes in public health care for nurses in Santa Rosa. When Sacry returned to become the first official public health nurse in the county in 1920, she was paid jointly by the school districts and the Red Cross. She worked in Sebastopol and the Sonoma Valley, as well as Santa Rosa. In the month of April in her first year, her report shows 128 home calls for "bed-side nursing," nine classes in home hygiene, and sixty-five school children examined in five clinics. In 1923 the Santa Rosa Board of Education, acknowledging that the need had been established, set up a school nursing program for Santa Rosa

Young doctors in the UC residency program's "Class of '41" at Sonoma County Hospital. Top row, left to right, physicians Robert Phillips, Dwight Barnett (the program's director), Raimond Clary, and Harding Clegg. Second row, dentist William Pearson and physicians Horace Sharrocks and William Rudee. In front, physician Ford Shepherd.

Dr. Edith Young was Sonoma County's Public Health Officer in 1949.

students, relieving the Red Cross of the responsibility. The second Red Cross nurse in the county, Mayme Peterson, organized the first Child Health Station. Miss Peterson and her Red Cross volunteer helpers saw an average of twenty infants and children at each weekly clinic.

When General Hospital was opened on A Street early in 1917, it was hailed as the first "modern" facility for paying patients. Until 1950, when Memorial Hospital was built, General would be the main hospital available to physicians for their private patients. In the 1930s and 1940s, it seemed to the medical community that General was overcrowded all the time—and, despite the best efforts of its administration, outmoded.

The hospital was owned as an investment by a group of Southern California dentists and run in its later years by Gladys Kay, the hospital administrator for thirty years beginning in the 1930s. Kay, who had no training in hospital administration, had been an ice skating champion in her native Canada before coming to Santa Rosa with her salesman husband Harry. She took on the impossible job of keeping General as current as possible.

There is a Gladys Kay legend in the medical community, oft-told by Dr. Frank Norman, Santa Rosa's physician-historian. Through the years, the story goes, Kay saved money in a shoebox, tucking away a portion of the hospital's meager profits until she had enough (or almost enough, anyway) to build a new hospital. She went proudly to the hospital owners to show them what she had accomplished, expecting praise and a better medical facility. But they pocketed her good work as profit and Kay had to be satisifed with some minor remodeling and wider halls to meet the new hospital codes.

After Memorial Hospital was built, General Hospital became the town's "alternative" hospital, utilitized by physicians for minor and less-serious major surgeries and by patients who preferred a more relaxed style of care to that offered by the new, ultra-professional Memorial.

The banks of the Russian River, from Healdsburg to the sea, had drawn vacationers to Sonoma County since the railroads created tourism as a secondary income source to the timber industry. The first visitors brought trunks and stayed the summer. But the widely advertised, turn-of-the-century "Triangle Trip" which brought Bay Area visitors in by one train and out by another, established the river area as a weekend excursion.

The Russian River was conveniently close to the Bay Area when the Depression lowered travel expectations, and throughout the 1930s resort business boomed. Murphy's Ranch was a good example of the kind of family resort that drew the same clientele back, year after year, to enjoy the beach and the sun.

Lee Murphy, son of the owner, tapped into another "draw" for visitors when he booked San Francisco jazz bands into his nightclub called The Grove in Guerneville. Murphy performed a coup by booking Glen Gray and his orchestra for an entire summer in the 1930s. The Grove featured bands like Sonny Dunham's and a few about-to-be-discovered locals including Santa Rosa musician Abby Rasor, whose band played the Grove in '37 and went on tour in '38.

At Guernewood Park, Gus Wright was doing the same. Guernewood had a young bandleader named Jack Winston, who played for dancing, and only the locals knew that he was Jack Winston Wright, son of the park owner. Jack enjoyed pre-war success in the music business before settling down to open a real estate firm in Guerneville.

From 1935 on, all the "Big Bands" were on tour. When they came to the Bay Area they would play all the satellite summer places including the boardwalk at Santa Cruz, Alameda's Neptune Beach—and the Russian River.

Rio Nido with, according to its sign, "Memories that Linger," was the main stop for the name bands. Rio Nido's owner Harry Harris brought Isham Jones in 1935. Jones played a lot of his own music including "I'll See You in My Dreams," "Swinging down the Lane," and "When My Dream

In 1936, *LIFE* magazine selected Santa Rosa as a "typical West Coast trading area" for an extensive city-wide survey of magazine reading habits. It was still small-city America. All the wildness of Prohibition, all the hardship of the Depression years, hadn't changed the character of Santa Rosa. Doctors and judges still walked home for lunch with their wives. Most women still stayed home and baked cookies, although some had taken up golf. For children it was still just about the best town in the world to grow up in—sunny, safe, and relatively prosperous.

There may be no better illustration of the kind of life Santa Rosa children were offered in the years before World War II than in their memories of a woman named Dagny Juell.

Miss Juell was the children's librarian at the Santa Rosa Free Public Library for thirty-five years. It was a measure of her undying interest, her warmth, and her professional skills, that the public library played a surprisingly important part in the lives of three generations of Santa Rosa's young people. Literally hundreds and hundreds of children who rode their bicycles or the "little yellow bus" to the library on Saturdays or summer days learned a code of behavior and a kind of value system from Miss Juell, along with their reading.

One of her "children," guided through the wonders of literature by her suggestions, remembered her as a small woman. "Not much taller than a child. She had a homely, elfin face with smile-crinkled eyes behind wire spectacles. She walked with a rolling gait, limping on a heavy shoe built up to correct a physical deformity.... She was always so bright and cheerful, there was no reason for pity. And after all, I thought, she had that whole wonderful roomful of books to read whenever she wanted to."[47]

Miss Juell—like the chief librarian in those years, Ruth Hall—was a shameless proselytizer for reading. One man's first memory of her is when she came to the Community Church in Windsor in 1935 to read stories at a Halloween party and "speak to the parents" about the importance of books in children's lives. He was an eager convert. "She understood little boys with uncanny precision," he later recalled. "Her selection was always the best book of the lot I carried home."[48]

Miss Juell was a stern critic. There were no Oz books in the Santa Rosa Library. And certainly no Tom Swift adventures or Nancy Drew mysteries or any of the other series that became so popular in the 1920s and 1930s. Comic books were taboo. But she sent each one of her clients home each week with a stack of books and she made reading an exciting adventure. There were reading contests in the summertime—and story hours.

"She always read the new books to us," one of her readers recalled. "I remember when she introduced us to Dr. Seuss. It was cold in that basement library in the winter and she had a little portable heater. It seemed cozy. My, she was awfully kind. And she instilled a love of reading in all of us. She made it a happy time for children."[49]

"We felt that library was the center of the universe," another recalled. "I can still see it—the children's room, the tree and the fountain next to it. It was a magic place. To this day, when I read—and I am never without a book—I think of Dagny Juell. That's where this habit was set in me, I know."[50]

Boat Comes Home." He had a fellow in the sax section who played a fine clarinet, name of Woody Herman. Ozzie Nelson, who married his vocalist Harriet Hilliard, played at Rio Nido also in that summer of '35.

The following year it was Phil Harris, and Ted FioRito's band. Before the decade ended the Rio Nido roster would include Del Courtney, Buddy Rogers, whose drummer was a "wild man" named Gene Krupa, and Woody Herman, leading the old Isham Jones band as his own.

No glory was greater than the glory days of the Russian River, when the Big Band sounds wafted downstream on a summer night.

It was cold in February of 1939. There was snow on the Bay Area's mountaintops—ten inches on Mt. Diablo. But the weather didn't stop 142,000 people from attending opening day of the World's Fair on Treasure Island.

It was conceived as a burst of jubilation for the end of the Great Depression, but it was also a final attempt to ignore the troublesome news from Europe, where Adolf Hitler was on the march. "The Pageant of the Pacific," as it was sometimes called, was a financial disaster and was forced to close early. But Bing Crosby sang there. And Irving Berlin led the crowd in "God Bless America." And Billy Rose's Aquacade had Johnny Weissmuller, who would be Tarzan, and a young swimmer named Esther Williams. And police ordered the dancers at Sally Rand's Nude Ranch to wear "bandanna handkerchiefs." And people saw themselves on television for the first time at the Science Pavilion. Those were the things people would remember, not the dollars lost.

The weather had warmed some by April when two special trains from Santa Rosa carried 4,000 citizens to "Sonoma County Day." E.J. "Nin" Guidotti, then chairman of the Board of Supervisors, was accorded the honor of pinning a redwood lily corsage on the lapel of Eleanor Roosevelt, who was visiting that day. Guidotti and Wallace

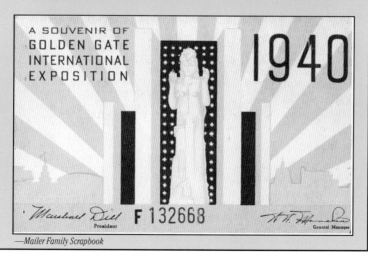

—*Mailer Family Scrapbook*

Ware, a former Santa Rosa attorney who had become an important figure in state politics and was serving then as a railroad commissioner, were the speakers at the ceremony. When Mae (Mrs. Joseph) Grace, the county's official hostess for the fair, became ill and couldn't attend, Olive Tauzer, wife of attorney C.J. "Red" Tauzer, took her place serving tea in the county's hospitality room.

Everyone went to the fair. The Healdsburg Chamber of Commerce members passed out 2,500 bags of the town's most important agricultural product on Prune Day. Sonoma County's young people won awards in the livestock exhibition, including Santa Rosa High School's Severa Wilford Jr, who took top honors for his sheep. Artist Al Sondag exhibited four large canvases in the Redwood Empire Building.

All that summer, Sonoma County residents, carrying picnic baskets and lunch pails, went to the fair. Small boys got lost on the Gayway. College students made plans weeks in advance to get in to see Sally Rand. Farm wives toured the electronic kitchens and everyone marveled at the Cavalcade of the Golden West, a pageant with a cast of hundreds, most of them on horseback. At home, business leaders beamed at the estimates of four million tourists to spread around Northern California. The fair made things happy. But only for a while.

By the summer of 1940, the fair's second season, Europe was at war. The British forces were evacuated from Dunkirk. Paris fell to the Nazis in June. In the Pacific, tensions mounted as Japan threatened Indochina. Off the Pacific Coast, a Japanese fishing boat was seized, its crew charged with espionage. As the World's Fair ended in September of 1940, so did the world as it had always been. For the second time in the century, war would bring change.

The way of life in the San Francisco Bay Area, Santa Rosa's small-town-America image, Sonoma County's farm-country value system, were all about to be challenged. If World War I opened Sonoma County to a wider world, this global conflict would fling open all doors to let that world come in. 🦋

Listen for the Warning! Pending adoption of a uniform air-raid warning signal system for the entire county, defense authorities here will utilize the old fire bell atop the former Fifth Street firehouse to warn Santa Rosans of impending trouble!

Three long and ten short taps on the huge bell will be temporarily used as the local air-raid warning signal, it was announced last night at civilian defense headquarters in the office of the district attorney.

Santa Rosa police officers will be charged with sounding the alarm, day or night, until such time as the uniform system of signaling is adopted. The huge bell, in disuse for several years, can be heard for several miles.[1]

War came to Santa Rosa and Sonoma County on a mild, overcast Sunday morning in December. Most people heard the news on the radio as shaky-voiced weekend announcers interrupted the 11 a.m. programming to tell of the attack on the Pacific Fleet in Pearl Harbor, Hawaii. With the news came panic. Were the Japanese planes still headed east?

The old fire bell, long silent and never intended for more than rallying the "fire laddies," was symbolic of how woefully unprepared the Pacific Coast was and how far removed the quiet farming community of Santa Rosa had been from the horrors of the war in Europe. The plight of the Poles, the Czechs, the London blitz were little more than news from far off places—until that Sunday morning in December.

The last "great" war had begun for Santa Rosans when their militia marched off to fight the Hun, down streets lined with schoolchildren waving flags. This time it came with the fear that a Japanese invasion of the Pacific Coast was possible, perhaps even imminent. The *Press Democrat* of December 9, 1941, had a giant red "EXTRA!" across the top and a headline reading "ENEMY HERE." There were submarine sightings at Dillon Beach, fighter plane alerts in San Francisco, and, in Santa Rosa, hurried meetings, hastily appointed block wardens, blackouts, tests

of that old fire bell, and the realization that, for all 12,000 citizens of this pleasant little town, as for the rest of the nation, the world had turned upside down.

It took only three days for the City Council to authorize purchase of a real air raid siren and to retire the old fire bell once more in favor of the sirens on the fire trucks until the new alarm could be installed. The blackouts were frightening events. City firemen and county forest rangers were called to "stand by"; as were ambulance drivers, their vehicles ready to roll. The newspapers were filled with alarms. And military information services, probably as panicked as everyone else, did little to soothe the fears. The "ENEMY HERE" headline, in fact, was predicated on a statement from Army information in San Francisco that two squadrons of Japanese planes, numbering thirty in all, had crossed the coastline west of San Jose the previous night and "reconnoitered" the Bay Area including the naval base at Mare Island. Every day of that first week "enemy planes" were sighted somewhere in the Bay Area. There were blackouts every night for seven nights.[2]

Within three hours of the attack on Pearl Harbor, the county's Defense Council, headed by District Attorney Toland McGettigan, met with Sheriff Al Wilkie, Santa Rosa Police Chief "Dutch" Flohr, and Sebastopol Police Chief Ed Foster, posting a twenty-four-hour watch over public utilities and other potential air raid targets. The hospital section of the Defense Council, chaired by Dr. E.D. Barnett, had met the previous Friday night to complete its organization plans, and it was "ready" with volunteer ambulance and truck drivers and an emergency plan for the county hospital.

By Wednesday, December 10, 1,300 men of the 17th Infantry—part of the Seventh Division, the oldest and most famous fighting unit on the west coast—were in Santa Rosa. They arrived in buses and trucks from Fort Ord and began the task of converting the Sonoma County Fairgrounds to an Army camp, with guard towers and official gates and secure perimeters.

The Poulsen building at Fourth and A streets, a grand structure by community standards, with a ballroom on the second floor, was designated as headquarters. Soldiers assigned to headquarters company slept in the grand ballroom and the hallways. A service company was billeted at the Armory Hall at Fourth and D streets. Bulldozers moved into the hop fields of the Laughlin, Talmadge, and Slusser ranches, building runways for the airport that Congressman Clarence Lea had been pleading for in government appropriations committees for several sessions. By Friday the funding was authorized and the land had been designated as the property of the U.S. Army Interceptor

Squadron, an auxiliary of Hamilton Field, until it became an independent base in 1944.

Blackout curtains were in place. One thousand men had been appointed as block wardens, equipped with helmets, armbands, and flashlights. Civilian defense personnel patrolled the darkened streets on bicycles. Stores, which had planned late openings for the Christmas season, closed tightly at 5:30 p.m. and all-night meetings of social organizations were canceled. Within a week, Santa Rosa had become a war town.

All military and government personnel were ordered to their posts. Recruiting stations opened on a twenty-four-

Soldiers were in Santa Rosa three days after Pearl Harbor. The first units came from Fort Ord as part of a hastily assembled Infantry "Coast Watch." Below, soldiers man a machine gun installation at the Army Air Field.

—*Barnett Collection*

—Keegan Family Collection

RCAF pilot William Keegan, Jr.

—Santa Rosa Veterans Memorial

Sailor Billy Montgomery.

*T*he names of Sonoma County servicemen known to be stationed in or near Pearl Harbor were listed in the newspaper—Santa Rosans Ken Eymann, a Naval officer on the *West Virginia*; Kingsley Browne, a machinist's mate aboard the *Oklahoma*; Jimmy Robinson, a flying officer stationed at Bellows Field; Malcolm Walt, aboard a minesweeper based in Honolulu. Readers were exhorted to keep "brave hearts" in the worrisome wait for word of their safety. Ironically, it was a young Santa Rosa man whose name did not appear in the "worry" columns who was the first Santa Rosan to die. The telegram to Mrs. Anna Hufft of Lincoln Street came in the second week, reporting the death of her twenty-year-old son, Billy Montgomery, aboard the *California*. Montgomery was one of three Sonoma County sailors who died at Pearl Harbor, none of them mentioned in the newspaper's list of concerns. George Maybee of Santa Rosa, and Rudy Theiller Jr. of Sebastopol, died on the *Arizona*,

but it was Montgomery who was, statistically, the first to be declared officially dead by military authorities. The government decision was a distinction that would see a street, a shopping area, and a high school take his name in years to come.

The first Santa Rosan to die in the European Theater was twenty-two-year-old William Keegan Jr., who was killed in action, flying out of a base in Scotland as a member of the Royal Canadian Air Force. Keegan had earned his private pilot's license with instruction at the Santa Rosa Municipal Airport before the war. He had planned to enlist in the RCAF with two Santa Rosa friends, Chip Giovanetti and George Giblin. But the Giovanettis and the Giblins dissuaded their sons from going to Canada to fight the Germans, so young Keegan went alone. Before the war ended, all three friends were dead—Giovanetti in a bombing raid and Giblin on his first mission over the oil fields of Ploesti in Rumania.[3]

hour basis and, with military service age limits changed, the minimum age was reduced to eighteen and the maximum raised from twenty-eight to forty-four. The men of Sonoma County stood in line to enlist. Santa Rosa's unit of the California Home Guard, made up of men who were either too old or unable to serve, turned out ninety-six men at a previously scheduled session leaders had hoped would draw at least twenty-five. Attorney Clarence "Red" Tauzer was the leader. Old soldiers responded to this call and to the call from the National Guard for a loan of their helmets, since the west coast fighting force was not equipped for all-out mobilization.

Santa Rosa Mayor Robert F. Madison urged citizens to keep calm and "continue your Christmas shopping as usual." He also tried to reassure Japanese residents they had "no cause for alarm," but his soothing words came on the same day (December 8) that FBI agents seized eight Japanese residents—non-citizens—in a preview of what lay ahead for Japanese-Americans.

Chief Flohr deputized volunteer guards who took turns keeping watch on Lake Ralphine and the pumping stations to keep saboteurs from poisoning the town's water supply. The Navy ordered twenty-two fishing boats, mostly shark fishermen anchored in Bodega Bay's outer harbor, tied up until further notice. California Highway Patrol Captain Harry Clodfelter also commanded a civilian defense force, to guard the county's bridges. The 17th Infantry deployed itself as a "Coast Watch," setting up outposts all along the north coast, from the Oregon border to San Francisco Bay. Armored vehicles, known as half-tracks, became a familiar sight on west county roads, rumbling through the coastal communities on their way to patrol the beaches where gun emplacements were being established. By spring the 17th Infantry moved out to Camp San Luis Obispo for overseas assignment. Men of the 17th, who opened the war walking guard duty at the fairgrounds, would go on to Attu in the Aleutians, to Kwajalein and Leyte; and to Okinawa, before the war was over.[4]

Santa Rosa's own Company K, a part of the 184th Infantry Regiment of the California National Guard, had already gone to war. Mustered in January of 1941, the men of Company K spent six weeks quartered in the old National Guard Armory on Fourth Street and in the Fifth Street firehouse left vacant when the fire department moved to the new station on A Street.

Just past midnight on March 16, they boarded a special train at the Northwestern Pacific depot for Camp San Luis Obispo and a succession of trainings and maneuvers and changes of address which would take them to the South Pacific for the final assault on Okinawa in 1945. The Santa Rosans were under the command of Captain Richard W. Robinson. His lieutenants were Arden Jewett, Robert Pelloux, Oswald Southworth, Walter Hockett, and Paul O'Neill. The sergeants were Warren Wilbur, Alfred Pisenti, Kenneth Webb, Charles Alexander, Jack Wallace, David Dodge, Elijah Groom, and Elbert Hausam. Some Company K men had already left their Guard unit to enlist in other branches of the armed forces. One of these was Corporal Bill Montgomery, the Navy gunner's mate who died at Pearl Harbor.

After the first week, when the actual position of the Japanese forces in the Pacific was ascertained, things calmed down in town. Men wagered 50 cents on pools to guess the hour of the next blackout. Housewives began baking to fill the soldiers' "need" for homemade cake. The Moose Lodge took over the organization of this project, asking for, and getting, 1,000 cakes a week from the city's kitchens. Every young soldier who didn't draw Sunday guard duty found himself with an invitation to dine with a Santa Rosa family.

—*Les Estes Collection*

The 74th Field Artillery, which was still using horse-drawn caissons, took over Rosseters' Wikiup Ranch north of Santa Rosa, below. At left, a soldier guards a bridge near Mark West Springs.

—*Les Estes Collection*

Mrs. A.M. Rocco, whose husband owned the Bank Club downtown, was the record holder, pledged to feed twenty-five soldiers per Sunday. Recreation halls were set up for the servicemen at the Episcopal Guild Hall at the Church of the Incarnation on Mendocino Avenue and at the Southern Methodist Church on Fifth Street. Alpha Barnes, a secretary at the Chamber of Commerce office, coordinated the dinner invitations, collected stacks of magazines and games, booked magicians and ventriloquists and tap dancers for the camp shows, and earned herself the affection of the soldiers and the nickname "Mom" from the 17th Regiment.

A Santa Rosa musician, Paul Marcucci, when asked to perform at a camp show, sat down and in an hour and a half wrote "Remember Pearl Harbor," a patriotic tune which became one of the rallying songs of the war. His friend Aubrey Brandon wrote the words. To show the Army's gratitude for their treatment by Santa Rosans, the Army Band played Marcucci's song on the steps of the courthouse the following Saturday.

Anti-Japanese sentiment was pervasive. The Chamber of Commerce established a special "Chinese Committee" which issued red, white, and blue silk ribbons with badges reading "I am Chinese," so those Asians would be spared the ordeal that lay ahead for Japanese-Americans. In a valiant attempt to make a public statement on loyalty, the Japanese-American Citizens League held a banquet in the second week of the war, honoring the thirty-five Nisei soldiers stationed in Santa Rosa with the 17th Infantry.

More soldiers were on the way. The ranch where John Rosseter raised thoroughbreds north of Santa Rosa was requisitioned by the Army. The 48th Field Artillery, twenty officers and 566 enlisted men, moved in. Camp Wikiup, as it

Private First Class Milton Walker, whose home was in Sonoma County, was one of the Infantrymen assigned to the Sonoma County Fairgrounds in December, 1941. Walker, who was a driver for officers, managed to take the staff car around to visit friends and relatives in Santa Rosa.

was known, was chosen because at this point, field artillery batteries were still using horses to haul cannon. Rosseter's luxurious stables became Army horse barracks. When the 48th moved out, it was replaced by Battery C of the 74th Field Artillery. On December 13, 1941, the Ohio National Guard, 107th Cavalry, activated in Cleveland, was on the train to California, to Camp Hunter-Liggett, near King City. By December 17 they were at Fort Ord. By January of 1942, they were in Santa Rosa, with troops deployed throughout the town. Some camped at the fairgrounds, where their 1,500 horses were stabled. Staff Sergeant Warren Williamson was a driver for the commander, Colonel Woods King. Williamson's quarters were in the Elks Building.5 The headquarters was the Occidental Hotel. Cavalry troops were assigned to Coast Watch—Troop D to Dillon Beach, Troop C to Bodega Bay—all the way to Eureka. Colonel King became a familiar figure in the community. A crowd of Santa Rosa residents stood at attention on the fringes of the Santa Rosa Municipal Airport in November of 1943 when he bade farewell to his soldiers with a full military review. King, whose transfer took him to the Far Eastern Theater, was succeeded by his brother, Lt. Col. R.T. King, who had been his executive officer. An armored truck served as a reviewing stand for the departing officer as the army band played "Strawberry Blonde," the unit's favorite waltz, and the troops massed on the runway to hear their commander's farewell speech.6

Later the men from the 107th Cavalry would fight in Europe, at Bastogne, at the famous "Battle of the Bulge." In April of 1942, the third battalion of the Texas National Guard, 144th Infantry, arrived in Santa Rosa, replacing the 17th Infantry. Another detachment from the 144th Infantry Regiment, inducted at Fort Oglethorpe, Georgia, arrived in Santa Rosa in November of 1942 to occupy the fairgrounds facilities and "watch" the coast.

Santa Rosa duty would not be a pleasant memory for at least one homesick member of the 144th. The camp was crowded. It was a cold, damp winter and the fog stayed until afternoon. Except for a weekend dinner in a Santa Rosa home, activity consisted mainly of training films and lectures, digging slit trenches and foxholes. California was a culture shock for these young men fresh from the Bible belt. Coming from Georgia and the mountains of Tennessee where liquor was a commodity that came from, as one former soldier termed it, "under the floor," they were amazed to find it available in "every drug store and every dry cleaners around the courthouse."7 The "Tennessee boys" were in Santa Rosa for three months, before the Coast Guard took over the duty of watching the coastline and they were shipped to the east coast.

The Naval Air Station's contribution to a parade and rally to sell war bonds was this Grumman fighter, rolling down Fourth Street.

—Frank Scott Collection

The Coast Guard had been involved in Coast Watch from the start. Small units of Coast Guardsmen were posted along the coast in early January of '42. The six who were to spend most of the war at Fort Ross arrived January 12. They brought dogs to aid in patrol of the beaches and deployed them among the soldiers on Coast Watch. In February of 1943, the Army pulled out and the Coast Guard assumed responsibility for the Pacific shores.

At Fort Ross it was a quiet war, but not a comfort post. The six men stationed there were assigned a three-room shack as headquarters. To occupy it, they had to run the sheep out and put doors on the building. They were instructed to build a kennel and dog house for a second group of search-and-patrol dogs. The dogs never arrived so the men moved into the dog house, which was better than the headquarters. The lookout north of the fort was the size of a telephone booth. Inside was a hand-cranked phone and a short-wave radio. Outside was a direction-finding device. That was all.

Once the airfields were in operation in Santa Rosa, the ocean air was filled with planes. The Navy Corsairs bombed the rocks with smoke bombs and flour sacks, shot sea lions, and sank the whistling buoy south of Fort Ross several times. The Coast Guard always reported them. To no avail. Still, the most excitement of the Fort Ross war was the Hollywood "invasion." In '44 Paramount Pictures trekked up the narrow coast highway to film scenes for their ghost story, *The Uninvited*, which starred Ray Milland and Gail Russell.[8]

The Army's 13th Engineers, billeted at Camp Wikiup, built the Santa Rosa Air Field. As an auxiliary base for the 174th Fighter Inceptor Squadron out of Hamilton Air Field in Ignacio, the new base was activated as a training facility, using P-39s and the distinctive P-38 fighters. The 312th Fighter Control Squadron, the only outfit which the Santa Rosa airfield could claim as truly its own, was formed from Hamilton. It set up its ground-air communication training program in June of 1943. The 305 members of the 312th remained in Santa Rosa until they were ordered to England and finally into Europe twelve days after D-Day to work with Patton's army on the road to Germany.

Santa Rosa Air Field remained under the command of Hamilton Field until April 1, 1944, when it was promoted from auxiliary status and became the home of the 434th Army Air Field Base Unit, a pre-combat training unit for fighter pilots, continuing to use P-38s as training vehicles.

A narrative history of SRAAF for the winter months (January to April) of 1945, obtained from the Air Force archives, chronicles the activity at the base. There were 1,500 enlisted men and 215 officers, excluding the flight

Santa Rosa Junior College's STARs, members of the Army's Specialized Training Assignment and Reclassification unit salute the colors in the quad in front of Analy Hall.

—1944 SRJC Patrin

trainees of which 156 started in January and 122 graduated in March, the discrepancy being explained in the narrative as "transfers and untimely deaths."

Two of the Army Air Corps men assigned to SRAAF were World War II rarities—soldiers assigned to their hometown. They were Temple Smith, a lieutenant in the 312th Fighter Control Squadron, and Sergeant William Barnett, a Sonoma County deputy sheriff in civilian life, who was attached to an intelligence unit at the airfield. Smith was very familiar with the base terrain, having worked for the Army Engineers during the base's construction while he was still a student at SRJC. There were 250 civilian employees at SRAAF, including 112 women. Pilot training, according to the narrative, was "hampered by bad flying weather" and the pilots spent considerable energy over the pool tables in the recreation room.

The Naval Auxiliary Air Station was constructed on a site on Sebastopol Road selected by officers at Alameda Naval Air Station. A second auxiliary airfield for Navy fliers was also built at Cotati. While Cotati was originally to be the site of the actual air base facilities, the decision to build at the Santa Rosa field was made because of drainage problems on the Cotati property.

The Santa Rosa Naval Auxiliary Air Station, part of the Alameda command, was commissioned on June 29, 1943, under the command of Lieutenant Frank Rolla Whitmore. War diaries of Alameda Naval Air Station indicate that bombing squadrons, torpedo squadrons, and fighting squadrons moved in and out of Santa Rosa, starting immediately upon commission. The squadrons stayed about a month, training while they awaited transportation, and, when the carriers came into San Francisco Bay, they were ordered to war. A permanent unit, Carrier Aircraft Service Unit 36, under the command of Lieutenant Ralph Bundy, arrived in October of 1943. In July of 1944 Lt. Bundy left, replaced by Lt. Commander Herbert Lovewell. In 1944 activity increased with two complete air groups (Groups Five and Six) moving in for training. In January of 1945 the

command of the Santa Rosa station was expanded to include an emergency field at Little River in Mendocino County, as well as the Cotati airstrip. At the height of its wartime activity, Naval personnel at Santa Rosa numbered 1,800 men.

While the Army Air Corps facility converted quickly to civilian use after the war, leaving the buildings and the mounds of packed earth called "Dutch hangars" where the P-38s were moored to what use a county airport could find for them, the Naval Air Station remained Navy property. Deactivated immediately after the war, it was opened again in 1952, during the Korean conflict, before being placed, once more, in the "outlying field" classification.[10]

In addition to the Santa Rosa and Cotati sites, the Navy purchased 3,300 acres at Skaggs Island in southeastern Sonoma County, west of Mare Island, as the site for a radio station which continued to operate after the war, under strict security. Naval histories say only that Skaggs Island was redesignated in 1962 as "Naval Security Group Activity," which took incoming messages from fleet and Naval shore installations in the Pacific areas.

In addition, there were officers in training at Santa Rosa Junior College. The Army's Specialized Training Assignment and Reclassification unit (STAR) used the classrooms at SRJC for, as one veteran put it, "aptitude testing and refresher courses in pre-engineering and girl watching." Attendance at SRJC had dropped from 670 to 235 almost overnight with the Pearl Harbor attack and the rush of college-age men to enlist. The campus demographics had changed markedly as the college president noted in a letter to a former student: "We have 235 civilian students, mostly women. We have three sophomore men and thirty-three freshmen men. The rest are women."[11]

Faced with its own war-time shortages, the junior college's administration and Board of Trustees were pleased to be chosen from among many candidates for the Army training unit. According to SRJC President Floyd Bailey, who included information about the program in his memoirs, the staff saw the program not only as a way to contribute to the war effort, but to make additions to the campus for the student boom they foresaw at the war's end. With the addition of the STARs in September of 1943, the college added sixteen faculty members to accommodate the 750 Army men. The servicemen required living facilities and SRJC's board obtained priorities on building materials and kitchen equipment which President Bailey said "violated many War Production Board regulations but they were convinced that the school officials were not trying to hinder the war effort."

SRJC's flight school, instituted in 1940, was moved to Ely, Nevada when the government ordered all flight training programs off the coast.[12] In April of 1943 the junior college signed a contract with the Navy to train fliers at the Ely facility, which accommodated 100 young men per class. After the SRJC program the future Navy fliers were sent on to St. Mary's College or the old Del Monte Hotel in Monterey for further classroom training and then to the Navy's pilot programs at Pensacola, Florida or Corpus Christi, Texas. SRJC's dean of men, Egbert Clark, moved to Ely to coordinate the program. Both the STAR program and the Ely Flight School were phased out in August of 1944.

Edwin Kent, county school superintendent, joined SRJC's faculty to coordinate defense work on the Santa Rosa campus. The college's industrial arts facility was leased to the government (for $1 per year) for round-the-clock ship-fitting, metal working, and electronics classes to prepare civilians for the Bay Area's defense plants. This twenty-four-hour pace continued only until the shipyards and plants were well-supplied, then classes were cut back and finally discontinued.

Santa Rosans proved as welcoming to the "fly-boys" as they had been to the infantry. Some of the town's big, old homes were converted to guest houses to accommodate the families of these pilots who came from all over the United States. Apartments were built over garages and in backyards. Everyone wanted to help make the servicemen comfortable.

The Hospitality House at 530 Third Street (located in the J.H. Williams Building which had previously been a lodge hall for Woodmen of the World and several other fraternal organizations) opened in September of '42 with more than 500 soldiers, sailors, and civilians at the dedication dance. It was a real community effort, financed by the United Service Organizations (USO) and the Works Progress Administration (WPA) and directed by the Chamber of Commerce with Dr. C.A. Sawyer, head of the chamber's defense recreation committee, as general chairman. Mary (Mrs. William) Berger was the hostess. Mrs. Ellsworth Barnett was "cookie chairman", a title which made her responsible for the hundreds of cakes and pies as well as cookies which flowed into the center from the ovens of women eager to help, often in the names of their own sons and grandsons who were servicemen.

The list of organizations whose members had volunteered to work at the center included all of the town's churches, the American Legion and the Veterans of Foreign Wars auxiliaries, the B'nai B'rith, the PEO Sisterhood, the American Association of University Women, the Druids, the Ladies of the Moose, the Business and Professional Women, Pocahontas Lodge, and the Daughters of the American Revolution. The new center had a dance floor, a stage big enough for an orchestra or entertainment by home talent, a game room, a reading room, washrooms, and "a powder room for the use of girls at the dancing parties," the newspaper reported.

Just as it happened in the morale-boosting movies made during WWII, romances bloomed at Hospitality House and could be cited as one of the factors contributing to Santa Rosa's postwar population boom. Servicemen who met their wives there, like Warren Williamson, became the new residents. Sgt. Williamson of the 107th Cavalry, who came from a small town near Cleveland, met "Bootsie"

Berger, whose father owned a cigar store on Fourth Street, at the Hospitality House. They were married before he went overseas. Williamson never went back to Cleveland. At war's end he returned to Santa Rosa where he owned a photo processing company for many years.

The American Legion turned the Armory Hall upstairs over the ice cream parlor at Fourth and D streets into an amusement center for servicemen. Owen Sweeten, a Healdsburg man with experience as a musician and entertainer, was in charge of programs in which soldiers and sailors were invited to join the local talent. Admission was free, to officers and enlisted men alike; 350 young women from Sonoma County signed up for the privilege of entertaining the troops, strictly chaperoned; and Legionnaires asked that the men contribute 10 cents a dance to help pay the costs of keeping the rec hall open.

The Santa Rosa chapter of American Women's Volunteer Services, organized in the first week of the war, was spurred on by Mae (Mrs. Joseph) Grace. Among the organizers were Helen (Mrs. Leon) Reynaud, Virginia (Mrs. Tom) Grace, and Geraldine (Mrs. Juilliard) McDonald. The AWVS had a busy motor transport division which provided rides for soldiers from their camps to the recreation hall, from downtown to their base.

Headquarters for the AWVS was in the Santa Rosa Hotel and the police set aside several parking spaces at Fourth and B streets for the women and their cars. Later the AWVS brought wounded sailors from the hospital at Mare Island to Santa Rosa homes for dinner. They also worked in the Hospitality House and the canteen, a drop-in spot for servicemen, on Fourth Street in the old Butler-Winans Pharmacy, which already had a soda fountain. With the addition of a juke box and some of Santa Rosa's young ladies, the canteen became a welcome respite for the members of the armed forces. AWVS members joined other organizations in providing refreshments. Sandwiches for hungry servicemen, in a time of rationing, required creative recipes. Egg salad with peanuts was a favorite.[13]

The Santa Rosa unit of the American Women's Volunteer Service was formed by Mae (Mrs. Joseph P.) Grace at the start of the war. Above, from left to right, Irma (Mrs. Vernon) Garrett, Virginia (Mrs. Thomas) Grace, Betty (Mrs. Franklin) Mecham, Helen (Mrs. Leon) Reynaud, Anna (Mrs. Roe) Barrett, and Mary (Mrs. William) Berger.

The venerable Saturday Afternoon Club, whose membership was by invitation only, generally considered the "society women's" club, lent its clubhouse at Healdsburg Avenue and 10th Street to the Army for the duration and it became the Officers' Club. In return for the town's hospitality, military units staged parades down Fourth Street.

The town went all-out for its military visitors at Christmas 1943. "Santa Claus has discovered a military secret," the newspaper reported, "and passed it on to the civilian population in and near Santa Rosa. He has obtained the name of every serviceman stationed near there and has warned Christmas party committees not to forget anyone." Parties were given by Santa Rosa civic organizations and lodges at the fairgrounds, the airfield, and the Naval Air Station. Food and gifts for men stationed at Camp Sebastopol, the former Civilian Conservation Corps camp at the foot of O'Farrell Hill, and those standing guard duty at

Bodega Bay and Jenner were delivered by special committees.

The Saturday Afternoon Club made the Army STAR unit at SRJC its special project. Helen Comstock, the club's president, promised that her organization would see that every one of the soldiers stationed at the junior college had an invitation for Christmas dinner. With the cooperation of the entire membership, plus the SRJC Mother's Club and the faculty, the promise was kept. Neil Daniels, public relations representative for the college, also credited "the enthusiastic and hospitable feminine segment of the civilian student body" with making the soldiers feel at home. The Associated Women Students gave a Christmas party for the soldiers—dancing, skits, and homemade cookies and punch. The troops on his post, Daniels told the newspaper, think "Santa Rosa is OK."

Santa Rosa Army Air Field had a comfortable working relationship with the community. *The Post Script*, the base's weekly newspaper, was printed at the *Press Democrat* and carried information about Santa Rosa's movie theaters and sporting events. The 312th Fighter Control Squadron also published a mimeographed newspaper, appropriately called *Static*, for the 250 communications specialists in training.

Dances for enlisted men brought young women from Santa Rosa, Healdsburg, and`Sebastopol to the base gymnasium to dance to the music of orchestras made up of men from the regimental band at Hamilton and even a dance band from the Santa Rosa Naval Air Station. Convoys took enlisted men to dances and entertainments at Cloverdale and Healdsburg each month and to the regular dances at Santa Rosa's Hospitality House each week. Officers, of course, danced at the Officers' Club. For those men who hesitated to get on the dance floor, Mrs. Lucy George, a Santa Rosa dancing instructor, came to the base with half a dozen young women and taught weekly classes, which progressed, in the words of the base history, "with increasing interest and attendance."

People, eager to be good neighbors and to aid in the war effort, helped in whatever way they could. John Carlson, who lived on Wright Road, learned there was a shortage of fishing gear at the base for all the men who wanted to try their hand at a Russian River steelhead. He donated poles and tackle. The Healdsburg Country Club opened its golf course to the men of the base. The Healdsburg Kiwanis Club donated funds for furnishing the recreation room and were rewarded with a tour of the base. The base basketball team, the "Badgers," played teams from airfields at Chico, Salinas, and Hamilton, but the true rivalry, the game known as "The Bucket of Blood" game, was played against the crosstown Navy, in SRHS gym. Both teams had a complement of former college and even professional basketball players and the game was played to a packed house.

A radio show on KSRO, with a variety of talent from the base, originated at SRAAF every other week. Musicians and singers from the base visited local organizations, like the Kiwanis and the Elks. The Army fliers joined community activities such as dancing to touring big bands like Ray Eberle's (with his vocalist Kay Starr) at the Melody Bowl on the corner of Santa Rosa Avenue and Bennett Avenue. A pass would get them to the Russian River resort area, where Mirabel, Rio Nido, and the Grove in Guerneville all featured name bands in the "season."

The war years, despite gas rationing, brought even bigger crowds to dance the summer nights away along the river. Two Santa Rosans, Harry B. Fetch and W.E. Barber, bought Mirabel Resort near Forestville and turned it over to a hustling young insurance salesman named W.C. "Bob" Trowbridge to manage. Trowbridge turned the dance hall over to Fred Plante, who had been running the Melody Bowl. From '41 to '45, with the county crowded with servicemen, Mirabel became a contender for the patronage of the younger set, featuring performers such as Lionel Hampton, Duke Ellington, Stan Kenton, Hoagy Carmichael and his Teenagers (who played a full month at Mirabel), and

Carmen Cavallero. When Cavallero played, a young Petaluman named Al Cernik, who had been singing with Santa Rosa bandleader Ralph Rawson at the Melody Bowl, came to ask for a chance to sing. Cavallero liked the sound and Al Cernik changed his name to Guy Mitchell and went on tour with the band, scoring several hit records in the 1950s.

The river resorts were a young musician's paradise. Sonoma County's finest, like Rawson and Abbey Rasor, Clyde Arrowood on string bass, Ernie Layton and Harold Gantner and Russ Mays on sax, clarinetist Glen Blair, Leroy Jewett on drums, Fred Jennings, Ernie Curtis, Stan Isaacs, Mel Hein, Bob Evans, and Pete Rugulo, who would later enjoy a long Hollywood career as a composer, arranger, and musician for films, did their apprenticeship in house bands and weekday bands at the river resorts. Ironically, Santa Rosa's best known resident bandleader, Anson Weeks, whose "Let's Go Dancin' with Anson" was a San Francisco trademark, never did play the River, except to sit in on an occasional day off.[14]

A collapsed nose wheel stopped the progress of this P-39 on a runway of the Santa Rosa Army Air Field.

While the community was attempting to make the military personnel comfortable, people were ever mindful of the reason the bases were there. Civilians had only to look to the skies. In addition to the Cotati and Santa Rosa air bases, the relative proximity of Hamilton Field and Alameda Naval Air Station kept the skies over Sonoma County filled with airplanes—and danger. Army Air Corps fighters and Navy dive bombers crashed with uneasy frequency off the ends of the runways and in the orchards and fields of Sonoma County. The first may have been the one in September of 1942 when a Hamilton Field pilot on a routine training flight crashed his P-38, which then exploded in a pear orchard on the Andrieux Ranch south of Sonoma. Residents never quite became accustomed to the scream of Navy dive bombers, flying low in close formation over house and farm. Nor did the sight of a pair of the distinctive twin-tailed P-38s or the single engine P-39s

engaged in a simulated dogfight fail to produce apprehension in onlookers. Too frequently, those dogfights ended tragically. On one occasion one of the planes, looping and diving high in the sky west of town, failed to come out of its dive. It crashed in an orchard near Dutton Avenue as shoppers, businessmen, and schoolchildren watched in horror.[15]

As the war wore on and more battle-fatigued aircraft were returned to stateside bases to be used in training, the accidents seemed to become more frequent. War diaries of Alameda Naval Air Station show the first crash near Santa Rosa was July 22, 1943. In October of the same year a 1000 TBM crashed at Tomales Bay. In January of 1944 there was another plane lost at Tomales Bay and an SB2C crashed at Bodega Bay July 14. The newspaper's account of this crash was typical of the reports which were standard front-page fare in the war years: Headlined "Dive-Bomber Hits Coast Hilltop in Training Maneuvers," the story quoted eyewitnesses who said four planes engaged in training maneuvers dived into a cloud together. "Three zoomed out but the fourth struck an obscured hilltop along the coast."[16]

A Navy pilot was plucked out of a treetop near Elk on the Mendocino Coast in July of 1944. His safe, if precarious, landing was reported on the same page of the newspaper that brought news of a second Navy plane's fatal crash and the death of an Air Corps pilot from the Santa Rosa airdrome in a crash north of Point Arena. That same week two Navy men died when their dive bomber struck a hilltop near Bodega Bay and two Santa Rosa teenage girls were cited for bravery after pulling an Army pilot from his crashed and burning plane. In the three month period from January through March of 1945, when storms and winter fogs left little flying time, nine men were lost in Air Corps crashes.

For the Army Air Corps personnel at SRAAF, crashes and frightening near-misses were almost routine. This partial list from the base's narrative history for the winter months of 1945 does not include belly landings, doors that fell off in flight, wing tips lost in collisions with ducks, taxiing accidents, and damage caused when pilots accidentally shot the tow target off and ran into it.

19 January: Second Lt. Carpenter, at 32,000 feet, dove his P-38 into the ground near Santa Rosa Army Air Field. The accident was fatal to Lt. Carpenter. The plane was a total loss.

19 January: Second Lt. Kramer successfully bailed out just east of Petaluma because of fire in the right engine of his P-38. No injury resulted to the pilot, but the plane was a total loss.

29 January: Second Lt. Black bailed out of his P-38 about five miles northeast of Cloverdale because of fire in the right engine. No injury to the pilot but the plane was a complete loss.

29 January: First Lt. Tatum crash-landed a P-38 two miles southeast of the field after he had tried to go around on one engine. The pilot sustained minor injuries and shock. The plane was a total loss.

10 February: Second Lt. McDonald chopped throttle when engine cut out on take off. The plane ran off end of runway, causing total loss of plane. No injury to pilot.

12 February: Second Lt. Toise was killed and his plane was a total loss. The engine cut out on take off causing the plane to crash one mile south of the field.

12 February: First Lt. Young and crew (Staff Sgt. Myhre and Cpl. Wheeler) bailed out over the ocean when fire was discovered in the engine. The two crew members were lost. The pilot was picked up.

26 February: Flight Officer Hall dove into the ground from 22,000 feet resulting in death of pilot and complete loss of plane. Cause of the accident was undetermined.

23 March: Capt. Armstrong and First Lt. Wooldridge crashed in Aeronica-65. Both pilot and passenger were killed. Plane was total loss.

24 March: Capt. Capps and Pvt. Riley in BT-18 were lost while on a search mission.

These deaths brought war even closer to Santa Rosa. Many of the fliers' wives, mindful of the hazardous duty,

P-38s were used for combat training by the Army Air Corps at Santa Rosa.

—*Harrison Rued Collection*

followed their husbands to Santa Rosa, sharing living quarters with Santa Rosans who opened their homes to the temporary residents. In many cases the rented room was that of the homeowner's own son, gone to war.

Other grim reminders were the ceremonies on the base to present medals to the families of Air Corps soldiers who had been killed or taken prisoners of war. Joseph Matheu of Maple Street accepted an air medal on behalf of his son, Lieutenant Daniel Matheu, who flew bomber missions over Europe before being taken prisoner by the Germans. Mary Guenza of Grange Road received an air medal for her son, Lieutenant Alfred Guenza, killed in the Middle East Theater.

Not all the soldiers stationed in Sonoma County during World War II were men. Two Rock Ranch, a radio interception base between Petaluma and the coast, was the duty post for forty-two members of the Women's Army Corps from 1943 until the war ended. The radio operators, whose job it was to monitor Japanese radio messages, were WACs who came to Petaluma from a training center in Kansas City, Missouri. One of the WACs, Ann Underkofler Hart, would later recall that she was on duty the day the atom bomb was dropped on Hiroshima. She didn't understand why she couldn't pick up a frequency she usually monitored. "I kept wondering," she recalled, "'Why doesn't this guy come on?' I found out why the next day."[17]

Two Rock, which had a full complement of male soldiers as well as the WACs, was one of two monitoring stations in Sonoma County. The National Security Agency's need to hear what the Chinese, Russians, and Indo-Chinese, as well as the Japanese, were saying among themselves, brought Army Intelligence and Signal Corps personnel to Two Rock in 1942. The Navy built their own receiving station on Skaggs Island in the southeastern corner of the county.

Soldiers and sailors cut a wide swath through Santa Rosa's social life. Les Estes came to town with the 74th

—Crevelli Family Collection

John Crevelli, age 15, on his authorized Western Union delivery bicycle at the corner of Third and Davis streets. The Crevelli family lived on Davis near Third, before the 101 freeway was built.

The black-bordered telegram was what families of servicemen feared most in the war years. John Crevelli was a ninth-grader at Santa Rosa High School, working as a Western Union messenger boy in 1944. He has painful memories of this method used by the military of notifying the next of kin.

"I delivered a number of tragic telegrams," Crevelli would later write, "but one in particular has been stuck, vividly, in my mind. Both the scene and the sounds haunt me. I had offered to work the morning of a major holiday, either Thanksgiving or Christmas, I can't remember which one it was. But that morning, about 11 o'clock, Mr. Stefani, the office manager, told me: 'Here's a real bad one to deliver on B Street.'

"So I knew the contents of the telegram as I parked my bike and walked into the apartment building at 616 B Street. Though I was only 14 years old, I remember thinking how cruel it was for the government to send such a telegram on a holiday. Before the apartment door on the second floor, I hesitated, listening to the sounds of what must have been a family gathering within, of people preparing for a holiday meal.

"The gentleman who came to the door was dressed as if he might have just come from church. He smiled when he saw me and announced to the people in the room, 'It's a telegram.' To me he said, 'Nobody should be working on this day.' Then he thrust his hand into his pants pocket and pulled out some change. In the spirit of the holiday, he gave me a 75-cent tip. That was big money to a fourteen-year-old in those days. I blurted out my 'Thank you' as he closed the door.

"I remained standing outside that closed door, confused thoughts flying through my mind. I felt guilty. I should not have taken the tip. I should have said, 'I'm sorry.' But I was only fourteen and what does a fourteen-year-old know of the protocol surrounding death? While I stood there, confused, from within the room I heard a woman scream 'Oh, no!' and the kind of crying that, thankfully, I have heard only a very few times in the ensuing forty-seven years.... The strongest argument against war I have ever heard was in the cry of that woman behind the closed door."[18]

Field Artillery and spent six weeks at Camp Wikiup in the spring of '42. Les's company had begun training at Fort Ord before Pearl Harbor, but it had been sent to Arizona immediately after the attack, before being assigned to Santa Rosa. The artillery, like the infantry, was assigned to guard powerhouses, bridges, and dams in the area. Estes remembers the stay in Santa Rosa "like a summer vacation."

He and his fellow soldiers went to Lena's to dance and to "a Chinese restaurant [Twin Dragons] where there was a blonde waitress." After six weeks at Wikiup, Estes' battalion went to Camp Heidle near Pt. Reyes Station and then to San Rafael, where it was relieved of its horses and converted to a motorized 105mm howitzer battalion. In the fall the battery was sent to Camp Roberts, then to Oklahoma, Texas, Louisiana, New York, and Europe.[19]

Lena's, the old Battaglia Hotel, had enlarged in the mid-'30s when Lena Bonfigli, a widow with three sons, bought the Torino Hotel property next door and expanded into the *bocce* alley. She put stucco on the old Italian hotel, added a dance floor, hired a trio, and opened for business in 1935. When the war came to Santa Rosa, Lena's was the town's only nightclub. "When the Navy was in town," Lena's son Alvin "Kewpie" Bonfigli recalled, "there would be sailors sleeping five deep in rooms upstairs." The dive bomber pilots wrote "Lena's Special" on their target bombs and "Mama Lena" got regular letters from "her boys" overseas.[20]

The Twin Dragons, Santa Rosa's most elaborate Chinese restaurant and bar, owned by Bertha and George Yee, was another favorite of the servicemen. Located at

Above, left, a group of "Rosie the Riveters," actually welders at Sausalito's Marinship yards. At far right, top row is Nell Codding. The wartime photo of the courthouse, at lower left, shows the airplane spotters' watchtower on the roof.

On the page at right, a Navy flier poses with the bomb his crew named after Lena Bonfigli, proprietor of their favorite Santa Rosa hangout. And Lena herself, standing fifth from left, poses with the sailors she called "my boys."

Third and D streets, it was new, having opened the first week of the war. The grand opening party, in fact, was held during a blackout. The Topaz Room, built during the war by Theron "Roy" Hedgpeth, was the town's fancy restaurant. The carpeted interior, the ceilings draped with parachute silk, the long mahogany bar, the crystal chandeliers: All were promises of an urbanity and sophistication the old farm town had not known before. Hedgpeth enhanced this rich image with a portion of his wife's valuable collection of fine china and crystal, displaying the Venetian glass and Dresden figurines in show cases behind the leather banquettes. This splendor was off limits to enlisted men. Only officers dined at the Topaz Room. There were other places servicemen did not go, but for other reasons. Military police stood guard at each end of the two-block street called Roberts Avenue connecting Third Street and Sebastopol Road west of the railroad tracks. Houses of prostitution plus some of the enterprising clientele of Mick's, a bar down the street, were considered harmful to the war effort.

War had altered the life of the town. Just as the old cannon on the courthouse lawn was shipped off as scrap metal to be melted down to make new weapons, so did the citizens "retool" for the new challenge. Civilians took SRJC's defense work classes and became defense workers. The gray Navy buses that carried workers to and from Mare Island became familiar sights. Civilians carpooled to Hamilton Field in Ignacio to work as airplane mechanics or in armaments, the sheet metal shops, and the fabric shops.

Others worked at Marinship, the shipyard on Richardson Bay at the north end of the fishing village of Sausalito where Bechtel Corporation was building ships named for famous Californians. The announcement that they would name ships for Marin historical figures William Richardson, William Kent, and John Muir prompted Clyde Edmondson, general manager of the Redwood Empire Association, to request that Bechtel so honor Sonoma

County's favorite sons—Luther Burbank, Mariano Vallejo and Jack London.[21] (Bechtel apparently ran out of ships before the trio of local heroes could be so honored.)

Those who didn't have a defense job also were doing their part. Civilian Defense organized a band of aircraft spotters who took turns standing watch over the skies in specially constructed towers with telephones and identification charts. Campaigns to sell war bonds began almost immediately after Pearl Harbor. In September of '42 a special showing of the sentimental wartime favorite film *Mrs. Miniver* at the California Theater raised nearly $50,000 for the war effort as Santa Rosa residents dug deep in the name of patriotism. A $50 bond bought a loge seat (Dr. John Fowlie, a Santa Rosa physician, made the news columns for buying the first four "high-priced" seats), a $25 bond, general admission. Banker Harold Bostock, chairman of the city's war-finance committee, ran successful War Loan campaigns in Santa Rosa. In the fall of 1943, Santa Rosans

—*Bonfigli Family Collection*

—*Bonfigli Family Collection*

Foremost among the "old soldiers" who answered the call to World War II was Major Burton Cochrane. Cochrane was a reserve officer who had received his commission before World War I, leaving Santa Rosa as a corporal and returning as a lieutenant. After the war he continued to serve as an officer in the Army Reserve, taking time from his accounting work and, later, his position at the Exchange Bank to attend training sessions.

When World War II began Cochrane was fifty years old. He went immediately to his superior officer and volunteered for active duty. He was told, his family

recalled, that "the Army has no need for decrepit old men of fifty." He returned to Santa Rosa, disgruntled but accepting. In June of 1942 the Army apparently changed its mind about Cochrane. They called him to active duty. And, more surprising to a man who had never even been a passenger in an airplane, they assigned him to the Air Corps.

Major Cochrane was part of an A-20 light bomber squadron that landed in Casablanca, participated in the invasion of Italy, helped to liberate France, and returned to Italy where, in 1944, columnist Ernie Pyle, the most celebrated journalist of WWII, caught up with him.

In his syndicated column of March 16, 1944, Pyle wrote one of his famous front-line sketches about Cochrane, a profile that was later published as part of Pyle's book, *Brave Men*.

"Major Burt Cochrane is executive officer of the squadron with which I've been living. He is not a flying man, but he takes most of the onerous duties off the shoulders of the squadron commander who is always a flying man.

"Major Cochrane is the perfect example of a man going all-out for his country. He doesn't want to be over here at all. He is fifty-five and a grandfather. But he fought through the last war, kept his commission in the reserve, and just couldn't picture himself not being in this one. He has been away from home three years.

"In civilian life, Major Cochrane is what you might call a gentleman cattle raiser. He owns about 300 acres in the beautiful rolling country north of San Francisco, not far from Jack London's famous "Valley of the Moon." The nearest town is Kenwood.

"He turns out about seventy-five head of beef cattle a year, has a lovely home, beautiful riding horses and lives an almost Utopian life. He left the city eight years ago and said he never knew what happiness was until he got out into the hills.

"Major Cochrane is quiet and courteous. Enlisted men and officers both like and respect him. He is so soldierly that he continually says 'Sir' even to me, although I'm a civilian and much younger than he."

lent the government $2,415,935—$112.75 in bonds and stamps for every man, woman, and child in town, $7.75 more than the national average. The money was judged to be enough to buy 2,945 "blockbuster" bombs.[22]

The triumphant return from Hollywood of Edna May Wonacott, the twelve-year-old Santa Rosa girl "discovered" and cast in Alfred Hitchcock's *Shadow of a Doubt*, was another fund-raising opportunity. The civic reception for the Fremont School student became a benefit when organizers of "Edna May Day" decreed that the courthouse plaza gathering would be a unique sort of war bond rally. Edna May, the daughter of a Santa Rosa grocer, Eley Wonacott, set the stage when she told Santa Rosa newspaper reporters she planned to buy war bonds with her first paycheck and that she would like to buy them in Santa Rosa. Her arrival in town was heralded by the Army Band. She was met by her school class, Mayor Ernest Eymann, and the war bond sales committee (ready to take her money) and a film crew from Universal Studio who planned to use the footage to promote the film. The highest bond bidder received a bound copy of Thornton Wilder's movie script autographed by the cast and crew. Another bond auction prize was a dress worn by actress Teresa Wright in the movie.

Despite the war, the Sonoma County Fair opened on the Labor Day weekend in '42 after fair president Joe Grace received permission from government and military officials to go on as planned before Pearl Harbor. The fair proved to be a splendid fund-raising vehicle for war-related enterprises. Record crowds attended, made to feel virtuous for doing so as horses raced for war bond purses. Ten days after the fair closed, a special three-day race meet, an unusual request granted by the State Racing Commission, was sponsored by United Service Organizations volunteers who, witnessing the success of the fair, planned the meet to raise money for the Hospitality House.

The Santa Rosa chapter of the Red Cross, which had remained active in disaster aid since it was organized in

World War I, was ready with volunteer ambulance drivers and first aid workers when the county defense committee met on the day of Pearl Harbor. The Santa Rosa American Women's Volunteer Service chapter took training classes. They learned first aid at Santa Rosa High School from Dr. Fowlie and automobile repair from Hayes Hunter in the high school auto shop. They studied their government-issued booklets and gave lectures in school classes and women's clubs on how to disarm an incendiary bomb.[23]

In the spring of 1942, Santa Rosa High School students staged a walkout to protest the firing of a favorite English and journalism teacher, Mary Frances McKinney, who was dismissed by the Board of Education when it became known that she was married to a Navy pilot. It was an unwritten rule, not only in Santa Rosa but in many school districts, that untenured female teachers had to be unmarried. If they became engaged before they had taught three years or more in the system, it was expected they would resign. Miss McKinney, who was actually Mrs. Dewitt Trewitt, needed the job, so when she interviewed for the position she neglected to say that she was a newlywed whose husband was in the Pacific. Hers was a badly kept secret. As adviser to the student newspaper, *The Santa Rosan*, "Petie," as she was known, worked closely with the students. There was even an oblique reference in one edition of the newspaper to her husband, referred to as "the admiral." When the administration took action, the students rallied to her cause.

Students left classes to gather on the lawn and steps of the school, and their leaders commissioned a sound-truck from a sympathetic businessman to broadcast throughout the town their outrage over the firing. The students were heard at a meeting of the school board. McKinney's dismissal was deferred, but she resolved the matter herself by submitting her resignation, effective at the end of the school year.

Wartime restrictions ranged from nuisance to outrage. The wartime law which prohibited non-citizens from visits to the sea coast chafed Santa Rosa fishermen whose birth records were lost when the courthouse was destroyed in the 1906 earthquake. In some cases, baptismal certificates sufficed to assure military officials of their loyalty. Others simply forswore salmon and crab for the duration.

There were more serious "nuisances." Wars create enemies and government security was tight. In Petaluma, a German-American businessman, known to be active in American Nazi affairs, was arrested. The county's large Italian population was affected by wartime strictures. The fact that Mussolini's Italy had sided with Hitler in the war in Europe made life difficult for those of Sonoma County's Italian immigrants who were not citizens. Under wartime alien laws they could not own a gun, not even for duck

A Vern Silvershield photograph of a war bond rally in front of the courthouse.

—*Jimmie FitzGerald Collection*

The Japanese American Citizens League marches proudly in the 1941 Sonoma County Fair Parade.

—Silvershield Family Collection

hunting. They were limited to travel within a certain radius of their homes, which often prevented them from working in the fruit and hop harvests, where labor was badly needed. The coastline prohibition meant that Highway 1 was the boundary they could not cross. In some coastal towns, this meant they could not conduct such routine business as visiting the post office or buying groceries. But the travail of the resident Italians was nothing compared to the fate of the Japanese-Americans.

Some Japanese were seized in the first weeks of the war, at the height of the Pacific Coast panic. Santa Rosa grocer Yoshio Nagase, whose store was on Second Street, was taken by the FBI on December 8, 1941. Kiyoshi Akutagawa was fixing the roof when they came to arrest him. One of the Taniguchi brothers was working in his orchard. His family would not have known he was gone if a friend hadn't seen him at the police station and managed to get him a change of clothes before he was taken to San

Francisco. Iwazo Hamamoto, owner of the Asahi Grocery which was then in Sebastopol, was gone before his eldest son, George, could get home from the orchard he was pruning, even though friends rushed to tell him the FBI was taking his father. When George, who had just turned eighteen, rushed into his family home he found that the lawmen had searched the house and ripped apart a crystal radio set he had built as a Boy Scout project, mistaking it for a transmitter.

The seizure of Japan-born residents that occurred simultaneously all over California was the first step in an elaborate program developed by the government for dealing with the supposed threat afforded by this alien presence on the Pacific Coast. The second step, the posting of Executive Order #9066, occurred in February of 1942. In what has since been characterized as a "land grab" move on the part of Caucasians in the Central Valley who wanted property controlled by Japanese farmers and who played upon the fears caused by the attack on Pearl Harbor, all persons of Japanese descent were ordered to leave the Pacific Coast. They had the option of moving inland on their own. If they could not, they would be relocated inland by the government.

It was a hard call for the Japanese-Americans in Sonoma County. George Hamamoto, left as the head of his family, remembered: "People began to make plans to move themselves, to go to Idaho or somewhere.... The ranchers who had trucks began getting them ready, putting shelters on them, and stoves. We didn't have a truck. We had a '36 Ford V-8, so I went out and bought a cattle trailer, changed the tires and tried to clean it up so we could live in it—my mother, my five brothers and sisters. I remember my uncle asking me, 'Where you gonna go? What will you do?'"[24]

Soon enough the realization that self-relocation posed serious problems slowed the travel plans. There was a Japanese community hall near Barlow's orchards in Sebastopol where the Japanese people gathered daily to discuss the best way to proceed. The Japanese American Citizens League, a fledgling organization, took a stand. Acknowledging the anti-Japanese feeling on the coast, the JACL counseled cooperation with authorities in a mass relocation program.

Thus, Sonoma County's Japanese-American families left on the train on a Saturday and a Sunday morning in May, bound for Merced, where the fairgrounds had been converted to a staging area.[25] Caroline Van Rensselaer, a recent graduate of Santa Rosa High School, was home from college that weekend. Her mother Catherine Van Rensselaer McCanse was a social worker who had been enlisted to help with the Japanese evacuation. She invited her daughter to join her, suggesting that she should witness what would be an historic event. Many years later, Van Rensselaer (married name, Ramberg) would write of that morning.

The Santa Rosa railroad depot, where the Japanese gathered for relocation. Note the blackout hood on the engine's headlight—a wartime measure.

—*Fred Stindt Collection, NWPRR Historical Society*

303

"The sleepy depot down at the end of Fourth Street was awake with action that morning. Hundreds of distraught people seethed around the parking area. Families loaded down with bedrolls and suitcases shoved through the crowd. They clung together, fearing to become separated—another worry added to the trauma of being forced to leave their homes.

"My mother stood on the sidewalk with her clipboard among the throng, struggling to understand Japanese names—Hasegawa, Ijichi, Furuji—as the people reported for assignment. Military police, fully armed and dressed for battle, politely directed the families to designated railway cars. There was no shouting. No one was prodded with a rifle barrel.

"To me, the mass of people was just a sea of anxious Orientals, until suddenly there was a face I knew. It was Fuji Murakami, a girl I had known and liked in high school, a rival in Latin, a classmate in dancing. I had always thought of her as 'one of us.' It was impossible to visualize her as a member of a sinister fifth column bent on sabotaging military installations. Then it struck me that all these people were no different than Fuji."[26]

An estimated 1,000 Japanese were evacuated from Sonoma that spring.[27] The day before the evacuation began Henry Shimizu, president of the Japanese American Citizens League, delivered a letter to the editor of the newspaper thanking Sonoma County residents "for the tolerance with which you have treated us." Shimizu wrote, "We are going into temporary exile, short I hope, with a smile, knowing that in this way we may be taking part in the defense of our country.... I hope to return to find all of you in health and prosperity."[28]

There was only one voice raised in protest to the evacuation, that of Erwin Penry, whose letter to the editor appeared two days after the Japanese left: "I believe the day will come when most people will consider the indiscriminate forced evacuation of American citizens who happen to be of Japanese lineage as one of the darkest blots on the history of the United States."[29]

Meanwhile, Sonoma County's Japanese residents were being "processed." Iwazo Hamamoto, who had been taken from his Sebastopol home by the FBI on December 8, 1941, rejoined his family at the staging area in Merced. (Others, like Mr. Akutagawa, were not reunited with their families until the end of the war was in sight.) There were other staging areas. San Francisco's Japanese went to Tanforan racetrack in San Bruno. Los Angeles's Japanese to Santa Anita racetrack. It was late September before they were moved out of the staging areas to hastily constructed government camps in Arizona, Colorado, Wyoming—ten in

At left, a truckload of Sonoma County Japanese men meet the train that would take them, eventually, to a camp in Colorado. In the photo at upper left, Martha Kameoka, at right, whose family lived in Petaluma, poses with a playmate outside the family's living quarters at Camp Amache.

all. Sonoma County people went to Camp Amache near the Colorado desert town of Granada.

Memories of Camp Amache are heavily weighted toward the dust, the cactus, and the rattlesnakes. The Japanese lived in barracks—families in one large room—and ate in mess halls. Washrooms, showers, and latrines were shared in a military manner. Despite barbwire and a guard tower, the families did create something of a homelike atmosphere. They hung curtains and planted trees and flowers, carrying water in buckets from the laundry room. Many of the young men volunteered for military service. Others were drafted. Many were assigned to military intelligence units, a fact considered ironic by their families who had been uprooted from their homes and farms and businesses and incarcerated because they were "dangerous." Several joined the famous 442nd Regiment, the most decorated fighting unit of World War II. Three Sonoma County men, Leo Kikuchi, Joe Yasuda, and Peter Masuoka, died in Italy with the 442nd.[30]

Relocation was particularly hard on the older men. Many came out of camp at the end of the war broken in body or in spirit, unable to recover the life they had lost. There is evidence that Sonoma County's relocated citizens fared somewhat better at the hands of their Caucasian neighbors back home than people from other areas. Most were able to reclaim the property they had left. In many instances neighbors and friends tended orchards and mended fences in the years they were away. The Murakami family had a chicken ranch in the Wright District just west of Santa Rosa. Cecil Rowe, who owned a service station and auto court north of the junior college, watched over their ranch in their absence. In some cases, feed companies looked after the chicken farmers' property, knowing they were good customers and would be good customers again when they returned.

Despite the FBI "raids" at the start of the war, Sonoma County law enforcement generally stood on the side of the Japanese-Americans, knowing them to be good citizens. Undersheriff Tom Money was in charge of labeling and storing "seized" property, kept safely until their return. Sheriff Harry Patteson personally promised members of Enmanji Buddhist Temple that no harm would come to their building while they were gone. Despite a couple of abortive arson attempts on the Sebastopol structure, which stood as a symbol of Japanese culture, Patteson was as good as his word.

––––––––––

It was nearly the end of the war when the government heeded the pleas of Sonoma County growers for help in the harvests. Italian prisoners of war, encamped at Benicia, were brought to work in the fields. But the needs were more than the government could supply and, in 1944, a German prisoner-of-war camp was established in the middle of the hop fields and prune orchards north of Santa Rosa. Military records indicate there were 6,000 war prisoners working as agricultural laborers in Northern California in 1944-1946. According to the rules of the Geneva Convention, prisoners of war could be paid no more than 80 cents per day for their labor. But American labor laws

––––––––––

Corporal Don Sullivan, the company clerk at the German prison camp, poses for a photo to send home to his family, marking his late-war assignment.

—*Don Sullivan Collection*

Horst Liewald, a German soldier, was captured in France and sent to Camp Windsor. After the war he returned to the United States and made his home in Santa Rosa. Below, the barbed wire and tent cabins of Camp Windsor.

prohibited the growers from paying less than the prevailing wage. The difference in what the government received for the men's labor and the 80 cents per day they paid out, put some $4 million in the U.S. Treasury in those three harvest periods.

Camp Windsor, the government's farm labor camp on Windsor River Road, was the site selected as the Sonoma County "branch" of the POW program run from Camp Beale in Marysville.31 The same utilitarian structures—lavatories, showers, dining hall, and recreation hall, and the floors and frames for tent cabins—built for migrant workers by the Farm Security Administration in 1937, the camp already had its own wells and septic system. It would need only a few strands of barbwire and an MP at the gate to make it a prison camp.

Walter Reuger, a Swiss native who spoke German, was hired by the growers as their business manager. Ranchers who had contracted with the government for prisoner labor had only to call Reuger's office a day ahead with a request, and trucks carrying the workers, large black PW's stenciled on the backs of their shirts, would arrive for work the next

morning. Earl Osborn, then vice principal of Healdsburg High School, worked the summer of '44 as Reuger's assistant, answering the phones, making up the work lists, and writing the reports to Camp Beale. The other half of the office was camp headquarters—one captain, several lieutenants, and half a dozen corporals who were the company clerks. The rest of the enlisted men were guards, accompanying the prisoners to their work places.32 Except for this handful of military personnel, Camp Windsor was run by the prisoners themselves. They cooked, cleaned, and attended to the carpentry and plumbing chores. They also ran the canteen where cigarettes, soap, razor blades, and sundries could be purchased with credits earned by the workers. Germans who spoke English became official interpreters while orders and assignments were posted in both languages.33 There were 1,500 prisoners that first summer, Osborn recalled, "and it wasn't enough. We didn't have near enough to meet the demand when the hop ranchers started calling for 300 or so at a time."

The first group sent down from Camp Beale were members of Field Marshal Erwin Rommel's proud Afrika Corps, captured in the desert campaign. The second group, mostly naval men from captured U-boats, were termed a "godsend" by the growers, one of whom remembers them as "able-bodied, intelligent young men" who were willing to learn the work of hop yard and orchard. They dug potatoes near the coast. They picked apples in Sebastopol and prunes in Santa Rosa and Healdsburg. They were supplemented at the end of the war by soldiers captured in Europe after the American invasion on D-Day. Horst Liewald was one of these.

Liewald was a veteran of the Russian front, captured in France in March of 1945. He was twenty-three years old when he arrived in the United States with a boatload of prisoners, docking in New York Harbor, ironically, on VE day, the day the war ended in Europe. He was sent first to Arizona and then transferred to Camp Windsor. He was assigned to pick hops on the Chester Frost ranch near

Healdsburg and became friends with rancher Frost. His memories of his American "prison" are not terrible. Happy to be out of the war, he found the camp a much pleasanter place than the German-Russian battle lines. Security was loose. Liewald remembers that military personnel at the camp were "practically non-existent." There were less than fifteen soldiers for a POW population of no more than 300 men. If the work parties were twenty men or less, no guard went to the fields with them. If it were a large group, a guard went along.

One of the favorite guards, Liewald said, was a private named Charlie who had a girlfriend in Windsor and spent more time with her than he did with his prisoners. One of Liewald's favorite Camp Windsor memories is of the day Charlie hung his rifle, his ammo belt, and his canteen on a prune tree limb and went off to see his girl. When the day's work was done, the POWs looked for Charlie for nearly an hour and, when the trucks came to pick them up, they tossed his gear into the truck and took it back to camp. Charlie claimed it the next morning.

Part of the fun of a soccer game at the camp was kicking the ball over the fence so a prisoner could climb the three sagging strands of barbwire and enjoy a few moments of "freedom" as he recovered the ball. Escape was unlikely, with a continent, an ocean, and at least one Allied nation between the prisoners and their homes. Two prisoners did get as far as Dillon Beach, where they were discovered in the barnyard on Walter Lawson's ranch. Nita Lawson remembered that her husband hailed a passing Coast Guard petty officer who borrowed Lawson's deer rifle and went looking for the escapees. "They gave up very willingly," said Mrs. Lawson. "They were so hungry—and one was so young that my heart melted. I wanted to feed them, but I was not permitted to. A lieutenant was called and came for them. He received quite a 'write-up' concerning his courage. The petty officer was not mentioned. They were trying to reach San Francisco where one had an uncle living. They hoped to board a ship for South America."[34]

The Germans were a familiar sight around the county. They sang as they were driven to their work and back in Army trucks. Before the war ended, they often gave the Hitler salute as they passed through a town. Small boys, standing beside the roadway as they passed, would mock them with a derisive imitation of their "Heil Hitler."

While fraternization between the prisoners and either military personnel or civilians was strictly forbidden, it did occur. The growers, grateful to have good help, often supplied cold drinks and cookies, although government rules prohibited such treats. They also kept the mess hall filled with Gravenstein apples in season and befriended many of the Germans. Liewald's friendship with grower Frost led the Healdsburg rancher to sponsor him when he returned to the United States in 1952 and applied for citizenship. Liewald lived in Santa Rosa for ten years, long enough for his son to graduate from Santa Rosa High School, before his job with an oil company took him to Oregon.[35]

———

Wartime in Santa Rosa meant the addition of knitting to the curriculum in Santa Rosa's elementary schools, the skill being intended to give children something to keep them from getting restless during blackouts and air-raid alerts. It meant the addition of meteorology, air navigation, principles of flight, and radio communication to the curriculum of the county schools. "A must for the air age," is what the county's superintendent of schools, Edwin Kent, called these classes.

In Santa Rosa High School's manual skills classes war meant construction of several hundred redwood boxes to be affixed to the city's lamp posts and the running boards of cars to hold first aid supplies. It meant parents reading to the children from the newspaper's careful instructions about unexploded bombs. It meant a special first aid class taught by the Ursuline nuns, and it meant practicing putting on gas masks.

The newspapers reminded Santa Rosans that two pounds of leftover cooking fat would provide enough glycerine for five anti-tank shells, that sixty empty toothpaste tubes had enough tin for all the electrical connections in a Flying Fortress, that a ton of waste paper would make 150 shell containers, that the Native Sons Lodge was collecting scrap iron in the city corporation yard at the DeTurk round barn on Donohue Street, and, always, that "The slip of a lip could sink a ship," and "Uncle Sam wants YOU!"

Wartime meant "Meatless Tuedays"; Victory Gardens in the backyards; saving your sugar stamps for Christmas baking; putting cars on blocks for the "duration"; and coloring the oleomargarine, which everyone called "Nucoa" for the most popular brand, with a packet of yellow food dye to make it look like butter. It meant knitting literally miles of regulation khaki yarn into caps and coldweather masks and gloves for the troops in the Aleutians.

For children, it meant maintaining absolute silence during news broadcasts, carefully peeling the tinfoil from gum wrappers and saving it in a giant ball to be compared, proudly, with the work of classmates. It meant learning the insignias—which stars and bars and stripes meant what ranks. It meant poring over *LIFE* magazine, and waving your arm off at passing troop convoys, wondering to what foreign place, never before heard of, the men were bound.

In 1944 the news from the front line became generally more cheerful, but the Bay Area suffered a frightful scare when, on a fine summer night in July, ammunition ships anchored at Port Chicago in Contra Costa County exploded. The blasts, which damaged the town of Port Chicago and killed more than 300 Navy men, Merchant Marines, and civilian workers, rocked residents from their beds in Santa Rosa and sent doctors, nurses, an ambulance, and two members of the Sonoma County War and Disaster Relief Council rushing to the scene.[36] The Port Chicago disaster was the worst munitions blast in North America since the Halifax, Nova Scotia, explosions of 1917. In the Navy's war diary for the Alameda base, there is an entry at 2225 hours, a call from a Lt. Snedeker who "reported a plane dropping a live bomb near his home." The explosion, the lieutenant said, "nearly blew him out of bed." A few minutes later a second explosion was reported by the base tower. Then the San Francisco radio stations began broadcasting the news from Port Chicago. Believed to be the work of saboteurs, the Port Chicago explosion may have been as close as the war came to the Bay Area.

There was a flurry of excitement in Santa Rosa in July of 1944 over word of the death of Germany's Field Marshal Erwin Rommel. First reports from the wire services indicated that Rommel had been killed when his staff car was strafed by a U.S. Army Air Corps plane. The gunner who made the "kill," the stories said, was a Santa Rosa resident named Harold Miller. The news that the reports were in error came later. Rommel was injured but not killed in the attack. And Miller was not the gunner.

The war in Europe ended on May 7, 1945. In Santa Rosa a firetruck drove up and down the city streets at 7:30 in the morning, draped with a banner announcing "GERMANY HAS SURRENDERED!" It was a Monday morning, a day the *Press Democrat* did not usually publish, but reporters, editors, printers, and pressmen rushed to the empty office and within an hour there were newsboys on the streets hollering "EXTRA! EXTRA! War in Europe over!" and Santa Rosans, off to store and office, could read all about it.

Welder Ras Bjornstad and his partner Bob Mitchell put an air compressor on their truck and, with an improvised gong, paraded through the downtown. Apart from this impromptu act of jubilation, there were no special celebrations. The *Press Democrat* was ready with special ads it had been holding for the occasion and regular advertising was replaced by giant victory V's, caricatures of a humiliated Hitler, and Norman Rockwell-like artwork heralding the return of the American soldier. But, apart from church services of thanksgiving, there were no scheduled festivities. There had been agreement among businessmen the previous week that the city would honor President Truman's request that rejoicing await the Japanese defeat.

That news came on the morning of August 14th. After four anguished years Santa Rosans were ready to celebrate. People poured into the streets, some shouting for joy, many in tears. Stores closed, stationery stockrooms were raided for streamers and confetti, and office workers emptied their wastebaskets into the streets as horns blared and sirens screamed. The city's firetrucks, draped with flags, roared through the downtown streets as cars, motorcyles, and bicycles fell in behind. Santa Rosans had dashed for the nearest liquor store to stock up the day before when the government, announcing that surrender was imminent, ruled that all liquor sales would be suspended for twenty-four hours after the official word.[37] They were ready to celebrate.

Unlike the larger cities, where VJ Day celebrations of the victory over Japan got out of hand, Santa Rosa's party was not marred by violence. In San Francisco, eleven people died and 648 were injured in the downtown "peace riot," and the Navy had to cancel all liberties and recall sailors to their stations to restore order. The celebrations everywhere, however, were a combination of joy and grief. The *Press Democrat* writer, recounting the events of August 14, wrote:

"Weeping mothers, many of them wives or mothers of servicemen in the Pacific, stood in the doorways and offered their thanks to God. Reporters rushed to the center of activity, recognized several mothers who in recent months had received those tragic telegrams from the War Department—'We regret to inform you that your son was killed....!' Tears streamed down their cheeks as they mingled with the milling throngs—grief-stricken by their own losses and thankful along with the rest that the lives of other sons had been spared."[38]

All attempts to organize the celebration failed miserably. Father Henry Raters of St. Rose's Catholic Church and most of the town's Protestant ministers tried to lead a thanksgiving service from the steps of the courthouse but could not make themselves heard over the sirens, horns, automobile backfires, and noise of thousands of firecrackers which had surfaced immediately and mysteriously, after being banned for the duration. Chamber of Commerce officials and Himmie Jacobs, Santa Rosa's perennial parade marshal, tried to assemble the horn-honkers and carloads of shouting, singing young people into a proper procession but they quickly gave up and scheduled a victory parade for the following afternoon.

"IT WON'T BE LONG NOW, RAGS"

SAARE RADIO & Appliance Shop

12 Mendocino Avenue   Santa Rosa   Phone 12

—Press Democrat Collection

WAR IN PACIFIC OVER!

THE PRESS DEMOCRAT

The Weather

Clear Wednesday and Thursday but with fog on the coast; little change in temperature; moderate to fresh northwesterly wind on coast.

Rainfall: seasonal, .00; normal .06 of an inch.

EIGHTY-NINTH YEAR—NUMBER 190   SANTA ROSA, CALIFORNIA, WEDNESDAY, AUGUST 15, 1945   TWO SECTIONS—FOURTEEN PAGES

ENTIRE NATION GOES WILD AS JAPAN'S SURRENDER ENDS WAR

Old Home Town Whoops 'Er Up--What a Day, What a Night!

SANTA ROSA'S downtown area seemed suddenly turned topsy-turvy yesterday, converted in a twinkling of an eye from a normal little business city into a jam-packed, paper-littered madhouse by a frenzied, cheering, sobbing, almost hysterical mob of people celebrating the end of the war. Young and old whooped it up for hour after hour, creating an ear-shattering din at its peak and quieting down only in the wee hours when auto horns wore out batteries and voices were hoarse. At left above is shown one of the hundreds of cars packed with cheering young people that roared up and down the streets; at right is a typical scene of the wildly cheering crowd in front of the courthouse. As a bevy of beautiful girls "adopt" a sailor while, by contrast, both the younger and older generation look on from the side.—(Press Democrat Staff Photos)

Gen. MacArthur to Be Commander of Conquered Enemy

'Cease Fire' Order Issued as Tokyo Gives Up Unconditionally, With All Powers Stripped From Emperor, to Wind Up World War II

WASHINGTON, Aug. 14 (AP)—The second World War, history's greatest flood of death and destruction, ended tonight with Japan's unconditional surrender.

Formalities still remained—the official signing of surrender terms and a proclamation of V-J Day.

But from the moment President Truman announced at 7 p. m., eastern wartime, that the enemy of the Pacific had agreed to Allied terms, the world put aside for a time woeful thoughts of the cost in dead and dollars and celebrated in wild frenzy. Formalities meant nothing to people freed from last of war.

To reporters crammed into his office, shoving now-useless war maps against a marble mantle, the President disclosed that:

Japan, without even being invaded, had accepted completely and without reservation an Allied declaration of Potsdam dictating unconditional surrender.

General Douglas MacArthur had been designated supreme Allied commander, the man to receive surrender.

There is to be no power for the Japanese emperor—although Allies will let him remain their tool. No longer will the war lords reign, through him. Hirohito—or any successor—will take orders from MacArthur.

Allied forces were ordered to "suspend offensive action" everywhere.

From now on, only men under 26 will be drafted. Army draft calls will be cut from 80,000 a month to 50,000. Mr. Truman forecast that five to five and a half million soldiers may be released within 12 to 18 months.

The surrender announcement set in motion a whole chain of events. Among them:

To a Japanese government which once had boasted it would dictate peace terms in the White House, Mr. Truman dispatched orders to "direct prompt cessation of hostilities," tell MacArthur of the effective date and hour, and send emissaries to the general to arrange formal surrender.

The War Manpower Commission terminated all manpower controls.

The navy piled a $6,000,000,000 cancellation of contracts on top of previous $1,200,000,000 cut in its shipbuilding program.

On the HOME FRONT

Mr. and Mrs. J. C. Biaggi, 465 Occidental road, received word recently that their son,

U. S. S. INDIANAPOLIS SUNK BY NIP U-BOAT

Cruiser Downed July 30 With 883 Crewmen Lost; En Route S. F. to Guam With 'Atoms'

FELELIU, Palau Islands, Aug. 5 (Delayed)—(AP)—The 10,000-ton cruiser Indianapolis was sunk in less than 15 minutes, presumably by a Japanese submarine, 12 minutes past midnight July 30—and 883 crew members lost their lives.

Petain Found

City Greets Historic News In Wild Frenzy and Racket

Shouting Crowds Turn Downtown Area Into Noisy Bedlam

Santa Rosa went mad—de-

PARADE IN DOWNTOWN AREA AT 2 P. M. TODAY

Santa Rosa businesses, bars, retail stores and all other

Surrender 'Swan Song' Of Hirohito

By contrast the official parade was a staid affair although it was still termed "the noisiest and certainly the most spontaneous parade in the old town's history."[40] It was a joint military-civilian effort as Army vehicles rolled along Fourth Street loaded with soldiers and civilians together, strict military procedure having taken a holiday. Calls for parade entries from KSRO and the *Press Democrat* brought soldiers from the Army Air Base, sailors from the Naval Air Station, Red Cross volunteers, nurses, veterans' organizations, hastily constructed floats with Uncle Sam and the Statue of Liberty, motorized troop carriers, staff cars, and the ubiquitous jeep.

There was still bad news to come, sons unaccounted for, crops to be harvested with not enough farm labor to do the job, more people than there were houses, apartments, or rooms in Santa Rosa; many problems to be solved. But the war was over. For those two midsummer days, joy reigned.

The war had produced enormous changes in Northern California. With Mare Island and Marinship and other Bay Area defense plants employing thousands of men and women, it sometimes seemed as if the entire southern United States and a good share of the midwest had moved in. The demographics of cities nearer the urban core changed markedly. Cities like Richmond and Vallejo, both of which had been quiet suburban towns in 1940, became beehives, with temporary government housing thrown up in every vacant space to shelter the new residents.

Santa Rosa and Sonoma County were on the fringe of the activity. But the impact of the war cannot be minimized. It was not just the expected toll that war takes, although 411 Sonoma County men died in WWII, seventy of them from Santa Rosa.[41] It was the "Big Change." At the start of the war Santa Rosa was an agricultural center of 12,000 people, emerging from the nation's worst Depression. War added some 7,000 soldiers and sailors and prisoners of war, and stirred them liberally into community life, creating a whole new mix.

One effect was the end of Santa Rosa's insularity. What WW I began for the farm boys, WWII did for the cow-town image. Citizens from neighboring towns, who had considered Santa Rosans somewhat snobbish, might have suggested that the war made them nicer. The alacrity with which the residents assumed a welcoming and accommodating mode, was unmistakable. The suspicion of the conservative farmers who had comprised the power base in the pre-war town had all but vanished in a rush of fear. The soldiers who came to guard the coast may have been the cousins and neighbors of the dustbowl migrants who had met bigotry and abuse less than a decade before. But now the newcomers were welcomed. Things had changed. ❧

With the war's end, the frightening story of the balloon bombs which had endangered the lives of Sonoma County residents could be told. Some 225 incendiary and "anti-personnel" paper balloons, released in Japan in the last nine months of the war, actually drifted over the continent, starting fires and, in one instance, killing six people on a church picnic in Lakeview, Oregon.

In the last year of the war, volunteer lecturers visited Sonoma County school classes and club meetings, warning people to stay away from any object they might see fall from the sky or stumble over on a country outing. But the volunteers did not know the full story. On the day after Japan surrendered, with censorship lifted, the Press Democrat told the story of five of the explosive devices finding their way to Sonoma County.

The first landed on a farm on Vine Hill Road, northwest of Santa Rosa, on January 4, 1945. A farmer was milking a goat in the barnyard when "a weird contraption plummeted from the sky." It landed in a stand of trees a few feet from man and goat. Army ballistics experts from Hamilton Field in Ignacio came to inspect the device, which was stored for two days in a reception room at the sheriff's office in the jail building at Third and Hinton streets. Newspapermen were invited by FBI agents, military authorities, and the sheriff to examine the bomb while being apprised of the rigid censorship that surrounded the discovery.

On February 23 another balloon, or "bomb-bag" as they were called, was sighted high in the skies over Santa Rosa and was trailed by Army pilots until it could safely be shot down. A month later, March 23, the remnants of another paper balloon were found near the quicksilver mine on Mount Jackson, northeast of Guerneville. On May 15 a balloon was found near Geyserville and in June, an incendiary bomb started a fire near Cotati. In addition to these, military authorities reported that several others passed over the county at the height of 20,000 feet or more, detected by coastal radar.[39]

Seeing the Future

Santa Rosa's 20th century began with an earthquake—an explosion of energy that changed the face of the city. At mid-century, there was another explosion of energy that would alter the state of affairs in Sonoma County even more than the natural disaster—the post-war population explosion.

Growth was not a political issue in the first half of the century. There wasn't enough of it to create controversy. Santa Rosa's population increased scarcely at all between 1900 and 1940—from 6,673 to 12,605 people, less than 1,000 per decade. In the 1940s, the population of the city grew by about 5,000. By 1955, there were 14,000 more. A trend had been established.

The boundaries of the city were pushing outward to accommodate the new residents. The pace was quickening. It would become increasingly more difficult to find that Santa Rosa where everyone "walked to church on Sunday with their Bibles under their arms." It would be preserved, in fact, only on movie film.

That image was what film director Alfred Hitchcock and screenwriter Thornton Wilder saw in 1942 when they came looking for a setting for their movie thriller, *Shadow of a Doubt*. This film, made on location in Santa Rosa that year, portrayed McDonald Avenue, the churches, the library, the courthouse, and the business district of the city as "Safe Haven, USA" and captured it for all time. It would become a nostalgia piece for those residents, once described as smug by outsiders, who were becoming less self-satisfied as the city grew and changed.

Hitchcock's suspense film plays the villain's worldy evil against the backdrop of "homey" Santa Rosa, a community of hard-working, church-going families known by their first names to the librarian and the traffic cop downtown. It was a place where men worked and read the newspaper at night while women baked cakes, and daughters dreamed of a bigger world while helping Mom with the dishes.

This may not have been far off the mark. In a 1940 survey for the School of Social Studies in San Francisco, a study group of Santa Rosans found "the chief qualification of a husband in Santa Rosa... is that he be a good provider and of the wife that she have the ability to make a good home for her husband and children."[1]

In 1939, there were 563 marriage licenses issued in Sonoma County (and 133 interlocutory decrees of divorce granted in superior court). Families were small. A computation based on the 1930 census showed only .66 children per married couple in the county, .11 percent of a child lower than the state average of .77. The low numbers were interpreted by the study group as indicators of a change in lifestyle—the start of the transition from rural to suburban, where children were "regarded as mouths, not hands"—and of the economic travail of the Depression years.

"The status of women and the home can almost be spoken of as one...," the study group reported. "While many women have managed to make a living and successfully bring up children at the same time, odds are certainly against them in the present age."

The 1940 survey found that traditional, rural values endured. Yet many saw the comfortable old ways as already passing. A grocer interviewed by the study group complained that cooking "is becoming a lost art.... We used to order great quantities of citron and all the makings for mincemeat at Christmas," he said, by way of example. "Then in later years, many cases of bottled mincemeats.... Now they want the pies already baked!" On the subject of the new interest in canned and prepared food, one housewife told the study group, coquettishly, "Men prefer our company to our food."[2]

The demographic changes brought to California and, more specifically, to the San Francisco area by World War II were impacting the northern edges of the Bay Area. If the seeds of change sown by World War II did not burst immediately into full, even overblown, bloom in Santa Rosa as they

The Alfred Hitchcock film *Shadow of a Doubt* portrayed Santa Rosa as an idyllic small city in the 1940s. In the montage of studio photos on the opposite page, townspeople gather in front of the courthouse to watch the filming of a scene on Fourth Street, upper left; director Hitchcock holds a street conference near the railroad depot, upper right; star Joseph Cotten meets Santa Rosa's police chief, "Dutch" Flohr, lower left; and Santa Rosa citizens play themselves in the funeral cortege scene at the close of the movie.

It was war and a government ceiling on the production costs of films that sent director Alfred Hitchcock to Santa Rosa in 1942 to make *Shadow of a Doubt*. When the War Production Board allowed producer Jack Skirball and director Hitchcock a total of $5,000 for sets, Hitchcock decided to return to a practice considered primitive in Hollywood. He took his cast and crew on location.

His conversion of a small city into a movie set made industry history. The editors of *LIFE* magazine, the photographic journal of American life in the '40s, were so excited about this innovation, they sent three photographers to document the making of a motion picture in wartime. The resulting photo essay appeared on six pages of the weekly magazine, prior to the film's release. The writer lauded Hitchcock for his thrift. "Accustomed to spending $100,000 for sets alone on a picture, he 'built' what sets he used for *Shadow* from old lumber for $3,000. He and Universal [Studio] did this by taking over the entire city (population, 13,000) for four weeks and converting it to a complete motion picture studio."[3]

Writer Wilder and the rotund English-born director had paid a visit to Santa Rosa in July of 1942. They had narrowed their search for the typical American hometown to two—Santa Rosa and Visalia. They chose Santa Rosa and Wilder literally wrote it into his screenplay—the courthouse in the middle of town, the ivy-covered stone library, the two-story Victorian home on the tree-lined street, the Gothic spires of the Methodist Church South at Fifth and Orchard streets, the soldiers on the street and in the 'Til Two Bar on the corner of Santa Rosa Avenue and Third Street, the townspeople playing themselves. They didn't have to change much. Only the house, the home of Dr. Clifford Carlson at 904 McDonald Avenue, had to be altered slightly. In his pride at having his home selected for the film, Dr. Carlson had it painted between the time of selection and the start of shooting. Hitchcock was aghast. He wanted the weathered look. He had his crew oil the house to take the shine off before the cameras rolled. The film also provided a brief Hollywood career for a Santa Rosa ten year old. Edna May Wonacott, whose father owned the College Market, across from the high school, was standing on a street corner with her cousins when Hitchcock, who was inspecting building facades,

spotted her. She played the too-smart younger sister in the film.[4]

The movie is considered by many critics to be Hitchcock's best and a classic of the film noir. Santa Rosa, along with Joseph Cotten as the sinister Uncle Charlie and Teresa Wright as his niece, is the star of the show. The camera pans slowly over the rooftops of the downtown, past the clock tower on the Bank of America building, past the policeman directing traffic at Fourth and Mendocino, and zooms in on McDonald Avenue. Teresa Wright walks along the downtown streets. The Red Top Taxi is there and the "Social and Club News" masthead on the *Press Democrat*'s section page. Gallen Kamp's shoe store in the Rosenberg Building, Arrigoni's Market, the train at the Northwestern Pacific

—*Virginia Grace Collection*

All My Sons' stars Burt Lancaster, left, and Edward G. Robinson on the steps of the Grace home on McDonald Avenue, 1948.

depot, the Western Hotel, the Petaluma & Santa Rosa Railroad depot, the interior of the American Trust Bank, and even bank manager Harold Bostock playing a bank clerk are all included in the film. Santa Rosa was proud to be chosen and her citizens repaid Hitchcock with hospitality and cooperation. When he needed a crowd to line the streets for the closing funeral cortege, he got his crowd of cheerfully underpaid extras.

The film was released in 1943, at the height of the war, and was distributed to servicemen wherever they had access to a movie screen. For Santa Rosa's men and women in Army camps and airfields, military hospitals and ships at sea, when Joseph Cotten spoke his lines distinctly into the telephone: "I want to send a telegram to Santa Rosa, California. That's right, Santa Rosa. Santa Rosa, California," it was a real homesick lump-in-the-throat, as Hitchcock brought them their town.

After *Shadow*'s success, location became a filmmaker's way of life and Santa Rosa and Sonoma County, chosen spots. The next year, cameras were back in Santa Rosa for a Don Ameche-Frances Dee wartime tearjerker called *Happy Land*. This film was historic on two counts. It was the movie debut for a winsome five-year-old named Natasha Gurdin, who was spotted by the director as she stood watching the filmmaking and eating an ice cream cone. The meeting began a long and productive film career for Natasha, whose name was changed to Natalie Wood. Also, it introduced Harry Morgan, who played the buddy of Ameche's fallen soldier son, to Santa Rosa, where he would maintain a residence in later years.

The Sullivans, a drama based on the real life story of five brothers who died on one ship, was filmed at a house on Morgan Street. The story of the Sullivan tragedy resulted in wartime prohibition against brothers serving together. In 1947, Loretta Young and Joseph Cotten starred in *The Farmer's Daughter*, filmed on location in Penngrove. Another important film, *All My Sons*, with Edward G. Robinson, Burt Lancaster, and Howard Duff, used Virginia and Tom Grace's McDonald Avenue home as a location in 1948. And the same Carnegie Library in Santa Rosa that had figured in *Shadow* brought filmmakers back in 1955 for *Storm Center*, a movie about censorship in which Bette Davis played a courageous librarian.

did in Vallejo and Marin City, they were, nonetheless, planted firmly in the fertile Sonoma County soil.

───────

When the war ended, Santa Rosans tried for several years to pretend that nothing had changed. The brewery whistle still hooted at noon and five o'clock; the highway to Portland still ran around the courthouse. But things were definitely different. There were new subdivisions springing up on the edges of town to provide housing for new residents, some of whom were the soldiers and sailors who liked the town the government had found for them. For the first time, with the Depression ended and gasoline and tire rationing over, the impact of the Golden Gate Bridge was felt. The Bay Area, filled to excess, overflowed into Sonoma County.

The Hillcrest subdivision on twenty hillside acres of abandoned apple orchard east of Franklin Avenue was the first post-war development. G. Aubrey Becker, who bought the land from the Devencenzi family in 1946, found that both surveyors and engineers were scarce, their services having been almost exclusively military for the previous four years. Building materials were also in short supply. Becker's wife Dorothy Bell Becker would later write in a brief history of the enterprise that nails were still rationed, by the pound, and the first houses had "battleship linoleum" in the kitchens.

The new streets were Crest Drive, an extension of Lewis Road; Hyland, the highest street; Danbeck, which was a contraction of Becker's name and that of his partner, Tom Daniels, who brought the former Murdock property into the development; Hexem, named for one of Daniels' Seabee buddies; Beverly Way, which was designated as "Glennwood" and changed when a resident removed the sign and posted what he apparently considered a better idea; and Gay, named for the Beckers' son, Glenn Aubrey III, called "Gay" as a child.₅

The dead-end streets that had plagued merchants who worried about traffic flow for so many years began to be pushed through to connecting streets. The necessary

extensions and bridges were constructed to make a workable pattern. The face of the town was changing as dramatically as its boundaries. Architecture, not a priority in the building of early Santa Rosa, had come into its own as a California art form. At the top of the list of Santa Rosa's pioneer 20th century architects was William Herbert, a graduate of Massachusetts Institute of Technology who opened his practice here before World War I, when he and Petaluma's Brainerd Jones were the leading architects between San Francisco and Portland. In a time when most people still sketched out their plans with a nail on the back of a shingle, Herbert had a difficult time establishing his practice. His first targets were school districts and he spent long hours convincing board members of rural schools of the wisdom of having their new buildings professionally designed.

His first Santa Rosa job was as an employee of another firm. He served as supervising architect for San

The postwar facade of Grace Brothers Brewery on Third Street. The brewery's Tap Room was a popular spot for civic meetings and men-only socializing

───────

315

Francisco architect W.H. Weeks on the construction of the new Santa Rosa High School on Mendocino Avenue, replacing the school that burned on Humboldt Street in 1921. He was also the supervising architect with the Weeks firm for the first buildings on the Santa Rosa Junior College campus, Pioneer and Geary halls, and he designed Garcia Hall on his own.[6] He also designed the Santa Rosa Fire House on A Street.

Herbert developed his own style, modifying, streamlining the Beaux Arts style popular in his school days at MIT. His designs incorporated the Spanish revival popular in California at the time. Good examples of his diversity were seen in the schools he designed—Luther Burbank Elementary on A Street, Cloverdale High School, and Park Side Elementary School in Sebastopol—and business buildings like the one at 527 Mendocino Avenue (built for Dr. Carl A. Sawyer, a chiropractor, in 1932). Herbert's design of his own family's home, at 1633 Austin Way, was typical of

his residences which, in the words of an architectural critic, "sit well along the tree-lined streets."

Santa Rosa's next architect, C.A. "Cal" Caulkins, Jr., was Herbert's partner for a short time when he first came to town. Caulkins designed Luther Burbank Auditorium, Tauzer Gymnasium, Analy Hall, and Bussman Hall at SRJC and, when Herbert closed his office in 1942 to join the Army Corps of Engineers designing military installations along the Pacific Coast, Caulkins assumed the mantle of Santa Rosa's favored designer. His most intriguing design was for buildings that were never built. In 1945, he drew preliminary sketches for a civic center in downtown Santa Rosa, along the creek. War memorial money available to the county would have been used to build a new county courthouse, a city hall, and a civic auditorium in a parklike setting. The Sonoma County Board of Supervisors turned it down, passing the decision about how memorial money should be spent to the individual communities. Santa Rosa's share built the Veterans Memorial Building on Bennett Avenue.[7]

Another young architect, J. Clarence Felciano, who was associated for a time with the Herbert-Caulkins firm, would make his own impact on the architecture of the town. Felciano opened his office in 1939 and in 1946 moved to the studio offices on Montecito Heights he called "Hilltop." Felciano designed St. Eugene's Church, Proctor Terrace School, the grandstand at the fairgrounds, and, when the courthouse and the jail were removed from the downtown, he would design the new county hall of justice and jail.[8]

The polio epidemic that swept the country in the early 1940s struck communities like Santa Rosa with a ferocity that startled physicians. Affecting mostly children and teenagers, it was the "plague" of that generation, leaving its victims seriously debilitated. It was a high profile disease, President Franklin Roosevelt having been crippled by it as a young man, and research into cause and cure was intense. But the disease seemed to ebb and flow at its own

Architect Cal Caulkins' grand plan to build a civic center including courthouse, city hall, and veterans memorial in a creekside park never passed the artist's concept stage.

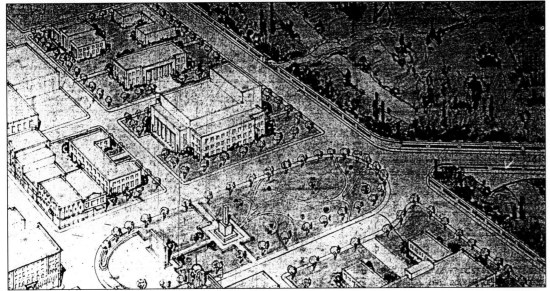

—*Press Democrat Collection*

time and pace, despite health officials' frantic efforts at prevention.

Poliomyelitis or infantile paralysis came to Santa Rosa and Sonoma County in epidemic proportion in the summer months of the early 1940s. The community rallied to fight it in the only ways available. In 1942 Ernest Finley, the *Press Democrat* publisher, organized a campaign to send two Sonoma County Hospital nurses, Edna Behrens and Gladys Main, to the Mayo Clinic in Rochester, New York to learn the "Kenny Method," a means of paralysis prevention named for Sister Elizabeth Kenny, the Australian nurse who had developed it. It involved the application of hot, moist wool pads to ease muscle tension in affected limbs and prevent the atrophy that caused life-long paralysis. The Santa Rosa Elks Club purchased and donated a large, tanklike machine known as an "iron lung" which "breathed" for patients whose lungs were damaged by the disease. County Hospital's iron lung was the only one in a four-county area. The hot packs for paralysis and the breathing aid were the only treatments known for the terrible disease.

In the summer of 1943, 101 people, most of them schoolchildren, were quarantined at Sonoma County Hospital with polio. Lionel Bourdens, age ten, was the first to be admitted with the disease. He was hospitalized on June 22, the first patient to be treated by the Kenny Method. The next day Dennis Tillotsen, five years old, was rushed to the hospital, already paralyzed. Augustine Bertoli, four years old; the Freese brothers, Edward and Eugene; Roy Gustafson of Sebastopol; Darnell Elgin, a seven-year-old from Healdsburg; the Skov brothers, Russell and Leighton—all hospitalized before the week ended.

Verve Pyke, a ten-year-old who lived on Steiner Court in Santa Rosa, died four days after his admission to the hospital, the first of five children to die of polio in Sonoma County that summer. Children from the six families on the Pyke family's two-block street, all of them playmates, were kept in isolation until the exposure period had passed.[9]

Jack Shea, a twelve-year-old at St. Rose School, a student leader and quarterback on the football team, was the 100th victim that summer. Shea, who became a successful and respected lawyer and political figure in Santa Rosa, was crippled for life by the disease. As an adult he recalled that there were so many children and teenagers hospitalized, they were placed in the hospital's morgue. The hospital lobby was filled with concerned classmates. "We had to shoo them away," one retired nurse recalled.[10]

It was a fearful summer for parents. Each edition of the newspaper brought word of new cases. The county health officer urged special sanitation precautions. Streams, particularly when the flow slowed in warm weather, were blamed for harboring the virus. Santa Rosa Creek was closed to all swimmers and waders. Matanzas Creek was also closed. By mid-summer, Doyle Park, the town's most popular play and picnic area, was closed to the public. Its location, between Matanzas and Spring creeks, was deemed dangerous. The reserve water supply from Lake Ralphine was diverted to "flush out" Santa Rosa Creek.

Children were banned from large public gatherings. Taking children to church services was discouraged, if not forbidden. Theater owners cooperated by canceling all children's movies. The Santa Rosa Public Library did not allow children to read on the premises but hurried them home with their borrowed books. Migrant workers' quarters, defense workers' living quarters, and trailer parks where people lived in close proximity were given special attention by health officers.

At times during that long hot summer of '43 there were as many as forty polio patients in Sonoma County Hospital at one time. By July 1, polio victims were being hospitalized at the rate of three to five per day. In the fall, with the return of cold weather, the epidemic abated. But polio would return again and again until the mid-'50s, when the first vaccine was developed by Dr. Jonas Salk.

Jack Shea at the age of twelve, before the polio epidemic of 1943 changed his life.

When Dr. Frank Norman, who would become the medical community's historian, came to Santa Rosa in 1948, there were sixty-five physicians in town. Dr. Robert Quinn was director of Oak Knoll Sanitarium for tuberculosis patients in 1948; General Hospital and the horse-and-buggy facilities of Tanner Hospital were all that was available for private patient care. Physicians like Norman, who were residents at County Hospital, received a thorough education. County was still primarily for the care of those who could not pay—except in special instances such as the polio epidemic of the early '40s. Since private physicians did not follow charity cases to County Hospital, the resident

The Tanner Hospital, a conversion of the old Mary Jesse Hospital, closed its doors the day the new Memorial Hospital opened.

—*Press Democrat Collection*

physicians received a wide range of experience. A large percentage of these residents entered private practice in Santa Rosa, as had their pre-war predecessors. Most started their private practice with established physicians, as Dr. Norman did with Dr. Leighton Ray.

Memorial Hospital was a community project. After World War II, with the town growing in a way it had not grown in the past four decades, the need for a new hospital was evident. Even with remodeling, General remained crowded and inadequate for the needs of a growing population. Tanner Hospital was clearly outdated. On the day that Memorial opened, Tanner closed its doors.

In 1946 a committee of the Chamber of Commerce addressed the problem and, boldly, went searching for a site. The committee chose a nine-acre cherry and walnut orchard on Santa Rosa Creek, at the end of a dirt road (later Sotoyome Avenue). The fund drive for the hospital was one of the most successful in Santa Rosa's history. The leaders were financier Fred Rosenberg, brewery owner Tom Grace, Judge Hilliard Comstock, attorney Finlaw Geary, merchant Kenneth Brown, auto dealers Herschel Niles and J. Henry Williams, newspaper publisher Carl Lehman, Sr., chamber manager Al Lewis, hop broker George Proctor, insurance agent Frank Luttrell, feed and grain merchant Maurice Nelligan, and inventor and entrepreneur Theron "Roy" Hedgpeth. A bridge was built across the creek at the site of the old Southern Pacific Railroad bridge.

Before the construction of the hospital could begin, the question of who would run it had to be addressed. The committee approached the Roman Catholic Sisters of St. Joseph of Orange, an order based in Southern California that had already established a reputation for the ability to administer hospitals throughout the state. Mother Louis, the head of the order, visited in 1947 to inspect the site and talk business. Mayor Obert Pedersen climbed a cherry tree in the orchard to pick her some ripe fruit—a nice hometown touch to begin a business venture—and an agreement was reached. In 1949, the sisters' task force

The effort to raise funds to build a new hospital began in 1946. The opening of Memorial Hospital, on the first day of 1950, was considered a community triumph.

moved in, headed by Sister Rita, the first administrator, and Memorial opened its doors to patients on January 1, 1950.

The black population of Sonoma County had increased, but not by much, in the '30s. The first real "community" wasn't formed until World War II brought an influx of southern blacks to Northern California to work in the Bay Area shipyards. This emigration changed the ethnic makeup of many Bay Area cities, notable among them Vallejo, where Mare Island drew workers and the quiet, mostly white Solano County city experienced a marked and diverse population explosion.

In Sonoma County, farther from the shipyards, the changes were slower and less dramatic. Alice and Gilbert Gray might be considered as examples of the first changes in Santa Rosa's ethnic makeup, subtle as they may have been. The Grays came to California from Texas in 1945, settling their family of nine children in the housing project at Marin City while Gilbert worked as a welder at nearby Marinship in Sausalito.

When the shipyards closed, Gray worked as a janitor during the week, played semi-pro baseball on weekends, and went to barber school. At completion of his course he signed on as a military barber at Hamilton Air Force Base, a job he would keep for twenty-seven years. By 1952 the Gray family moved out of the "projects" with enough savings to buy a house on Petaluma Hill Road in Santa Rosa.

The reception from the predominately white, conservative community "wasn't too bad," Alice Gray recalled later. "Of course," she added, "there weren't enough blacks to make any difference in those days." The Grays could count on their fingers the number of black families in Santa Rosa when they arrived—the Wyatts (Mr. Wyatt worked at Sears Roebuck), Jessie Love, who was a warehouseman, Evelyn and Paul Jones, Bertha Phillips, Ruth and Jimmie Carter (Ruth worked at Corrick's and Jimmie was the downtown shoe shine man), and Platt Williams, who was a student at SRJC when the Grays arrived.

There was a church group which met in Love's home, a mission of the Village Baptist Church begun in 1951. This congregation soon became the Community Baptist Church. But the establishment of the Sonoma County Chapter of the National Association for the Advancement of Colored

People, founded by Gray and Williams, was still several years away.[11]

In 1942 Ernest Finley died, leaving the *Press Democrat* in temporary disarray. Carl Lehman, the business manager, stepped into the breach and became the newspaper's temporary publisher. Herbert Waters, who had started at the newspaper while he was still a high school student, was running the news department.

By 1948, Ruth Woolsey Finley, Ernest's widow, had taken over as the newspaper's publisher, with her son-in-law Evert Person as assistant publisher. They discovered

the publishing company was in debt to its wire service, United Press, and to its paper suppliers. With their counsel, Mrs. Finley agreed to hire a man known to west coast journalists as a newspaper "doctor" to fix what ailed the county's leading newspaper. William Townes brought a new

kind of journalism to Santa Rosa.

The old news staff had substantial political connections. The police reporter was the coroner; until Herbert Slater's death the previous year, the political columnist was the state senator; the sports editor was the assistant county clerk; and the editor, Herb Waters, was a leader of the local Democratic party and ultimately a candidate for state senate, while still serving as editor. Townes ended these conflicts of interests and, under his management, the *Press Democrat* expanded its circulation area to Lake and Mendocino counties and became a regional newspaper. Charles Carson became managing editor and Mike Demarest was hired to write a daily column, bringing a brand of sophisticated wit the paper had not offered readers before.

In terms of physical change, the war hit Santa Rosa with the impact of the earthquake of '06. At the decade year, 1950, Santa Rosa was a new town, more new in more ways than the rebuilt city of post-earthquake years. The 1950s might be considered Sonoma County's "Era of Good Feeling." The decade began with countywide effort to locate both a Ford plant and the U.S. Air Force Academy here. Sonoma County Airport was among the serious contenders in 1954 as a site for the academy, as was the Sonoma Valley, which had its war-hero resident, General of the Air Force H. H. "Hap" Arnold, in its corner. Neither effort was successful. The Ford plant was built in Milpitas and the Air Force Academy in Colorado Springs, Colorado.

Still, business boomed in the postwar economy. A new Sears Roebuck store at Seventh and B streets, built in 1948, was the largest retail store in the "Redwood Empire," a term coined in 1924 when the Redwood Highway opened. The term was enjoying a new vogue as business, like the newspaper, began to think regionally.

If business boomed at the war's end, social life exploded. Following a national pattern, Santa Rosans

—John LeBaron, Press Democrat Collection

Farm editor Mike Pardee, above, was part of the *Press Democrat*'s plan to become a regional newspaper. Pardee's weekly "Howdy, Neighbor" features reached out to rural Sonoma, Lake, and Mendocino counties in the late 1940s and early 1950s. At far left is 1953 column by Mike Demarest. Demarest's daily feature was the first of its kind for a Santa Rosa newspaper.

Song Wong Borbeau stands in a doorway of the Third Street restaurant she owned with her husband Charles Borbeau. Song inherited the Jam Kee from her grandfather, who started the restaurant in Santa Rosa's Chinatown.

celebrated prosperity by dining out and giving parties. The Topaz Room, built during the war, was still the fanciest place in town, but diners also filled Eisenhood's on the other side of the courthouse and the modernized versions of the old Italian hotels, Lena's and Guidotti's. Hagel's on Santa Rosa Avenue had its faithful clientele, as did Marico's, an updated version of a roadhouse on the highway just south of Wikiup. Golden Bear Lodge in Adobe Canyon off Sonoma Highway competed with the Green Mill in Cotati for the most lavish smorgasbord in the county. The Seven Seas on Fourth Street and Claude Dingman's Fisherman's Port on outer Mendocino Avenue were the choices for seafood. In the early '50s, Jim Mills bought Fisherman's Port and converted it to a steak house he called Mills' Patio. Economy-minded families and students on a budget patronized the dining room at the Occidental Hotel where dinner was all-you-could-eat for $1.50.

For Chinese food there were the ornate Twin Dragons, which had a cocktail lounge, and Jam Kee, with its old-fashioned wooden booths. Jam Kee was all that remained of Santa Rosa's Chinatown. There Song Borbeau and her husband Charles knew the customers by name and Song maintained her reputation for smoking the finest barbecued pork east of Canton. Warren Wright's coffee shop near the White House department store at Fourth and B streets, was the summer spot for strawberry pie. Mac's, the town's first kosher-style delicatessen, opened in the block east of the courthouse in the early '50s.

Out-of-town visitors would almost certainly be driven to Occidental, the tiny west county town that had become famous for its family-style Italian food. There was not one but three Italian restaurants—the Panizzeras' Union Hotel, Fiori's, and Negri's—in Occidental, earning it the nickname "Calorie Gulch."

To keep apace of the social whirl, one had only to read the *Press Democrat*'s women's section, expanded in 1950. Publisher Townes hired an Oregon journalist named Roby Gemmell as part of his plan to save the newspaper.

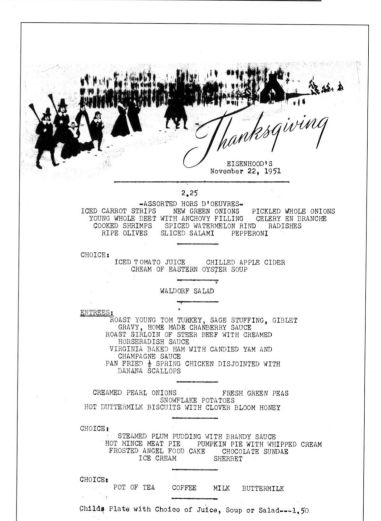

Eisenhood's Restaurant on Exchange Avenue on the west side of the courthouse, was where the service clubs met for lunch and, along with the Topaz Room east of the courthouse, filled most of the dining-out needs of downtown Santa Rosa.

Roby Gemmell, above, was the editor of the newspaper's women's pages for twenty-five years.

School sports was a big part of young people's social life. Below, Santa Rosa High School's baseball team and rooters at a game with Tamalpais High. Back row, second from right, is Quinto Furia. To his right, Gloria Carpenter, Sally Farrar, Connie Barnett, and Joan Peterson. Front row, from left, Leonard Mayer, George Mancini, Jim Carlson, and J. Svendsen.

His orders to her were to put as many names in the newspaper as would fit. Gemmell, for the next twenty-five years, complied. Her pages were filled with photographs and stories of charity balls and social functions, complete with lists of those attending and descriptions of what the women (and sometimes even the men) were wearing. Being named in her column, called "Bib 'n Tucker," was, for some, the pinnacle of social success. But Gemmell prided herself on being democratic and no social event, not birthday parties for one-year-olds nor an evening of bridge, was turned away. Gemmell and her assistant editor, Gladys Sergent, wrote astonishing amounts of social news: weddings, travel plans, house tours and teas, garden parties, PTA functions, church bazaars, and Bluebirds on nature hikes.

After World War II, the GIs who enrolled at Santa Rosa Junior College were catalysts for the start of a "naughtier" era in young people's entertainments. Spring and summer afternoons at the river, at Healdsburg's Camp Rose or Palomar, at Hilton and Mirabel—the closest swimming beaches to Santa Rosa—became "beer parties." Weekend nights, after football and basketball games, the older students, taking their young friends along, went out for a good time.

Often their quest for amusement took them to the Boots 'n Saddles on Sonoma Highway at Brush Creek Road where the regulars kept beer mugs with their names on them—or to Sonia's. Halfway to Calistoga on Porter Creek Road, Sonia's called itself a "resort" but was mostly a bar, the kind of place that in earlier days would have been called a roadhouse. It was opened in 1945 by Sonia and George Jaure, who had been professional dancers in pre-war Europe. They brought a touch of old-world sophistication and Sonia's quickly became a Friday night destination for Santa Rosa's college crowd.

For Santa Rosa youth of the '40s and '50s, life still centered around a single public high school and the junior college. So did a portion of the adult social life. Sporting events at the two schools routinely attracted capacity crowds as the town came to root for the orange and black Panthers of the high school and the red and blue Bear Cubs of SRJC. The high school's sports rivalries with Petaluma and Vallejo and SRJC's with College of Marin occasionally produced encounters that required police arbitration, but mostly the mischief was just that—painting the giant plaster of Paris chicken at the south entrance to Petaluma orange and black, or kidnapping the Marin yell leaders for display at the traditional pre-game bonfire in the Bailey Field parking lot. SRJC's post-war football teams, beefed up by the war veterans who were returning to school fully grown, enjoyed great success, establishing the school as an athletic power among the state's junior colleges.

Semi-pro teams, both football and baseball, drew large crowds of fans in the late 1940s. The Santa Rosa Bonecrushers football team, composed of former high school and college athletes, had enthusiastic support from the town but could not best their county rival, the mighty Leghorns of Petaluma, organized in '48 by Gene Benedetti

—Gloria Oster Collection

322

(a former SRJC star who was manager of the Petaluma Cooperative Creamery), Bob Acorne, and George Norwood. The Leghorns were awesome. In '49 and '50, they were the second-highest scorers in the country.[12]

In 1948, major league baseball's Pittsburgh Pirates brought their farm team from the Far West League to Santa Rosa for one exciting season, during which Sonoma County baseball fans had a chance to meet Pirates' co-owner Bing Crosby and to preview the pitching talents of Vernon Law, an eighteen-year-old fastballer from Idaho who would be pitching in the major leagues the following year. Another Pirates' prospect was a SRJC pitcher, John Fitzgerald, who would later coach at Cardinal Newman High School. The Pirates brought a touch of baseball class to the Doyle Park diamond, building wooden bleachers and even box seats. Both were almost always full.

In '49, the Pirates dropped the franchise and the team became the Santa Rosa Cats, still competing in the Far West League. It was a tough schedule, infielder Ralph DeMarco would later recall. The teams they played included Klamath Falls and Medford and Willows and Oroville. The bus trips were long and the money was scarce. In 1950, when the Cats folded, many of the players, including DeMarco, played for the Rosebuds, the town team long supported by Santa Rosa baseball's trio of stalwarts: Denny Moore, Willie Rossi, and Norm Maroni.

Still living in the center of a rural county, Santa Rosans maintained their interest in fishing and hunting. The Sonoma County Sportsmen's Club had been organized in 1921 and, through the years, had been active in the protection of the Russian River and its creek tributaries as fishing streams. Club members studied fish habitat with an eye to preservation, stocked streams, policed them for

SRJC's Big Game was always the one with neighboring Marin JC. At top right, students prepare for "Marin Week." At right, the Bonecrushers, Santa Rosa's semi-pro team of the postwar years was, like its rival Petaluma Leghorns, made up of former college and high school players.

—*Santa Rosa Junior College Collection*

—*Grace Family Collection*

Above, outdoor writer Walt Christensen. Below, the after-school scene at the Winkin' Lantern, a 1940s Fourth Street malt shop.

pollution, and monitored the annual steelhead runs. In addition, they reared and planted thousands of pheasants and quail in Sonoma County habitat and urged strict enforcement of game laws.[13]

Herbert Slater's outdoor column had been one of the most popular features in the *Press Democrat* for forty years. After his death in 1947, Walt Christensen, a gunsmith who had long been involved in Sportsmen's Club work, took over the writing of his "Rod and Gun" column. Christensen would write the popular newspaper feature, that not only told people where the fish were biting and who had bagged what game but advanced the cause of wildlife conservation and protection for another forty years.

Student theatrical productions also attracted large audiences. The work of directors George Andreini and Julio Francescutti at the junior college would fill Burbank Auditorium, and at Santa Rosa High School there was a remarkable drama instructor named Glen G. Guymon, who made high school plays an important element in the community in the late '40s and '50s. Guymon had come to SRHS in 1936 from Uintah High School in Vernal, Utah. Under his tutelage, Santa Rosa's debate team was a frequent winner in the National Forensic League's competitions and his ambitious productions brought literally thousands of dollars in support from community clubs and individuals. Much of his success was made possible by many friends who worked in the film industry, including former students. His 1949 production of *Life with Father* used costumes loaned by Warner Brothers from the movie version. Through his Hollywood connections, he was also able to bring high-profile entertainers to the school.

What Bouk's had been to the teenagers of the '30s, The Winkin' Lantern, also on Fourth Street in the first block east of the courthouse, was to the teenagers of the '40s—the after-school gathering place. Known fondly to its patrons as "The Wink," the sandwich shop owned by Marguerite and Oliver Ramsey from 1941 to 1946 was the province of the high school and junior college set.

Young people of the war and postwar years tested their social skills under the watchful eyes of sponsoring adults. Many displayed their manners as well as dancing skills at the Cotillion parties. The Santa Rosa Golf and Country Club's formal holiday dance for what was officially known as the club's "Younger Set" was attended by 100 or more teenagers. The Redwood Roller Rink on Santa Rosa Avenue was a less formal gathering place. But few dates or outings ended without an obligatory trip—or two, or twenty—around the courthouse. The unique configuration of Santa Rosa's downtown streets which took both north and southbound traffic in a half circle around the imposing county government structure was ideal for the car-crazy kids of the postwar years who drove round and round the circle, stopping to visit friends in a custom that was known as "cruising" or "tooling."

—1949 SRHS Echo

Time had not diminished the country's love affair with the automobile. With the end of gas rationing teenagers were firmly affixed in their cars, or the family car. Drive-in movie theaters such as the Redwood at Wilfred crossing south of town and the Village east of Montgomery Village near Reservoir Drive opened in the late '40s and early '50s. Drive-in restaurants became the new gathering places. The two earliest in Santa Rosa were Morrow's on Sebastopol Road and the Cock 'n Bull on Mendocino Avenue, just north of the junior college. The important one, however, was the one at College Avenue and Fourth Street that became the acknowledged hangout for high school and college students for more than a decade. Originally known as Quinley's, it was built in 1947 by contractor Hugh Codding. Owner Al Quinley had a similar establishment in Petaluma. In 1950 Quinley sold to partners Kenneth Wells and Gordon Lemon, who owned a chain of drive-ins in the Bay Area, headquartered in Richmond. They renamed it Gordon's.

Quinley's Drive In at College Avenue and Fourth Street was the social center for young people. It became Gordon's Drive In in 1950. At right, opening day at Quinley's, 1947.

—1949 SRHS Echo

A montage of "old, familiar places" for Santa Rosa's young people of the early 1950s: the drive-in movies, the drive-in restaurant, and the roller rink.

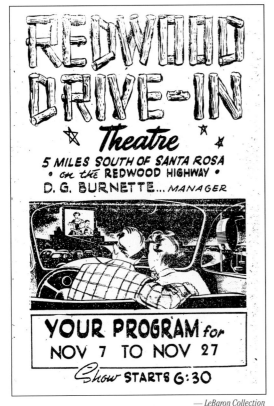

— LeBaron Collection

—Nanci Burton Collection

Gordon's traffic patterns provided a great advantage. There were driveways into the parking area from both College and Fourth, so that the "hot-rodders" and "cruisers" of the period, after their turns around the courthouse downtown, could make several slow loops through the area to check the action before committing to a burger, fries, and a Coke—maybe a lemon Coke, or one with a squirt of cherry syrup.

The biggest physical change was the freeway—which wasn't really a freeway. Santa Rosans had been restive about the path of Highway 101 since it became apparent that the automobile had come to stay. The major north-south coastal artery was Santa Rosa Avenue, south of the courthouse, and Mendocino Avenue, north of the courthouse. Northbound drivers were guided to a right-hand semi-circle around the county's central office building in the center of the plaza, on a one-block street called Hinton Avenue. Southbound drivers went to the right along Exchange Avenue to Third Street and Santa Rosa Avenue. In the Depression years there was little hope of changing this traffic pattern, although there was talk of a future realignment which would not go through the heart of the city.

Back in 1938, when the Depression economy was starting to mend, the *Press Democrat* conducted the first poll, or straw vote, of its readers on the subject, asking if the new Highway 101 bypass should be to the east or the west of Santa Rosa's downtown. The overwhelming majority voted for a western route. The question to be addressed was: How far west? An immediate conflict arose between the city officials and the engineers from the State Division of Highways. A bypass, the engineers said, should be built at the far western edge of the community. They suggested a route which followed Wright and Fulton roads.

Santa Rosa's business community did not agree. At the very word "bypass" the Chamber of Commerce seemed to shudder, collectively, and merchants like Fred Rosenberg objected strenuously. Getting the trucks off the courthouse lawn was one thing. Routing potential customers away from the business district was something else entirely.

Engineers warned a decision to build the bypass close in would split the town in half. But businessmen feared tourists wouldn't stop. In 1939, in a special election, the voters cast ballots on a proposed route along Wilson Street, the closest street to the NWP railroad track. Merchants along lower Fourth Street, led by the patriarch of Santa Rosa's Italian community, Natale Bacigalupi, worked to defeat the route and succeeded.

Then World War II intervened. Money for roads was channeled into the "war effort," and until 1944, there was little or no talk of a bypass. When the route was finally selected by the City Council it took sections of Davis Street, South Davis Street, and small portions of Ripley Street, Lincoln Street, and Cleveland Avenue. It was even closer to town than the previously suggested route. It was just three blocks from the courthouse.

The state engineers made another proposal which caused the merchants to protest. They suggested the bypass be a "freeway," a comparatively new term for a road with limited access and no stop lights. They could eliminate dangerous intersections, the engineers said, by elevating the roadway. Community leaders again refused to hear the experts. There would be no "giant viaduct," they said, no "highway on stilts" in Santa Rosa. It was clear they didn't want motorists to go by too fast. In fact, it seemed, they didn't want them to go by at all.

Citizens protested the decision. Writing to the newspaper's "Let the Public Speak" column, they advised Santa Rosa was making the mistake every city in the world was then trying to avoid, namely building a highway through the city instead of around it. One writer blamed "selfish interests" for the decision, another warned Santa Rosans did not approve of the "butchery" of their city. Still another suggested sarcastically the business community might be

best served by leaving 101 alone and moving the courthouse. At the end of 1948, a newspaper reporter summed up the year as one which "has changed the face of Santa Rosa more than any year since 1906." It was, he wrote, "the year they sawed the town in half."

The "freeway" which opened in May of 1949, with bands and dignitaries and horsemen and hoopla, was barely an expressway. There were seven stoplights: Sebastopol Road, Third, Fourth, Fifth and Ninth streets, College Avenue, and Steele Lane. Less than two years later, in February of 1951, Santa Rosa City Manager Sam Hood spoke

The highway 101 bypass cut a swath through Santa Rosa in 1949. This aerial view, looking south shows the new highway, center bottom to top left; the railroad top to bottom at right; and Third Street crossing left to right in the center. The large buildings next to the creek at top center are the Grace Brothers Brewery.

—*Sonoma County Library*

327

—LeBaron Collection

The 101 freeway from Petaluma heads north from Wilfred crossing to Santa Rosa in the mid-1950s.

serious. And the merchants who blocked the western route and the elevated roadway had found the "present freeway has not affected their business one way or the other." Hood described Assistant State Engineer John H. Skaggs as "a voice lost in the wilderness" urging out-of-town or overhead construction. "There is more cross traffic on the state highway," Hood said, "than there is on the highway itself. If the Highway Commission were to recommend a freeway outside Santa Rosa, I doubt there would be one voice raised in objection," said Hood. But it was too late.

The increased flow of traffic was a concern of the entire Bay Area. In the early '50s there was a movement for a second crossing of the Golden Gate as well as proposals to bridge the bay elsewhere. A self-taught engineer named John Reber proposed to divide the bay with earthwork dams topped by highways and railways. The result would be the formation of two fresh-water lakes apart from the bay. The Reber Plan garnered considerable support and was the subject of wide debate although it was abandoned in favor of the San Rafael-Richmond Bridge, which was under construction by 1955.

The long-awaited county airport finally became reality in the summer of 1946. The Army had deactivated the Santa Rosa Army Air Field in April, and in July the county took over on an interim permit from the Army, under which it operated the airport until title was acquired. Harrison Mecham, who had been with the Army Corps of Engineers at Hamilton Field, was appointed the first airport manager and served in that capacity until he retired in 1964.

Postwar commercial air service began in 1947 when Southwest Airways made its first flight into Sonoma County Airport. In 1953, Southwest became Pacific Air Lines. The company operated in California, Oregon, and Nevada and flew Fairchild F-27s and Martin 404s. In the 1950s, it served Sonoma County with four scheduled stops per day, two northbound, two southbound, carrying both passengers and air freight.[14]

to the San Francisco Commonwealth Club about the mistakes Santa Rosa had made. The "selfish interests," Hood said, had forced the ground-level highway rather than a viaduct and created a roadway which was "a detriment to the through highway users."

There had been five deaths and forty-seven injuries, Hood told the San Francisco audience, since the bypass opened. Increased speed had made the accidents more

When Memorial Hospital opened in 1950 on creekside land on the old Southern Pacific right-of-way, property that had been the Hahman family's cherry orchard, it opened new lands for speculation. The hospital occasioned a burst of expansion and improvement. An automobile bridge replaced the railroad bridge over Santa Rosa Creek and the railroad right-of-way became a street. Named Montgomery Drive for young Billy Montgomery, the sailor on the *USS California* who died at Pearl Harbor, the new street opened the prune and walnut orchards east of Santa Rosa to development.

Nowhere in the Bay Area, or perhaps the state of California, are the effects of the post-World War II building boom seen more concisely than in the story of one ambitious Santa Rosa developer and his construction exploits of the 1950s, which would be recited like a litany for the next forty years. He came out of the Seabees with his $400 discharge pay in his back pocket, the story goes, and changed Santa Rosa more dramatically and more quickly than any change that had come before, with the possible exception of the '06 quake.

The man was Hugh Codding, a native Santa Rosan who had dabbled in construction and development before the war. Building several small houses for speculation sale near the corner of E Street and Bennett Avenue on streets he named McKinley and Georgia for the man he bought the property from and the man's girl friend, Codding displayed a whimsical approach to development that would characterize him for the rest of the century.

His first postwar project was a small subdivision he called Brookside Terrace, between Sonoma Avenue and Doyle Park. His next was more ambitious, a development of the Parsons orchard between the Grace Tract and the Rural Cemetery. The gates to the Parsons ranch opened off Franklin Lane and a dirt lane wandered through the orchard to the Gothic farmhouse on the hill which had been built in the 1880s. Ike Parsons, who owned the ranch in 1946, was the second generation of his family to live in the house. The

Parsons had raised draft horses on the ranch, mostly Shires, the largest of the horse breeds. The magnificent animals, some six-feet high and 2,200 pounds, won prizes at fairs and horse shows throughout the west. When the automobile ended the day of the draft horse, Ike Parsons converted his pastureland to prune and apple orchards. But the town was stretching out to meet the country and, when Codding came in '46 offering to buy his flat land, Ike Parsons sold it to him for $1,100 an acre.

Codding borrowed $10,000 from the Exchange Bank to build homes and an under-one-roof shopping center, a smaller version of one he had seen in Sacramento. He called it Town & Country Village and sold it when it was half-finished to an investor named Mario Gracchi for $100,000. With his new-found financing, Codding bought the Hahman prune and walnut orchard on Farmers Lane and, in 1949, started another, larger, shopping center. The decentralization of Santa Rosa was underway.[15]

The opening of east Santa Rosa brought other developers. In 1950 Charles Cornish and Eugene Personett began work on a 145-home subdivision between Mont-

Developer Hugh Codding, above, would become a symbol of the postwar building boom. Below, a drawing of Town 'n Country, his first shopping center.

—1955 SRHS Echo

329

—Press Democrat Collection

—David Frey Collection

gomery Drive and the creek which they called Sherwood Forest, with street names—Robin Hood, Little John, Marian—in keeping with the theme. James Blackwell, Jr., whose major addition to the city would be his Blackwell Tract south of the fairgrounds, developed the Edgemont subdivision south of Sonoma Avenue near Franquette Avenue, adding Carvel Drive and Rocklin Drive to the map.

Meanwhile, Codding was buying more walnut and prune orchards, negotiating with the banks and property owners for the land from Santa Rosa Creek along the old Southern Pacific railroad right-of-way toward the rural lane called Summerfield Road. He surrounded his shopping center across the Farmers Lane bridge from Sonoma Highway with 2,600 homes which sold faster than he could lay the foundations. He attracted national attention with his flamboyant construction stunts. He built a house in less than four hours, a church in five hours and sixteen minutes. He named his triumph Montgomery Village.

Codding's promotional exploits earned him notice from *Time* and other national publications. If Henry Doelger was the dean of California's tract housing boom, young Codding was the *wunderkind*. He thrived on the attention. And so did his business. When Montgomery Village shopping center opened in 1950 there were twelve businesses. By its second anniversary there were eighty-two. The Saddle 'n Sirloin restaurant was opened in 1952 by Al Quinley, who had owned Gordon's Drive In. Clyde Chesney, who would earn his reputation as an exemplary restaurant host by stopping at every table and greeting every diner, purchased the "Saddle" soon after it opened and ran it for many years. The Village Pool, built by Codding and operated by a membership association, opened in '52 also, with an aquacade and a sports carnival in the shopping center.

At top left, Hugh Codding stands in the center of a lineup of the original merchants of his Montgomery Village on the shopping center's second anniversary in 1952. The photograph at left shows Don Frey's Village Super Market in the first of the Village buildings in 1950.

—Wanda Ruegamer Collection

—Codding Collection

In one fateful day in 1955 the population of Santa Rosa went from 18,000 to more than 30,000 with the annexation of the Montgomery Village area. The agreement to annex was not easily achieved but rather the result of a compromise which ended a five-year war between Codding and city officials.

The question was, who would control the inevitable growth of Santa Rosa. Codding's rapid success had caused a substantial amount of concern in the city. There were differences between city and county building standards and city officials mourned their lack of control over what was going on just outside their city limits.

But the political power of the county was shifting, not so subtly, away from the agricultural forces and the merchants, spelling the end of Santa Rosa as a farm town. The new politics belonged to the men who were financing the building boom. The town's banks, its one savings and loan, a new mortgage company, and their chief executives—Charles Reinking at the Exchange Bank, James Keegan at American Trust (later, Wells Fargo), Bank of America's Joseph Lombardi, Santa Rosa Savings & Loan's J. Ralph Stone, and Sonoma Mortgage Corporation's Henry Trione, plus Mead Clark Lumber Company owner Elie Destruel: these were the new power brokers. Trione's mortgage company, which had started after the war in a hole-in-the-wall office with a rented desk, chair, and typewriter, quickly became an important factor in the growth of the community. The young man from Humboldt County was already recognized as an important financial force. Trione and his family would prove to be among the most civic-minded of Santa Rosa citizens, ready to provide funds for city beautification, for parks, and for education as Sonoma County grew.[16]

The early years of Montgomery Village's development were punctuated with Codding's publicity stunts. At upper left, Codding and his mother Ruby Jewell Codding Hall are interviewed by KSRO's Jim Wilkey. Upper right, flagpole sitter Wanda Ruegamer looks down from her Village tower. At left, Codding Construction Co. crews swarm over the house he built in less than four hours.

—Codding Collection

—Doug Bundock, Press Democrat Collection

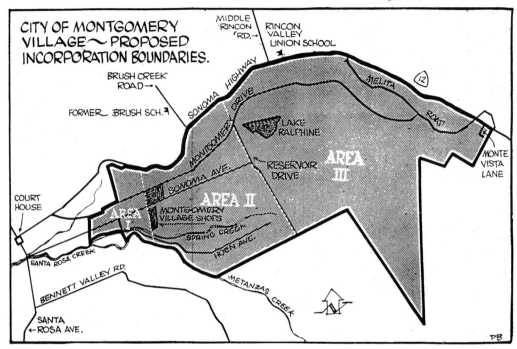

CITY OF MONTGOMERY VILLAGE ~ PROPOSED INCORPORATION BOUNDARIES.

The City of Montgomery Village never came to be. Codding struck a deal with city officials and the Village was annexed to Santa Rosa in 1955.

Hugh Codding was also a pivotal figure in the town's political life. His adversary was big, bluff good-natured city manager, Sam Hood, who was the perfect foil for Codding's grandiose schemes. Under Hood's direction, the city began to acknowledge and plan for the growth that was occurring. The council adopted a master plan and moved to annex seven areas: the Monroe District, the south side where Blackwell was building homes, portions of Bennett Valley and Rincon Valley, Montecito Heights, and the northside, including subdivisions developed by Lewis Meyers and Gene Service in the Elliott Avenue area and Montgomery Village.

Codding alone decided to fight City Hall. The annexation proposal, which he regarded as a takeover, opened an old wound suffered when one of Hood's predecessors, Ross Miller, had taken the City Council on a

field trip to view a Codding foundation the city's inspector deemed substandard, and the council had ordered the newly constructed house torn down. The twenty-nine-year-old developer, who had learned his trade working as a plumber with his stepfather and taking construction courses at night before he became a Seabee, had defended his work and accused the city of trying to put him out of business. He had vowed never to build another house in Santa Rosa's city limits. Now, faced with an annexation proceeding, he remembered that vow and refused to entertain the city's overtures, openly enjoying the power his success gave him over government and glorying in the reputation he was getting for thumbing his nose at City Hall.

Montgomery Village, however, lacked two important factors for continued growth. If Codding were to successfully expand into Bennett or Rincon valleys, he would need a water supply and sewer facilities. The city could offer both. But Codding was young and rich and having a good time. He announced he would build his own sewer plant, develop his own water sources. And he would incorporate his Montgomery Village into a separate city which would challenge Santa Rosa's future.

Montgomery Village residents, spurred on by their brash hero, began collecting signatures for incorporation. With Codding's holdings in the shopping center, the necessary assessed valuation seemed assured. Then, in an eleventh-hour meeting with Hood and the city engineer, Robert Van Guelpen, Codding acknowledged that the task he had set for himself in providing adequate water and sewage facilities might not be possible. A deal was cut. The city relaxed its position that the Village streets had to be brought up to city standards before annexation. And Hood agreed on a greatly reduced fee for sewer connection.

Codding stopped in at radio station KSRO and broadcast an urgent message to the residents of his "new city." He was taking his name off the petition for incorporation, he said. The next day the newspaper told the story. Without Codding's signature there was not enough assessed valuation to qualify the Village for incorporation. The annexation that followed was a mere formality. The decision had been made at that Sunday morning meeting. Montgomery Village would be part of Santa Rosa.[17]

North Korea invaded South Korea in June of 1950 and the United States sent thousands of troops to South Korea in response to a United Nations call. Once again, Santa Rosa's young men and women went to war. And war came once again to Santa Rosa. In July of 1952, Alameda Naval Air Station, overcrowded with the rush of Naval Aviation squadrons to the Pacific Coast, reactivated the Santa Rosa Naval Auxiliary Airfield. Carrier Air Group Two, which consisted of 800 men who were already veterans of three tours of duty on two carriers, was assigned to the base.

Navy Crew Chief Ray Anders hangs his laundry on a fence at the reactivated Naval Air Station. There was no PX and no amenities when the Navy returned to Santa Rosa in 1952. Below, Santa Rosa residents view the Navy's newest planes at an open house in 1953.

—Ray Anders Collection

They found it wasn't easy living. The field had been closed since 1945 and there were no services. Ray Anders, a crew chief, who was on the first bus that arrived from Alameda, remembered, "There was nothing there. No commissary. No PX. No laundry. No movie. No barber."

Anders, who married the girl (Betty Daulton) whose family lived across the street from the main gate, recalled later how the Navy men improvised. "There was a barber across the street and a grocery store on Wright Road called Bernie and Woody's [Berniece and Woody Pollard's neighborhood market] that was our commissary." Two barracks were reopened. Married officers found housing in the community. Bachelor officers rented two bungalows at the corner of Fresno and Finley avenues, a housing complex known to its occupants as "The Snake Farm."[18]

The pilots were flying Corsairs and Sky Raiders. They were also converting to jets. The Panther jet, a simple, one-engine jet aircraft with no afterburner, was first used for training at Santa Rosa. Barely settled in, the air group was sent out for a second tour on the *USS Boxer* that would prove more than harrowing. The men were within thirty days of coming home again when a bomber crashed on the

—*Frank Scott Collection*

333

Clayt Williams' tavern on Fourth Street near Farmers Lane, its walls hung with old signs and rusty farm implements, was among the many businesses that profited from having the Navy in town.

flight deck and the *Boxer* became a subject for enemy propaganda. The Communists put out the word they had sunk the *Boxer*. To disprove the claim, the Santa Rosa squadrons propped up the flight deck with beams and flew for ten more weeks. "Half the town was in Alameda to welcome us home," Anders recalled.

The Navy once again enhanced the economy of the town. Each squadron had a favorite hangout. The fighter squadrons divided themselves between Lena's, El Rancho, and the Alibi, a bar on outer Fourth Street near Farmers Lane. The attack squadron met at the Seven Seas. They all knew Clayt's, the creekside watering hole decorated with horse collars and old signs reminiscent of Jake Luppold's Senate Saloon of an earlier era. And they all knew the way to Gordon's Drive In.

In the two years the field was open, the Navy shared the base for two weeks each summer with Air National Guard squadrons from the western states. Two fighter wings, which translated to sixty to 100 pilots and support crews, came for training. The impact of the Korean War, adding about 5 percent to the population of the town for the duration, was much less than what had occurred in World War II. But, as in WWII, a surprising number of men

stationed in Santa Rosa came back to make their home. Some, like Anders, found wives here. Others just liked the possibilities in the growing community.

Not all the government installations left Sonoma County at the end of the Korean War. The Army Signal Corps' west coast radio interceptor station—commissioned at the start of WWII when the National Security Agency determined a need to hear what the Japanese, Chinese, Russians, and Indo-Chinese were saying when they talked among themselves—continued its "top secret" operation at Two Rock Ranch, as did the Naval radio interceptor station at Skaggs Island south of Sonoma.[19]

The Central Intelligence Agency joined the ranks of Sonoma County's "listeners" after WWII with a hilltop installation off Eastside Road near Forestville. The CIA employed some fifty people as analysts at the listening post, many of them foreign-born, all of them versed in at least two languages, one of which was Russian or Chinese, all of them pledged to silence about what they did, for whom, and why.[20]

The 1950s was the decade of Coyote Dam, which harnessed the Russian River above Ukiah for water and flood control, and the "Master Plan for Sewering the Greater Santa Rosa Plain," which allowed for the beginnings of westward expansion which would continue throughout the century. But the city itself was still home-owned. Fourth Street was full of little stores whose owners still made good livings selling only millinery, only ice cream, only lingerie—a testimony to the fact that oldtime shopping patterns had not yet changed. Even Montgomery Village was more of the same little shops, family owned—Ruth and Jack Rollins' Fireside Stationery, Archie Cash's Men's Wear, Gartin's Cleaners. It was not yet a chain-store town.

Santa Rosa of the '50s was a fine place to live. People didn't lock their doors. Parking spaces could be found in front of whatever little shop you were patronizing. There

A "before" photograph, above, is this 1920s view from Proctor Heights looking southwest toward Santa Rosa, over the Sonoma Road and the orchards and fields that would be the Grace Tract and Montgomery Village. On the following page is the "after" view of the same vista—an aerial photograph of the same area made by Charles Ackley from above Rincon Valley.

was a traffic cop at the intersection of Fourth and Mendocino (for many years it was former police chief Watt Maxwell), who would often greet pedestrians by name and pass the time of day.

But change was in the air. Safeways were replacing many of the small grocery stores and meat markets. Sears Roebuck was pulling in customers from as far away as Humboldt County. The concept of a regional shopping area, promoted by the *Press Democrat*'s Townes and continued by his successor as general manager, Dan Bowerman, was much discussed. The farm town of the '30s had passed through the war years and emerged with fancier ideas.

The annexation of 1955 would prove to be the pivot point for the swing into these new attitudes. In the next official census Santa Rosa's population of 17,902 would rise to 31,027, a much greater percentage increase than that of the county as a whole during that period.[21] Now, nearly one in four Sonoma County residents was a Santa Rosan. The urbanization of the rural county had begun in earnest, with Santa Rosa leading the way.

In 1955, the first year of its second century, Julio Carrillo's one-square-mile town, laid out so carefully around the Hispanic-style plaza he felt was necessary to a proper city, was abandoning its farm-town image to take its place among the growth-oriented, medium-sized urban centers of the San Francisco Bay Area. ❧

Sources & Notes

Research for this book has come from a mosaic of community resources: archival research utilizing primary and secondary sources; oral histories employing interviews and remembrances; plus many sources that may have been sent off to storage by the owners, then retrieved just for this book.

Seeking same or next-day reports of events to capture the tenor of the times, the authors did extensive research into the newspapers, particularly the *Press Democrat*, through the fifty-year period. The Santa Rosa *Republican*, the Santa Rosa *Herald*, and the Santa Rosa *Independent* were also consulted, as were selected newspapers from other communities.

Letters noted in this volume were written to or owned by the authors, unless otherwise noted. The oral research is based on interviews done by the authors over the eighteen-year period this and the previous volume were in preparation. Much material has been drawn from the use of private sources. Individuals, students, and organizations have generously shared their unpublished manuscripts, family scrapbooks, collections, and written memoirs. These often include pamphlets, programs, dedication information, minutes of meetings, plans for property development, and other items of historical interest.

The increasing number of MA theses available through Sonoma State University or the PhD dissertations available at Bancroft, Berkeley, or Sonoma County Library relating to the history of Santa Rosa and Sonoma County have been helpful. Many were consulted; some were used and are noted. Resources for Sonoma County were researched at California State Library, Sacramento; Bancroft Library, UC, Berkeley; California Historical Society, San Francisco; and Society of California Pioneers.

For general and specific information, the U.S. Census and Census Field Notes provided valuable ethnic, agricultural, and population information; the Santa Rosa Water Works maps (1877-1947); the building permits (1941-44, 1947-51) and assessment rolls of the city (1867-1964) as well as information available at the County Recorder's office provided demographic resources. Directories of Santa Rosa and Sonoma County; church histories; lodge and club histories; Sonoma County Genealogical Society, cemetery records; SRJC and SRHS yearbooks; Santa Rosa telephone directories (1907-1956, some missing years); License Register (1909-1922, some missing years) covering saloons, junk, milk wagons, cigar dealers, etc. educated us on the miscellanies of the community. Local publications such as the *Sonoma County Labor Journal* (1922-36, not complete); *Nulaid News* (1927-29); *Sonoma County Farm Bureau Monthly*; the journals of Sonoma County Historical Society: all gave us information on the economic developments of the town. Most of these sources are available in the Sonoma County Library. Other helpful library sources can be found in "Sonoma County History—a Bibliography and Union List" (Sonoma County Historical Records Commission: May 1990).

The need for information on the Depression, schools, court cases, the Army and Navy bases in Santa Rosa and Sonoma County and Santa Rosa City government required research into government documents. These included U.S. Works Projects Administration information (California State Library, Sacramento); Statistical and Municipal Reports of the City of Santa Rosa; court cases (Hall of Justice, Sonoma County and State Law Library, Sacramento); records at Sonoma County Department of Education and Santa Rosa City Schools; minutes of the City Council; and copies of the charters, City of Santa Rosa; information from numerous departments of Sonoma County; research in the National Archives, Washington, D.C. and Suitland, Maryland; Naval Archives at the Washington Navy Yard; and Air Force Archives at Bolling AFB, Washington D.C.

Previous histories of Santa Rosa, covering this period of time, were utilized in this book. These include Ernest Finley's *History of Sonoma County* (Press Democrat, 1937); Honoria Tuomey's *History of Sonoma County, California* (Clarks, 1926); Thomas Gregory's *History of Sonoma County, California* (Historic Record Co., 1911); Finley's *Santa Rosans I Have Known* and Historia, Ltd.'s first publication, *Santa Rosa, a Nineteenth Century Town*.

There is not space to acknowledge the dozens of general sources examined for information on the state of the nation and the state of the state for this fifty-year period. Specific sources are listed herewith.

CHAPTER ONE

1. Originally this church had been built as a Christian Church.
2. Letter from "Jessie" to her sisters "Lillie and Hattie" in Sacramento, April 27, 1906, LeBaron Collection.
3. *Press Democrat*, April 18, 1962, interview with earthquake survivor Bob Wheeler.
4. *Democrat-Republican*, April 21, 1906.
5. Many years later, in the 1950s, Minerva stood tall at the front of Woody's Secondhand Store at Fifth and E streets.
6. Ernest Finley, ed. *History of Sonoma County, Golden Gate Bridge Edition* (Press Democrat Publishing Co., 1937), p. 280.
7. *The Fresno Bee*, October 20, 1974.
8. *Santa Rosa Republican*, May 8, 1906.
9. Letter from Victoria Bamford to her sister Elizabeth Jones in Potter Valley, April 19, 1906, Betty Bamford Trailer Collection.
10. City of Santa Rosa Municipal Report, year ending July 4, 1907.
11. James Berkland, Santa Clara County geologist who made a study of the earthquake, estimated that 150 died in Santa Rosa. Research by Gladys Hansen, San Francisco City Archivist, also indicates that death totals were much higher than originally reported.
12. *Report of the Relief Committee, Santa Rosa Cal., 1906* (Press Democrat Publishing Co., 1906) followed by the *Report of the Relief Committee, April 20, 1906, to July 4, 1907* (Santa Rosa Municipal Report, 1907).
13. Ibid.
14. *Press Democrat*, June 5, 1906.
15. *Democrat-Republican*, April 23, 1906.

CHAPTER TWO

1. *San Francisco and North Pacific Railway Company, 17th Annual Report* (Year ending June 30, 1906 (John Monahan & Co.). Also, Stanley T. Borden, "Petaluma & Santa Rosa Electric Railroad," *The Western Railroader*, Vol. XXXIII, No. 4 (April 1960), p. 26. Also, *Press Democrat*, Feb. 8, 1917.
2. Later these two became the California and the Roxy, respectively.
3. Former NWP employees' presentation to the Sonoma County Historical Society, January 1988.
4. Ibid.
5. The CNW, which was the Donahue family's San Francisco and North Pacific railroad, and the narrow gauge North Pacific Coast, its name changed to the North Shore, joined under one ownership by the Marin County entrepreneur, Arthur W. Foster, in the 1890s.
6. *Press Democrat*, August 9, 1910.
7. *Petaluma Argus*, August 9, 1910.
8. *Press Democrat*, May 9, 1909.
9. Ibid.
10. *Commercial Car Journal* (June 1981).
11. *Press Democrat*, November 1, 1912; July 19, 1913; May 3, 1914.
12. Andy Triaca, interview, May 1986.
13. *Press Democrat*, June 11, 1916.
14. *Directory of Santa Rosa, Petaluma and Sonoma County*, (Press Democrat Publishing Co., 1924).
15. Doble and his wife Alene moved to Santa Rosa's Holland Heights in 1950. Doble continued to work on his dream that steam would one day replace gasoline as a source of fuel for American automobiles until his death in 1961.
16. *Press Democrat*, July 12, 1914. The Redwood Empire Association records give the year as 1911, but without documentation.
17. *Press Democrat*, May 11, 1916.
18. *Press Democrat*, March 27, 1927; June 22, 1927; March 11, 1928; June 3, 1928.
19. According to former county public works director Don Head, engineers, working on the widening of Santa Rosa Avenue in the 1980s, would discover that sections of that old highway had been, in fact, paved twice in the same time period, raising questions about the quality of the initial work.
20. *Redwood Empire Travel-eer*, Redwood Empire Association, February-March 1929, p. 7.
21. Ibid.
22. *Press Democrat*, March 18, 1927.
23. James D. Hart, *A Companion to California* (Oxford University Press, 1978), p. 377.
24. John van der Zee, *The Gate* (Simon & Schuster, 1986), p. 63.
25. Hart, p. 164.
26. Finley's oft-repeated exclamation has become part of the lore of California journalism.
27. Finley, *History*, pp. 444-445.
28. *Press Democrat*, April 27, 1937.
29. *Press Democrat*, quoted February 17, 1966.
30. Ibid.
31. Guglielmetti family scrapbook, courtesy Merie Guglielmetti.

32. *Press Democrat,* July 27, 1919; August 24, 1920.
33. Exhibition flights were often attempts to reach new heights. As early as 1912, pilot Weldon Cooke, with many Santa Rosans watching, reached an altitude of 2,500 feet.
34. *Press Democrat,* September 4, 1919.
35. R.E. Fisher, chairman of the aviation committee of the California Developmental Association, speech at a luncheon at the Occidental Hotel, May 18, 1929.
36. *Press Democrat,* May 9, 1929; January 30, 1931; February 25, 1931.
37. *Sonoma County, a Preliminary Survey by Members of a Study Group in the School of Social Studies,* 1940, Myer Cohen, Staff Chairman, p. 90.
38. Joann Mitchell, "Role of Clarence Lea in Federal Regulation of Aviation" (unpublished graduate paper Sonoma State College, 1970). Also, historical data from Sonoma County Airport, courtesy airport assistant manager Robert Becker.
39. Borden, p. 26.
40. The last passenger train on the Northwestern Pacific line was not a train at all but a Budd car from Willits to Eureka in 1958. *The Redwood,* the last passenger train from Eureka to San Rafael, made the down trip for the last time on November 9, 1958, per Fred Stindt, *The Northwestern Pacific Railroad,* Vol. I (Kelseyville, CA: by the author, 1964), p. 55.

CHAPTER THREE

References 1-14 are from the *Press Democrat:* (1) March 23, 1917; (2) October 22, 1914, November 16, 1914; (3) April 7, 1917; (4) April 16, 1918; (5) March 26, 1918; (6) September 7, 1918; (7) February 27, 1918; (8) Letters home from Sonoma County men and women serving in France appeared in the *Press Democrat* throughout the fall and winter of 1918-19; (9) Ibid.; (10) September 26, 1918; (11) October 9, 1918; (12) October 16, 1918; (13) November 16, 1918; (14) November 2 to November 15, 1918.
15. Letter from Frances Grimm Little, March 12, 1989. Mrs. Little, interview, March 28, 1993.
16. Burgess Titus's memoirs were written over several years. Titus died in 1992. The original is in the possession of his family.

17. *Press Democrat,* November 3, 1918.
18. Whether Bloomfield escaped completely is unknown but the flu was often late to strike in rural areas. Ukiah's most serious period was in January of 1919.
19. *Press Democrat,* February 2, 1919.
20. California State Department of Health Services, Death Records.

CHAPTER FOUR

1. Finley, *History,* p 368. Sonoma County was tenth in the nation in agricultural production ($29,770,620) in the 1930 census. In 1920, the county ranked eighth in the nation in agricultural income ($32,300,632); also, *Press Democrat,* February 19, 1933. Other statistical information can be found in the *Fourteen* and *Fifteenth Censuses of the United States,* (Agriculture reports for the Western States, 1922 and 1932).
2. *Press Democrat,* March 6, 1955.
3. *Agricultural, Industrial and Scenic Resources of Sonoma County.* Published by *Sonoma County Herald,* 1919.
4. Adair Heig, *History of Petaluma, a California River Town* (Scottwall Associates, 1982), p. 114.
5. Finley, p. 369.
6. Ibid.
7. Heig, p. 117.
8. Phillip Naftaly, "Jewish Chicken Farmers in Petaluma, California 1904-1975," *Western States Jewish History,* Vol. XXIII, No. 3 (1991), pp. 231-247.
9. Ibid., p. 247.
10. Sonoma County Department of Agriculture, *Agricultural Crop Report to the Board of Supervisors and the State Department of Agriculture,* submitted annually.
11. U.S. Department of Commerce, Bureau of the Census, *United States Census of Population and Agriculture* (Agricultural Products of Sonoma County, 1850-1935) California.
12. Harold Bruner, interview, April 10, 1981.
13. John Talbot, "Recollections of a Vanished California Industry," *The Far Westerner,* Stockton Corral of Westerners (October 1987).
14. Vern Wood, interview, July 1989.
15. *Press Democrat,* December 14, 1918.
16. *Press Democrat,* August 31, 1921, quoting

circular handed to hop pickers.
17. Joseph Maddux, interview, June 1976.
18. Vern Wood, interview.
19. Robert W. Bussman, interview, Stockton, California, July 1989.
20. Valerie Hagerty, quoting *Hopper* magazine (unpublished student paper, SRJC, 1981), p. 11.
21. Walter Tischer, interview, Sebastopol, 1976.
22. Haraszthy was commissioned by the California Legislature to study European vineyards. His report, titled *Grape Culture, Wines and Winemaking,* was published in 1862.
23. Joseph Vercelli, interview, 1981. The numbers of 42,000 acres in 1920 and the 256 wineries the same year come from Vercelli, a wine historian.
24. Cooperative Extension Work in Agriculture and Home Economics, State of California, *Statistical Information on Sonoma County Agriculture, 1899-1944.* University of California, Berkeley, 1944-45. Although a state survey done in 1936 shows that the peak year for production was 1930, there is evidence that the 34,000 acres of grapes shown in Sonoma County that year were misleading. The survey did not take into account vines that had been removed after the "bust" of 1926.
25. *Republican,* September 27, 1922.
26. *Press Democrat,* January 30, 1921.
27. *Press Democrat,* September 17, 1926.
28. *Press Democrat,* November 22, 1933.
29. Dewey Baldocchi, speech to North Coast Grape Growers Association, Healdsburg, 1992.
30. Louis Foppiano, "Grape Tidings," a publication of Foppiano Vineyards, Vol. II, No. 3 (summer 1982).
31. Vercelli, interview.
32. LeBaron, Blackman, Mitchell and Hansen, *Santa Rosa, A Nineteenth Century Town* (Santa Rosa: Historia, Ltd., 1985), p. 69.
33. *Press Democrat,* December, 5, 1924.
34. Land that his family would later donate to the city as Juilliard Park.
35. Theresa Guenza, interview, and Rita Carniglia Hall, interview, September 1982.
36. Now part of Hunt-Wesson Foods, Hunt Brothers moved from Santa Rosa early in the 20th century to establish bigger canneries and processing plants in the

Sacramento Valley.
37. *Press Democrat,* May 23, 1928.
38. At the time of publication it was operated by Hotle's grandson, Robert Burdo.
39. *Press Democrat* library, weather files.
40. Walter Tischer, "Notes on the history of the apple industry," Sebastopol, 1976.
41. *Press Democrat,* November 5, 1929; November 28, 1929; March 25, 1930.
42. *Press Democrat,* January 28, 1931.
43. *Press Democrat,* June 1, 1932.
44. The seed farm property was sold by the Rohnert family in 1960 to developers Paul Golis and Maurice Fredericks who developed the first phases of the planned community of Rohnert Park.
45. *Press Democrat,* July 17, 1936.
46. *Press Democrat,* January 15, 1935.
47. *Press Democrat,* February 27, 1937.
48. *Press Democrat,* "Empire Farms," May 15, 1955; July 1, 1956.
49. Finley, *History,* p. 368.
50. Frank Anthony Speth, "A History of Agricultural Labor in Sonoma County, California" (unpublished MA thesis, University of California, 1938), p. 19A.
51. Sonoma County Department of Agriculture, *Agricultural Crop Report to the Board of Supervisors and the State Department of Agriculture, 1955.*
52. Ibid.

CHAPTER FIVE

1. *Pacific Rural Press,* May 1932, has figures to show farm towns led urban centers in per capita retail sales in California.
2. A portion of the rebuilt cannery burned in 1909 and the operation was moved to a new building at Third Street and the railroad in 1917.
3. Edwin M. Bent, compiler, *The Official Program, Fourth of July, 1908* (*Press Democrat* Print).
4. "Printed Population Schedules, examination of Census field notes," courtesy Dee Blackman, November 1978, and Meryl King, 1976.
5. Many of the responses from 250 elderly citizens questioned about the "most important person" in Santa Rosa in their lifetime named Frank Doyle. Authors' survey, 1975.
6. University Street became Talbot Avenue when the bridge across Santa Rosa Creek

was built in 1935.

7. *Press Democrat*, July 20, 1922.

8. Site of the Fourth Street Safeway.

9. Thomas Grace reopened the brewery in 1958. In 1966 the brewery was sold to Maier Brewing Company of Los Angeles. The Santa Rosa brewery closed forever in 1967. This and other Grace Brothers history can be found in John Burton's extensive research project.

10. Letters, Chamber of Commerce Archives.

11. *Christian Science Monitor*, October 21, 1987. News of the impending visit can be found in the *Press Democrat*, October 20, 1915.

12. *Press Democrat*, October 23, 1915.

13. Letter from Charles Black, quoting Ford Motor Company's history, December 7, 1989. Also, Ken and Pat Kraft, *Luther Burbank, The Wizard and the Man* (New York: Meredith Press, 1967), p. 205.

14. Walter Nagle, year-end report, 1915.

15. Fechtelkotter would later shorten his name to Fetch.

16. *Press Democrat*, February 6, 1915.

17. Saare family scrapbook, Alice Saare Collection. Also, *Republican*, August 8, 1922.

18. According to radio historian Stan Bunger of San Francisco's KCBS, most stations in cities of comparable size were "out on the plains" outside the reach of bigger stations. Interview, February 1989.

19. Frank McLaurin, interview, and Hilmar Cann, interview, February 1989.

20. Strobino had an unusual background for a businessman. Between 1905-1920 he was a labor organizer and agitator, a pioneer of the Italian Socialist Federation, a member of the Industrial Workers of the World, and a friend of Emma Goldman and "Big Bill" Haywood.

21. Dan Peterson, Bette Patterson, and Gerrie Peterson, *The Old Post Office and Federal Building, Past and Present* (Sonoma County Bicentennial Commission, 1976). The post office building was moved two blocks north to a site on Seventh Street in 1979, where it was converted to the Sonoma County Museum.

22. Cannon went on to extend his newspaper empire to the *Portland Oregonian* and, by 1915, the *Reno Gazette*.

23. *Press Democrat*, April 29, 1923.

24. Frank Arrigoni and Louis Traverso, interview, October 20, 1985. Arrigoni's Market was an institution that lasted nearly 40 years, selling to the Nabor brothers in 1975.

25. Traverso's Market was in the redevelop-ment area for the Santa Rosa Plaza in the 1970s and was moved by the agency to B Street between Second and Third streets. At the time of the move, Louis's sons Gene and Bill and Enrico's son George became partners. Rico's wife Adeline ran the deli in the new store.

26. Joan Perry Ryan, interview, March 1992.

27. *Press Democrat*, January 19, 1926; November 29, 1934; April 19, 1936.

28. Ted Gambogi, "Notes on the history of the basalt quarries," LeBaron Collection.

29. From William Kortum's interview with A.J. Camozzi, a quarryman, as quoted in Nancy Olmsted's "History of Paving Blocks along San Francisco's South Beach Waterfront" (San Francisco Redevelopment Agency, 1991).

30. *Santa Rosa Digest*, Santa Rosa Chamber of Commerce, Vol. I, No. 6 (November 14, 1924).

31. *The Press Democrat's 1924 Directory of Santa Rosa, Petaluma, and Sonoma County*, p. 11.

32. *Press Democrat*, September 27, 1928.

33. The house would be a subject of much controversy in the 1980s and 1990s after it was damaged by fire and moved.

34. Three more Pedersen "sons," Ken, Paul, and Richard, great grandsons of the founder, became the fourth generation in what was one of the oldest continuing family businesses in Santa Rosa.

35. Ralph Stone joined the board of directors of Santa Rosa Savings & Loan in the 1940s. In 1958, he became president of the S&L, which later merged with Great Western.

36. In 1964 Marjorie and Kenneth Brown's son Corrick Brown, musical director of the Santa Rosa Symphony Orchestra, became a partner as did store manager Leonard Curry. Curry retired in the 1980s. Corrick's son Keven Brown became the fourth generation management in 1992.

37. When Clem retired in 1964 Elwin's son Gerry bought his share. After the 1969 earthquake, the store relocated on Fifth Street just a few doors from where the original Flagler's stood before the 1906 quake. In 1990, Hardisty's moved to Montgomery Village.

38. Harold Bruner sold the art business in 1970 but continued to work there until his retirement in 1972, the same year the shop moved to Cleveland Avenue. Bruner Radio (and later TV) moved to its Mendocino Avenue location in 1957. Bud's son William C. Bruner became owner of the business when his father died in 1982.

39. Clark Mailer sold the store in 1981 and the building was remodeled to accommodate an arcade of small shops with apartments upstairs.

40. Jean "Dusty" Destruel, interview, May 1993.

41. Rosenberg's closed in 1988.

42. Bert Callwell, interview, 1987.

43. Of all these, only Tuttle's survived as this book went to press. Medico sold to Bill's Drugs chain in 1983, and again to Long's in 1993. Farmer's Empire closed in 1993.

44. Ira B. Cross, *Financing an Empire, Banking in California*, Vol. IV (San Francisco: S.J. Clarke Publishing Co., 1927).

45. Joseph Lombardi, interview, May 1978.

46. Leonard Talbot, interview, at age 89, in 1987. Hannaford & Talbot sold to First California Company in the early 1960s.

47. *Press Democrat*, November 28, 1925; June 13, 1926; November 17, 1927; October 20, 1928.

CHAPTER SIX

1. Page Smith, *America Enters the World, A People's History of the Progressive Era and World War I*, Vol. VII (McGraw-Hill, 1985), p. 784.

2. Joseph Vercelli, Sonoma County wine historian, interview October 1983. In 1914, according to the *Press Democrat*, July 18, 1914, quoting the county assessor, there were 229. There were 150 wineries in 1915 according to a pamphlet produced by Sonoma County for the Panama-Pacific Exposition, courtesy Donna Born.

3. *Press Democrat*, February 12, 1901.

4. *Press Democrat*, September 21, 1918.

5. Kevin Starr, *Inventing the Dream, California through the Progressive Era* (Oxford University Press, 1985), p. 153.

6. *Press Democrat*, October 2, 1919.

7. *Press Democrat*, October 16, 1920.

8. Emil J. "Nin" Guidotti, interview, February 1982.

9. *Press Democrat*, December 7, 1930.

10. *Press Democrat*, September 7, 1923.

11. *Press Democrat*, November 26, 1921.

12. Guidotti, interview.

13. *Press Democrat*, November 3, 1925.

14. Guidotti, interview.

15. *Press Democrat*, April 19, 1931.

16. *Press Democrat*, February 18, 1928. Also, Tom Money, former undersheriff, interview, 1975.

17. *Press Democrat*, January 30, 1923.

18. *Press Democrat*, April 2, 1931.

19. *Press Democrat*, April 19, 1931.

20. *Press Democrat*, September 16, 1922. *Republican*; September 27, 1922; October 6, 1922.

21. Money, interview.

22. *Press Democrat*, March 2, 1927. Also, Roy Michie, interview, July 3, 1983.

23. Raford Leggett, interview, December 1983.

24. *Press Democrat*, May 5, 1923.

25. Edith and Beatrice Gemetti, interview, December 1983.

26. Letter from Wes Caughey, Storm Lake, Iowa, October 28, 1987. Also, "A Face from Sonoma County," *The Journal*, Sonoma County Historical Society, No. 3 (1980), p. 3, interview with Fred Barnes.

27. *Press Democrat*, May 23, 1934; November 30, 1934; February 7, 1935; May 24, 1935.

28. Leighton Ray, M.D., interview, September 1977. Also, *Press Democrat*, November 10, 1929; January 12, 1930.

29. *Press Democrat*, April 9, 1931.

30. *Press Democrat*, February 6, 1935.

CHAPTER SEVEN

1. The last lynching occurred in 1933 in San Jose when a mob seized the men who murdered the young scion of a well-known mercantile business.

2. Lynching participant, interviews, December 1985 and August 29, 1989. Oral history, sealed until ten years after the participant's death, in the Sonoma County History Room, Sonoma County Library.

3. Spud Murphy was on trial for the rape in a San Francisco court when the Santa Rosa lynching occurred. He was found guilty by a jury that deliberated only twenty minutes.

4. Crowds gathered outside the jail for several days. On December 6, a mob of 3,000 had attempted to storm the doors of the jail; Mayor Rutherford ordered a fire truck to stand by at Fourth and Hinton to prevent mob action.

5. Lynching participant, interview.

6. The species of tree used for the hanging has been a point of contention ever since the event occurred. Many remembered it as an oak tree. Neighbors identified it repeatedly as a locust.

7. *Petaluma Argus*, December 11, 1920.

8. Lynching participant, interview.

9. *Press Democrat*, June 1, 1922.

10. *Press Democrat*, February 26, 1933.

11. *Press Democrat*, May 5, 1933; September 16, 1933; November 4, 1934.

12. Melvin "Dutch" Flohr, interview, 1975.

13. *Press Democrat*, July 25, 1935.

14. Leonard Talbot, interview, 1986.

15. Russell Denner, interview, 1986.

16. *San Francisco Chronicle*, July 16, 1935.

17. *Press Democrat*, July 16, 1935; September 13, 1935.

18. Sonoma County Records, Case Nos. 612C and 613C, Hall of Justice, Sonoma County. Also, California Appellate Reports, No. 18,

1912, State Law Library, Sacramento, p. 75.

19. In 1922 Governor-elect Friend Richardson and his family spent Christmas Day with Dr. Burke.

20. *Press Democrat*, August 4, 5, and 12, 1910.

21. *Press Democrat*, April 14, 1923.

22. Pio served 28 years in the Men's Colony in San Luis Obispo. He was discharged in 1977—to the Sacramento area.

23. San Quentin Museum Records, March 5, 1954.

24. Both were convicted although evidence later indicated that they had been victims of perjury. Mooney served 23 years in prison before he was pardoned in 1939. Billings' sentence was commuted in 1939. He was pardoned in 1961.

25. Herbert Waters, interview, October 1987.

26. San Francisco still had four newspapers: the *Examiner* and the *Chronicle* in the morning, the *News* and the *Call-Bulletin* in the afternoon; Santa Rosa had two, the *Morning Republican* and the *Press Democrat*.

27. Brown would later serve two terms as governor of California.

28. Accounts of the 1949 trial and the theories that were explored later came from newspaper accounts and from a series of interviews with Charles Raudebaugh, crime reporter for the *San Francisco Chronicle*, who covered the murder story.

29. In 1981, a biographer of Jimmy "The Weasel" Frattiano, a Mafia enforcer, quoted him on the subject of the DeJohn killing. Frattiano pinned it on a Chicago mobster named Dominic Galiano who told Frattiano he was under orders from a mob boss who was attempting to take over organized crime in San Francisco.

30. *Press Democrat*, June 3, 1954.

31. John Schubert, "Blue Lights and Red Faces," (Prostitution in Downtown Santa Rosa), *The Journal*, Sonoma County Historical Society, No. 5 (1990), p. 4. Also, in 1907, District Attorney Clarence Lea noted at least ten "houses of ill fame" in the area of First and D streets. He warned the "prominent people" who leased out these buildings for immoral purposes, *San Francisco Call*, December 29, 1907.

32. *School of Social Studies Survey*, p. 65.

33. Walton Bean, *California, an Interpretive History* (McGraw-Hill Book Co., 1973), p. 387.

34. *Press Democrat*, November 11, 1923; *Republican*, November 12, 1923.

35. Ibid.

36. Information on the Green House was obtained in interviews with Sonoma County residents who asked not to be identified, 1990.

37. *Petaluma Argus*, September 9, 1925.

38. *Press Democrat,* February 27, 1974.

39. Marilyn Josi, director of the Sonoma County Law Library, verified the terms of earlier judges.

40. The next Superior Court addition to the county would not occur until 1966, when Joseph P. Murphy, Jr. became the fourth judge. Mahan had been appointed to succeed Geary at his retirement in 1957. When Comstock retired in 1964, he was succeeded by another muni judge, F. Leslie Manker. The fifth seat was established in 1974 and filled by the appointment of Rex Sater. In 1993 there were ten Superior Courts in Sonoma County.

41. Court records show the divorce was granted July 17, 1917.

42. Dennis Keegan, speech to Sonoma County Bar Association, 1990.

43. Nick DeMeo, interview, June 1991.

44. *Press Democrat*, April 29, 1952. Also, Edwin Anderson, interview of John Moskowitz on history of Geary, Spridgen & Moskowitz law firm.

45. Some smaller justice courts remained in effect after 1955. By 1968, all justice courts in the county had become part of the municipal court system.

46. John Schubert, "Ellen Fleming: Sonoma County's First Lady of the Court," *The Journal*, Sonoma County Historial Society, No. 2 (1990), p. 10. The first woman appointed to municipal court was Gayle Guynup in 1983.

47. It also earned Dolan a place in women's history. In later years her photograph and biography would be included in a special "Herstory" calendar published by Idaho Planned Parenthood in 1985.

CHAPTER EIGHT

1. Paul Mancini, interview, 1987.

2. *Press Democrat*, March 22, 1931.

3. The disaster increased community awareness of the problems of the hoboes and also intensified surveillance by railroad, city, and county law enforcement officials.

4. *Survey by the School of Social Studies*, pp. 241-43. Also, U.S. Department of Commerce, Bureau of the Census, "Sonoma County Population, Farm Operators, Use of Farm Land, Size of Farms, Value of Farmlands, Buildings, and Irrigated Farms, 1900-1944."

5. *Survey by the School of Social Studies*, p. 15.

6. Dee Blackman, "One View of Women in the 1930s: The Cult of True Womanhood Updated" (unpublished term paper, 1973), p. 12.

7. *Press Democrat*, August 19, 1930.

8. Pauline Goddard, "The Impact of the Work Projects Adminstration (WPA) in Sonoma County" (unpublished MA thesis, Sonoma State University, 1976). Goddard lists seventy-three miles of road and eighteen bridges.

9. Goddard, quoting Mayor Jep Valente of Sonoma, p. 49.

10. Ibid, p. 87.

11. Ibid, p. 70.

12. Martin Coorpender, president of the Luther Burbank Chapter of the National Association of CCC Alumni, interview, 1990.

13. A.P. Noyes, city manager, Report to the City Council, March 8, 1938.

14. Verna Case Tischer, interview, September 1979 and 1985, and Louise Johnston, 1979.

15. *Press Democrat*, July 13, 1933.

16. *Press Democrat*, April 22, 1934.

17. Leonard Talbot, interview, October 1987.

CHAPTER NINE

1. Carey McWilliams, *Factories in the Field* (Little, Brown and Co., 1939), p. 242.

2. Ibid. p. 240.

3. *Press Democrat*, May 1, 1932.

4. *Press Democrat*, July 30, 1935; *Western Worker*, August 5, 1935.

5. *Press Democrat*, July 30, 1935.

6. Ibid.

7. *Press Democrat*, July 31, 1935.

8. *Western Worker*, August 5, 1935.

9. *Press Democrat*, August 6, 1935.

10. *Press Democrat*, August, 9, 1935. Also, Sonoma County Records, Hall of Justice, Sonoma County Case No. 217-88.

11. *Press Democrat*, August 13, 1935.

12. McWilliams (p. 242) says the mayor, a member of the Legislature, and other officials as well as the American Legion participated. Numerous other sources confirm the Legion's role in the incident.

13. Sonoma County Records, Hall of Justice, Sonoma County, Superior Court, Dept. 1, Case No. 2030-C, August 17, 1936.

14. *Press Democrat*, October 27, 1936.

15. *Press Democrat*, October 27, 1936.

16. *ACLU News* (Fiftieth anniversary publication reprint of 1936 newspaper), Vol. XLV, No. 6 (August-September 1980).

17. McWilliams, p. 242.

18. Ibid.

19. Ibid. p. 243.

20. Los Angeles did send workers in 1936 and many stayed because growers lobbied federal agencies for work projects to keep workers through the winter.

21. *Press Democrat*, August 20, 1936.

22. *Press Democrat*, July 30, 1935.

23. Speth, p. 63.

24. Sonoma County Records, Hall of Justice, Sonoma County, Superior Court, No. 8468, October 17, 1923.

25. In 1932 the Appeals Court upheld Fujita.

26. Lucas Benigno, Joe Rivera, and Felisa Asuelo, interview with representatives of the Filipino community, May 1991.

27. Danny Cardona, former president of the Sonoma County Filipino-American Association, interview, May 1991.

28. *Sonoma County Farm Bureau Monthly*, Vol. I, No. 4 (June 1918).

29. Speth, p. 64.

30. *Press Democrat*, March 18, 1914.

31. Finley, p. 368; p. 371.

32. *Press Democrat*, March 31, 1936.

33. *Press Democrat*, February 9, 1938.

34. Ibid.

35. *San Francisco News*, editoral quoting Wilford Howard, January 5, 1938.

36. Opal Garrett Young, interview, June 1979.

37. Joe Young, interview, June 1979.

38. Glen Crownover, interview, July 1986.

39. Charles Coates, interview, June 1979.

40. References 40-48 are from the *Press Democrat*: (40) January 16, 1909; (41) May 2, 1917; (42) September 16, 1914; (43) February 5, 1915; (44) June 21, 1918; (45) July 2, 1919; (46) Letters to the Editor, February 1924; (47) January 15, 1934; (48) September 2, 6, and 9, 1942.

49. Walter Tischer, interview, February 1980.

50. Talmadge "Babe" Wood, interview, 1987.

51. Benny Carranza, Rafael Morales, Lolita and Tony Tamayo, and other former *braceros*, interview, May 1987.

52. *Press Democrat*, August 12 and 14, 1955.

CHAPTER TEN

1. Joann Mitchell, "The Career Biography of Clarence Frederick Lea" (unpublished MA thesis, Sonoma State College, 1971). In 1958 the Federal Aviation Agency encompassed Lea's ideas with few changes.

2. Hubert Scudder was the fifth Congressman to serve in the first half of the century, being elected when Lea retired in 1948.

3. The friends would work together again, in the Legislature, when Reindollar was elected state senator from Marin County.

4. *Press Democrat*, January 7, 1921; January 13, 1937; March 1, 1934.

5. *Press Democrat*, April 23, 1926.

6. Bean, p. 365. Also, Ross Dematre, Clarence

McIntosh, Earl Waters, eds., *The Rumble of California Politics*, 1848-1970 (John Wiley & Sons, 1970), p. 214.

7. *Rumble*, p. 200.

8. Courtesy of Denis Edeline, First District congressional aide.

9. *Press Democrat*, March 27, 1935.

10. Wallace's observation was a favorite story of his successor, Donald Head.

11. *Press Democrat*, January 7, 1920.

12. *Press Democrat*, April 4, 1920.

13. *Press Democrat*, July 10, 1920.

14. *Press Democrat*, August 10, 1920.

15. *Press Democrat*, September 12, 1920.

16. Donald Head, former county director of public works, interview, July, 1993.

17. Hall was the mother of developer Hugh Codding, who served as mayor and councilman in Santa Rosa in the 1960s.

18. Four years later, in 1957, a group of Sonoma County officials died in a plane crash on their way to visit Miller at his Arizona ranch. Dead in the crash were Ken Carter, manager of the Sonoma County Fair, Chris Beck, chairman of the fair's board of directors, and Lou Basso, the fair's concessionaire.

19. Sonoma County Records, Board of Supervisors.

20. *Press Democrat*, November 18, 1930.

21. Assembly Bill 1021.

22. *Press Democrat*, August 1, 1920; July 8, 1921.

23. *Press Democrat*, October 26, 1913. Also, City of Santa Rosa files, Municipal Reports, 1917-18.

24. *Press Democrat*, editorial, February 18, 1910.

25. *Press Democrat*, October 10, 1911.

26. Senator Slater helped change registration laws to allow women to simply certify that they were "over 21." The law went into effect in March of 1912, the month before the election.

27. Santa Rosa Police Department pamphlet, 1913.

28. Although the newspaper called this a "first," there is evidence that there were earlier women jurors such as July 12, 1913, in Petaluma Justice Court when an all-women panel found "one of their sex" guilty of battery and fined her $1. This, too, was called a "first."

29. City of Santa Rosa Records, courtesy of Kitty Frisbie.

30. *Press Democrat,* August 4, 1915; November 19, 1915.

31. *Pacific Municipalities*, California League of Municipalities, Vol. XXXI, No. 9 (September 1917).

32. *Press Democrat*, May 19, 1920; June 26,

1920; February 17, 1921; March 2, 1922.

33. Santa Rosa was far from a pioneer in this concept, even in its own region. The first recorded instance of a city manager appointment was in Ukiah in 1904 when the post of "chief executive officer" was created. This history-making event, according to historians, "went virtually unnoticed at the time."

34. *Press Democrat*, May 3, 1923.

35. *Press Democrat*, December, 4, 1924.

36. *Press Democrat*, May 1, 1926. Dunbar had served as a state assemblyman in 1903-04.

37. Finley, p. 335.

38. *Press Democrat*, December 16, 1928. His opposition called him a "dictator," charging that he had rehired Cozad; that he favored the California Willite Company; that he had purchased a turbine for the city from Steiner's partner, *Press Democrat*, October 15, 1924.

39. City of Santa Rosa Records, Municipal Report, 1917-18.

40. *Press Democrat*, January 1, 1925.

41. Field notes from consultant Anne Bloomfield, made in preparation for an historical survey of the City of Santa Rosa, 1991.

42. Jim Davis, retired SRFD captain, compiled the department's history.

43. Bloomfield, notes.

44. *Press Democrat*, April 2, 1930.

45. Succession of council members was provided by the city manager's office, City of Santa Rosa.

CHAPTER ELEVEN

1. Floyd P. Bailey, *Santa Rosa Junior College, 1918-1957* (Santa Rosa Junior College, 1967), p. 1.

2. *Press Democrat*, December 5, 1917.

3. The school received full accreditation by the Western College Association in 1955.

4. Bailey died in 1968. *The Years of the Presidency of Randolph Newman, 1957-70* (Santa Rosa Junior College Foundation, 1988).

5. Robert Dodds, *History of a Partnership* (Exchange Bank, 1980), p. 14. Twelve million dollars in scholarship funds had helped more than 25,000 students as of 1993.

6. *Press Democrat*, April 1, 1922.

7. *Press Democrat*, May 5, 1923.

8. *Press Democrat,*, March 17, 1968.

9. *Press Democrat*, November 3, 1922.

10. Harvey Sullivan, Martha Erwin, Raymond Clark, and Henry Abel, recollections as quoted in the SRHS Foundation Newsletter, Vol. II, No. 3 (Summer 1990).

11. James B. Conant, *The American High*

School Today (McGraw Hill, 1919).

12. *Press Democrat*, October 7, 1922. It would be the only public high school in Santa Rosa until 1958 when Montgomery High opened in Montgomery Village east of Santa Rosa.

13. Interview with Martha Erwin, October, 1984.

14. The authors' "most important person in Santa Rosa" questionnaire gave almost as many votes to Miss O'Meara as to her illustrious brother-in-law Doyle.

15. Dr. Frank Keegan, family history of his grandmother.

16. Monograph on history of the Ursuline Order in Santa Rosa, *Press Democrat* Library.

17. Sweet's College Reunion, recollections and interviews, November 1983. Sweet's closed in 1935.

18. Irene Faoro, interview, 1993.

19. Brush and Wallace schools were both converted to residences. The old Rincon School site, across from Calistoga Road is a condominium complex.

20. In 1993, with 42 districts, Sonoma County was still a leader among the non-rural counties in California.

21. Two of these small rural schools have been re-incarnated in their districts. The third school in the Bennett Valley District, built in 1978, was named Strawberry and, in 1991, a new school in the Mark West District was named Riebli School.

22. Ed Riebli, interview, 1976. Also, Sonoma County Office of Education, Book of Deeds, No. 248 (1955), p. 408.

CHAPTER TWELVE

1. Letter from Robert Herbert, retired Naval architect and son of architect William Herbert, November 1989.

2. Letter from C. Raymond Clar, retired state forestry official and Russian River area historian, to Guerneville merchant Kysee Horn, 1985. Clar went on to say that, as a Santa Rosa High School student who "commuted" from Guerneville in the early 1920s, "We outlanders felt the superior indifference keenly."

3. Burgess Titus, memoirs.

4. Peter Dreyer, *A Gardener Touched with Genius: The Life of Luther Burbank,* (Coward, McCann and Geoghegan, Inc, 1975), p. 215.

5. *Pacific Rural Press*, August 14, 1909.

6. In an interview in 1968, Elizabeth Burbank also told "visitor" stories including one about a woman who boldly plucked a blossom as she walked through the garden.

"May I see it please?" Burbank is quoted as saying. "That's the first bloom on that plant."

7. *The Stark Story,* Stark Nurseries' 150th anniversary, a special publication of the Missouri Historical Society (September 1966), p. 29.

8. Dreyer, p. 128.

9. *San Francisco Examiner,* January 27, 1925, p. 11.

10. There is disagreement on where the story first appeared. In 1950 a writer named Frank Piazzi wrote for *Coronet* magazine claiming to be the one who broke the story. Although Dreyer doubts Piazzi's claim, it seems probable that his story of interviewing Burbank for an article in the *Republican* is correct, since Waite recalled that he made the visit to Burbank after seeing a story in the *Republican* about his unorthodox religious views.

11. Ken and Pat Kraft, *Luther Burbank* (Meredith Press, 1967), pp. 244-45.

12. Dreyer, p. 272.

13. Dreyer, p. 275.

14. The honor to Burbank of celebrating Arbor Day on his birthday was proposed early in the century but not made official by the California Legislature until 1947.

15. The landmark Presbyterian Church was demolished in 1959, when the Adventists moved to Sonoma Avenue. Johnson Street subsequently became Seventh Street.

16. Information about the organization of this church and other churches came from a series of church histories compiled and published by the *Press Democrat,* 1963-65.

17. After the re-routing of North Street the one block section in front of the church and beside Fremont Park became Hope Street.

18. This church building became the Christian Life Center after the arrival of Pastor Watson Argue in the 1960s and, when the new center (later the Luther Burbank Center for the Arts) was built, the city purchased the Steele Lane building for a recreation center.

19. Ernest Finley, *Santa Rosans I Have Known* (Press Democrat Publishing Co., 1942), p. 85.

20. This was the Diocese of San Francisco. The Diocese of Santa Rosa was not established until 1962. Father Raters retired in 1961.

21. *Republican*, August 24, 1922.

22. Lillian Green, Everett Shapiro, and Evelyn Gurevitch, interviews, May 1993. The congregation moved in 1963 to a new temple on a site on Mayette Avenue. Information comes from interviews with congregation members.

23. Joe Catalani, interview, 1985.
24. Dan Bonfigli, interview, December 1986. Also, Frank Bastoni, several interviews through the 1970s and 1980s.
25. *Press Democrat*, February. 9, 1926.
26. *Press Democrat*, November 16, 1923; February 16, 1924.
27. Song Borbeau, interview, February, 1985. Jam Kee eventually moved to a converted two-story house on Fifth Street. It was destroyed by fire in the 1990s.
28. *Press Democrat*, October 25, 1924.
29. Fred Daniels, interview, May 1975.
30. Wallace Ware, *The Unforgettables* (Hesperian Press, 1964), p. 45.
31. The Fountain Grove label was sold to Martini & Prati Winery where it continues to be produced.
32. Typescript history of the Monroe Club, courtesy of Clarence Freitas, 1985.
33. March 30, 1932, was designated as "Ripley Day" in Santa Rosa.
34. Finley, *History*, p. 376.
35. Billie Newman Keegan, who worked behind the fountain at Bouk's as a high school student, interview, July 1992.
36. *California Pythian Star* (Souvenir Edition— Grand Lodge, May 16-20, 1921), p. 8.
37. Jack Bookwalter, "Taking in a Show at the Tower," *The Journal*, Sonoma County Historical Society, No. 1 (1993), pp. 9-13.
38. *Press Democrat*, June 29, 1915; August 17, 1915.
39. Harold Bruner, notes on Sonoma County artists. Also, *Press Democrat*, March 14, 1934; April 11, 1937.
40. Maurice Lapp and Robert Sondag, compilers, *Alphonse Sondag, "California Mission Painter"* (SRJC Bicentennial "200 Series," 1976).
41. Trombley's wife Erlene, who played the harp, and concertmaster Walter each continued to play with the orchestra for fifty years.
42. *National Football League Record Book* (1992). The forty points (six TDs, four PATs) Nevers scored in 1929 stands as the NFL scoring record for an individual player in a single game.
43. Letter from Aubrey Brandon, December 1983.
44. Clarence "Cook" Sypher, interview, March 1977. Also, Bailey, p. 101.
45. Drs. William Rudee, Horace Sharrocks, Leighton Ray, Lee Zieber, interviews, July 1985. Also, Dr. Frank Norman, speech on the occasion of the 90th anniversary of the Sonoma County Medical Society, May 17, 1978.
46. Robert Tuttle, DDS, interview, June 1993.

47. Caroline Ramberg, "Miss Juell," written for *Flashback*, a publication of Geets Vincent's autobiography class, SRJC, 1992.
48. Letter from John Crevelli, retired history instructor, SRJC, March 1993.
49. Nancy Noonan Berto, interview, March 1993.
50. Laila Storch Friedmann, interview, March 1993.

CHAPTER THIRTEEN

1. *Press Democrat*, December 9, 1941. The *Press Democrat* did not publish on Mondays, which accounts for the day's delay in the warning.
2. Later it would be ascertained that there were no Japanese planes over California; that, indeed, the Japanese had no aircraft capable of reaching the California shores.
3. Frank and Dennis Keegan provided the family information about their brother.
4. Records of the U.S. Adjutant General's Office, World War II operations reports, 1940-1948, National Archives, Suitland, Maryland.
5. Warren Williamson, interview, December 1985.
6. *Press Democrat*, November 30, 1943.
7. Dick Miles, interview, December 1985.
8. The authors are indebted to the late Kaye Tomlin, a member of the pioneer Call family of Fort Ross. Tomlin was a child in World War II. He spent summers with his Call relatives at the fort and came to know the Coast Guardsmen. He later made meticulous notes about that period and was planning a 50th reunion of the post when he died in 1992.
9. Letter from Robert Samuels, December 1978.
10. Alameda Naval Air Station war diaries are part of the WWII Naval archives at the Washington Naval Yard, Washington, D.C.
11. Quoted in Bailey's *History*, p. 40.
12. Flight schools had to be at least 150 miles inland. Source of information on SRJC's wartime role is Bailey's *History*.
13. Virginia Grace, interview, 1987.
14. Peggy Weeks Austin, interview, August 1982.
15. Personal accounts of several former SRHS students.
16. *Press Democrat*, July 15, 1944.
17. *Press Democrat*, August 14, 1985.
18. Letter from John Crevelli, retired history instructor, SRJC, February 1991, on the occasion of the United States entrance into war in the Persian Gulf.
19. Letter from Les Estes, April 20, 1989.
20. Alvin "Kewpie" Bonfigli, interview, December 1986.

21. *Press Democrat*, September 3, 1942.
22. *Press Democrat*, October 3, 1943.
23. Virginia Grace, interview.
24. George Hamamoto, interview, May 1988.
25. The actual dates were May 16 and 17, 1942.
26. Ramberg's writings were published in *Flashback* and, subsequently, in the *Press Democrat*. As a result, Fuji Murakami Kamatani of Los Angeles and Ramberg communicated by telephone and letter for more shared memories.
27. *Press Democrat*, May 12 and 17, 1942.
28. *Press Democrat*, May 15, 1942.
29. *Press Democrat*, May 19, 1942.
30. The annual Teriyaki Barbecue at Enmanji Buddhist Temple in Sebastopol was begun after the war by returned Japanese-Americans as a memorial to these three young men.
31. Information supplied by MSgt. Alan Doty, Wing Historian, Headquarters, 9th Strategic Reconnaisance Wing, SAC, Beale Air Force Base, CA.
32. Clipping from unidentified newspaper supplied by Maria Reuger, widow of the camp manager, 1977.
33. Rudolph Betz, former prisoner at Camp Windsor, interview, *Stars & Stripes*, Germany, May 24, 1992. Also, subsequent telephone interview with Betz.
34. Letter from Nita (Mrs. Walter) Lawson, July 1977.
35. Letters from Horst Liewald, July 1977, September 1989, February 1990, and subsequent interviews.
36. *Press Democrat*, July 18, 1989.
37. *Press Democrat*, August 15, 1945.
38. *Press Democrat* extra edition, August 14, 1945.
39. *Press Democrat*, August 16, 1945.
40. Ibid.
41. Santa Rosa Veterans Memorial records.

CHAPTER FOURTEEN

1. *School of Social Studies Survey*, p. 57.
2. Ibid., p. 61.
3. *LIFE*, January 25, 1943.
4. Edna May Wonacott Green, interview, *Press Democrat*, November 1982. Wonacott came away from *Shadow* with a movie contract. She had a small role in *The Bells of St. Mary's*.
5. Letter from Dorothy Bell Becker, October 1992.
6. There is disagreement on this point. Herbert's family gives him full credit; Bailey's *History*, and plaques on the buildings cite Weeks as the official architect. Preservation architect Dan Peterson gives

credit to both.
7. Caulkins' plan was lauded by *Press Democrat* editors in 1945 but was never formally considered by the Board of Supervisors.
8. This is the jail built in the 1960s, not the one opened in the 1990s.
9. Throughout the summer of 1943, almost every edition of the newspaper carried stories of polio victims and suggestions for prevention.
10. Jack Shea, interview, April 1985.
11. Alice and Gilbert Gray, interview, January 1992.
12. *Petaluma Argus Courier*, on the occasion of the 1983 reunion of the team. The Crushers scored 551 points in the 1949 season.
13. *Press Democrat*, "Rod and Gun," November 24, 1974, .
14. V.T. Hitchcock, deputy county counsel and former Pacific Airlines pilot, and John Kirkland, assistant airport manager, memorandum on airport history, February 9, 1965.
15. Hugh Codding, interview, *Golden Gate North* (Spring 1973).
16. *Press Democrat*, December 4, 1988. Trione would donate a million dollars worth of property to the state for inclusion in Annadel State Park and was one of the founders of Luther Burbank Center for the Arts.
17. It was a measure of Codding's popularity with Village residents that he could exercise such control.
18. Ray Anders, interview, June 1993.
19. Two Rock Ranch Station became a Coast Guard Training Station in the 1960s. Skaggs Island remained a Navy post.
20. The CIA's "Listening Post" land was later divided between Ya-Ka-Ama Indian Culture Center and Santa Rosa Junior College's Shone Farm agricultural education facility.
21. County population (1950-1960) went from 103,405 to 147,375.

Index